087338

D0304067

Popular Music ar

?

POPULAR MUSIC AND LOCAL IDENTITY

ROCK, POP AND RAP IN EUROPE AND OCEANIA

Tony Mitchell

Leicester University Press
London and New York

87338

Leicester University Press
A Cassell Imprint
Wellington House, 125 Strand, London WC2R 0BB
215 Park Avenue South, New York, New York 10003

First published 1996

© Tony Mitchell 1996

British Library Cataloguing in Publication Data
A CIP catalogue record for this book is available from the British Library.
ISBN 0 7185 0019 9 Hardback
      0 7185 0016 4 Paperback

Library of Congress Cataloging-in-Publication Data
Mitchell, Tony, 1949-
    Popular music and local identity : rock, pop, and rap in Europe
and Oceania / Tony Mitchell.
        p. cm.
    Includes index.
    ISBN 0-7185-0019-9 (hardback). – ISBN 0-7185-0016-4 (pbk.).
    1. Popular music – History and criticism. 2. World music – History
and criticism.   I. Title.
ML3470.M57   1996
781.63–dc20   95-53293
                                                                  CIP
                                                                  MN

Typeset by BookEns Ltd, Royston, Herts.
Printed and bound in Great Britain at Redwood Books, Trowbridge, Wiltshire.

Contents

Acknowledgements

This book is a series of palimpsests of my own as well as others' texts. Chapter 1 still retains a few traces of 'Performance and the Postmodern in Popular Music', an article published in the US *Theatre Journal*, vol. 41, no. 3, in October 1989. It was my first foray out of Performance Studies into Popular Music Studies, and I am grateful to Sue Ellen Case and Enoch Brater for supporting what was rather a left-field venture for a Performance Studies journal, and to my wife Diane Powell for the photos which accompanied the article, and for her continuing support.

Chapter 2 started life as a paper given at a conference entitled *Continental Shifts: Globalisation and Culture*, held at the University of Technology in Sydney in August 1991, and I am grateful to Elizabeth Jacka for providing the impetus for it, as well as for publishing it under the title 'Towards an Ethnography of World Music' in *Continental Shifts*, published by Local Consumption Press, Sydney, in 1992. A revised version later appeared under the title 'World Music and the Popular Music Industry: An Australian View', in the US journal *Ethnomusicology*, vol. 37, no. 3, in the autumn of 1993, and I thank Jeff Todd Titon for his editorial advice and suggestions.

Chapter 3 was initially presented as a conference paper at the first Australian Cultural Studies Association conference at the University of Western Sydney in December 1991, and was published in that conference's proceedings the following year. I later gave a revised version of it at the International Association of Popular Music (IASPM) conference on Central European Music in Prague in July 1992, the proceedings of which were published in 1994. This conference was my first encounter with the extraordinary international network of IASPM, and was organized by Aleš Opekar, to whom I owe a great deal for his help and advice about the Czech rock music and rap scene. I am also grateful to Richard Middleton for his editorial advice in publishing a version of the Czech paper in *Popular Music*, vol. 11, no. 2, in May 1992. I would like to thank Jan Jirasek, President of the Sydney Chapter of the Australian Czech and Slovak Cultural Association, for his help and friendship. Meeting President Havel in Sydney in 1995 is one of my most treasured memories.

At the Prague IASPM conference I also met Vincenzo Perna, whose comments about the Italian hip hop scene inspired me to research and write an article which became the basis of Chapter 4. Vincenzo read and corrected a draft of this article, which was published under the title 'Questions of Style: Italian Hip Hop and its Social Contexts', in *Popular Music*, vol. 14, no. 3, in October 1995. I also presented different versions of it as papers at IASPM conferences at Southern Cross University, Lismore, New South Wales, in July 1994, and at the University of Strathclyde, Glasgow, in July 1995.

Chapter 5 originated as a paper at the International Communications Association conference in Miami in 1992, and was published in an early form as 'World Music, Indigenous Music and Music Television in Australia', the first article in the first issue of *Perfect Beat*, the Australian and Pacific popular music journal established by Philip Hayward at Macquarie University, Sydney, in 1992. As a friend, an editor and an active member of the renascent Australia–New Zealand branch of IASPM, Phil has been an important influence, and a major force in putting Popular Music Studies in Oceania on the world map. Another early version of the Australian chapter was published in *Media, Culture and Society*, vol. 15, no. 2, in April 1993, and I am grateful to John Corner, whom I met at the Miami conference, for engineering this. I would also like to thank Ian Maxwell for his willingness to share his work on Sydney hip hop.

Chapter 6 is a revised amalgam of three articles originally published in *Perfect Beat*, in which Phil Hayward's encouragement and influence was again a major factor. Phil, Roy Shuker and I co-edited *North Meets South: Popular Music in Aotearoa/New Zealand*, a special book-issue of that journal on New Zealand music which appeared in January 1994, containing my reflections on independent music and Maori and Polynesian music in Aotearoa/New Zealand. These were based on conference papers presented at the first Australia and New Zealand IASPM conference, which I organized at the University of Technology, Sydney, in July 1993, and at the international IASPM conference at the University of the South Pacific, Stockton, California, an unforgettable event organized by US IASPM chairperson Paul Friedlander. A version of 'He Waiata ne Aotearoa' appeared in the Stockton proceedings, published in 1995 as *Popular Music – Style and Identity* by the centre for Research on Canadian Cultural Industries and Institutions in Montreal. The title was slightly mis-spelt and the author was credited as 'Akona te reo' (Learn the Language), but I bear no regrets about this sleight of hand towards Will Straw, who has been an inspiration. The first version of my accounts of the soundtrack of *Once Were Warriors*, the *Proud* project and Crowded House's *Together Alone* was published in *Perfect Beat*, vol. 2, no. 3, in July 1995. I am particularly grateful to Roy Shuker and Colin McLeay for their regular correspondence and exchange of material about New Zealand music, and to Karl Neuenfeldt for his generous supply of material and information on anything he thought might be relevant. I would also like to thank Meaghan Morris and Graeme Turner for their advice on my initial outlines of this book, and Janet Joyce of Cassell plc for her editorial encouragement and support.

Tony Mitchell
Bundeena, NSW, Australia, 1995

Introduction

This book explores and interrogates interactions between the global configurations of contemporary popular music and local music scenes in Italy, Central Europe, Australia and Aotearoa/New Zealand. It also surveys indigenous musical production in relation to the importation and appropriation of US and British musical idioms related to pop music, rock music and hip hop culture. The largely Anglo-American industrial trade routes which continue to dominate the global popular music industry are often portrayed by writers on popular music as forms of cultural imperialism which displace and appropriate authentic representations of local and indigenous music into packaged commercial products commodified for ethnically indeterminate, but predominantly Anglocentric and Eurocentric, markets. This book sets out to examine and challenge this cultural imperialism thesis as an overly simplistic means of representing the often complex cultural and political issues involved in local versions of imported music cultures. Arjun Appadurai has defined five spheres of influence in which the flow of communication in the global cultural economy operates: ethnoscapes, mediascapes, technoscapes, finanscapes and ideoscapes.[1] All of these spheres relate directly to the global production and consumption of popular music, and in this book I am particularly concerned with the first and the last of Appadurai's categories. Ethnicity and ideology are important aspects of contemporary popular music, giving it a sense of defining local identity, particularly when it is confronted with broader narratives of globalization and nationalism.

Instances in which traces of 'colonial discourse' can be seen in musical forms in which migrant and indigenous cultures appear to be spoken for by culturally dominant Anglocentric power groups do none the less occur, as in the case of Paul Simon's *Graceland* album, which is examined in Chapter 2. But a number of examples in which local musical cultures and subcultures absorb and appropriate US, Jamaican, Latin American and English paradigms into hybridized local musical contexts in a kind of 'reverse appropriation' are also examined. In the process, notions of musical identity, authenticity, indigenous music, appropriation and originality are interrogated through the analysis of ethnically and geographically specific expressions of hybrid cultural forms, as well as in the context of migrant musical diasporas.

All four countries covered in this book, two in Europe and two in Oceania, are marginal localities in relation to the phenomenon known as world music. The hybridized local representations of rock, pop and rap music in the Czech Republic, Italy, Australia and Aotearoa/New Zealand primarily reflect the cultural and social concerns and conflicts of their local contexts, while also aspiring, or being forced by commercial pressures, to operate in the global market. In this process of globalization, the localized concerns of music-making in each of these countries are embedded in representations of a national imaginary which none the less can be seen to contain distinctive features. The use of a piano accordion and Czech-language lyrics by the punk group Tři Sestry (Three Sisters) can be seen as a distinctively Czech aberration from globally recognized norms of punk rock. The Italian rapper Papa Ricky, who combines the dialect of Lecce and the ragga-based musical inflections of British reggae artists like Linton Kwesi Johnson and Apache Indian, is none the less a rhetorical representative of an unmistakably national and regional Italian cultural youth movement. Yothu Yindi, the Yolngu rock group from North-East Arnhem Land in outback Australia, who include didjeridu and clap sticks, bodypainted traditional dancers, and both Aboriginal and Anglo-Australian musicians, are seen as international cultural ambassadors of a particular image of Australia. The abrasive, hard-core political raps of the Maori hip hop group Upper Hutt Posse, who combine Maori language with samples of US Nation of Islam leader Louis Farrakhan, represent oppositional practices in the geographically isolated context of Aotearoa/New Zealand. In the two European instances, distinctively oppositional local and regionally marked idiolects collapse into national cultural movements with a strong linguistic identity. In the Australasian instances, micro-conflicts between a post-colonial, Anglocentric cultural hegemony and heterogeneous tribal (Aboriginal, Maori) forms of indigenous cultural expression come into conflict. In all four cases, national 'vernacular expressive cultures'[2] are constructed through music by means of a hybridization of local and global musical idioms.

Chapter 1 provides a context for the local case studies of the later chapters, periodizing Western rock and pop music into four eras of development and influence: a rock and roll tradition established in the 1950s, the various forms of rock music which developed in the 1960s, the impact of punk rock and reggae in the 1970s, and the diverse and multiple musical forms which emerged in the 1980s, including the widespread use of digital sampling in rap, hip hop, dance music, techno and other hybrid forms of pop music. The role of nationalist rhetoric in British rock music and African-American musical forms is examined in terms of the preservation of cultural hegemonies which rely on the exclusion of 'other' expressions of musical idioms seen as inherently Anglo-American or Afro-American. This leads to a brief examination of global manifestations of hip hop which have combined borrowed US idioms with local cultural and linguistic inflections. The multicultural aspects of French hip hop in particular are surveyed as examples of appropriation and hybridization of a form of sometimes multilingual musical expression which provides a powerful mode of address for predominantly migrant subcultures in localized contexts.

The different activities of Western musicians such as David Byrne, Brian Eno, Peter Gabriel and Paul Simon and the emergence of hip hop, house and various forms of dance music suggest that the exploration and appropriation of 'other' forms of non-Western music in Africa, Latin America and Asia at the end of the 1980s was a response to a perceived atrophy in the inherited forms of Western rock and pop music. In the words of Simon Frith, by the 1980s it had become 'no longer possible to make a startling rock statement',[3] and this perceived 'postmodern condition' of fragmentation and breakdown of 'master narratives' in popular music led both to a widespread tendency towards pastiches and recyclings of earlier forms and idioms of popular music, and to an exploration of Third World musics.

Chapter 2 surveys the sudden geographical diversification of the Western popular music industry in the late 1980s, and attempts to map the trade routes of world music which were established by the end of the decade, with Paris and London, and to a lesser extent New York, as the principal trading bases. The use of the term 'world music' as a marketing category is analysed in relation to the production values of the Anglo-American and French popular music industry, and the global prevalence of Western aesthetic and technological pop norms even in indigenous musics. World music is examined as what Steven Feld describes as 'an encoding of multiple significances' in relation to its musical diversity, academic designation, use as a commercial marketing term and dialectics of isolation and hegemony, resistance and accommodation.[4] The political dilemmas of representing Third World music and musicians in the Anglo-American pop mainstream are also examined, along with the positive results of the increased accessibility of the West to non-Western musics which the world music phenomenon generated. Notions of national popular music are investigated in relation to the musical diasporas of European-based 'ethnic' musicians, the appropriation of different forms of African music in exile in Paris as French by French cultural institutions, and the sometimes uneasy alliance between indigenous forms of popular music and the world music industry. The importance of locality in music-making in what John Street has identified as industrial base, social experience, aesthetic perspective, political experience, community and scene is also examined.[5]

Chapter 3 offers the first of four case studies of 'national popular musics' which have absorbed the prevalent influences and idioms of Anglo-American popular music and hybridized them with national and local idioms and content. The case of the Czech Republic, where rock music operated as a dissident and often criminalized cultural practice under the Communist regime, despite a frequently expressed disdain for politics by some prominent Czech musicians, is only partially representative of the role of rock and pop music in formerly Communist Central European countries and the former Soviet Union. Czech rock under Communism offers an argument for the political significance of rock music outside the parameters of world music in the context of its historical suppression, emphatic public expression and appropriation of dominant Western musical forms. In the former Czechoslovakia, rock music can be interpreted as having played a major part in political events like Charter 77, the Velvet Revolution and the ascendancy of President Havel, himself a rock fan, who appointed Frank Zappa as a special cultural adviser to the Czech government, and invited Lou Reed and the Rolling Stones to perform in Prague.

This chapter examines Czech rock and pop in the context of the reflection and appropriation of Anglo-American forms of pop music in Central Europe, an area marginalized from dominant trends and influences owing both to a lack of access to music technologies and to an institutional suppression of the music which guaranteed its continuing politicization. The diminished politicization of Czech rock and pop since the Velvet Revolution is also examined in the context of the music scene which has emerged in Prague in the 1990s.

The second case study explores the modalities of appropriation, hybridization and authenticity in the development of distinctively local and indigenous forms of rap, ragga and hip hop music in Italy. Like the Czech Republic, Italy has been largely unrepresented in either world music or Western popular music narratives, with the exception of occasional novelty songs and the over-hyped and un-distinctive Italo House phenomenon of the early 1990s. Initial Italian rap recordings and performances in English gave way in the 1990s to the use of regional dialects by individual rappers such as Papa Ricky and regional 'posses' like Almamegretta, Africa Unite, Mau Mau, 99 Posse, Sud Sound System and others, many of whom are associated with 'underground' social clubs which function as more than simply music venues.

A survey is made of this new movement in Italian hip hop, which combines the influence of Jamaican ragga music, Afro-American and Latino rappers, and has developed alongside a resurgence of 1970s-style mass oppositional political activity in Italy, which it both reflects and provides a soundtrack for. The importance of the *centri sociali* (social centres) as both venues and nurturing places for the development of indigenous Italian rap styles and idioms is discussed, and contestations about the *centri sociali* as indicators of authenticity against the appropriation of hip hop in pop contexts are discussed. The musical lineage of Italian rap, which could be seen to extend from seventeenth-century opera *recitativo* to Mediterranean folk music and Italian punk rock, is also examined. Much Italian rap, although taking the form of hybrid 'stylistic exercises' influenced by African-American rap, is also an alternative mode of social and political discourse which speaks out about local social problems such as homelessness, unemployment and police repression, and attacks targets such as political corruption, the mafia and the Northern League. The use of regional dialects and instrumentation serves as a cultural repository for tribalized local cultural forms, and gives Italian rap a folkloric dimension which distinguishes it from rap music in many other Western countries.

The third case study deals with Australia. Since the 1988 bicentenary of 'invasion day', or the British occupation of Australia, a heterogeneous, multicultural national identity comprising Aborigines, the descendants of Anglo-Saxon convicts and migrants from more than a hundred European, Asian, South American and African countries has become increasingly marked in Australia. This heterogeneity is reflected in the popular music of the country, although rarely acknowledged by the popular music industry, which maintains a hegemony of Anglocentricity, and still adheres to an outmoded concept of 'Oz rock'.

The emergence of the Aboriginal group Yothu Yindi, and a number of other Aboriginal and non-Anglo musicians who combine rock and indigenous musical idioms (Sunrize Band, Kev Carmody, Tiddas, Not Drowning Waving) has transformed the prevalent national image of 'Oz rock'. While this reflects to some extent a growing awareness and sensitivity among white Australian listeners towards Aboriginal and non-Anglo musics, it also generates dilemmas surrounding assimilation, appropriation and hybridity which are similar to those involved in World Music. Yothu Yindi inscribed themselves on Australian national consciousness with their song 'Treaty', a call for politicians to honour a promise to formulate a formal agreement between Aborigines and white Australians. Their 1993 album *Freedom* features US avant-garde guitarist and producer Bill Laswell, combines European techno-oriented dance music with reggae, pub rock and the *yidaki* (didjeridu), and celebrates the abolition of the concept of '*terra nullius*', and the acknowledgment of Aboriginal sovereignty of Australia signalled by the 1992 Eddie Mabo case. Kev Carmody's 1993 album *Blood Lines* illustrates the widespread country music influence on Aboriginal rock, together with a strong appropriated influence of the mbaqanga music of the townships of South Africa. But the varying responses of white Australians to Aboriginal rock musicians indicate that they still 'must steer a course between the cliffs of essentialisation on one side and assimilation on the other'.[6] The continuing difficulties of defining any distinctively and idiosyncratically national forms of Australian rock music apart from the Aboriginal rock music hybrid of Yothu Yindi and others is also discussed.

The fourth case study is of Aotearoa/New Zealand. The nineteenth-century English author Samuel Butler set his Utopian novel *Erewhon* ('Nowhere' spelt backwards) in Aotearoa/New Zealand, reflecting a sense of profound geographical isolation and a perceived lack of national identity in this former British colony. In 1990 Aotearoa/New Zealand celebrated the sesquicentenary of the signing of the Treaty of Waitangi between Maori and Pakeha (Anglo-Saxon settlers), and has been undergoing the transformations and conflicts of an official government policy of biculturalism, which has seen a strong imprint of Maori language and cultural forms on the local vernacular culture. This biculturalism is reflected in the contemporary popular music of Aotearoa/New Zealand, where there is an increasing prominence of Maori and Polynesian rap, reggae, blues, soul, funk, dance and rock music, recorded on local labels such as Tangata, Deepgrooves, Southside and Tai E, set up to promote Maori and Polynesian popular music, which often appropriates a variety of Afro-American musical paradigms and blends them with traditional indigenous musical forms of *waiata* (song) in distinctive and idiosyncratic ways.

Cultural imperialism arguments which have been raised in relation to American influences on Aotearoa/New Zealand popular music are examined in relation to both distinctive *pakeha* musical idioms which provide local variations on forms imported from the UK and USA, and Maori and Pacific Islander musical hybridity. Aotearoa/New Zealand's geographical isolation intensifies an idiosyncratic interaction between local 'micromusics' and globally dominant popular music genres. The year 1991 marked a decade of operations for the independent Aotearoa/New Zealand recording label Flying Nun, which has succeeded in establishing the country's rock music as a fragile but growing international force, with particular interest being generated among independent music subcultures in the USA.

Conflicts between the global concerns of an Anglo-American-dominated popular music industry and the local concerns and constituencies of popular musicians in the Czech Republic, Italy, Australia and Aotearoa/New Zealand can be contextualized in terms of the emergence of hybrid musical idioms exemplified by the use of traditional Czech musical and linguistic forms within its rock music, regional dialects in Italian rap music, an increased focus on traditional Aboriginal sounds and icons in Australia, and a renewed growth of self-reflective forms of Maori and Pacific Islander popular music in Aotearoa/New Zealand.

The world music phenomenon, which has proved to be a durable one in popular music of the 1990s, both as a marketing strategy and as a musical genre, has functioned as a positive form of cultural influence in terms of providing momentum and inspiration for the indigenous and often dissident musics of ethnic minorities throughout the world. It has also helped to establish a musical language of hybridity, in which traditional, authentic and indigenous musical forms are combined with global musical idioms. As a result, the local distinctiveness of particular 'national popular musics' can be preserved alongside a potential global accessibility which preserves what Frith identifies as 'what is most interesting about music - its blurring of insider/outsider boundaries'.[7]

Notes

1. A. Appadurai (1990) 'Disjuncture and Difference in the Global Cultural Economy', *Public Culture*, vol. 2, no. 1 (spring), pp. 6–7.
2. P. Gilroy (1991) 'Sounds Authentic: Black Music, Ethnicity and the Challenge of a Changing Same', *Black Music Research Journal*, vol. 10, no. 2, p. 126.
3. S. Frith (1987) 'We Win Again', *Village Voice* (29 December).
4. S. Feld (1992) 'Voices of the Rainforest: Politics of Music', *Arena*, nos 99/100, pp. 166–7.
5. J. Street (1995) '(Dis)located? Rhetoric, Politics, Meaning and the Locality', in W. Straw *et al.* (eds) *Popular Music - Style and identity* (Montreal: The Centre for Research on Canadian Cultural Industries and Institutions), pp. 256–7.
6. J. Castles (1992) '*Tjungaringanyi*: Aboriginal rock', in P. Hayward (ed.) *From Pop to Punk to Postmodernism: Popular Music and Australian Culture from the 1960s to the 1990s* (Sydney: Allen & Unwin), p. 32.
7. S. Frith (1993) 'I Am What I Am', *Village Voice* (3 August).

1

Modernism and Nationalism in English and Afro-American Popular Music

Appropriation and crossover

The history of Anglo-American rock and pop music is a history of appropriations, often involving the adoption and transformation of African-American music into successful popular configurations by white musicians. The concept of musical appropriation is a contested one, and ranges from scenarios in which a musician 'borrows' (or copies, or steals) a phrase or style or sound or inflection from another musician, to a whole genre or historical movement of music being perceived as deriving from an earlier style or genre (for example, 1990s grunge music as a recycling of 1970s punk rock, 1990s jungle as a reworking and combination of reggae and techno). The history of popular music is a constant flow of appropriations in which origins, and notions of originality, are often difficult, if not impossible, to trace. While the ownership of individual songs by composers is protected by copyright against musical theft, the ownership of, for example, guitar riffs, phrases or idiosyncratic sound styles is virtually impossible to protect. The historical development of blues music, for example, involves the adoption and proliferation of new modes and styles of guitar playing whose origins are often difficult to trace.

Appropriation is often seen as a kind of betrayal of origins, and musicians perceived as copying other musicians' styles or inflections are often criticized as derivative or even dishonest. It is also often associated with an assumed exploitation of weaker or subservient social or ethnic groups by more dominant and powerful groups, as in the history of appropriation of black American musical forms by white musicians, and seen as a process akin to colonization. But appropriation can also be applied to a process of adoption of socially dominant forms of music by economically weaker and less developed minority societies, such as the adoption of US country music by Australian Aboriginal musicians. This process is sometimes referred to as 'reverse appropriation', which is what later chapters in this book are largely concerned with.

The emergence of rock and roll in the mid-to-late 1950s in the USA (and later Britain) involved to a large extent musicians like Elvis Presley and Bill Haley appropriating and copying the rhythms and vocal styles of African-American rhythm and blues (with a bit of Cuban rhythm thrown in for good measure). Presley's and Haley's success occurred within the dictates of an entrenched white hegemony in the music industry of the time that made it necessary for black musicians to deploy 'crossover' strategies to gain success with the predominantly white audiences for popular music, a process of musical and cultural compromise which Nelson George has equated, with particular reference to Berry Gordy's Motown label, with 'the death of rhythm and blues'. George argues that the growing mainstream commercial success of African-American music since the Second World War, which paralleled the increasing integration of the black community in the USA into white society, and their pursuit of white values and goals, meant that

> black culture, and especially R&B music, has atrophied. The music is just not as gutsy or spirited or tuned into the needs of its core audience as it once was. Compare the early Aretha Franklin to Whitney Houston. Franklin's music always relied heavily on the black inner-city experience, and especially on the black church. When she forgets that, she stumbles. Houston is extremely talented, but most of her music is so 'colour blind', such a product of eighties crossover marketing, that in her commercial triumph is a hollowness of spirit that mocks her own gospel roots.[1]

While it is difficult to disagree with this viewpoint, George's conceptualization of crossover is based on implicit notions of musical roots, authenticity, and a community basis – what George refers to as ' "real" black music by blacks'[2] – which have begun to be questioned as idealizations of a musical past in which music-making is perceived as having a direct and uncomplicated connection with social, cultural and often racial community expression, unmediated by business and industrial factors. The term *crossover*, which George states was institutionalized by CBS records in 1976 as a policy referring to 'the sale of black hits to whites',[3] has become a frequently used term in the music industry in a wide range of contexts. It usually denotes a recording artist's shift from a sometimes ethnically defined niche market into a broader mainstream market, and often carries with it strong implications of 'selling out', abandoning one's roots or deserting one's original musical constituency or fan-base. As with appropriation, use of the term *crossover* is often based on purist and essentialist notions of authenticity and musical stability exemplified by those who, for example, criticized Bob Dylan for adopting electric guitars into his folk music in the late 1960s, or Miles Davis for incorporating rock and funk elements into jazz, or Philip Glass for employing minimalist classical music in popular contexts.

Such criticisms are usually predicated on notions of musical authenticity which regard a particular form of music (folk, jazz, minimalism) as possessing an inherent truth, value, tradition and originality which places obligations on performers not to deviate from the implicit rules inherent in these elements. These notions often amount to fixed and traditional orthodoxies (even when the music is non-traditional, like minimalism) which fail to account for often radical processes of evolution which particular musical forms undergo in relation to both technological developments in the music industry and the pressures of commercialization. Musical authenticity often becomes synonymous with paying one's dues as a musician, with earning the right to sing the blues, with street credibility. It is also often related to notions that musical forms such as blues, jazz, rhythm and blues, gospel, soul, and rap, all of which had (to varying degrees) origins in African-American communities, are valid only when performed by black musicians.

The appropriation of African-American roots music by a white-dominated popular music industry, white performers and white musical commentators is not inherently unauthentic or treasonable, although it is sometimes conceptualized as such in terms of an essentialized truth value given to African-American music. This sometimes involves assumptions that 'black' music played by white musicians and historical accounts of it by white musical commentators are inherently derivative and second-rate, as in George's comments about blues:

> The black audience's consumerism and restlessness burns out and abandons musical styles, whereas white Americans, in the European tradition of supporting forms and style for the sake of tradition, seem to hold styles dear long after they have ceased to evolve.
>
> The most fanatical students of blues history have all been white. These well-intentioned scholars pick through old recordings, interview obscure guitarists, and tramp through the Mississippi Delta with the determination of Egyptologists. Yet with the exception of Eric Clapton and maybe Johnny Winter, no white blues guitarist has produced a body of work in any way comparable to that of the black giants. Blacks create and then move on. Whites document and then recycle. In the history of popular music, these truths are self-evident.[4]

But these 'self-evident truths' are based on spuriously generalized, homogenized notions of black and white creation and documentation, which are little more than simplistic ethnic stereotypes. While George's justified anger at the injustices, exploitation and neglect suffered by African-American musicians is a continual factor in his argument, his assumptions about both black and white musicians and their audiences are essentialized to the extent of caricature. It is also worth noting that the efforts of white blues musicians like Clapton and Winter and many others in promoting blues music and musicians brought increased recognition to a wide range of black American blues artists in the 1960s in Britain and the USA. Similarly, there has been a revival of blues music amongst both black and white audiences in the 1990s, much of it generated by white musicians and promoters, which has seen veteran seventy-year-old bluesman John Lee Hooker produce four top-selling albums, assisted by a number of white musicians like Van Morrison, Bonnie Rait, Roy Rogers and Jimmie Vaughan. While blues music has often been predicated on earning 'the right to sing the blues', as a song sung by Billie Holiday puts it, and on the expression of suffering associated with the deprivation and curtailment of freedom involved in African slavery and its heritage in the USA, these social origins were soon industrialized and blues became a musical style which has been appropriated around the globe.

The 'British invasion' of US-dominated pop music in the 1960s, which developed contemporaneously with Motown and went on to dominate Anglo-American pop music, was the result of English groups like the Beatles, the Rolling Stones, the Animals, the Yardbirds and others playing cover versions of black American blues and rhythm and blues songs, before venturing into their own more commercially viable, pop-oriented compositions. While this 'invasion' is sometimes criticized as an unauthentic appropriation of African-American roots, it was based on an admiration and respect for blues music which sometimes verged on the religious.

The postmodern condition and how pop ate itself

Since the 1950s, dominant global formations of rock and pop music have tended to oscillate between (and combine) developments from American and British trends, which have provided a dominant influence on rock and pop music in other countries throughout the world. In 1987 Simon Frith signalled four peak periods in postwar Anglo-American rock and pop music: rock and roll, which reached its zenith in 1956–57; rock, which reached a height of sophistication in 1966–67; punk rock, which emerged as a form of social and ideological revolt in 1976–77; and the various diversified forms from pop to hip hop on both sides of the Atlantic which had emerged in 1986 and 1987.[5]

In the years since 1986, the multiple diversifications of pop music formations and genres have continued to proliferate, often recombining in the process in new hybrid formations, so that by 1995 the range of popular music sub-genres is constantly being extended, and has become almost impossible to quantify. The diversifications, apart from the standard retro-oriented AOR (Adult-oriented Rock) and MOR (Middle of the Road), on which many radio stations base their entire programme outputs, include folk, blues, and country, all of which have enjoyed revivals in interest in the 1990s; heavy metal and its offshoots such as thrash, hardcore, death metal, gothic and grunge; the open-ended, 'other'-

embracing label of world music; the various strands of hip hop and rap; house and dance music, and its various rave culture offshoots acid house, deep house, and techno, dance, trance, Hi NRG, handbag, ambient, acid jazz, jungle, trip hop, etc.; reggae, raggamuffin, dancehall, dub and other derivations; funk and disco, and variations and combinations of all the above.

By 1987 the 'master narrative' (to use Lyotard's term) of dominant Anglo-American rock music had split up into a series of fragmented, decentred musical forms which sometimes corresponded to or overlapped among particular youth subcultures. Frith described this phenomenon, quoting *ID* magazine, as 'a culture of margins around a collapsed centre ... the pop-world version of the "postmodern condition"'.[6] In 1995 this 'master narrative' could be said to have split into a network of discrete, separate but interrelated forms similar to a complex molecular structure. Each sub-genre may still be related back to a core concept of 'popular music' (a term of almost infinite breadth of definition), but is probably best defined in its own terms and within its own musical and social parameters.

Frith's four periods of post-rock-and-roll popular music could be equated with a tradition, which largely consisted of white rock 'n' roll musicians appropriating African-American roots; a modernist period, in which hybrid forms such as acid rock, progressive rock, hard rock, soft rock, art, symphonic and glam rock extended rock music further away from its roots; a new and socially oppositional traditionalism, in which more minimalist, stripped-down forms like punk rock, reggae, soul and ska, asserted themselves (mostly in the UK) in an attempt to find new roots; and a postmodern era, in which a multiplicity of genres of both black and white musical forms appropriated, recycled, pastiched, mutated and recombined earlier and contemporaneous genres and sub-genres. According to Frith, any sense of a clearly linear, historical progression in guitar-based rock music had ceased as early as the late 1970s, by which time it had become almost exclusively self-reflexive and self-referential: 'By the end of the 1970s there was no music a rock musician (however young) could make that did not refer back, primarily, to previous rock readings; the music was about itself now, whether it liked it or not.'[7]

By the mid-1980s, rock music had split into various forms of pop and dance musics, including house, hip hop, techno – almost anything except 'rock', which became an outmoded term, while 'pop' enjoyed a revival of interest in the UK – in a process in which, as Iain Chambers indicated, 'Pop's past stops being a mausoleum of picturesque relics and turns back into a contemporary reservoir of musical possibilities'.[8] This recycling of past forms often crossed racial and ethnic boundaries: rap groups like Public Enemy sampled 1970s British glam rock icons Queen as Grandmaster Flash had done before them, while funk superstar James Brown became the most heavily sampled artist by both black and white artists in popular music history, and eclecticism and a seemingly borderless bricolage of pop music history became the order of the day.

The concept of postmodernism made a resounding entry into the discourse of anglophonic Cultural Studies in the mid-1980s, hard on the heels of the publication of Jean-François Lyotard's *The Postmodern Condition* (1984) and the works of Barthes, Baudrillard and other French post-structuralists on subjects such as simulation, the death of the author, the mythologies of mass media and the loss of history, and the US Marxist literary critic Fredric Jameson's famous essay 'Postmodernism, or the Cultural Logic of Late Capitalism' (1984). According to Lyotard, unifying, totalizing 'master narratives' of knowledge and interpretation in Western philosophy had fragmented and decentred into a series of Wittgensteinian 'language games' in which specialized areas of knowledge operated independently of one another.[9] In an often quoted (and often misunderstood) passage, Lyotard is critical of the cult of ephemera and consumerism and the superficial chaos and indeterminacy which results from postmodernity, in which

> Eclecticism is the degree zero of contemporary general culture: one listens to reggae, watches a Western, eats McDonald's food for lunch and local cuisine for dinner, wears Paris perfume in Tokyo and 'retro' clothes in Hong Kong; knowledge is a matter for TV games. By becoming kitsch, art panders to the confusion which reigns in the 'taste' of the patrons. Artists, gallery owners, critics and the public wallow together in the 'anything goes', and the epoch is one of slackening.[10]

One of the results of this eclecticism, as Jameson pointed out, was an increasing predominance of fragmentation, pastiche, incorporation, appropriation and outright plagiarism as an overriding feature in contemporary art forms, supplanting the notion of the original author, and expressing 'the erosion of the older distinction between high culture and so-called mass or popular culture'.[11] Other optimistic exponents of postmodern theory celebrated ambiguity, ephemerality, indeterminacy and the power of playfulness, and provided legitimization within the discipline of Cultural Studies and elsewhere in academia for the study of a wide range of forms of popular culture with a degree of aesthetic depth formerly accorded the canonic products of high culture. Self-appointed elucidators of postmodernism like David Harvey, whose book *The Condition of Postmodernity* appeared in 1989, addressed readers who, in Meaghan Morris's words, wanted

> to know 'what happened' ... in Western societies during the 1980s – why some places boomed while others suffered, why yuppies flourished while poverty and homelessness increased, why conservative regimes came to power, and what all this had to do with *Blade Runner*, pink and blue buildings, Lyotard, Cindy Sherman and a crisis of representation.[12]

But, as Morris points out, Harvey's aesthetic smorgasbord of surfaces, crises of meaning, flux and flow which celebrates postmodernism as a phenomenon existing largely outside of historical and geographical constraints, failed to acknowledge, among other things, the political realities analysed by feminism and post-colonialism. His neglect of dilemmas of gender, race and ethnicity, and non-western perspectives, indicates that his and many other versions of postmodernism may simply have become 'a privileged space for Marxist self-reflection'.[13]

By the beginning of the 1990s, there was an almost unilateral retreat from postmodernism within the broad field of Cultural Studies, within which, as Roy Shuker has pointed out, popular music studies is embedded.[14] The concept of postmodernism began to be questioned both as a useful theoretical tool and as an all-embracing, non-specific 'condition', and perceived as something of a runaway train, although some of its key precepts, such as the fragmentation of knowledge and the collapse of philosophical 'master narratives', continued to be acknowledged. A major problem was that postmodernism itself had become a 'master narrative' that was loosely applicable to almost any form of social or cultural practice: the more heterogenous and hybrid the form of activity under study the riper it was for conceptualization in terms of pastiche, intertextuality, bricolage, montage, etc. Applications to political practices were more difficult; as Dick Hebdige acknowledged, a good deal of postmodernist theory and practice 'aestheticise[d] politics'.[15]

Exponents of British Cultural Studies like Dick Hebdige were quick to point out that dominant forms of Anglo-American rock and pop music, as formations of popular culture, seemed to exhibit some of the classic features of the postmodern condition in the course of their rapid development since the Second World War. This was partly due to rock and pop's connection with the fashion industry and youth subcultures, and reliance on popularity charts, which, among other factors, made for rapid ephemerality. In moving from 1950s rock and roll to the multiplicity of sub-genres that had sprung up by the mid-1980s, pop music was seen to have exhausted its own 'master narratives' and embraced and appropriated a multiplicity of genres and artforms in a postmodern process of pastiche, intertextuality and incorporation, spearheaded by the increasing practice of digital sampling.

Jameson cited English punk rock group the Clash and US art-rock ensemble Talking Heads as examples of postmodernism in popular music, contrasting them with what he saw as earlier 'modernist' examples of the Beatles and the Rolling Stones, although this distinction seemed vaguely historical rather than relating to particular musical genres.[16] As Andrew Goodwin later pointed out, these four rock groups could be categorized more convincingly in terms of popular music forms and traditions as 'realist' (the Rolling Stones and the Clash) and 'modernist' (the Beatles and Talking Heads). Goodwin regarded most postmodernist attempts to account for popular music as notable more for what was excluded than what was incorporated,[17] and saw the application of postmodern theory to popular music as verging on the syllogistic: 'The logic that one typically finds is this: postmodernism employs eclecticism and intertextuality; rock music is eclectic and intertextual, *ergo*, rock music is postmodern. But what does this tell us about rock music or postmodernism, other than that they might explain *each other*?'[18] Much postmodernist analysis of rock and pop, as Goodwin has shown, has tended to deal with the 'high culture' end of popular music, concentrating on avant-garde figures such as Laurie Anderson, David Byrne, Brian Eno and Philip Glass, who are all arguably marginal to the principal developments of rock and pop music. Glass's repetitive minimalism, which developed out of the music of avant-garde composers like Lamont Young, Terry Riley and Steve Reich, and involves incursions into opera, remains entrenched in classical distribution circuits, despite the enormous popularity in the mid-1970s of Mike Oldfield's derivative minimalist composition *Tubular Bells*. The attempted 'art into pop' crossovers of string quartets like the Kronos Quartet, who play music by Jimi Hendrix and others, the Balanescu Quartet, with their Kraftwerk adaptations, and the Brodsky Quartet's collaborations with Elvis Costello, are attempts to 'classicalize' pop rather than blurring barriers between art and pop. Brian Eno's ambient music and production of a range of music groups from Africa to Russia, it could be argued, has little connection with his participation in the 1970s art-rock group Roxy Music. David Byrne's 1989 mock-Mahler composition *The Forest* for stage director Robert Wilson could be seen as more of a 'crossover' from 'pop into art' than the reverse, and Laurie Anderson's subsequent performance art works have never managed to repeat the surprising British pop chart success she had with 'O Superman' in 1983. All these musicians, it could be argued, have a more direct connection to modernist manifestations of avant-garde art forms than to amorphously defined concepts of pop postmodernism.

In the early 1990s, a process of revisionism began to set in amongst postmodernist Cultural Studies analysts, re-implementing notions of modernism. This coincided, as Goodwin has pointed out, with the inscription of postmodernism as a category within the music industry itself at the end of the 1980s, when Music Video Awards were given for 'best postmodern video' (REM, Sinéad O'Connor), and the term became a marketing category vaguely synonymous with modernist art rock, 'alternative' or 'independent' music, incorporating almost any left-field group from the Cure to Sonic Youth.[19]

The development of digital sampling in the 1980s was a major factor in postmodernist formulations of a perceived end of a historical cycle in rock music leading to a direct and open plundering and recycling of previous music, as pop began 'eating itself' in an endlessly intertextual cycle which seemed quintessentially postmodern. The expression 'Pop Will Eat Itself', which was adopted by a British thrash-dance rock band who combined sampling with hard rock and dance music, was first used by *Melody Maker* journalist Simon Reynolds, and became a catchphrase to describe the cannibalistic tendencies of rock and pop ushered in by sampling, which Reynolds designated as heralding 'the end of music'.[20] Reynolds saw the futurist 'sound-byte' culture which sampling introduced, along with the death of the author and its concomitant copyright problems, as a reflection of

> what's already happening in popular culture: the death of the Song, to be replaced by the de-centred, unresolved, in-finite house track; the brain-rotting vortex of quick-cutting in video and TV; the supercession of narrative, characterization and motivation by sensational effects. Blip culture means the death of sequential, linear thought, an erosion of people's ability to plan and manage their lives. There is only a NOW that is either blissed out, or dread-ful (dread is a kind of jouissance-in-negative, a slow subsidence into uncontrol and panic).[21]

The apocalyptic and existential consequences which Reynolds saw in sampling began to seem less far-reaching as copyright control over samples began to become entrenched, house music became superseded by the instant ecstasy of rave culture, and ideological concern about the depoliticization and postmodern fragmentation of contemporary culture as reflected in pop music subsided. But this subsidence did not prevent the continuance of moral concerns about drug-taking and noise control in rave culture. As Sarah Thornton has pointed out, media-fuelled moral panics associated with house music and rave culture, which culminated in the Criminal Justice Act in the UK in 1994 making it illegal to play music with 'repetitive beats' in public places, indicate that these newer forms of popular music involved socially transgressive and oppositional aspects linking them to 'modernist' underground rock music subcultures of the 1960s.[22] The disintegration of 'master narratives' in popular music could be seen to contain the seeds of regeneration, and to fit notions of a 'changing same' expressed by Paul Gilroy in his study of the diaspora of African music.[23]

In 1993 Jeremy J. Beadle's book *Will Pop Eat Itself?* examined 'pop music in the soundbite era', and celebrated sampling, the agit-pop antics of British group the KLF, and pop music's endlessly regenerative powers. Beadle saw pop's self-consumption in rather simplified terms as a manifestation of both modernism and postmodernism:

> 'Pop' as we understand it was ... born around 1955 or 1956, and reached a point where it seemed exhausted about thirty years later. The digital sampler proved the ideal tool for pop to take itself apart, thus arriving at modernism and post-modernism simultaneously. If this seems far-fetched, remember that in most 'higher' art both modernism and post-modernism took the basic

constituents of the form and placed it in a new context. Context is all. The major difference is that modernism in 'high' art drove the public away in vast numbers. Clearly that didn't happen with pop music.[24]

Beadle saw M/A/R/R/S's 1987 number one British hit 'Pump Up the Volume', which used more than thirty samples from other records, as a modernist (and also presumably postmodernist) watershed in popular music history, a portent of pop deconstruction comparable to Arnold Schoenberg's invention of the twelve-tone scale in classical music:

> 'Pump Up the Volume' was the result of careful consideration of recorded sound, acknowledging that this, rather than any musical system, is the basis of pop music, and an attempt to see what happened if you broke that down to its constituent elements and – like Picasso or Schoenberg or T. S. Eliot – started to rebuild the same basics in a recognizable but different manner.[25]

Rather than celebrating pop music eating itself, Beadle's essentially superficial reading of the surface developments of British pop in the late 1980s celebrates pop undoing itself, becoming self-conscious and self-aware, and overcoming its own fragility and ephemerality by continuing to regenerate itself in the pursuit of 'perfect pop'. But his conflation and confusion of modernist and postmodernist tendencies amounts to little more than another attempt to explain pop music in the language of high culture.

The Pet Shop Boys and pop modernism

One British pop group who perhaps more than any other survived a transition from perceived postmodern fragmentation into a more modernist configuration is the Pet Shop Boys. From their beginnings in the mid 1980s, they celebrated pop's surface ephemerality, as Simon Frith noted:

> Pet Shop Boys make music to please in a way that seems deliberately, almost tauntingly easy. They use their machines as if following a manual, setting up a simple phrase, talking idly over it; their trademark is a streamlined, nonabsorbent, synthetic texture, the crucial hooks embedded in an appearance of grandeur that doesn't survive close attention. The Pets' music is all surface and no depth, and in terms of the late '80s British pop aesthetic it should, therefore, be worthless – they're on the wrong side of the ideological divide.[26]

But as Goodwin has shown in his study of the Internet newsgroup of Pet Shop Boys' fans, the group's tantalizing use of camp irony and unashamed adoption of mainstream pop aesthetics appeals to a significant number of intellectuals and gay listeners in the UK, USA and Australia who contribute to often highly critical and informed debates about the group's recorded output, song lyrics and sexuality.[27] Such debates indicate that the group has continued to produce music that is far from 'worthless' by successfully pursuing an aesthetic of 'perfect pop' crossed with disco music within the mainstream of contemporary popular music, while gradually foregrounding their gay concerns in the process (singer Neil Tennant finally 'outed' himself in 1994). Their 1993 album *Very* concluded with a poignant and wistful post-AIDS version of the Village People's 1970s gay disco anthem 'Go West', blending it with Pachelbel's Canon, and turning it into a gay anthem of the 1990s (it was used as the theme song of the 1994 Sydney Gay and Lesbian Mardi Gras). In 'Yesterday, When I Was Mad', they examined prominent myths about their own perceived use of irony, ambiguity, their reliance on studio technology, and survival of almost a decade of pop trends. On the single release of the song, which laments an absence of sincerity, the group included a plangent and seemingly unironic version of Noel Coward's 'If Love Were All', perhaps acknowledging that, like Coward, they were forced to admit that theirs was merely 'a talent to amuse'.

One issue the Pet Shop Boys continue to treat with irony is their incorporation by 1990s rave culture, which they regard as dull and worthless. *Very* included a free supplementary album of dance music mixes entitled *Relentless*, and their single release of their TV-related hit 'Absolutely Fabulous' included what was described as a 'boring soulless dance mix'. In a review of *Very*, Ann Powers acknowledged the Pet Shop Boys' 'genius at rescuing the "disposable" pop soundbytes treasured by audiences in bedrooms and on dancefloors' and their realization 'that pop's political effect, while sometimes experienced as real, ultimately stays within the realm of imagination'.[28] Despite its wit, frivolity and irony, the Pet Shop Boys' music began to find a kind of political engagement, not just in the gay politics of songs like 'Can You Forgive Her?', but also in the recognition of class privilege and homelessness in 'The Theatre', which describes people sleeping on the street outside the London West End theatre where *Phantom of the Opera* is playing, and in 'Young Offender'. Likewise, the use of Soviet imagery in the video of 'Go West' suggests strongly that there is a serious side to the hedonism which their music is often seen to espouse. This indicates a shift from perceived postmodern expressions of stylish surface ambiguity towards a more modernist, even realist concern with social issues.

The Pet Shop Boys' continuing commercial success, and increasing fascination for highbrow commentators on pop music, suggests that the multiple forms of post-postmodern pop music may have regenerated themselves into modernist manifestations which are best considered discretely in a case-by-case approach. While many of the regenerative qualities of pop music largely involve appropriating a succession of different styles as they become fashionable, the Pet Shop Boys show that the inbuilt obsolescence and inherent ephemerality of pop can be utilized in intelligent and socially meaningful ways.

Nationalism in British pop and the music press

The various trends and regenerations of trends in British popular music are largely signalled by the weekly music papers *New Musical Express* and *Melody Maker,* two vastly influential organs who initiate new styles, break new bands, dictate taste, and establish the credentials of what style magazine *The Face* has called 'a righteous pop nation'.[29] The national success of British pop groups in the mid-1990s like Blur, Oasis, Suede and the Boo Radleys has been largely due to their acclaim in the nationalist British music press, but also to the way in which they have reshuffled some of the principal musical tendencies of the history of British pop music since the 1960s, from the Beatles and the Kinks to the Jam and the Clash. In the late 1980s, the kind of Beatles pastiche that these groups express would have been celebrated as postmodern, but in the mid-1990s it seems more like a narrow form of introspective pop nationalism and nostalgia.

In an incisive and wide-ranging study of nationalist tendencies in mid-1990s British rock and pop music and the music media entitled 'What Do *They* Know of England?', Martin Cloonan identified six aspects of a self-defining Britishness: a concern with recycling notions of working-class and punk 'realizm' exemplified by Blur's use of greyhound racing imagery and assumed Cockney accents; a conflation of British and English music so that the latter is seen as exclusively representing the former; the exclusion of Asian groups, Jamaican reggae groups and black rappers from notions of Englishness; a predominant ethos of 'laddishness' despite the increasing number of women in English bands; a prevalent anti-American ethos typified by Blur's disdain for the USA fuelled by their lack of success there, and Julie Burchill's claim that British pop groups are the main reason for being proud to be English; and a widespread nostalgia for previous eras of British world pop dominance like the 'Swinging Sixties', illustrated by the repeated recycling of 1960s pop icons like Dusty Springfield. Cloonan relates these nationalist tendencies to a nationalist spectrum ranging from neo-Fascist manifestations of xenophobia to the appeal of 'white bread' 1980s British singers like Morrissey to racists, the English Conservative Party's Europhobia, a non-articulated Englishness assumed in jungle, techno and rave music, and even the left-wing nationalism of folk-punk troubadour Billy Bragg.[30] These tendencies appear to be linked by an overriding concern with national identity and self-definition in the face of perceived threats from the USA and Europe, and an expression of English national pride through pop music, most strongly typified by Blur. As David Runciman said of Blur, whose 1994 album *Parklife* the *Independent on Sunday* called 'the most exciting album since the Beatles' *Sergeant Pepper*',

> Their own particular collage of our pop heritage, a mix of music hall whimsy and sweeping ballads, punky anthems and jokey references, borrows from everywhere and brings to mind everyone, not just The Beatles, The Who and The Kinks, but The Jam, The Buzzcocks and Madness as well. . . . But here, as elsewhere, the heightened Englishness which makes *Parklife* such a wonderful record is likely to be their undoing. Blur don't like America, and Americans don't much like those who don't like them.[31]

The cosy provincialism and national musical self-referentiality fostered by the British music press has its disadvantages outside national boundaries. The exponents and advocates of British pop may be convinced it is the best in the world, and sneer at the pop of other countries, especially their European neighbours, but success in the USA, a market which accounts for nearly forty per cent of the world's record sales, is still all-important, just as it was for the Beatles.

An article in the March 1995 pop monthly *Mojo* explored why no new British act had had any success in the USA since 1985 and asked 'why the Yanks think British music sucks'. The conclusion was that the rise of grunge, described as 'America's own punk movement', as well as home-grown US country music, rap and hip hop meant there was enough national product for British imports to be considered irrelevant. A Boston radio station manager known as 'Oedipus' was quoted saying that *Melody Maker* and *NME* created 'artificial stars' in the UK who were promoted too fast and too early and were unknown in the USA because they were out of touch with audiences and not prepared to work on promoting themselves. Suede – known as the London Suede in the USA as a Baltimore-based jazz singer trademarked the name Suede – were seen a case in point, acting like superstars on their US tour and making very little impact, while their two support bands, the Irish group the Cranberries and the US group Counting Crows, carried on touring and sold millions of albums.[32]

One way in which British rock culture maintains its rather fragile hegemony is by asserting domination over the non-US anglophonic world and the rest of Europe, whose rock music, despite the growth of MTV Europe, is still almost unilaterally ignored in Britain and regarded as foreign, dated, derivative, and subject to pernicious Europop influences. In an article on Europop written in 1990, Paul Morley makes the presumptuous assumption that 'Rock music has never been taken seriously on the continent as it is in Britain and America', and criticizes the popularity in Europe of the more trite Anglo-American pop stars like Jason Donovan (who is, of course, Australian) as an indication of 'a sluttish willingness on behalf of millions to keep wanting entertainers that were built up around money chasing money around a block of clichés'.[33]

Morley claims that even successful European rock groups like Kraftwerk, Can, Yello, Boney M and Abba are among the top fifty pop groups of all time because of their self-mocking misapplication and mistaken copying of Anglo-American styles, and that through 'their different levels of wrongness, their varying ways of missing the point: accidentally, they become interesting, sometimes more than interesting'. Making little distinction between different countries and cultures of Europe, he concludes piously that European pop music is simply a shallow, mechanical re-creation of Anglo-American models, and 'the sound of people who have little to think about because they have everything they want, and they just don't care'.[34] A similar view of European rock music was expressed by expatriate Australian writer Andrew Mueller in a *Melody Maker* article about Belgian group dEUS, another group perceived as misapplying a variety of Anglo-American rock styles in an accidentally interesting way, who were signed by Island Records in 1994:

> while the people of continental Europe are probably the most avid, even fanatical consumers of rock 'n' roll and its attendant culture in the world, their attempts to participate in it, to exert any influence over it, have been distinguished mainly by their haplessness. Indeed, when numbering the great European rock groups, an inability to count beyond nought has scarcely been a disadvantage. When you think Euro-rock, you think mistimed gestures, badly copied poses, lyrics that would make a cat laugh, and white socks.[35]

Asked by Mueller 'What makes dEUS the first decent rock band in European history', group leader Tom Barman replied, without irony, 'A lot of it has got to do with having a good accent'. Barman not only sings in almost perfect American English, but dEUS's music is full of pastiches of US rock influences from Tom Waits and Captain Beefheart to Pavement to the Velvet Underground, REM, Faith No More, Nirvana and numerous others in a listener-friendly mélange which allows reviewers to display their knowledge of rock history. In a climate where British pop is ignored in the USA, it is curious that dEUS's European rehash of significant moments in American rock history has been embraced in Britain. Their name derives from a song by the Icelandic group the Sugarcubes, one of only two European rock groups to enjoy success in the 1990s in the British music press. Both the Sugarcubes and the Swiss industrial group the Young Gods sing mostly in English, and preserve distinctly 'arty' associations which correspond to received English notions of European rock culture. Barman explained this European artistic orientation to the *NME*:

> The one thing that we noticed when we came to Britain was the cynicism and careerism of all the bands there. Everyone is desperate to get signed and to be famous. That's cool in a way, but it means there are very few original bands around – everyone copies the classic rock star way of doing things. In Belgium

and Holland bands are much more in it for good vibes, creativity, and doing something new.[36]

Although dEUS's originality appears to be based on the audacious range and diversity of musical influences that have been perceived by their anglophonic listeners, their novelty could be said to reside in an arresting variation on eclectic British pop norms which rely on what Runciman has described as 'shamelessly ... plunder[ing] the past for anything that might be cobbled together to make the perfect pop record'.[37]

Hip hop and 'populist modernism'

A distinctly influential American form of popular music which has had few successful exponents in the UK, rap and the broader rap, graffiti and break-dancing sphere of hip hop culture it belongs to, has produced international resonances which confirm the increasingly parochial nature of British pop. Grandmaster Flash's 'old school' rap recording, 'Adventures of Grandmaster Flash on the Wheels of Steel', which first appeared in 1981, is arguably the first use of sampling to appear on record in the history of popular music, which gives rap a special position in relation to pop eclecticism. Rap's hybridization of Jamaican toasting and Puerto Rican beats with the traditions of the African griots, the ritual insults of signifying, the dozens, and other forms of black American street culture, as well as disco and funk musical elements, together with its appropriation of a wide range of other musics, black, white, popular and 'serious', and television themes, advertising jingles and video game soundtracks through sampling, cutting, mixing and scratching, has caused it too to be seen within the academy as a ideally postmodernist phenomenon. Richard Shusterman, for example, in his essay 'The Fine Art of Rap', argues that rap's 'eclectic pastiche and cannibalization of past styles ... is central to the postmodern' and 'inimical to modernism's rationalised, disembodied, and formalised aesthetic'. Prefacing his essay with a quote from Shelley about 'rapt Poesy', portraying rap DJs as 'musical cannibals of the urban jungle' and message rappers as 'artists and poets' and comparing rap's appropriations to the paintings of Duchamp, Rauschenberg and Warhol, Shusterman aestheticizes rap into a new form of high culture. Claiming that rap's original manifestations in the South Bronx and Harlem in the late 1970s were, like modernist art, 'not intended for a mass audience', he none the less attempts to incorporate its often confusing and contradictory confrontational politics into a coherent postmodernist aesthetic. Praising the 'authenticity and power of [the] oppositional energy' of Public Enemy and Ice-T,[38] he argues: 'A fascinating feature of much underground rap is its acute recognition of the politics of culture: its challenge of the univocal claims of white history and education; and its attempt to provide alternative black historical narratives which can stimulate black pride and foster emancipatory impulses.'[39]

The imagined coherency of this historical project of cultural politics must surely make rap a modernist phenomenon, given postmodernism's loss of history and collapse of 'grand narratives'. This is affirmed by Paul Gilroy, who argues that the reclamation of black history in rap music and other hybrid cultural expressions of a 'black Atlantic' diaspora lie outside the concerns of postmodernism, which he regards as 'another Eurocentric master narrative from which the history and experience of blacks remain emphatically absent'.[40] Gilroy has proposed the notion of an 'Atlantic diaspora' of black music in which the use of historical musical forms through sampling and re-appropriation is not parody or pastiche but a reconstruction of black histories, 'folding back on themselves time and again to celebrate and validate the simple, unassailable fact of their survival'. Regarding music as 'the centre of black vernacular culture',[41] Gilroy posits the idea of a black 'populist modernism' which focuses on 'music and dance which have handled the anxieties and dilemmas involved in a response to the flux of modern life', generating 'a cohesive but essentially defensive politics and a corresponding aesthetic of redemption from racial subordination'.[42] Gilroy has usefully diagnosed three separate strands of US rap music, involving the 'self-conscious racial pedagogy' of African-American nationalist rap (KRS1, X Clan, etc.), the 'carefully calculated affirmative nihilism' of 'gangsta' rap (Ice Cube, Above the Law, etc.) and the 'ludic Afrocentrisms' of the 'Native Tongues' movement (Jungle Brothers, De La Soul, A Tribe Called Quest, etc.). He finds that this latter movement 'effectively contrasts the local (black nationalism) with the global (black internationalism) and Americanism with Ethiopianism'.[43] Acknowledging the ideological difficulties and confusions of the first two categories of rap's often misogynist, homophobic, violent, anti-Semitic, anti-Asian and anti-white sentiments, Gilroy attempts to construct a modernist, rationalist project for hip hop as 'black music' situated within a broad African musical diaspora.

'Black music' and nationalism

The term 'black music' is a problematic one, which is difficult to define in musicological or anthropological terms, as Philip Tagg, among others, has pointed out.[44] It has essentialist connotations, establishing connections between skin colour and music, and is often given ideological expression in African-American hip hop culture. As Gilroy has indicated, it is often linked with a 'radical utopianism' and 'a heavily mythologised Africanity that is itself stamped by its origins not in Africa but in a variety of pan-African ideology produced most recently by Afro-America'.[45] This enables African-American cultural critics like Greg Tate, founder of the quasi-nationalist Black Rock Coalition, to define 'black music' as 'our mother tongue', and claim that:

> Black music, like black basketball, represents an actualisation of those black ideologies that articulate themselves as antithetical to Eurocentrism. Music and 'ball both do this in ways that are counterhegemonic if not counter-supremacist – rooting black achievement in ancient black cultural practices. In the face of the attempt to erase the African contribution to world knowledge, and the diminution of black intelligence that came with it, the very fact of black talents without precedent or peers in the white community demolishes racist precepts instantaneously.[46]

An illustration of the kind of utopian, counter-hegemonic rhetorical strategy Tate is proposing might be the 1992 film *White Men Can't Jump*, and its soundtrack, *White Men Can't Rap*. Aligned to these vaguely defined notions of black musical culture is the loosely conceived idea of the Hip Hop Nation. According to Jeffrey Louis Decker, this term was first used in 1988 by the New York intellectual weekly *Village Voice*, which has a predominantly white readership, and later legitimized by the US music industry organ *Billboard* in 1991. Decker uses it in the sense of

> an 'imagined community' that is based less on its realisation through state formation than on a collective challenge to the consensus logic of the U.S. nationalism. The language of nation is appropriated by the hip hop community as a vehicle for contesting the changing discursive and institutional structures of racism in America. ... Hip hop nationalism, like black nationalism generally, provides an imaginative map and inspirational territory for African-Americans who wish both to end the institutionalised legacy of slavery and to create self-sufficient, organically-based organizations such as black businesses and Afro-centric school curriculums.[47]

Decker's rather narrow definition of the term forms part of an homogenizing rhetorical strategy in which he invokes Gramsci's concept of the 'organic intellectual' to propose a recontextualization of 1960s black American militancy for the 1990s, and to 'valorise the great ancient civilisations of North Africa as both the origin of all Western civilisation and the inspirational glue that binds the diverse black American community together'.[48] In this context, the Hip Hop Nation becomes a vague and amorphously local relation to other African-American nationalist projects. These include Afrika Bambaataa's Zulu Nation, the Five Percent Nation – which numbers rappers Rakim, Brand Nubian and Poor Righteous Teachers among its members, and which Nelson George has described as rising 'out of a spiritual vacuum in the black community' and lacking 'philosophical underpinning'[49] – and the Nation of Islam it is predicated on, whose anti-Semitic leader Louis Farrakhan is frequently sampled in rap music. These 'nationalist' organizations attempt to link African-American culture with 'ancient black cultural practices' in Africa, Egypt and the Islamic world, but as Gilroy has commented:

> There is a sense in which the new varieties of nationalism no longer attempt to be a coherent political ideology. They appear more usually as a set of therapies: tactics in the never-ending struggle for psychological and cultural survival. In some non-specific way, then, a new idea of African-ness conveniently dissociated from the politics of contemporary Africa operates transnationally and interculturally through the symbolic projection of 'race' as kinship. It is usually a matter of style, perspective or survivalist technique, before it becomes a question of citizenship, rights or fixed contractual obligations.[50]

In the USA, this imagined nationalism manifests itself in local, even parochial tropes such as the family, 'homies' or the 'hood' (neighbour-hood), while black (or, for that matter, brown) cultures outside of the USA are rarely, if ever, acknowledged; the USA becomes the whole world in an Americocentrism masquerading as Afrocentrism. It is difficult if not impossible, for example, to make any useful or direct connection between the individualistic 'tribalisms' of the Hip Hop Nation, as Andrew Ross attempts to in his romanticization of post-LA riot gangsta rap, 'Tribalism after LA', and the 'federalism, secessionism, and demands for regional autonomy and cultural pluralism that are sweeping the spectrum of 5,000 nations that inhabit the world's 190 states'.[51] Such a connection is vastly different from the more local discovery that the 1992 LA riots, which involved Latinos and Koreans as well as African-Americans, were 'truly multiethnic' although their direct connection with hip hop culture was more significant. Ice-T and Ice Cube both claimed the lyrics of their songs had predicted the riots (especially the latter's racist track 'Korean Black'), and Public Enemy's Chuck D's widely quoted statement that 'rap music is black America's CNN' was re-invoked by the US media as an indicator of the power of rap as a vehicle of information and activism within black American communities. Ross's argument, however, for the social origins of hip hop seems more rhetorical than actual, the stuff of neo-Marxist phantasmagoria:

> Hip hop, from the first, has been a *social* movement, which has come to bear all of the full-blown contradictions of a counterculture in its own right. Having emerged in the Bronx as an explicit alternative to gangland culture, hip hop's subsequent rise to international prominence has been shaped by the tension between its status as socio-political commentary, and its status as a commodity. On the one hand, it has been a medium for recording popular memory, for renovating activist histories and ideas, for renewing nationalist and postnationalist consciousness, and for shaping the attitudes and sensibilities of youth culture as black music and style always have done. On

the other hand, the successes of its independent record industry have encouraged the growth of a black entrepreneurial sector that exploits social prejudice – as nasty as they wanna be – as unscrupulously as the lords of narcotraffic exploit social poverty and despair.[52]

Ross's 'countercultural' characterization of hip hop echoes the white hippie libertarianism of the Woodstock Nation of the 1960s, while his lament for its *realpolitik* of commercial exploitation seems to overlook the constant demands for 'getting paid' which have featured throughout hip hop from its beginnings. And rap's effect on 'postnational consciousness' was all too clear during Ice Cube's 1993 Sydney concert, when he expressed patronizing surprise at the existence of a local hip hop scene – referring as much to his audience's dress codes as to his support group, multicultural Sydney rappers Sound Unlimited – and amazement that rap music had travelled so far from the USA. In apparent acknowledgement of Ice Cube's influence on local hip hop culture, rumours of a possible local gang war at his concert had circulated in local music papers. That they remained only rumours was evidence of Sydney's largely imaginary membership of the Hip Hop Nation.

Likewise the sight of Ice-T exhorting an almost all white, and predominantly middle-class, audience in Sydney in 1989 to stop taking crack and to stay away from hand guns and street gangs, while aggressively deprecating gays and pruriently manhandling his on-stage women dancers, seemed an acutely 'postnational' irony. (Although its effect on male members of the audience's behaviour towards the women in the audience and on their way home after the concert through the largely gay area of Oxford Street was not so ironic.) Returning to Australia three years later, Ice-T asked his four thousand-strong audience (who had paid more than $30 a head for a ticket) 'Is Sydney the motherfuckin' capital of the hip hop world?' 'Hell, yeah!' replied the audience, willing to indulge in any degree of suspension of disbelief, and encouraging Ice-T to refer to 'the Koori [Aboriginal] brothers' of whom there was hardly a single representative in the house.[53]

Rap music may have become a global phenomenon, with practitioners in many different countries around the world, as feature articles in the *New York Times* and *Time* magazine acknowledged in 1992, but its US manifestations seem to remain resolutely local, dominated by New York versus West Coast rivalry. A 1994 'ultimate history' of rap, commemorating fifteen years of hip hop, in the Afro-American style magazine *Vibe*, a black nationalist venture founded by jazz musician, television producer and cultural entrepreneur Quincy Jones, began by attempting to debunk numerous myths about the origins of hip hop,[54] and ended with an article proclaiming the superiority of West Coast rap over the East, as if this was the most pressing current issue in hip hop culture.[55] While it is undeniable that since the LA riots Los Angeles rappers have managed to inscribe inner-city ghettos like Watts, South Central and Compton on the international map of popular music more indelibly than any East Coast rappers, this is simply continuing evidence of a US domination of global popular music which rap has inherited.

The myths debunked in *Vibe*'s rap survey included hip hop's origins in the South Bronx (the West Bronx and the influence of Jamaican reggae sound systems need to be considered), its initial audiences being gang members ('ordinary kids' according to Kool Herc), that it was exclusively 'a black thing' ('racially diverse', including African-Americans, Afro-Caribbeans, Latinos and what Afrika Bambaataa called 'progressive minded' whites) and that its original manifestation was exclusively hardcore rap ('a free-form expression', according to Grandmaster Flash).[56]

This apparent need for a revisionist and more expansive and racially inclusive history of hip hop could be seen as an attempt to distance the 'old school' origins of rap from what Bambaataa refers to as the 'musical apartheid of the late 1980s' and the often violent, nasty and sexist manifestations of a number of 'new school' rappers. According to Bambaataa, 'In the early 80s, everything was progressive. People listened to funk, soul, reggae, rock, calypso, hip hop all in the same place.'[57] This heterogeneous mix of different musics portrays hip hop's origins as an all-embracing, heterogeneous, Utopian culture, as well as corresponding to current moves among rappers back to the influences of the 'old school' of Bambaataa, Grandmaster Flash, Kool Herc, Melle Mel, Kurtis Blow and others.

The year-by-year breakdown of significant hip hop events which follows in *Vibe* is a fairly orthodox, standard history. No mention is made of Gil Scott-Heron, the Last Poets, Latin hip hop, or any rap music outside of the USA, and the Sugarhill Gang's 'Rapper's Delight' is presented as the starting point of the fifteen-year history, because 'its wide release made hip hop instantly international'.[58] Emphasis is placed on legitimations of rap and hip hop through signings to major labels, the establishment of recording companies like Tommy Boy and Def Jam, advertising endorsements and coverage on radio and television and in the print media, as well as in movies and in book-length academic studies. Only three women rappers are mentioned – Queen Latifah, Salt-N-Pepa and Sister Souljah – the first two because of their commercial success, the latter only because she was featured on the cover of *Newsweek* in 1992 owing to President Clinton's response to her controversial comments about violence in the black community.

On the other hand, the survey does not stint at some of rap's controversial moments like the violence at Run DMC's 1986 Long Beach concert, Public Enemy's Professor Griff's anti-Semitic statements in 1989, when he said Jews were responsible for 'the majority of wickedness that goes on across the globe',[59] the perceived influence of Tone Loc's 'Wild Thing' on the New York Central Park rape in 1989, the controversy of

NWA's (Niggaz With Attitude) 'Fuck tha Police', 2 Live Crew's obscenity trial, Slick Rick's convictions for attempted murder, the perceived racism of Ice Cube's *Death Certificate*, Kriss Kross's offence to the memory of Hiroshima with *Da Bomb*, and (white-founded) rap magazine *The Source*'s internal scandal. What emerges is a problematic history which is none the less linked to a sense of black pride and African-American solidarity (the only white rappers to be mentioned are the Beastie Boys, whose interruption of the 1987 Grammy Award with a tape of Public Enemy's 'Timebomb' – which is also the title of the history – is included, along with their number one album *Licensed to Ill...*).

Vibe's hip hop history puts emphasis on anniversaries: the magazine's own first anniversary celebrations in August 1994 (at which Sugarhill Gang performed 'Rapper's Delight') the fifth anniversary of the Universal Zulu Nation in 1979, and its twentieth anniversary in 1994. As a project of African-American incorporation, it bears similarities to Quincy Jones's 1989 album *Back on the Block*, which combined three generations of black American jazz, gospel, soul, funk and rap musicians, presenting what Gilroy described as 'a powerful and necessary argument for the seams of continuity that, although invisible to most, connect the discrete, generational styles found in African-American musical culture'.[60] But by attempting to focus its willy-nilly, syncretic eclecticism within an unconvincing hip hop framework, the album, in Gilroy's opinion, loses itself in a totalizing vagueness, portraying a US-based Afrocentric nationalism as ethnic absolutism:

> Old and new, east and west simply dissolve into each other or, rather, into the receptacle provided for their interaction by the grand narrative of African-American cultural strength and durability. However compelling they may be, Jones's appropriations of Brazilian rhythm and African language are subservient to his need to legitimate African-American particularity. The promise of a truly compound diaspora, even of a global culture, that could shift understanding of black cultural production away from the narrow concerns of ethnic exceptionialism recedes rapidly.[61]

In her essay 'Nationalist Thought in Black Music', Kristal Brent Zook attempts to forge a more concrete and less idealized notion of Afrocentrism in the USA by incorporating marketing strategies and critical discourse. Linking the history of rap with the history of nationalism, Zook argues that African-American nationalism

> is not just a metaphoric or aesthetic vision which appears in the creative product, but it is also that which informs the actual material mechanisms of cultural production itself (i.e. the marketing, promotion and distribution of this product). ... rap confirms a sense of imagined, metaphorical community, but ... this fantasy of 'home' is simultaneously constructed materially through the very modes of production, marketing, and the critical discourses which surround it.[62]

This allows her to represent Quincy Jones, Spike Lee and the successful clothes designer Karl Kani as well as collaborations between Ice Cube and Chuck D, along with Nelson George's involvement in the 'Stop the Violence Movement' and the self-produced black American film renaissance as examples of 'economic nationalism' and resistance to and subversion of what she regards as 'white appropriation and theft of Black creativity' in the history of rap. This black cultural retrieval may be an attempt to reassert an African-American ownership of hip hop against claims like those of Dick Hebdige in his book *Cut 'N' Mix* that 'nobody can own' hip hop because of its diverse fusion of elements,[63] but it is difficult to see it as an expression of nationalism. As Gilroy comments in relation to Nelson George and others:

> Rap is a hybrid form rooted in the syncretic social relations of the South Bronx where Jamaican sound system culture, transplanted during the 1970s, put down new roots and in conjunction with specific technological innovations, set in train a process that was to transform black America's sense of itself and a large proportion of the popular music industry as well. How does a form which flaunts and glories in its own malleability as well as its transnational character become interpreted as an expression of some authentic Afro-American essence? Why is rap discussed as if it sprang intact from the entrails of the blues? What is it about Afro-America's writing elite which means that they need to claim this diasporic cultural form in such an assertively nationalist way?[64]

Similarly, claims for black American 'economic nationalism' are difficult to sustain, given events like the Zulu Nation's marketing of T-shirts with slogans stating 'Bitches ain't nothin' but ho's and tricks', the exorbitant prices of clothing marketed by Kani and 4 Acres and a Mule, well beyond the reach of working-class African-Americans, and the resort to violence against Korean street-sellers who market cheap imitations of these products. This type of 'economic nationalism' often appears spiritually bankrupt and morally ugly, and its incorporation as 'nationalism' a chimera. Likewise Spike Lee's marketing of Malcolm X products to black youth in the wake of his controversial 1993 film, which angered activist poet and music critic Amiri Baraka, seems a return to 1970s 'blaxploitation' strategies. As Zook points out, nationalism in an African-American context is 'a complex, contradictory, dynamic, historically loaded, "scary" word',[65] but her simplifications of it are little more than rhetorical.

As a dominant discourse, or 'grand narrative', nationalism is as useful to describe manifestations of popular music as postmodernism. But discussion of African-American nationalism in relation to rap and hip hop highlights the inseparability of music from national and ethnic identity, however they are conceptualized. As Mark Slobin has stated, 'music is at the heart of individual, group and national identity, from the personal to the political, from the refugee mother's lullaby to the "Star Spangled Banner" at the baseball game'.[66]

Attempts to 'rescue' rap music as a metaphorical expression of black American nationalism are often provoked by attempts by white writers to discredit hip hop, or suggest that it addresses only white audiences. The 1992 *Newsweek* cover story entitled 'Rap and Race', for example, published in the wake of Bill Clinton's censure of Sister Souljah's satirical suggestion that white people rather than black people be killed in ghetto gang wars, and Dan Quayle's condemnation of Ice-T's song 'Cop Killer', claimed that rap was being marketed to a predominantly white mainstream audience: 'rap is locating white insecurity about race – and black insecurity about class – and selling it back as entertainment. As a tidy projection of the messy fears people live under, rap gives its white audience a chance to explore – and ignore – them.'[67] But rather than indulging in a softening process to ensure palatability for white audience in order to achieve the crossover success that Motown had done in the 1960s, the *Newsweek* article suggested that rap aimed for the vicarious thrills of violent threats and danger, 'to curry favour with a white audience by showing rebellion'.[68] The tongue-in-cheek apotheosis of this perceived hard-core marketing strategy might be Ice-T's 1993 album *Home Invasion*, a nasty series of brutal and violent raps aimed directly at white listeners, whom Ice-T saw as 'eavesdroppers' on black rap music, or Ice Cube's 1992 album *Death Certificate*, which *Sydney Morning Herald* reviewer Jon Casimir described as

> covering the full spectrum of the politics of hatred. Jews, Koreans, gays, the army, police, whites, blacks, and women of all kinds are dealt with in the same numbingly aggressive way. In the US, the album has sold in the millions. ... The biggest problem in dealing with the record is that if you couldn't speak English (or rap's approximated version), you'd be listening to one of the finest albums in the idiom, a furious and compelling collection of rolling grooves, clever samples and awesome rhythmic delivery.[69]

The moral panic about rap music generated by the *Newsweek* rap cover story came hot on the heels of David Samuels's *New Republic* article which claimed that white acceptance had killed off hip hop's potential to operate as an influential cultural form of racial politics. In the light of the rise of rap videos to the top of MTV ratings as the most popular form of music television among white US youth between eighteen and twenty-four, Samuels claimed:

> whatever its continuing significance in the realm of racial politics, rap's hour as innovative popular music has come and gone. Rap forfeited whatever claim it may have had to particularity by acquiring a mainstream white audience whose tastes increasingly determined the nature of the form. What whites wanted was not music, but black music, which as a result stopped really being

either. ... The ways in which rap has been consumed and popularised speak not of cross-cultural understanding, musical or otherwise, but of voyeurism and tolerance of racism with the complicity of both blacks and whites.[70]

Such claims that white audiences have hijacked the cultural constituency of black US rap have the ring of wish-fulfilment about them, and appear to be responses to a perceived separatism in African-American rap. (Samuels seemed to be responding in particular to the anti-Semite remarks expressed by Professor Griff.) Such variations on the old 'sell-out' argument overlook the continual connection rap has had with 'getting paid', marketing strategies and commercial exploitation, and its vast black and non-Anglo constituencies of listeners and practitioners both within and outside the USA. Far from 'rap's hour' being over, it has proliferated and diversified to a bewildering extent, as Gilroy indicates:

> One of the things I find most troubling in debates about rap is that I do not think anyone actually knows what the totality of its hyper-creativity looks like. I am a compulsive consumer (user, actually) of that culture, but I cannot keep up with the sheer volume of hip hop product any more. I do not know if anyone can. There is simply too much of it to be assimilated and the kinds of judgments we make have to take that volume into account. It is a flood – it is not a flow, it is a flood, actually – and just bobbing up and down in the water trying to gauge its depth, tides and currents is not very fruitful.[71]

This sense of excess and over-saturation also indicates that, like predominantly white forms of pop music, the hybrid manifestations of rap music continue to regenerate themselves, and are resistant to most conceptualizations and periodizations which attempt to divide them into moments, hours or epochs. Most of these attempts continue to insist on the socially marginal and politically oppositional qualities of rap and hip hop and regard it as a coherent expression of African-American culture. But as Gilroy has noted, 'Hip hop's marginality is as official, as routinised, as its overblown defiance; yet it is still represented as an outlaw form', and he identifies a need to interrogate 'the revolutionary conservatism that constitutes its routine political focus but which is over-simplified or more usually ignored by its academic celebrants'.[72]

The increasing number of scholarly articles on rap music by academics is one symptom of this celebration of the marginality of rap in which a taste for the vicarious thrills of African-American hip hop becomes synonymous with academic hipness. In an 'appreciation' of gangsta rap published in *Critical Enquiry*, for example, Tim Brennan offers his critique as an answer to what he sees as the deficiencies of the growing literature of previous rap criticism. Exaggerating the strength of various forms of opposition to rap, Brennan castigates much academic analysis of it for a deficiency in feeling and for being overly concerned with rap's history and sonic structure rather than the listening experience it offers.

Finding that Shusterman's 'smart' postmodernist view of rap 'acts too much the agent of alien black youth in the fuddy-duddy surroundings of the academy',[73] Brennan argues that rap's appeal lies in its excessive output, chaotic and dissonant 'tonal clashes' which 'please by being unpleasant' and its modernist 'deep structure of African intertextuality ... in which African-American achievement and struggle are recorded and promoted'.[74] He then unconvincingly attempts to locate rap's politics beyond the blatant and often confused political rhetoric of many rappers in 'the interstices', where expressions of 'cultural uplift' can be found in relation to hedonism, religion and business entrepreneurialism, and where 'the messy politics the poor live, or those who mouth for them'[75] are represented. In attempting to reply to a series of negative criticisms of gangsta rap, Brennan works himself into a corner of obfuscation and patronizing expressions of an assumed ghetto hipness.

A more wide-ranging example of simplifying academic celebration is Nelson George's 'Chronicle of Post-Soul Black Culture', which places rap music and hip hop culture within an open-ended historical continuum of African-American musical, cultural, sporting, criminal and political events from 1971 to 1992. George begins with Melvin Van Peebles's underground film *Sweet Sweetback's Baadasssss Song*, which he sees as projecting 'rebellious black heroism in visual terms that will echo in pop music iconography 20 years later'.[76] In the following two decades, George argues, African-American culture evolved 'from gospel-and-blues rooted with a distinctly country-accented optimism to assimilated-yet-segregated citified consciousness flavoured with nihilism, Afrocentrism, and consumerism.'[77] This covers a multitude of contradictory elements and builds them into a homogenized historical totality, in which not a single female rapper is mentioned. (Tricia Rose subsequently challenged the masculine focus of George's history in a letter to the *Village Voice*, where it was originally published.) As Brian Cross emphasizes in his otherwise breezy and uncritical history of LA hip hop, 'The culture of the gang, the culture of the vato, the pachuco and westie, Eurodisco, skate culture, house, Rastafarianism and Islam all contribute to the vocabulary of hip hop. ... In 1993 it has become exceedingly difficult to talk about hiphop as a unitary phenomenon.'[78]

George's syncretic chronicle of African-American hip hop culture, offered as a guide to African-American identity, also contains a number of events which have exerted influences well outside the USA, combining with local indigenous cultural formations into transnational hybrids which are interfaces between African-American and other local cultures. This 'globalisation of vernacular forms' as Gilroy has called it,[79] is usually not acknowledged by commentators on African-American culture, or, when it is, is often dismissed as 'derivative', as in Shusterman's judgement of French rap music.[80] Rappers from the African continent like black South African Prophets of da City, who have been denouncing the suffering and injustice in black ghetto townships since 1983, or the Senegalese group Positive Black Soul, would appear to be ideal exponents for exchange programmes of Afrocentricity in the USA, but any interest in them outside their countries of origin seems restricted to Europe. Similarly, the hard-line militant rhetoric of the Palestinian rap group Shehadin (Martyrs), who advocate suicide and bomb attacks against Israelis, and their sternly moralistic Islamic stance, expressed in a song entitled 'Order your Wife to Wear a Veil for a Pure Palestine', described by David Hudson in the *Guardian* in August 1995, makes US Nation of Islam rappers seem mild by comparison.[81] The willingness of white as well as black US commentators to claim hip hop and rap as an authentic expression of US popular culture, and assertions like Brian Cross's that 'the black community is definitely the community of origin of the music',[82] have led to its institutionalization as an exclusively North American phenomenon.

Hispanic rap in the USA

The concern of many African-American critical commentaries on rap music to embed it in black nationalist projects causes them not only to neglect or overlook international manifestations of rap music but also to gloss over the multicultural aspects of US hip hop and ignore non-anglophonic rap closer to home. The participation of Puerto Rican graffiti artists such as Futura 2,000 and break-dancers like the Rock Steady Crew in the initial developments of hip hop in the Bronx in the late 1970s, and the Latino rap movement which developed in East Los Angeles in the 1980s, for example, are rarely if ever acknowledged. As Juan Flores has pointed out:

> Puerto Ricans have been involved in hip hop since the beginning, since it first emerged in the streets of Harlem and the South Bronx nearly twenty years ago. Along with their African-American counterparts, 'Puerto Rocks' (as Puerto Rican hip-hoppers came to be called) were an intrinsic part of the forging of expressive styles which have become the hallmark of an entire generation, and have diffused throughout the country and worldwide. While the relation of other cultural groups to rap has been one of adoption and rearticulation, Puerto Ricans have been present as initiators and co-creators, such that their recent history as a community can be tracked by way of reference to their participation in the trajectory of the genre.[83]

Flores calls for a revision of hip hop history which acknowledges the 'cultural interaction between black and Puerto Rican communities' that has been involved and which is obscured in claims for the multiculturalism of hip hop, but black American communities seem unwilling to make this concession. Raegan Kelly, on the other hand, characterizes

Chicano hip hop more realistically as 'a separate but parallel story', relating it to celebrations of difference by multicultural LA rappers like Funkdoobiest, the Samoan Boo-Yaa Tribe, and the Irish-Americans House of Pain.[84] Even Tricia Rose in her widely acclaimed 1994 book on the 'marginality' of rap music and its expression of 'Afrodiasporic' American culture, *Black Noise*, while noting the participation of Latinos in hip hop, and expressing the hope that future books will deal with 'more globally focused projects' like Latino rappers in LA and New York, Chinese and Japanese break-dancers in Hong Kong and the French, German, British and Brazilian rap scenes,[85] devotes only half a paragraph to US Hispanic rappers. Rose, whose book is important in dealing extensively with female rappers and addressing the masculinist bias of African-American hip hop, name-checks the LA-based Kid Frost and Mellow Man Ace and Panamanian rapper El General before moving on to discuss Cypress Hill, a group which tends to conceal its Hispanic and Italian roots for commercial reasons, but which Rose claims 'serve[s] as an explicit bridge between black and Hispanic communities that build on long-standing hybrids produced by blacks and Hispanics in New York'.[86] Mitchell (1996: 33)

In a 1991 interview with Brian Cross, Cypress Hill, whose music is mainly about the delights of smoking marijuana, and who consist of a Cuban, a Chicano and an Italian-American from Southgate, Los Angeles – not New York as is often supposed – declared that they made their music 'for everybody, not just people in New York or LA or of one race, everybody ... the niggas, the Mexicans, the Chinese, white kids, it don't matter', going on to describe Kid Frost as a 'sucka' for his espousal of a Latin audience.[87] In 1993 they refused to be interviewed for a feature on Chicano rappers in the LA music monthly *Option* unless they were featured on the magazine's cover. The *Option* article, by Lorraine Ali, dealt with the immense difficulty rappers like Frost, Ace, the Hispanic MCs, Proper Dos, and an estimated twenty or thirty other Latino hip hop groups with recording contracts have in gaining recognition, even among Latino communities in the USA. The article cites Cypress Hill as the only Latino rappers to have made the 'big time', and having 'borrowed from Chicano culture without saying thanks'.[88]

Kid Frost's 1990 gangsta-style rap 'La Raza', an adaptation of the early 1970s El Chicano hit 'Viva La Tirado' by African-American bandleader Gerard Wilson, on his album *Hispanic Causing Panic*, became something of a Latino anthem, claiming 'It's in our blood to be an Aztec warrior'. He raps mainly in English for greater accessibility, using lardings of Calo, Hispanic slang derived from prisons. Frost, whose real name is Arturo Molina Jnr, uses many of the braggadocio trappings of African-American gangsta rap, posing for photos with a gun in his hand, using spoken word and musical samples and rapping about ghetto life, police harassment, getting paid, prison and urban violence. But he also uses Latin percussion and calls for peace and unity in 'La Raza', which declares himself 'Chicano and I'm brown and proud', as well as initiating community projects in Los Angeles. Also notably absent from his raps is any deprecating reference to women, as he explained to Brian Cross: 'I never, never on any record disrespected women or somebody's mother 'cause that's not done in the Hispanic community.'[89] In 1991 he organized Latin Alliance, a joint venture of Latino rappers including the Cuban Mellow Man Ace (also known as U. Reyes, 'The Brother with Two Tongues', who specializes in macho posturing and party rap), the Puerto Rican group ALT and others in an album which featured a version of War's 1970s hit 'Low Rider'. While the latter was a minor hit, the album failed, but in 1992 Frost produced and performed on 'City of Fallen Angels', a benefit single for the Los Angeles riots relief funds which featured Jesse Jackson, Arsenio Hall, Young MC, the Crenshaw Church Choir and others in a black–Hispanic crossover community project.

Lorraine Ali has described the difficulties faced by Latino rappers like Frost, who have to play down their ethnicity to avoid alienating significant sections of their own community as well as non-Latinos, and for whom the rhetoric of 'brown and proud' or the Hip Hop Nation is not a simple option:

> For Chicano rappers, talking about La Raza is more complicated. Latinos are broken up by cultural barriers within the Hispanic world: Cubans didn't grow up like Mexicans, who didn't grow up like Puerto Ricans or Salvadoreans. Unlike African-Americans, whose tribal roots became tangled up and ripped apart during the savagery of the slave trade, Hispanic cultural borders remain intact and strong in this country. So when the rhetoric of Latino rappers becomes nationalistic, it's not just black or white audiences they may alienate – it can be other Latinos.[90]

None the less, Frost has arguably had an influence outside the USA, not just in Latin America but in Europe. Italian rappers, whom I shall be discussing in Chapter 4, were in all probability inspired by his use of Spanglish to abandon their attempts at rapping in English and begin using first Italian and then regional dialects. (Frost visited Italy in 1992 and improvised freestyle raps with a number of Italian rappers, and Italian rap, like Frost's, is largely free from any 'dissing' of women – for similar cultural and community reasons.) A *New York Times* feature in 1992 on the spread of rap around the world describes how Claudio Yarto of Calo, the only successful Mexican rap group at the time, was so inspired by Frost's visit to Mexico City in the mid-1980s that he used a tape of Frost's performance to teach himself to create rap music.[91] Both these examples suggest that the idea of a Hip Hop Nation may be really meaningful in any global sense only when it is applied outside the USA.

Global rap: the view from the USA

A *New York Times* article on rap outside the USA, by James Bernard, is an important document in terms of mapping global configurations of rap from an American perspective. Bernard sets out to examine what he describes as 'The American art form ... hopscotching the globe', and question how well rap has translated outside 'an American context where rap and race are inextricably bound'. Comparing rap's 'democratic' nature to that of punk rock (which, it is worth recalling, originated in Britain, not the USA), he identifies one of its main universal properties as bearing witness, citing approvingly the Australian rappers Sound Unlimited Posse's little-known B-side 'Paradise Lost', about the mistreatment of Aborigines, and Brazilian Ademir Lemos's rap about 'fishnets', the youth gangs in Rio. Other elements of rap Bernard identifies as exportable are its orientation towards protest and 'boastful self-awareness', and he concludes with the suggestion that a test of the existence of an international rap community might be if L. L. Cool J. ever felt inclined to 'diss' a Russian rapper. Cold War models still appear to predominate in this 'new world order' of rap.[92]

Assumptions of (African) American ownership and dominance of rap music continue in the series of brief reports from different countries which follow Bernard's article, although Daisann McLane's feature on the veteran Trinidad Calypso toaster Alric Farrell (also known as Pretender) acknowledges rap's debts to its fifty-year-old 'Forgotten Caribbean Connection', as well as its more ancient heritage in the African griots. McLane also points out how rap has cross-fertilized Jamaican dancehall, Haitian compas, Dominican merengue and Trinidadian calypso, before concluding that all these musical forms are part of an 'African-American tradition'.[93]

Brief reports follow about the hip hop scenes in Russia, China, India, Japan, West Africa, Eastern Europe, Britain, France and Mexico. Steven Erlanger characterizes Russian rap as a temporary Western fad which has been converted into apolitical, escapist, fashion-oriented, and even overtly violent and racist local manifestations, which have to overcome the difficulties of adapting the Russian language to the American rhyme patterns of rap, and lack its black underclass.[94] Nicholas D. Kristoff cites British popsters Wham! as the chief influence on a virtually non-existent Chinese rap scene, and identifies only one Chinese rapper, Dou Wei, a former heavy metal rocker.[95] Edward Gargan can likewise offer only one rapper in India, the Bombay-based Baba Seghal, whose main influences he ascribes to MTV Asia and Vanilla Ice.[96] Steven R. Weisman estimates the existence of forty Japanese 'Hammer Wannabes', with the biggest rap hit in Japan being 'Talking Nonsense' by a group called Scha-dara-parr, whose name consists of nonsensical syllables. Japanese rap is portrayed as a vehicle for aggressive political messages, snatches of English, and self-parody, and as sounding 'like its American counterpart, perhaps because the language suits rap's staccato chops'.[97]

Kenneth B. Noble's survey of West Africa deals only with Abidjan, in the Ivory Coast, where clubs feature local rappers imitating their favourite American rappers, who are featured on a weekly music television show. Rap is also portrayed as a replacement for the decline of Ghanaian high-life music and Nigerian ju-ju.[98] In Eastern Europe, Burton Bollag claims, rap 'blandly imitates the American original', but expresses the concerns and observations of post-revolutionary Eastern European youth, such as sex, drugs and poverty (in the case of the Prague group Rapmasters, poverty exacerbated by being surrounded by wealthy Western tourists). Like Russian, the polysyllabic nature of Slavic languages is regarded as an obstacle to the clear-cut rhythms and rhymes of rap.[99]

In Britain, Simon Reynolds portrays the rap scene as similarly derivative of American models, and largely confined to a submerged underground scene dominated by a 'celebratory and multiracial' rave culture. Reynolds sees British rap as having hybridized into ragga, hip-house, techno, and more compound musical forms like the ambient-soul-funk-reggae of Massive Attack.[100] In William Schomberg's survey of Mexico, Calo is presented as the only Mexican rap group and as posing no threat to American rappers, leading him to conclude that 'there is hardly a hip-hop explosion in Latin America' – an assumption that, even on available evidence in the USA, is questionable to say the least.[101]

The overall impression conveyed by this multiple *New York Times* feature, compiled completely by Anglo-American journalists, is that rap is an exclusively African-American artform which has been badly imitated in other countries, and its US origins and domination remain unchallenged by any of its derivative international manifestations, even in Britain. The sole exception to this norm is John Rockwell's survey of French rap, which he states

> comes by its own roots honorably, with real anger emanating from depressed minority neighborhoods and direct traditions of spoken music in the West African griots and North African muezzins of its former colonies. If hearing rap in French strikes some Americans as inherently fancified, the language's felicitous rhymes make for some dazzling wordplay.[102]

Rockwell profiles three prominent French rappers: the Senegalese emigrant M. C. Solaar, whom he unflatteringly compares to M. C. Hammer, the hardcore NTM, whom he compares to Public Enemy and the Sex Pistols, and the largely North African, Marseilles-based IAM (Imperial Asiatic Men), whom he describes rather unenthusiastically as combining 'Egyptian mythology, Muslim pride and the strains of rai, a kind of Algerian pop, to sometimes energising effect'. French rap is accorded some of the prerequisites for an authentic, roots-based existence, but criticized for displaying residues of Europop and the French chanson tradition, and lacking the 'hard-driving funk pulse of the best American groups'. The implication is that any indigenous national or local characteristics are, like language difficulties, inherent obstacles to the achievement of this American artform.

Jay Cocks's article 'Rap Around the Globe', which appeared in *Time* magazine two months after the *New York Times* feature, confirmed a lingering American curiosity about international appropriations of rap, which Cocks described as 'now possibly the most successful American export this side of the microchip, permeating, virtually dominating, worldwide youth culture'. Quoting M. C. Solaar saying 'Parisian rap is pretty much a US branch office. We copy everything, don't we?',[103] Cocks put paid to any suspicions that French rap cultures was posing any threat to US domination. (An article by Dan Glaister in the British *Guardian* in 1994 quoted Solaar saying almost the opposite: 'Sometimes I'm proud to say I'm doing French music, French rap, because none of the tracks we do are imitations. We listen to West Coast, Acid Jazz, hip hop, hard core ... and we do something totally different. We have influences, but we know we are living in France'.[104]) Re-juggling the global rap scenario slightly, Cocks surveyed innocuous teenage hip hop fashions in Japan, the ideological, dialect-based posses emanating from the computer-linked social centres around Italy, potentially dangerous political fantasies in Brazilian rap and a predominantly dance-oriented Russian scene, concluding that British-based ragga might offer 'the first serious challenge' to US rap's primacy.

Assumptions in both the *New York Times* and *Time* articles that rap music is confined to national borders, but subject to continuous assessment in terms of American norms and standards, mean that both accounts of global rap have little value outside of their assertion that rap is an inherently African-American musical genre with its own fixed properties and features. Little attempt is made to understand the various foreign adaptations of the genre in the context of the musical language of individual countries, or even in terms of a fusion of transnational and hybrid influences.

Both articles confirm what Ian Steaman's liner notes to leading New York independent rap label Tommy Boy Records' 1993 international rap compilation *Planet Rap* called 'the American monopoly on rap superiority'. These liner notes incorporated information from the *New York Times* article in listing the names of prominent rap groups from the UK, Japan, Australia, France, Canada, Denmark, Sweden, Italy, South Africa, Brazil, Germany, Holland, Belgium, Spain, Greece, the Czech Republic, the former USSR, India, Mexico and China. This broadening of the global perspective was not matched by the predominantly lightweight, all-male musical contents of *Planet Rap*, however. The compilation featured only four of twelve tracks in languages other than English (IAM from France,

MD MCs from Brazil, Articolo 31 from Italy and Microphone Pager from Japan) and even included a US rapper (Coolio, who subsequently won a Grammy Award in 1996 for 'Gangsta's Paradise'). It almost seemed designed to highlight the derivative aspects of international rap, and contained some mystifying selections: the completely unknown Melbourne group Mama's Funkstikools was chosen to represent Australia over the far more prominent and distinctive Sound Unlimited; the juvenile Italian pop-rap group Articolo 31's rap about street fights among *motorino* (Lambretta)-riding middle-class teenaged street gangs, described as 'a raw street tale of gangs and turf fights' was chosen in preference to far stronger examples by at least a dozen other Italian posses or individual rappers; and the rather pedestrian English track by the London Posse took precedence over more forceful rappers like Credit to the Nation, Blaze or Fun^Da^Mental. Norway and Sweden were represented by English-language rappers, while the Brazilian group MVP, who contributed a rather lightweight samba-pop rap, was based in New York, and the rather gimmicky Japanese group Microphone Pager was presented as apeing black American fashions. That left the Irish ragga-rap group Scaryeire, the black South African rappers Prophets of da City, and IAM to offer the only distinctive and incisive cuts on the album, which predictably failed to sell in any significant quantity and ended up in bargain bins.[105]

Some developments in francophone rap

In the 1990s, a vast range of different local and regional forms of rap have developed globally, combining US influences with local musical formations, to the extent that, as the Italian radio announcer and music critic Luca De Gennaro stated in the liner notes to a 1992 compilation called *Italian Rap Attack*, 'Rap is a universal language, in whatever language it happens to be in, and whatever part of the world it is produced'.[106]

The crossover success of French rapper M. C. Solaar in the anglophonic world has focused some attention on a significantly Afrocentric, multicultural and migrant francophone hip hop scene, which as Miguel D'Sousa has indicated, has been developing since Afrika Bambaataa's European tour with Public Enemy, the Rock Steady Crew and others in 1982.[107] Solaar's guest appearance on Gang Starr rapper Guru's ground-breaking 1993 jazz-rap *Jazzmatazz* album with a track entitled 'Le Bien, le Mal' (Good and Evil) brought him to the attention of New York hip hop aficionados, despite the language barrier, and was perhaps partly due to long-standing connections between Paris and African-American jazz musicians such as Miles Davis. He was later featured on the *Rebirth of Cool Volume 3* jazz-rap compilation, and invited to collaborate with US jazz musician Ron Carter to produce 'Un Ange en Danger' (An Angel in Danger) on the 1994 jazz-rap AIDS benefit compilation album *Stolen Moments: Red Hot and Cool*. Meanwhile his first album, *Qui Seme Le Vent Recolte le Tempo* (Who Sows the Wind Reaps the Beat), released in 1991, had drawn some attention in England, and by the time his second album, *Prose Combat* (1993), was released in the English-speaking world, he was being fêted in the British music press (even featured on the cover of *Straight No Chaser*). He gave a concert in London in December 1994, which was attended largely by francophiles and French expatriates with little connection with hip hop culture, indicating the more intellectual cultural appeal Solaar tends to have in comparison to US rappers.

One has to speak fluent French to fully appreciate the highly literate verbal wit, wordplay and quick-fire onomatopoeic runs in Solaar's raps, which are peppered with hip Anglicisms and name-droppings from Rimbaud, Rousseau and Lacan to Sylvester Stallone, Arnold Schwarzenegger and former Italian goalkeeper Dino Zoff. None the less, the cool jazz and film soundtrack samples and loping beats which his DJs Jimmy Jay and Boom Bass lay down behind Solaar ensure that the musical aspect of his output is consistently varied and engaging. Solaar combines the 'edutainment' elements of West Coast rappers Boogie Down Productions with an 'art into pop' intellectualism in dealing with subjects like racism, war, AIDS and police harassment along with less political subjects like the fashion industry, Westerns (in a pastiche of Serge Gainsbourg's 'Bonnie and Clyde'), philosophy and human relations.

More culturally sophisticated than any of his US counterparts and completely free of expletives, sexism and racism, Solaar is sometimes accused of addressing an educated elite rather than the social, political and cultural concerns of la Goutte d'Or, the Paris suburb and immigrant African subculture he comes from. His eclectic use of the French language has even been invoked by right-wing Minister of Culture Jacques Toubon as a model for his campaign for a restricted and protected usage of the French language free of the corruptions of slang and anglicisms. But as Solaar has indicated, his relatively correct and literate usage of the French language is a deliberate tactic to counter American rap's bad reputation: 'I wanted to correct all the cliches about rap. ... People used to think we were just robbing, stealing, selling drugs ... the image was coming from the US. So the first album was in well-written French. No slang, good subjects and sometimes just poetry'.[108]

Solaar's fellow rapper Soon EMC, originally in the rap group 501 Posse, imposes less control on his anglicisms, and likewise began to cross over into the anglophonic world with his 1993 album *A Tout ... Point de Vue* (From Every Point of View). Although not as smooth, wide-ranging or witty in his word play as Solaar, Soon EMC uses a similar jazz- and funk-oriented musical idiom which he calls 'rap jazz soul' in a series of boasting and constantly self-defining raps which also deal with political issues such as hunger, poverty, ghetto life, pollution and neo-Nazis. He stresses the pluralism of his perspective, especially in the collective rap '500 One for All', about the Quartier Nord district of Paris, and the distinctively intellectual, culture-oriented nature of francophone rap:

> Francophone rap is really different from Anglophone rap. The message is the same, because I think it's possible to say everything in rap music today ... but in France the reality is totally different. You have to go to school, then college, then university, because France is a country of culture, literature, poetry, writers, good food and fashion! ... France is a country with a big culture, and it's important for people in France to recreate this culture in the lyrics. And that's why Solaar, Soon EMC, IAM, we write, we choose our words, because it's important for people to understand what we say. It's not just rap for raps, it's rap for the message, rap for the writer, for the mind.[109]

The Marseilles group IAM's massive two-and-a-half hour 1993 double album *Ombre est Lumière* (Shadow is Light), which has also been released in France in two different single-album versions, is in many ways the unacknowledged masterpiece of Francophone rap, but despite being produced in New York by prominent sound engineer Nicholas Sansano, who has produced albums by Public Enemy and Sonic Youth, it is virtually unknown in the English-speaking world. One of the group's tracks is entitled 'Reste Underground' (Stay Underground), which illustrates their underground status as well as the sense of darkness, gloom and obscurity which permeates *Ombre est Lumière*, a title which suggests that the light of knowledge can issue from the shadows and darkness of Marseilles.

IAM comprise one French national, two members of Spanish origin, and one each of Senegalese, Italian and Algerian origin, and the multicultural nature of the group in itself offers an affront to anyone with xenophobic inclinations. IAM characterize Marseilles as 'The Planet Mars', the title of the group's debut 1989 album, and emphasize its separation from the rest of France as a seaport with large numbers of immigrants from Spain, Greece, North Africa and Egypt. The group's raps are spiced with Italian, Spanish and Arabic slang, and address issues such as racism, unemployment, war, drugs, poverty and local identity. Their song 'Où Sont les Roses?' (Where are the Roses?) begins with a French explanation of the Italian tricolours, samples a Neapolitan song and includes an argument in Italian about emigration in its portrayal of the historical shift in Italian immigrants in Marseilles from the market gardeners who were victims of racism to the present perpetrators of racist views. 'Le Soldat' (The Soldier) samples helicopter blades and Middle Eastern music in dealing with the Gulf War, while 'Mars Contre Attaque' deals with unemployment and the lack of government spending in Marseilles. But IAM also have their lighter moments; like M. C. Solaar (who quotes approvingly their concept of a 'mental hold-up' in *Prose Combat*), they sample Serge Gainsbourg on 'Je Ne Veux Plus Voir

Personne en Harley Davidson' (I Never Want to See Another Harley Davidson Rider). On 'La Méthode Marsimil' a mock lesson in Marseilles dialect is interrupted by an American voice exclaiming 'Damn! I wish I could speak French', which has obvious resonances for anglophonic listeners. Unlike Solaar and Soon EMC, IAM do not include the texts of their lyrics in the album, and there is little to guide non-French speakers through the forty tracks of *Ombre est Lumière*, which feature a dramatic array of samples, from Marseilles football chants to Arabic, French and African and Italian songs. The group's aim is to address francophonic listeners in West Africa, Canada and Belgium as well as in France, and their all-embracing, open brand of multicultural hip hop moves from specific local concerns to universal ones.[110] In musical terms, *Ombre est Lumière* rivals any rap album to have come out of the USA in the 1990s in its inspired reflection of Marseilles as a multiethnic city of racism, unemployment and neglect.

Another multi-ethnic francophone group is the Lausanne-based Sens Unik, who are of Swiss, Turkish, Tunisian, French and Spanish origin, rap in French and Spanish and snippets of English about multiculturalism, food and holidays and debunk Swiss stereotypes in their album *Chromatic* (1994). Also on the Lausanne-based Unik label are the ironically named Geneva-based ragga-jazz-rappers Silent Majority, who rap in English, Jamaican patois, French and Swahili, as well as featuring the Spanish-language rap of MC Carlos from Sens Unik. Silent Majority sometimes use four languages in the same song to express 'international truths in a tribal style'. Characterizing themselves as 'funky multilinguals', they embody the concept of rap as a global idiom and a universal language.

Also celebrating Francophone multiculturalism are the more pop-oriented Alliance Ethnik, whose 1995 album *Simple and Funky* and single 'Respect' – which includes vocals by Vinia Mojica, a female backing vocalist with US 'native tongue' group De La Soul, and remixes by De La Soul and US rappers Gravediggaz – were released by Virgin in the UK. Containing French and Arabic members, Alliance Ethnik overemphasize the funk component of their music, as well as the extent of their ethnic diversity, beginning the album with messages of respect from a range of places including Vietnam, Portugal, Senegal, the USA, Germany, Spain, former Yugoslavia, Jerusalem and Italy over a sample of Courtney Pine's 'Children of the Ghetto', before settling into a largely self-congratulatory and anonymously mono-ethnic jazz-soul-funk groove, with blandly universal titles like 'L'Union du Son', 'Salsalliancia' and 'Psycho Funk de l'Alliance' and undistinctive French lyrics.

The growing number of francophone and multilingual rappers indicates that French rap has developed its own 'diaspora' which includes migrants from Africa, Algeria and the Arabic world. In other European countries such as Germany, Italy and Spain, rap and hip hop were initially slow in taking root within indigenous expressions of popular music, but significant numbers of local groups rapping in their native language have emerged in the 1990s after an initial phase of imitative English-language rap. In 1993 Mark Pennay described a divided and largely middle-class German hip hop scene aware of the few social affinities it had with US hip hop:

> the fledgling genre of German rap is currently the scene of a three-way contest, between the somewhat dictatorial enthusiasts still active since the early 1980s, younger hip hoppers inspired by a second, later wave of rap influences (the post-1989 trend), and the political fringe seeking an urgently-needed format for antifascist political messages. Over and above this lies a gloss of pure pop makers, who without commitment to either the core hip hop culture, nor the antiracist cause, have taken up the music of the moment. It is currently too early to say which group will win out.[111]

As an example of the first tendency Pennay cites Advanced Chemistry, a trio of Haitian, Ghanaian and Italian origin, who have examined the dilemma of foreign-born German citizens as well a defending 'old school' hip hop. Die Fantastischen Vier (the Fantastic Four) were one of the first groups to rap in German, and went on to achieve mainstream pop success, while Mastino represent a hard-core political fringe who shifted its allegiance, as a number of Italian groups did, from hard-core-punk to a fusion of hip hop, techno, jazz, metal and progressive rock. As we shall see in later chapters, hip-hop cultures in Australia and Aotearoa/New Zealand have similarly been divided between commercially oriented, old school and new school tendencies, indicating a number of shared universal elements in appropriations of rap styles around the globe.

Because distinctively localized appropriations of rap music and other forms of pop and rock music throughout Europe and Oceania lie outside the territory of dominant Anglo-American music industry and critical discourses of popular music, they are seldom heard or reported, except occasionally as a way of reaffirming dominant musical models such as US rap. One of the aims of this book is to rectify this situation. If a transnational, totalizing 'master narrative' capable of including popular music from all over the world were possible, it might find expression in Vesa Kurkela's proposal of the end of national musics in 'music as late-modern collage':

> Music as late modern collage refers to musical life, where national and transnational features, local and global music are, on the one hand, living side by side and, on the other hand, continuously forming various fusions. ... In this case cultural change is seen as a complex process, where global and local do not form an antithesis. On the contrary, the very process of binding people together into a global, transnational culture leads to an increasing sensitivity to the local particularities of social life.[112]

In terms of dominant discourses on popular music, whether they be postmodernist, Afrocentric, nationalist, multiculturalist, diasporic or otherwise, Kurkela's concept offers a way of considering popular music around the globe which at once affirms its distinctively local features while acknowledging its links to globally dominant influences. The remainder of this book will be concerned with non-Anglo-American musical appropriations and manifestations, and how notions of local identity and cultural change can be constructed around them in the light of their perceived Anglo-American influences. But first, the following chapter considers the phenomenon of world music, and the global extensions of popular music it offers into previously uncharted musical territories.

Notes

1. N. George (1988) *The Death of Rhythm and Blues* (New York, E. P. Dutton), p. xii.
2. *Ibid.*, p. 106.
3. *Ibid.*, p. 150.
4. *Ibid.*, p. 108.
5. S. Frith (1987) 'We Win Again', *The Village Voice* (29 December), p. 106.
6. S Frith (1988a) *Music for Pleasure* (London, Polity Press), p. 150.
7. S. Frith (1984) *Sound Effects* (London, Constable), p. 162.
8. I. Chambers (1987), *Urban Rhythms: Pop Music and Popular Culture* (London, Methuen), p. 199.
9. J. Lyotard (1984) *The Postmodern Condition – A Report on Knowledge* (Manchester University Press), p. xxiv.
10. *Ibid.*, p. 76.
11. F. Jameson (1985) 'Postmodernism and Consumer Society', in H. Foster (ed.) *Postmodern Culture* (London, Pluto Press), p. 185.
12. M. Morris (1992) 'The Man in the Mirror: David Harvey's "Condition" of Postmodernity', in E. Jacka (ed.) *Continental Shift: Globalisation and Culture* (Sydney, Local Consumption Press), p. 26.
13. *Ibid.*, p. 46.
14. R. Shuker (1995) *Understanding Popular Music* (London, Routledge), p. vii.
15. D. Hebdige (1988) 'Who Put the Bomp?', *New Statesman* (5 February), p. 30.
16. Jameson (1985), p. 111.
17. A. Goodwin (1990) 'Popular Music and Postmodern Theory', *Cultural Studies*, vol. 5, no. 1, pp. 177, 181.
18. *Ibid.*, p. 176.
19. *Ibid.*, p. 187.
20. S. Reynolds (1990) *Blissed Out: The Raptures of Rock* (London, Serpent's Tail), p. 171.
21. *Ibid.*, p. 161.
22. S. Thornton (1994) 'Moral Panic, the Media and British Rave Culture', in A. Ross and T. Rose (eds) *Microphone Fiends* (London and New York, Routledge), 1994, pp. 176–92.

23. P. Gilroy (1991) 'Sounds Authentic: Black Music, Ethnicity, and the Challenge of a *Changing* Same', *Black Music Research Journal* vol. 10, no. 2, pp. 111–35.
24. J. Beadle (1993) *Will Pop Eat itself? Pop Music in the Soundbite Era* (London, Faber), pp. 6–7.
25. *Ibid.*, p. 148.
26. S. Frith (1988b) 'Pet Shop Boys: The Divine Commodity', *Voice Rock & Roll Quarterly* (spring) p. 7.
27. A. Goodwin (1995) 'Surfing with the Pet Shop Boys', unpublished paper, International Association for the Study of Popular Music (IASPM) conference, University of Strathclyde, Glasgow.
28. A. Power (1993) 'Camp Counsellors', *The Voice* (2 November), p. 73.
29. D. Runciman (1994) 'Mods, Yes, but not Cons', *The Modern Review* (October–November), p. 8.
30. M. Cloonan (1995) '"What Do *They* Know of England?" Englishness and Popular Music in the mid-1990s', unpublished paper, IASPM conference, University of Strathclyde, Glasgow.
31. Runciman (1994), p. 8.
32. B. Flannagan (1995) 'No Milk Today . . .', *Mojo* (March 1995), p. 42.
33. P. Morley (1990) 'The Smile of David', *New Statesman and Society* (22 June), p. 45.
34. *Ibid.*, p. 46.
35. A. Mueller (1995) 'The Definite Arty Cool', *Melody Maker* (18 February), p. 7.
36. In J. Cigarettes (1994) 'Squash Racket', *New Musical Express* (30 April).
37. Runciman (1994), p. 8.
38. R. Shusterman (1991) 'The Fine Art of Rap', *New Literary History*, vol. 22, no. 3, pp. 613–32.
39. *Ibid.*, p. 625.
40. P. Gilroy (1993) 'One Nation under a Groove', in *Small Acts: Thoughts on the Politics of Black Cultures* (London, Serpent's Tail), pp. 37, 42.
41. *Ibid.*, 'Introduction', p. 5.
42. *Ibid.*, 'One Nation under a Groove', pp. 37, 45.
43. *Ibid.*, 'It Ain't Where You're From, It's Where You're At', p. 127.
44. P. Tagg (1989) '"Black Music", "Afro-American Music" and "European Music"', *Popular Music*, vol. 8, no. 3.
45. Gilroy (1991), p. 118.
46. G. Tate (1992) 'Silence, Exile, and Cunning: Miles Davis in Memoriam', in *Flyboy in the Buttermilk*, (New York, Simon & Shuster), p. 86.
47. J. L. Decker (1994) 'The State of Rap: Time and Place in Hip Hop Nationalism', in A. Ross and T. Rose (eds) *Microphone Fiends* (London and New York, Routledge), pp. 100, 118.
48. *Ibid.*, p. 11.
49. N. George (1994) *Buppies, B-Boys, Baps & Bohos: Notes on Post-Soul Black Culture* (New York, HarperCollins), pp. 247–8.
50. P. Gilroy (1993) 'It's a Family Affair', in *Small Acts*, p. 195.
51. A. Ross (1992) 'Tribalism after L. A.', *Art and Text*, no. 43 (September), pp. 92, 100.
52. *Ibid.*, p. 60.

53. I. Maxwell (1994) 'Discourses of Culture and Nationalism in Sydney Hip Hop', *Perfect Beat*, vol. 2, no. 1 (July), pp. 1–2.
54. F. Owen (1994) 'Back in the Days', *Vibe*, vol. 2, no. 10 (December–January), p. 68.
55. C. Coker (1994), 'How the West was Won', *Vibe*, vol. 2, no. 10 (December–January), pp. 78–81.
56. Owen, (1994) p. 67.
57. In Owen, (1994) p. 68.
58. H. Allen (1994) 'Timebomb', *Vibe* vol. 2, no. 10 (December–January), p. 71.
59. *Ibid.*, p. 74.
60. Gilroy (1991), p. 132.
61. *Ibid.*, p. 133.
62. K. Zook (1992) 'Reconstructions of Nationalist Thought in Black Music and Culture', in R. Garofalo (ed.) *Rockin' the Boat: Mass Music & Mass Movements* (Boston, South End Press), pp. 256, 263.
63. D. Hebdige (1987) *Cut 'N' Mix: Culture, Identity and Caribbean Music* (London, Methuen), p. 158.
64. Gilroy (1993), p. 125.
65. Zook (1992), p. 257.
66. M. Slobin (1992) 'Micromusics of the West: A Comparative Approach', *Ethnomusicology*, vol. 36, no. 1 (winter), p. 3.
67. J. Leland (1992) 'Rap and Race', *Newsweek* (29 June), p. 52.
68. *Ibid.*, p. 49.
69. J. Casimir (1992) 'Review of Ice Cube, *Death Certificate*', *Sydney Morning Herald* (18 February).
70. D. Samuels(1992) 'How Whites Took the Rap', *Sydney Morning Herald* (15 February) (reprinted from *The New Republic*).
71. Gilroy (1993), p. 200.
72. P. Gilroy (1994).' "After the Love Has Gone": Bio-politics and Etho-poetics in the Black Public Sphere', *Public Culture*, vol. 7, no. 1 (fall), p. 51.
73. T. Brennan (1994) 'Off the Gangsta Tip: A Rap Appreciation, or Forgetting about Los Angeles', *Critical Inquiry*, vol. 20 (summer), pp. 675–6.
74. *Ibid.*, pp. 680–2.
75. *Ibid.*, p. 689.
76. George (1994), p. 9.
77. *Ibid.*, p. 7.
78. B. Cross (1993) *It's Not about a Salary ... Rap, Race and Resistance in Los Angeles* (London, Verso), p. 63.
79. Gilroy (1991), p. 134.
80. Shusterman (1991), p. 630.
81. D. Hudson (1995) 'Islamic Rap Tops Pop Charts with Songs of Hate', *Sydney Morning Herald* (6 August), p. 13 (reprinted from *The Guardian*).
82. Cross (1993) p. 63.
83. J. Flores (1994) 'Puerto Rican and Proud, Boyee!: Rap Roots and Amnesia', in A. Ross and T. Rose (eds), *Microphone Fiends* (London and New York, Routledge), p. 90.
84. R. Kelly (1993) 'HipHop Chicano: A Separate but Parallel Story', in Cross (1993), p. 74.
85. T. Rose (1994), *Black Noise: Rap Music and Black Culture in Contemporary*

America (Hanover, Wesleyan University Press), pp. xiv–xv.
86. *Ibid.*, p. 59.
87. Cross (1993), p. 59.
88. L. Ali (1993) 'Kid Frost and Chicano Rap', *Option* (November–December), p. 70.
89. Cross (1993), p. 192.
90. Ali (1993), p. 69.
91. W. Schomberg (1992), 'Mariachi Meets the "Street" ', *New York Times* (23 August), Section 2, p. 23.
92. J. Bernard (1992) 'A Newcomer Abroad, Rap Speaks Up', *New York Times* (23 August), Section 2, p. 1.
93. D. McLane (1992) 'The Forgotten Caribbean Connection', *New York Times* (23 August), p. 22.
94. S. Erlanger (1992) 'Of Dog Cosmonauts and Leather Jackets', *New York Times* (23 August), p. 22.
95. N. Kristoff (1992) 'At the Boundaries of the Permissible', *New York Times* (23 August), p. 22.
96. E. Gargan (1992) 'Vanilla Ice in Hindi', *New York Times* (23 August), p. 22.
97. S. Weisman (1992) 'Hammer Wannabes Spouting Nonsense', *New York Times* (23 August), pp. 22–3.
98. K. Noble (1992) 'A King Yields to a New Messenger', *New York Times* (23 August), p. 23.
99. B. Bollag (1992) 'The Curtain Parts, And Rap Emerges', *New York Times* (23 August), p. 23.
100. S. Reynolds (1992) 'Underground, But Not Forgotten', *New York Times* (23 August), p. 23.
101. Schomberg (1992).
102. J. Rockwell (1992), 'Felicitous Rhymes, and Local Roots', *New York Times* (23 August), p. 23.
103. J. Cocks (1992) 'Rap around the Globe', *Time* (19 October), p. 74.
104. D. Glaister (1994), 'C'est cool!' *Guardian* (29 November).
105. Various (1993) *Planet Rap: A Sample of the World*, Tommy Boy Records.
106. In F. Liperi (1994), 'L'Italia s'è desta. Tecno-splatter e posse in rivolta', in M. Canevacci *et al.* (eds) *Ragazzi senza tempo: Immagini, musica, conflitti delle cultura giovanili* (Genova, Costa & Nolan), p. 193.
107. M. D'Sousa (1994) 'Soon EMC: Solve the Mystery', *3D World*, Sydney (17 October), p. 18.
108. Glaister (1994).
109. In D'Sousa (1994), p. 18.
110. K. Laing (1994) 'The Europeans', Radio National, Australian Broadcasting Corporation (21 August).
111. M. Pennay (1993) 'Rap and Racism in Germany', Sydney, unpublished paper.
112. V. Kurkela (1994) 'Music Culture as Collage: The End of National Musics?', in A. Opekar (ed.) *Central European Popular Music: Proceedings from the International Conference Prague 15–17 July 1992* (Prague, IASPM), p. 112.

Discography

Alliance Ethnik, *Simple & Funky*, Delabel, 1995.
Blur, *Parklife*, EMI, 1994.
dEUS, *Worst Case Scenario*, Island, 1994.
Guru, *Jazzmatazz Volume 1*, Crysalis/EMI, 1993.
Kid Frost, *East Side Story*, Virgin, 1992.
—*Hispanic Causing Panic*, Virgin, 1990.
IAM, *Ombre est Lumière*, Delabel/Virgin, 1993.
Ice Cube, *Death Certificate*, Priority, 1991.
Ice-T, *Home Invasion*, Priority, 1993.
Latin Alliance, *Latin Alliance*, Virgin America, 1991.
The Pet Shop Boys, *Very/Relentless*, Parlophone, 1993.
Quincy Jones, *Back on the Block*, Qwest, 1989.
M. C. Solaar, *Prose Combat*, Polydor, 1993.
—*Qui Seme le Vent Recolte le Tempo*, Polydor, 1991.
Sens Unik, *Chromatic*, Unik Records, 1994.
Silent Majority, *La Majorité Silencieuse*, Unik, 1994.
Soon EMC, *A Tout ... Point de Vue*, EMI France, 1993.
Various, *Planet Rap: A Sample of the World*, Tommy Boy, 1993.
—*Stolen Moments: Red Hot and Cool*, Red Hot/MCA, 1994.

2

World Music: Beating through the Jungle

The cultural imperialism thesis

Arguments about the appropriation of indigenous popular music often construct a simplistic opposition between 'margins' of authentic local cultural expression and a 'centre' controlled by market and commoditization forces in the global music industry. These arguments are frequently defined in terms of the imposition of Anglo-American music on the rest of the world, and the exploitation of traditional, culturally distinctive and often politically oppositional forms of 'roots' music by globally dominant Western market forces, recording industries and musicians. They are usually linked to what has been referred to as the cultural imperialism thesis, which claims that the power of market capitalism – dominated by the USA, Japan and Western Europe – not only 'dumps' its own cultural products on an unsuspecting world but appropriates, technologizes, contaminates and commodifies the cultural products of Third World and economically weaker nations and channels them into a global economy which denies recognition or reward to the products' originators. As John Tomlinson has indicated in his book on the subject, the cultural imperialism thesis originated in the 1970s as a left-wing academic shorthand term to describe what was seen essentially as a one-way process of economic and cultural dominance spreading from a single centre of power across the globe. This ideology was bluntly expressed by Tunstall as follows: 'The cultural imperialism thesis claims that authentic, traditional and local culture in many parts of the world is being battered out of existence by the indiscriminate dumping of large quantities of slick commercial and media products, mainly from the United States.'[1] Tomlinson argues that by the end of the 1980s the term 'imperialism' needed to be replaced by 'globalization', indicating a far more disorganized, random process involving 'interconnection and inter-dependency of all global areas which happens in a far less purposeful way' and which 'weaken[s] the cultural coherence of all individual nation-states, including the economically powerful ones – the "imperialist powers" of a previous era'. This meant that while the cultural and social identity of small nations was still dominated by the larger forces of international information technology, these forces operated in a remote global sphere where notions of identity could not be articulated. Tomlinson concluded, however, that the cultural agency involved in the demands of small nations for a voice in the world implicit in the notion of cultural imperialism was still a valid starting point for theorizing about global communications.[2]

Examples of the cultural imperialism thesis in popular music are put forward in the book *Music at the Margins*, a collective study of indigenous local popular musics compiled by the International Communication and Youth Consortium which appeared in 1991. Borrowing its frame of reference from the musicologist Alan Lomax, *Music on the Margins* explores '"the cultural imperialism hypothesis," an assumption that the predominantly one-way flow of cultural products "from the west to the rest" threatens to produce a cultural "grey-out". In the case of popular music the hypothesis projects a sort of Michael Jackson world takeover of musical expectation and expression.'[3] The various authors of this book offer a series of case studies of 'peripheral' popular musics in Greece, Israel, Eastern Europe, the USA, Jamaica, South Korea, Nigeria, India and elsewhere, which are portrayed as locally significant, 'authentic' cultural products promoting social change, and are resistant to the prevalent 'economic internationalism' of popular music. But as Simon Frith points out in a 'Critical Response' included as an appendix to *Music on the Margins*, the book demonstrates the increasing interplay between hybridized local musics and global market forces and musical forms, but does not use its findings to go beyond its cultural imperialism thesis.[4] In his book *Understanding Popular Music*, Roy Shuker has summarized cultural imperialism arguments and suggested three major points to consider in opposition to any application of the thesis, unilateral or otherwise: that since the 1950s, Anglo-American popular music has become a universal and international youth culture which has often been adopted in socially oppositional ways; that local musical production cannot be seen as directly equivalent to local national cultural identity, or imported music as alien; that imported musical influences are ubiquitous, and 'local musicians are immersed in overlapping and frequently reciprocal contexts of production, with a cross-fertilization of local and international sounds'.[5]

As a static and often rigidly imposed criterion identifying and condemning instances of musical exploitation of Third World countries by First World capital, the cultural imperialism thesis is frequently used to criticize ethnic musical appropriations by Anglo-American or English rock musicians from Elvis Presley and the Rolling Stones to Paul Simon, David Byrne, Peter Gabriel and Sting. While it is undeniable that aspects of exploitation and possibly unjustifiable appropriation can be found in some of the output of some of these musicians, such discoveries do not take us very far if they stem from a unilateral disapproval of a First World musical 'centre' exploiting Third World musical 'margins'. Most Third World musics are already 'contaminated' by their own appropriations of First World musical influences, and most First World musics contain Third World (or at least African and Latin American) influences, so relations between the two are never simple and always mediated by complex interplays of intercultural cross-fertilizations.

Arjun Appadurai has argued that the increasingly shifting, haphazard and disorganized global developments of capitalism and the inter-nationalization of mass media make the imposition of hegemonic notions of a central economic and cultural domination of vulnerable, fragile margins untenable:

> The new global cultural economy has to be seen as a complex, overlapping, disjunctive order, which cannot any longer be understood in terms of existing centre–periphery models (even those which might account for multiple centres and peripheries). Nor is it susceptible to simple models of push and pull (in terms of migration theory), or of surpluses and deficits (as in traditional models of balance of trade), or of consumers and producers (as in most neo-Marxist theories of development). Even the most complex and flexible theories of global development which have come out of the Marxist tradition ... are inadequately quirky and have failed to come to terms with what Lash and Urry have called disorganised capitalism ... The complexity of the current global economy has to do with certain fundamental disjunctures between economy, culture and politics which we have only begun to theorise.[6]

In his introduction to *Rockin' the Boat* (1992), a collection of essays on the political impact of rock and popular music in the USA and a number of other countries around the world, Reebee Garofalo has summarized the inadequacies of the centre–margins cultural imperialism thesis as it relates to the field of popular music. Drawing on studies by Roger Wallis and Krister Malm (1984), Dave Laing (1986), Steven Feld (1988), and Andrew Goodwin and Joe Gore (1990), Garofalo criticizes the thesis as a 'vague and limited ... analytical tool' which relies on an equation between the historical colonization of the Third World by Western nations and the complex structure of transnational and multinational media and music marketing organizations. It also equates economic power with cultural effects:

> there is a tendency to privilege the role of external forces, while overlooking the internal dynamics of resistance and opposition that work against domination. In addition to underestimating the strength and resiliency of indigenous cultures, this tendency assumes audience passivity in the face of dominant cultural power and neglects the active, creative dimension of popular consumption. ... Finally, the notion of cultural imperialism rests on the premise that the 'organic' cultures of the third world are somehow being corrupted by the 'unauthentic' and 'manufactured' cultures of the West.[7]

Pointing out that the 'big six' major transnational record companies that control two-thirds of the international music business (and increasingly more as they absorb 'independent' record labels) – EMI, Polygram, BMG–RCA, SONY–CBS, MCA and Time–Warner–WEA – are owned by British, Dutch, German and Japanese conglomerates respectively, with only the last being US-owned, Garofalo questions the US economic basis of the cultural imperialism thesis. (Although this in no way diminishes the fact that these companies, all of whom have branch companies in South America, Europe, Asia and Africa, market predominantly Anglo-American music throughout the world.) He also questions equating the industrialization, commercialization and technological mediation of music with economic power, control and imperial ownership, and the related construction of international pop music audiences for singers like Michael Jackson as dupes of imperialist forces. The African and multicultural basis of rock and roll and much American popular music has also cross-fertilized the music of non-Western countries to an extent which seriously challenges any implied notions of purity in these musical cultures. Garofalo invokes Wallis and Malm's term 'transculturation' to describe the interaction between international rock music and local national and indigenous musics which has become particularly evident in the phenomenon of world music, which Goodwin and Gore have described 'as Western pop stars appropriating non-Western sounds, as third world musicians using Western rock and pop, or as the Western consumption of non-Western folk music'.[8] The following study of world music and 'peripheral' forms of popular music is predicated on the observations of Garofalo, Frith and others referred to above.

Mapping world music

In the context of the global economy of the popular music industry, the category of world music represents a very small subculture, predominantly produced, marketed and consumed in Europe and the USA; although usually commanding a vast groundswell of consumption in the musics' countries of origin, often through local audio cassette distribution networks. The book *Rhythms of the World*, published by the BBC in 1989 to supplement a television series of the same name, contains a map of world music which covers thirty-three different regions, ranging over Eastern Europe, the Caribbean, Africa, Latin America, the USA and Pakistan. A third of the musics and musicians listed are African, while Latin America, including the largely New York-based salsa and the Miami-based Latin hip hop, occupies more than another third. Western Europe, the USSR, almost the whole of Asia and Australia remained uncharted, or untargeted, territory.

The term *world music* came into currency in the popular music industry in 1987 as a generalized marketing tag referring to popular music originating in countries outside the normal Western (and predominantly Anglo-American) trade routes of popular music. In this sense the term covers a vast range, incorporating, as Steven Feld has indicated, 'any commercially available music of non-Western origin and circulation, as well as ... all musics of dominated ethnic minorities within the Western world'.[9] It was launched as a new category of popular music by eleven independent British, European and American record labels specializing in music from Third World countries, including Globestyle, Earthworks (which was later amalgamated with Virgin), Charly, Sterns, Mango, Cooking Vinyl, Globestar, Oval Records and Hannibal.[10] This distribution network aimed for a commodification of 'other' musics in a way which involved what Feld has described as 'music for/of/in a market; music of the world to be sold around the world'.[11] There is an implicit sense of homogenization in this notion, an idea of a shrinking world in which diverse and heterogenous musical cultures are being brought together, but it is arguable that local 'indigenous' musics have been able to maintain their specificity and distinctiveness, despite the increase of global influences. As Appadurai has pointed out, 'at least as rapidly as forces from various metropolises are brought into new societies they tend to become indigenised in one or another way: this is true of music and housing styles as much as it is true of science and terrorism, spectacles and constitutions.'[12] One recent example of a highly distinctive cross-fertilization between African-American and African musical cultures which illustrates the vital, innovative and unexpected results which world music can produce is *Talking Timbuktu*, a musically seamless collaboration between the white US blues guitarist Ry Cooder and traditional Malian guitarist Ali Farka Toure, which was the highest-selling album on world music charts in Europe, the US and Australia in 1994. The album revealed Toure as a prototypical blues guitarist, and exposed the African origins of Cooder's very Western country blues and slide guitar playing, the synthesis of both producing an excitingly distinctive hybrid which struck a chord with Western and non-Western listeners alike. It also demonstrated that, far from being marginal, African music was central to the history of Western rhythm and blues and rock and roll; in the words of Toure quoted on the album's liner notes: 'For some people, when you say "Timbuktu" it is like the end of the world, but that is not true. I am from Timbuktu, and I can tell you that we are right at the heart of the world.'[13]

Some of the principal musical territories mapped by world music by 1990 include rai music from Algeria, mbalax from Senegal, the griots of Mali and Guinea, Ghanaian high-life, Nigerian ju-ju, soukous from Zaire, jit and chimurenga from Zimbabwe, mbaquanga and Soweto jive from South Africa, qawwali from Pakistan, zouk from the Antilles, soca from Trinidad, salsa from New York and Central America, and more obviously hybrid forms like the Anglo-Indian bhangra and ghazals and Franco-American cajun and zydeco. One factor which unites these musics under the rubric of world music is what Feld has called 'senses of commodified otherness, blurred boundaries between exotic and familiar, the local and global in transnational popular culture'.[14] By the late 1980s, most 'world' musicians were using the sophisticated electronic and digital means of sound production developed in Western rock and pop music, and many of them were using rock instruments and Western guest musicians and producers. These homogenizing factors ensured a sense of familiarity to the Western listener, and made notions of musical purity in relation to local or ethnic musics impossible to entertain, but, despite the blurring of boundaries involved, produced a wide range of stimulating and excitingly hybrid sounds.

It is important to differentiate between the cartographic image of world music, which represents a global economy within a Eurocentric and highly fashion-oriented popular music industry, and world musics which are defined as objects of ethnomusicological study. In this context, as Feld has pointed out, world music can become an oppositional label which challenges the hegemonic equation of music with Western European art music.[15] It can also become a way in which sometimes extinct or highly modified forms of ethnic musics can be either frozen into idealized products supervised by the ethnomusicologist, or combined with ambient electronic music to become a form of exotic sonic wallpaper. The highly popular *Deep Forest* album, which combines UNESCO ethnographic recordings of pigmy chants (also called 'Deep Forest') with programmed keyboards and drum machines by Belgian producers Michel Sauchez and Eric Mouquet, who are credited with the 'original idea' of the project, is one example of this. Released in 1992, *Deep Forest* begins with a deep, soporific, French-accented voice intoning over an ambient-style organ wash reminiscent of Serge Gainsbourg's 'Je T'aime (Moi Non Plus)': 'Somewhere in the jungle are living some little men and women. They are our past and maybe they are our future.'[16] The unintentional comedy of this exotic but highly popular dance-trance album, which at times manages to make the pigmy voices sound like the Chipmunks, the cartoon vocal group of speeded-up voices, is almost matched by *Sacred Spirit*. Subtitled 'Chants and Dances of the Native Americans', *Sacred Spirit* is a mixture of 'all original Native American material' and densely layered ambient music produced in 1994 by an anonymous but apparently well-known musician, who refers to himself only as 'The Fearsome Brave', and promises to make 'a donation ... to the Native American Rights Fund for each record sold'.[17] While both these albums contain undeniably pleasant music, they also convey an increasing tendency of some forms of world music towards 'sugaring the pill' to render indigenous ethnic music more palatable to Western ears.

But this Western 'sugaring' influence occurs to lesser degrees in most other forms of world music. Ambient musician Brian Eno's involvement as producer, co-writer, keyboard player and backing vocalist (along with Peter Gabriel, who also plays 'fake organ' on one track, and percussionist David Bottrill) on two albums by the powerfully distinctive exiled Ugandan singer Geoffrey Oryema, for example, poses a dilemma in terms of an over-indulgence in accessible sonic indicators. Oryema's father was a senior minister in Idi Amin's government and was secretly executed in 1977, forcing the singer into exile in Paris. The 1990 album *Exile* features Oryema's richly plangent singing and playing of the *lukeme* (thumb piano), *naga* (seven-string harp) and acoustic guitar, with very little accompaniment (usually only bass, percussion, guitar or backing vocals), and all the songs are in his native language, Acholi. In 1993 the more popular *Beat the Border* was released, produced by Bottrill, with a denser line-up of Western musicians accompanying Oryema, and with ambient-styled keyboards particularly prominent, less *lukeme* and *naga*, and the opening and closing songs of the album sung in English. The vagueness of Australian music critic Bruce Elder's description of the album, comparing it to the bland and vaguely mystical Gaelic ambient music of Enya, matches the blurred and indeterminate sonic associations of the music: 'Eno's influence has produced music which is immediately accessible ... and which is a kind of African answer to Enya. This is music which floats. It is music which seems to reach into some kind of mythical heartland and quietly expresses worlds of seductive meaning which hover between exuberance and immense sadness.'[18] This crossover album brought Oryema more international exposure (he was particularly popular at the Womadelaide World Music festivals in Adelaide, Australia in 1994 and 1995), but its distinctiveness suffers from a blurring of the borders between its indigenous and Western musical components.

The term *world music* has had its detractors: Ian McCann, for example, in his liner notes to Zairean singer Ray Lema's 1990 album *Gaia*, refers to it as 'that insulting term for non-Western pop'.[19] In his introduction to *The Virgin Directory of World Music*, which divides the field into Africa, Europe, the Middle East and Indian Subcontinent, the Far East and Pacific, the Caribbean, South America and North America, Philip Sweeney also criticizes the term

for its combination of a meaninglessly wide field of reference, with a capricious and subjective actual application, but it is also understandable. No better short term has yet been proposed, and thus the term World Music has taken on a quite sturdy life of its own, which is one of the reasons it forms the title of this book. The clinching reason is its nearest rival, The Virgin Directory of World Popular and Roots Music from Outside the Anglo-American Mainstream is somewhat lacking in *élan*. It is also still lacking in precision.[20]

As an academic label, world music is sometimes seen as a capitulation to the dictates of the commercial popular music industry, although it is usually problematized in most academic studies. One example where this occurs, at least implicitly, is in the book *World Music, Politics and Social Change*, a collection of papers by members of the International Association for the Study of Popular Music (IASPM). This book is largely a cultural geography of local musics from non-Anglo-Saxon countries which remain outside the commercial circuits of world music, but, as its editor, Simon Frith, notes in his introduction,

> all countries' popular musics are shaped these days by international influences and institutions, by multinational capital and technology, by global pop norms and values. Even the most nationalistic sounds – carefully cultivated 'folk' songs, angry local dialect punk, preserved (for the tourist) traditional dance – are determined by a critique of international entertainment. No country in the world is unaffected by the way in which the twentieth-century mass media (the electronic means of musical production, reproduction and transmission) have created a universal pop aesthetic.[21]

Hybridization and transculturation: the Bhundu Boys

Local musics' interaction with norms of international entertainment and a 'universal pop aesthetic' has meant that any ethnographic claims of authenticity in these local forms by musicologists are confronted with the hybridization of these forms as a result of their 'contamination' by Western technological and musical influences. But this interaction has been a continuous historical and highly productive process, as John Collins and Paul Richards in their study 'Popular Music in West Africa (1981)' explain:

> If ... it is the long-established characteristic of a trade-dominated social formation constantly to absorb 'new' and 'alien' cultural influences, much as a new fashion in commodities stimulates trade, then the 'modernisation' and 'Westernisation' rejected in the name of musical 'authenticity' or which 'syncretism' is supposed to graft on to the traditional, are terms empty of meaning.[22]

Collins and Richards show that the adoption and indeed fetishizing of Western musical instruments such as the guitar, banjo, accordion, trumpet, clarinet, saxophone and piano began in West Africa in the early part of the twentieth century, and the electric guitar, organ and synthesizer were quickly introduced after they became the dominant code of rock music in the 1960s. They also show how merchant capital had an important influence on the construction of contexts for the performance and meaning of West African popular music forms like ju-ju and high-life, as well as on the evolution of traditional music forms, and this in turn influenced the impact which these West African musics, among the first to cross over into the West, had on European popular music. In a later essay, Collins argues that contemporary African music has resisted cultural imperialism in three ways: by indigenizing musical genres based on foreign influences, by creative incorporation of black dance music from the New World, and by continuing the African tradition of protest music. Collins puts a case for regarding the influence of New World forms of black dance music on contemporary African music as a form of 'cultural feedback' of transatlantic music which left Africa during the diaspora and has now returned.[23] Paul Gilroy makes a similar point in relation to the transcultural hybridity of the transatlantic diaspora of Afro-American music, arguing that 'the unashamedly hybrid character of these black cultures continually confounds any simplistic (essentialist or anti-essentialist) understanding of the relationship between racial identity and racial non-identity, between folk cultural authenticity and pop cultural betrayal'.[24]

One of many examples of African hybridization and musical transculturation on the world music scene is provided by the Bhundu Boys – a group from Zimbabwe who play 'jit' music, have successfully toured Australia four times and have attracted a large following with their infectiously looping and flowing, polyrhythmic, electric-guitar-based dance music. In live performance, the group uses no identifiably African instrumentation, and began its career as a teenage band in Harare (then Salisbury) in the late 1970s playing cover versions of country songs and rock music by the Beatles, the Rolling Stones and the Eagles. (This choice of repertoire was largely due to the fact that the Smith regime in Rhodesia had banned native Shona music from live performance, as Andrew Martin has pointed out.[25]) In 1986 and 1987 the Bhundu Boys, whose name means 'Bush Boys', after the guerrilla fighters who supported Zimbabwean Prime Minister Robert Mugabe, undertook three extensive British tours, playing the pub-rock circuit normally frequented by up-and-coming new independent rock bands. They gained some success on the British independent rock charts with their first two albums, recorded in the Shed Studios in Harare and released on the independent Scottish label Disc Afrique, whose manager, Owen Elias, 'discovered' the group, and was instrumental in importing them to Scotland, where they began from scratch an attempt to crack the British market. After one of their albums, *Shabini*, had topped the British independent charts in 1987, and they had played a fifty-date British tour, culminating in the support slot for Madonna at Wembley Stadium, they became the first African band to obtain a contract with the multinational record company WEA.

WEA insisted that they should sing in English and they released *True Jit* (1987), an album tailored for accessibility to the Western pop market and described by the disc jockey Andy Kershaw, one of the group's main British promoters, as a 'smoother Euro-friendly sound'. The majority of the songs on *True Jit* were sung in English rather than Shona, the group's native language, and the album was recorded in London by a British producer. *True Jit* sold reasonably well in Britain, and the group was able to co-produce its next album, *Pamberi!* (1989), in Harare. Songs on this album were mostly in Shona, and the *mbira*, the traditional Zimbabwean thumb piano on which the rhythms of Bhundu Boys' and many other Zimbabwean musicians' music is based, was incorporated into the mix. But the album failed to make significant sales, despite the fact the group was nominated as 'best live band in Britain' by *Time Out* magazine in 1990. The group's attempt to cross over into the increasingly Westernized and techno-oriented world music market seemed to be coming to grief, and Rise Kangona, the group's lead guitarist and founder member, stated at the time, 'we've tried dance mixes, house mixes ... but it's very difficult to compete. It's very frustrating.'[26] WEA dropped the Bhundu Boys, who went back to Disc Afrique, and released a live album recorded in one of their regular venues, King Tut's Wah Wah Hut in Glasgow, cheekily entitled *Absolute Jit!* (1990).

It would be easy to regard the Bhundu Boys' declining success in recording market terms as another example of cultural imperialism at work, but they have continued to show a remarkable resilience in maintaining an international following as a live act. When they toured Australia in 1990 they were instantly popular, and *Sydney Morning Herald* music critic Bruce Elder cautioned his readers, 'miss them and be doomed to an eternity of regret'.[27] Returning the following year, they played to an enthusiastic audience of six thousand in an open-air concert in Sydney, despite being without their lead guitarist Biggie Tembo, who had left to pursue a solo career. (In 1992 Tembo released an album on Cooking Vinyl called *Out of Africa*, recorded with local musicians in Shed Studios in Harare, but lacking the polyrhythmic intensity of the Bhundu Boys' music, while the title track and another called 'Harare Jit' indicated its relative paucity of ideas.)

Tembo's and the Bhundu Boys' British and international success was of national importance in Zimbabwe. This was illustrated in the 1990 BBC TV series on African music, *Under African Skies*, where Tembo, wearing a WOMAD T-shirt, lectured to local musicians at a Harare music school on strategies for developing Zimbabwean popular music in the West. But, in a country where 15–20 per cent of sexually active people are HIV-positive, sexual promiscuity is a problem of major proportions, and this is reflected in the concerns of some of the local music. Like many Zimbabwean groups, the Bhundu Boys' repertoire includes songs in Shona which contain advice on moral issues. As the singer Paul Metavire stated in a Finnish Broadcasting Corporation documentary, *The Soul of Mbira*, 'our music is different from overseas music. It teaches us moral lessons and tells us how to behave, whereas songs from overseas are only for entertainment.'[28]

The Bhundu Boys' music could be seen as combining both local and overseas tendencies, but, partly owing to its international lifestyle, the band began to lose members to AIDS. In 1991 bass player David Mankaba died of the disease, his replacement, Shepherd Mangama, died the following year, and in 1993 vocalist and keyboards player Shakespear Kangwena also succumbed to AIDS. None the less, in 1993 the group still seemed capable of regeneration, releasing their most Westernized album to date, this time on British independent label Cooking Vinyl, entitled *Friends on the Road*, which was recorded mostly in English, and celebrated 'chance encounters with a diverse group of singers and musicians, recorded in snatched moments over the last two years'. In it they collaborated with English dance group Latin Quarter, and revisited their international country music origins, including a version of Johnny Cash's 'Ring of Fire' (with a rap in Shona added as a coda), and two other songs with country singer Hank Wangford, as well as a song by country singer Don Williams, 'My Best Friend'. The group's trademark sounds, rhythms and infectious energy, joy and positivity are still stamped on the album, although the tracks they perform without the help of Western musicians tend to be the most successful. Their popularity in Australia as an irresistibly entertaining and danceable live band increased notably: their fourth tour of Australia and Oceania in 1993 was by far their biggest, including more than twenty-five dates and even a projected tour of Papua New Guinea. Reviewing one of their gigs at the Moruya Golf Club on the south coast of New South Wales, Elder commented on the uniquely disparate and heterogeneous audience for the group's music:

> From the opening moment when light, tripping notes showered from Rise Kagona's guitar, the golf club came alive. There was no self-conscious 'cool' here. People leapt to their feet and started dancing. Long-haired hippies from the hinterland gyrated and whirled. Clean-cut bank clerks and shop assistants embraced and jumped and laughed. Hardened old golfers put their arms around their tidy wives and swayed and smiled. For most of the audience, this was music from an alien culture sung in a language they did not understand. Yet their response, so spontaneous and so refreshingly uninhibited, was a demonstration of just exactly how music really can become a universal language.[29]

The infectious danceability and 'universality' of the Bhundu Boys' combination of jit, pop and country music in live performance raises issues relating to the function of the international popular music industry as a mediating outlet for largely ephemeral musical commodities whose use and exchange value is limited by consumption contexts where there is scant regard for the music's conditions of origin. In his study of cultural geography, *Maps of Meaning*, Peter Jackson states: 'the politics of consumption are rarely straightforward. For white, middle class teenagers, listening to the Bhundu Boys or the latest Bhangra band can seem more like "musical tourism" than a genuine expansion of musical consciousness. For the history of black music is a history of exploitation and appropriation.'[30] But it is also possible to see such musical exploitation and appropriation in a different light. The Bhundu Boys have adapted Anglo-American rock music forms and produced an open-tuned, distinctively African electric guitar idiom. This makes possible a cross-fertilization of Zimbabwean music with the range of popular dance musics in the Western world and paves the way for mass marketing of other music from this source, such as the chimurenga ('music of the struggle') of the politically militant Zimbabwean musical mentor, Thomas Mapfumo. In 1989 Island's Mango label released Mapfumo's album *Corruption*, while in 1990 the Virgin Earthworks label released two volumes entitled *Zimbabwe Frontline*, featuring Mapfumo, the Four Brothers and a number of other Zimbabwean bands. This marketing of Zimbabwean music, together with films like Michael Raeburn's *Jit* (1991) which feature it, contribute to make it far less of a 'music from an alien culture' for the Western listener.

Bhangra and 'Asian beat': diasporas adrift

Anglo-Indian bhangra music has outlived its brief elevation by the English popular music press into the fashionable limelight of popular ethnic dance music in Britain in the late 1980s and become an established social index of cultural practices among young people in Indian and other Asian communities. (In using the term 'Asian' I acknowledge Peter Jackson's observations that the term is of dubious value and fails to reflect the diversity of nationalities, religions and language amongst Britain's Asian communities, and that it expresses the homogenizing ideology of an dominant Anglo majority.[31]) Rick Glanvill characterized bhangra as follows in his liner notes to the Nachural Records 1993 compilation *East 2 West: Bhangra for the Masses*: 'Bhangra became to the young Asian community what reggae was to Seventies black British youth – an assertion of a cultural identity discrete from that of an establishment giving them grief, a rejection of the stale, passive culture of their parents, and a movement that was both rebellious and great fun.'[32] Based on centuries-old traditional Punjabi harvest folk dance music played on the *tumbi* and *dholak* (which replaced the earlier use of the *dhol*) percussion instruments, bhangra (which derives from *bhang*, or hemp) went through three successive waves of development in Britain: as dance pop music played on synthesizers, guitars and drum kits in migrant Indian communities in the late 1970s, incorporating house and dance music and drum-machines in the 1980s, and combining with rap, sampling and Jamaican ragga or dancehall rhythms in the early 1990s to become bhangramuffin. This latter phenomenon became popular throughout Asia, with recording artists like Malkit Singh releasing 'raggamuffin mixes' of bhangra songs through labels like Oriental Star, and even reached the Indian community in Australia. (The weekly world music programme on Australian youth radio station 2JJJ features a monthly bhangra top ten, and 'Masala Mix', an hour-long weekly programme of bhangra, Hindi and Tamil music began on Sydney community radio station 2SER in August 1995.) Releases like the 1992 'Wham Bam!', a Bhangra remix which samples the dance floor hit 'The Power' by black American pop group Snap – as do a number of other bhangra hit songs – showed that bhangra, like many other forms of world music, was appropriating Western pop music technologies and forms, proving what Sabita Banerji has described as 'the commercial viability of Westernised Indian, rather than Indianised Western pop music. Music which is rooted in the original culture of the new generation, but which is an unequivocal expression of the British experience.'[33] As with many other forms of music originating in migrant ethnic minorities, British bhangra had its advocates for traditional authenticity who criticized the substitution of the *dhol* drum with drum machines, and saw British bhangra as a betrayal of the original cultural values of the music.

The commercial viability of British bhangra became particularly apparent in 1993, with the emergence of Apache Indian, also known as Steven Kapur, a Birmingham-based Anglo-Indian ragga-rapper, who combined bhangra influences with reggae and pop, and whose name derives from Jamaican ragga artist the Wild Apache Supercat. As Kim Burton and Sairah Aiwan have pointed out, Apache Indian has never claimed to be a bhangra singer, but a number of bhangra artists displayed a faint undercurrent of hostility towards his use of Afro-Caribbean ragga with bhangra influences as a vehicle for polemical songs about Asians living in Britain.[34] After his third single, 'Arranged Marriage', crossed over from reggae charts into the British pop charts, and he appeared on the television programme 'Top of the Pops', both the English music press and major record labels suddenly discovered 'Asian beat' as a major new British musical phenomenon. *New Musical Express* writer Steven Wells profiled Apache Indian as 'Britain's first Asian pop star' representing 'the *true* sound of multi-racial Britain' in January 1993. Apache Indian had in fact already achieved prominence as a reggae star in Jamaica, India, Pakistan and elsewhere, and 'discovered he was an international pop star' long before his British success. This *NME* story on Apache Indian was not a cover story (although a photo of him did appear in a tiny inset in the corner of the cover), for reasons which Wells suggested related to 'thousands of NME readers who don't buy the paper every time it has a non-white face on the cover'.[35]

Apache Indian's 1993 debut album *No Reservations*, recorded in Bob Marley's studio in Jamaica, was released on Island records, and combined Indian film music, bhangra and dancehall dub with politically oriented raps about the dangers of AIDS, alcohol and racism and the injustices of the caste system and arranged marriages. It was primarily addressed to Anglo-Indians and Asian migrant communities in Britain, but West Indian and white audiences also responded to its ragga beats. In an article about the fiftieth anniversary of Bob Marley's birth in 1995, Adam Sweeting portrayed Apache Indian as a leading exponent of a new boom of a hybrid form of British reggae which still had strong roots in Jamaica. If Marley were still alive, he suggested, he might be more inspired by Shabba Ranks and 'the "bhangra-muffin" of Apache Indian, whose roots lead circuitously back to Jamaica, amongst other places' than 'the likes of China Black, Pato Banton and the revitalised Aswad'.[36]

As a result of Apache Indian's sudden popularity in England, a vast submerged subculture of music by Anglo-Asian groups and performers in Britain was exposed, as outlined in a special report on 'Asian Beat' by Dave Simpson in *Melody Maker* in February 1993. This report (again, not a cover story) was prompted by a letter to the paper at the end of 1992 by a Middlesex reader who accused *Melody Maker* of racism for ignoring the Asian music scene. Simpson's article revealed a cultural economy of thousands of albums, mostly low-priced cassettes, by Anglo-Asian groups, sold in Britain through corner shops and Asian grocery stores, which were not recognized by Gallup polls and therefore had no impact on pop music charts and got no mainstream media coverage.[37] In a lengthy cover story in October 1994, *Billboard* profiled bhangra recording labels Multitone, which had been set up in 1979, and Nachural, established in Birmingham in 1991, both of which had become subsidiaries of BMG as the bhangra market emerged as a significant presence in Britain. But *Billboard* also pointed out that ninety per cent of bhangra's sales were still carried out through 'ethnic independent retailers' and hence established bhangra acts which were able to sell between 60,000 and 75,000 units still had to impact on the UK charts.[38] Apart from Apache Indian, whose *No Reservations* sold an estimated 160,000 units worldwide, only Cornershop, an Anglo-Indian punk rock group based in Leicester, and Fun^Da^Mental, a multi-ethnic hard-core rap group fronted by Pakistani musician Aki Nawaz, had managed to make any impact outside the exclusively 'ethnic' underground economy of bhangra and 'Asian beat', chiefly by virtue of performing songs in English. But this situation soon changed.

Nawaz was one of the founders of Nation Records, which specializes in what has been variously described as Anglo-Asian 'world dance fusion', 'ethnic techno' and 'radical global pop'. In 1993 Nation released a highly multicultural dance album by the flamboyant Asian-inflected ragga-techno group Trans-Global Underground, entitled *Dream of 100 Nations*, which went to number one on the British Independent charts, suggesting that 'Asian beat' had begun to cross over. As David Hesmondhalgh has pointed out in his study of the label, the first single from the album, 'Templehead', which combined acid house piano with samples of a Tahitian gospel choir, spoken word segments proclaiming 'music is a

universal language', and 'prototypical unity chants', had been a novelty
success in 1992 in British dance clubs. Relying heavily on the romantic
rhetoric of global unity, Oriental spirituality and primitivism, multiculturalism and visual exoticism, Trans-Global Underground, who wear
oriental masks, pharaoh costumes and African jewellery in performance,
feature belly-dancing Jewish-Moroccan singer Natacha Atlas, who also
has Spanish connections, and plays on the ambiguities of her multi-
identity. Atlas's 1995 solo album *Diaspora* combines Arab, Turkish and
Jewish musical styles, and features an Egyptian orchestra, samples of
Grandmaster Flash and 1970s rock group Iron Butterfly, a didjeridu and
other sounds, along with highly exotic, 'orientalist' publicity images
which recall Yemenite world music star Ofra Haza. Often criticized for
her belly-dancing and exploitation of exotic imagery, Atlas and Trans-
Global Underground produce tensions and contradictions between their
use of exotic ethnic stereotypes and their apparent advocacy of critical
multiculturalism. These tensions in their politics of representation are
amplified in the ambient instrumental music of Loop Guru, who have
released two albums on National Records, and consist of two Englishmen
who have adopted the Indian names Salman Gita and Jamud,
appropriating extensive Indian samples and musical influences in their
output. But as Hesmondhalgh points out, this ethnically heterogeneous
label none the less maintains a strong commitment to anti-racist politics,
particularly through the rap artists it has signed, such as Fun^Da^Mental,
Sikh rappers Hustlers HC, the Asian Dub Foundation, and black South
African group Prophets of da City. But attempts by Nation Records to
insert their output into the Asian corner shop distribution circuit in
Britain proved unsuccessful, indicating that, despite their multicultural
inclinations, their artists have an audience which lies predominantly
outside the trade routes of British-Asian ethnic communities.[39]

With increased media and major label interest, 'Asian beat' began to
achieve a higher profile not just in Britain but also throughout Asia. In
August 1993, *NME* featured a double-page colour spread on Apache
Indian's first tour of India, where he discovered that, thanks to MTV
Asia, he had become a major celebrity who required vast security
arrangements and commanded an apparent Indian fan base which rivalled
Michael Jackson's. Accompanied by a media circus including Jamaican
film-maker Don Letts, who filmed the proceedings, he performed to a
crowd of fifteen thousand, descending on to the stage in a crane, and
attempted to get audience participation in a song attacking the caste
system. After a planned meeting with Mother Teresa had to be cancelled,
he was received by Ghandi's granddaughter, who compared his potential
in India to that of her grandfather. He was humbled by the poverty he
witnessed in his first trip to his country of origin since he was seven years
old, and his naive response took on almost messianic overtones. His
eagerness to help the hungry masses of India led him to devise a song

called 'Stop the Corruption', after he had identified this as India's most major problem, but it was clear that his status as a musical role-model returning briefly from the diaspora had little to do with the social realities of India. As Roger Morton, the author of the *NME* article, indicated:

> In Britain, Apache might have settled into his role as a symbol of Indian pride and black-Asian togetherness, but in India his position is far more uncertain. As the first Indian from abroad to make it as a huge pop star in his roots country, Apache is being given unprecedented attention. And Steven Kapur, self-raised on the teachings of Bob Marley and Ghandi, wants to use his spotlight to change things. But how far India is prepared for an ex-welder from Birmingham to tell them where to move on to is another matter.[40]

The song entitled 'Movin' On' which Morton refers to suggests rather archly and ingenuously that sectarian violence in India between Hindus, Muslims and Sikhs must stop, and that the three groups should stop burning down temples and mosques and 'live as one'. It also exhorts the people of India to stop using the Indian crisis for religious and gang violence, and that 'an eye for an eye make[s] the whole world blind.'[41] A new version of the song which Apache Indian wrote and performed later that year, protesting against the election of British National Party MP Derek Beackon to the seat of Tower Hamlets in Millwall, an area with a large Asian population, seemed more appropriate to his role as a political rapper in a primarily British-Asian musical constituency. This version of the song was performed as an initiative in support of Tower Hamlets Asian community groups, and initially intended exclusively for broadcast on Radio One, but released as a single owing to public demand. After a second, more problematic trip to India, Apache Indian appeared to reach an awareness of his limitations, and it was a more humbled figure promoting his second album, *Make Way for the Indian*, in 1995, playing down his Asianness:

> In the beginning people started calling me the Ghandi of Pop and I'm trying to keep away from that. I'll talk about certain things like the problems of caste and arranged marriages, just because that's a part of me really, not to try and solve the problems of the world as far as Asians are concerned. It kind of got heavy that way so I've kind of kept away consciously from specific Asian issues on this album. I think I don't have to keep waving the Indian flag all the time. Hopefully the tracks will just stand up: It's either a good hip hop track or it's not, or a good reggae track or it's not, and afterwards you see it's an Asian guy.[42]

Consequently, as the title indicates, *Make Way for the Indian* is a decidedly pop-oriented mixture of boasting and toasting, with collaborations with a number of British and American reggae artists and production on two tracks by the ubiquitous US rhythm section Sly and Robbie. There is also a strong jungle influence, with bass and drums predominant, following on from Apache Indian's 'ragga jungle' collaboration in 1994 with the much criticized 'King of Jungle' General Levy on a single, 'The New Style'.[43] Only 'Ansa Dat' (a ragga version of 'Answer That', not an Indian-language expression), which criticizes guns, has any political orientation, while a number of other tracks show religious and spiritual concerns. There is only one track with any real bhangra influence, the decidedly lightweight 'Boba', a collaboration with Pandit Dinesh of the East India Company and Chumni of bhangra group Alaap. The album considerably weakens George Lipsitz's rather portentous claim that Apache Indian 'uses performance to call into being a community of Punjabis, Jamaicans, South Asians and West Indians', and that 'venerating Mahatma Gandhi and Bob Marley rather than Winston Churchill or George Frederick Handel ... [he] creates problems for nation states with their narratives of discrete, homogenous, and autonomous culture, but he solves problems for people who want cultural expressions as complex as the lives they live every day.'[44] The burden of characterizations such as this, which pay scant regard to Apache Indian's music, and the novelty appeal of his bhangramuffin hybridity, evidently caused Apache Indian to seek a more discreet, and less noticeably Asian, form of ragga, drawing on predominantly Jamaican influences which distinguish him less from other British and Jamaican reggae performers. But as Kudwo Edshun suggested in a review of Apache Indian's 1993 single 'Arranged Marriage', 'Apache Indian is a critical lure. Because he's more interesting in theory than in hearing, people don't realize how dull he really is.'[45]

In an apparent attempt to rival Apache Indian's triumphant return to his country of origin, the more abrasively revolutionary Anglo-Asian rap group Fun^Da^Mental undertook a tour of Pakistan in 1993 to film a music video for their single 'Countryman', this time with a reporter from the *Melody Maker* in tow. 'Countryman' is the story, told in Jamaican ragga style, of an Asian man who emigrates to 'the promised land' from his village and family in the Indian subcontinent, and his experience of degrading housing and employment, racism and unemployment in a nation built on immigrant labour. The song concludes the 'countryman' will rise through hard work, commitment, religion and love. Samples of racist comments about Asian immigrants are mixed with Indian film music, while the B-side, 'Tribal Revolution', calls for black revolution from Kingston to Brixton, and from Bombay to LA, to 'the roll of the dhol'. Fun^Da^Mental's 1994 debut album *Seize the Time*, a hard-core collection of abrasively rhetorical attacks against racism, the mass media, corporate banking and other capitalist and colonialist targets, celebrations of 'mother India' and Muslim beliefs and anti-pacifist exhortations of 'a revolution of the mind', combines samples of skinhead racist messages, radio talkbacks on immigration and messages from Nation of Islam leader Louis Farrakhan. Its blend of full-frontal leftist cant and visceral beats led *Melody Maker* to describe it as 'the most inflammatory album since [Public Enemy's] *Fear of a Black Planet*'.[46] Although addressing Asians, Arabs and black people generally throughout the world, it operates primarily within a British context. The group's Muslim leader Propa-Ghandi (also known as Aki Nawaz, former drummer of Southern Death Cult and co-director of Nation Records), who reputedly supports Iran's *fatwah* against writer Salman Rushdie, tends to cover his face and mouth with a Palestinian guerrilla-style *kafia* head scarf in live performance, but is always vocal about political issues in interviews, explaining the group's name and political agenda as follows:

> I don't really like fanatics but I can also see that a lot of fundamentalist groups are like freedom fighters and then the people in power come along and paint them with a different and more negative brush. I look at the Third World that is supposedly in 'crisis' and I see people who have actually worked out how to fight the system and are being called fundamentalists or subversives because they are succeeding.[47]

At the time of their visit to Pakistan, Fun^Da^Mental consisted of leader Propa-Ghandi, Pakistani rappers Goldfinger and Lallaman, and West Indian DJ 'D'. Propa-Ghandi had previously been the subject of a television programme, *Punjabi Hip Hop*, which had chronicled his musical journey through India and Pakistan to meet with prominent traditional musicians. As he told *Melody Maker*, he wanted Fun^Da^-Mental's video to reflect the Third World realities of life in Pakistan, in contrast to Apache Indian's show-business-styled visit to India: 'When Apache Indian went to India, he went with an entourage and he stayed in big hotels. That's bullshit, man! Fun^Da^Mental talks about the street and it wants to be walking through the street, not driving down it in a f***ing [sic] limousine.'[48] He forbade his group to stay in comfortable hotels, preferring to attempt to live at the same level as Pakistan's poor, with the result that most of them suffered severely from heat, insect bites and dysentery. After an attempt to film at a fortress at Lahore without police permission resulted in Goldfinger and Lallaman being detained by police, and differences of opinion between Propa-Ghandi, who announced his intention to return to Pakistan 'and do something for people who really need somebody fighting for them', and the others, who retained their commitment to fighting racism in Britain, the group split up. On their return to Britain, Goldfinger and Lallaman formed a new group, also called Fun^Da^Mental, and played at a Rock against Racism gig in Leeds, while Propa-Ghandi and 'D' continued to perform in Britain under the name Fun^Da^Mental. Eventually Propa-Ghandi obtained legal rights to the name, and the other faction changed theirs to

Detrimental, eventually, in 1995, releasing a single, 'Babylon', which was almost indistinguishable, in its anti-racist concerns and use of Asian music samples, from Fun^Da^Mental, who had to remix *Seize the Time* to edit out the voices of Goldfinger and Lallaman. Detrimental later released three of their own versions of 'Countryman', indicating that their animosity towards Fun^Da^Mental was continuing.

In 1995, Fun^Da^Mental returned to Pakistan to shoot a documentary video to accompany their second album, a series of instrumental remixes of tracks from *Seize the Time* entitled *With Intent to Pervert the Course of Injustice!* This time they were accompanied by *NME* writer Steven Wells, whose subsequent lengthy and emotive article dwelt almost exclusively on his upset stomach, insect bites, exhaustion and inability to 'adopt a studiously neutral, detached, professionally journalistic attitude'.[49]

With Intent to Pervert the Cause of Injustice! contains no new material, but its global focus on oppressed indigenous people is indicated in its dedication to Aotearoa/New Zealand rapper DLT and 'the inspiring Maori youth of Auckland and people of the land', as well as the Wreck Bay Aboriginal Community in Australia and 'the intoxicated wisdom of the Aborigines in Adelaide Square', South African rappers Prophets of da City and the Nation of Islam, among others. A note also thanks 'all traditional music/musicians around the world who have inspired us, not just musically but politically'. The final track is a highly polemical unaccompanied poem entitled 'Global Tales', which attacks oppression in Africa, Asia, Australia, Canada and South Africa. This suggests a homogenizing notion of world music as the united cries of oppressed peoples which the music on the album, with its incorporation of Pakistani devotional chanting, traditional bhangra, Ethiopian cow horns and other samples of indigenous musics such as a didjeridu, attempts to comple-ment. But the album's political perspective on global colonial oppression relies almost exclusively on extra-musical features expressed in its poem and liner notes, and its association with the lyrics of Fun^Da^Mental's previous album *Seize the Time*.

Both the misplaced adulation and euphoria arising from Apache Indian's Indian tour and the disastrous outcome of Fun^Da^Mental's first Pakistani trip illustrate the predicament of deracinated Anglo-Asian musicians, and confirm their position, like that of many other musicians who are included under the label of world music, as hybrid musical groups rooted in a migrant culture. Their experiences indicate the unreasonable expectations of diasporic musicians wishing to speak directly for or to their countries of origin, although their musical influences on developments in popular music in those countries have been evident.

Musical migration, 'ouverture' and sonic tourism

The Canadian ethnomusicologists Line Grenier and Jocelyne Guibault have been critical of tendencies among ethnomusicologists to idealize and historically freeze Third World musical cultures. As global technology, communications and migration have had a shrinking and homogenizing influence on world cultures, they argue that non-Western 'others' can no longer be the exclusive objects of ethnographic study, since many of them are dynamic, interactive and polyphonic subjects. Transnational migration has brought about accompanying shifts in the field of popular music. The largely white, Anglo-Saxon and nationally defined musical subcultures identified by British cultural studies ethnographers like Stanley Cohen, Paul Willis and Dick Hebdige in the 1970s and 1980s have expanded into more multi-ethnic 'sites of difference' which call for a combination of micro-analyses of local practices and pan-global macro-analyses. Such analyses 'consider the Other in the context of the world political economy'.[50]

The jet-setting Paris-based West African music producer Ibrahima Sylla could be seen as a personification of some of the pan-global practices current in the world music scene. Sylla speaks Arabic, French, Wolof and Bambara. He developed an interest in Cuban music in the 1970s and began importing salsa records to Paris from New York before starting to produce records by African singers like Youssou N'Dour, Salif Keita and Ismaël Lo, who have since become major figures in world music. While recording for the Western European market, Sylla regards Africa as his main market, and contrasts the glasnost-like concept of 'ouverture' with the compromising 'denaturalizing' effect of the world music market on some African musicians: 'you should record in Paris, you should open your music up. When I say "open up" [ouverture] I mean make it accessible to other people, especially the West. One mustn't confuse "ouverture" with "de-naturalizing" [denaturer]. African music will remain African music. But we can make openings so that other ears can accept it.'[51] This binary dynamic places the Western listener in the privileged position of being a musical *flâneur* able to tune into new sonic adventures, often sung in a language he or she does not understand. The tourist-like position in which this places the world music listener is illustrated by the publication in 1994 of *The Rough Guide to World Music* by a London-based publisher normally concerned with economical tourist guides for young travellers. This seven-hundred-page tome, far too heavy for the average backpack, divides the world into thirteen territories, starting with the Celtic World and concluding with Australia and the Pacific. The latter is by far its shortest section, consisting of an account of Aboriginal rock music and its traditional background by Marcus Breen (in which 'kangaroo' is mis-spelt throughout), and an interview with British composer David Fanshawe about the music of the various countries of

Oceania – a brief and sketchy tourist's impression. A series of lightweight, accessible magazine-styled feature articles, interviews and discographies focusing largely on traditional musics, the *Rough Guide* is an encyclopedic reference work which appears to take for granted the open-ended, all-embracing nature of world music. But it is also highly selective, as the quote from Hijaz Mustapha which prefaces it indicates: 'Four fifths of the world cannot be wrong.' As a result, the section 'from the Baltic to the Balkans' does not include the Czech Republic or Slovakia, or any rock or pop music in those regions, and 'the Mediterranean and Maghreb' includes a chapter on Spanish flamenco but nothing on Italian music of any kind. On the other hand, there are three lengthy sections on African music, and one each on North and South America, the Caribbean, the Indian subcontinent, the Far East and the Nile and the Gulf, indicating that the Rough Guide concept of world music, like the BBC's, is predominantly Third World and oriental music.[52]

Song lyrics of much world music make no strong interpretive demands on the anglophonic listener, although the practice of printing English translations or summaries of lyrics on CD sleeves is becoming standard. But, as Vincenzo Perna has indicated, often the desires of the listener to find out more about the music's context is not catered for by liner notes or explanations:

> What about the poor listener, trapped in a jungle of sonic codes? Does one really have to 'acculturate oneself' in order to be able to appreciate world music? Clearly the immediate attraction of much world music lies purely in its exoticism, and its strangeness and novelty has led many of us to discover astonishing sonic landscapes. But without detracting from the right to listen in whatever way one likes, I think many listeners feel the desire – often frustrated – to go beyond first impressions. I mean 'go beyond' not just in relation to strictly musical information, but particularly information about the conditions in which the music has originated and developed. In this case the music, not unlike a novel or a film, can open a door through which one can glimpse a new world.[53]

Steven Feld's concept of 'interpretive moves', through which the listener identifies and links new musical experiences to an accumulated musical and social experience, is useful in this context.[54] It is possible for a reasonably experienced listener to world music to identify music not only by singer but also nationally. Zimbabwean chimurenga has a particular sonic and rhythmic identity which differentiates it from Zairean soukous, the griot tradition of Mali or South African mbaqanga, for example. Sylla's notion of 'ouverture' also ensures a modicum of 'listener-friendly' familiarity in the use of recording studio technologies and instrumentation – usually guitar and keyboards – which facilitate the 'interpretive moves' of the Western listener.

This recipe was particularly successful on Salif Keita's *Soro* (1987), an album which launched this Malian griot on to the European music market and became a defining album of world music without alienating African consumers in the process. Keita who had not recorded for seven years, since his 1980 album *Wassolon-Foli*, recorded in the US and combining reggae and traditional Mali music. Keita is an albino African descendant of the medieval noble Soundjata Keita family and is a Muslim. This, combined with his quasi-sacred status as a griot or traditional storytelling singer often patronized by royalty, gives him a highly exoticized sense of 'otherness' to Westerners that fuels the form of imaginary cultural stereotyping that Edward Said has referred to as orientalism.[55] This is particularly evident in a music video of him on a desert mountain top dressed in robes like a Muslim spiritual leader singing the song 'Souvareba' from *Soro*. The main dynamic of the clip involves a group of seemingly adoring, white-robed women approaching the singer up the mountain, while Keita displays an odd series of jerky hand movements (slightly reminiscent of Joe Cocker) which suggest a gestural code of signification inaccessible to the Western listener, thus heightening the sense of mystique. Keita was invited to perform Cole Porter's song 'Begin the Beguine' (a dance of African origin) on *Red, Hot and Blue*, an American music video programme devised by Leigh Blake and John Carlin to support AIDS research, which was broadcast on International AIDS Day in 1990 on a number of Western television networks. As the only African performer among the twenty popular British and American artists featured in the programme, Keita's presence served to remind Western viewers of the gravity of the AIDS problem in Africa, and to provide a strong interactive context for African popular music. His performance, however, in a studio-bound clip directed by Zak Ove and featuring African dancers, a red colour wash, flames and some very perfunctory-looking hand gestures, was rather lacklustre.

Keita's albums after *Soro* included more Western elements: *Amen*, released in 1991, was recorded in Paris and Malibu, and produced by jazz musician Joe Zaiwanul, who also played keyboards and supervised computer and keyboard programming on the album, giving it a more accessible, jazz-oriented focus. The album featured rock guitarist Carlos Santana and jazz saxophonist Wayne Shorter, but the mix of Western jazz and rock with Malian griot songs is an uneasy one, tending towards a turgid, over-lush sound. A pop-oriented love song, 'N B'l Fe', indicates a commercial, crossover orientation. Keita, like a number of other African musicians on the world music scene, is now based in Paris, a growing centre for transculturation for African musicians. This is reflected in his address of a new French-based audience. His 1989 album *Ko-Yan*, which failed to capitalize on the commercial success of *Soro*, included a song in French entitled 'Nou Pas Bouger' (We Won't Move), about African emigrants in France resisting threats of deportation. Musically, this album was a hybrid which seemed to lose the benefits both of Western instrumental and recording technology and of residues of Malian traditional music.

A certain degree of exoticization in representations of Third World music in the West is inevitable. As Roger Armstrong, co-director of Virgin Globestyle, has commented, this is part of the process of marketing it as pop music: 'A lot of the stuff we do on Globestyle is essentially the pop music of the country, but as soon as you transpose it into the West, it sounds exotic. People don't understand the language, or the social or musical context. But at the same time, because it's pop music, it has that accessible quality to it. Pop music is pop music, whatever language it's in.'[56] The exoticization of world music through video, CD packaging and advertising increases the mystique of the music to the Western consumer, and a purely superficial approach to the music by the listener is often taken for granted by recording companies.

Algerian rai: Thursday night fever

Discrepancies between the oppositional social and cultural contexts of some world music and the incomprehension of Western listeners are particularly apparent in the construction of Algerian rai music in the West. Rai, or 'opinion music' which takes its name from a chant of approval roughly equivalent to 'yeah', is a highly controversial, anti-traditional form of Algerian popular music. Deriving from the music of female Bedouin singers of the 1920s and 1930s, it is a hybrid form combining Moroccan and Spanish flamenco elements with African rhythmic influences. It often features trumpet, violin, accordion, electric guitar and synthesizer with an often erotic improvised vocal style which originated in Oran, Algeria in the late 1970s, and celebrates passion and sexuality, and alcohol – taboo subjects in Muslim Algeria. The music's concern with eroticism and sexual freedom from both a male and a female perspective, and its personification of its singers as Chebs and Chabas – 'young' and 'good looking' men and women – has caused problems of censorship and open hostility in Algeria. These culminated in the death of rai singer Cheb Hasni at the hands of an angry crowd in Oran in September 1994. Hasni, an up-and-coming singer following in the footsteps of the acknowledged 'king of rai', Khaled, was shot twice by Islamic fundamentalists. His funeral was attended by forty thousand people, including a number of women, who are forbidden under Islamic law to attend funerals.

Khaled, a 1993 French television documentary by Jean-Paul Guirado, captured some of the dilemmas and controversies of rai, profiling Khaled (formerly Cheb Khaled) in exile in France, watching and responding to video recordings of interviews with his parents and fans in Oran, and nervously waiting backstage to perform at the prestigious Paris Olympia.

Khaled's song 'El Harba Wine' ('Where to Flee?') had been used as a theme song in Algeria in a 'rai rebellion' by anti-government protesters, and as a result Khaled had virtually been forced into exile in Marseilles. In Guirado's film, some of Khaled's Algerian fans accuse him of betraying rai by concentrating on playing it for Westerners in Western contexts, and a group of young Oran rappers acknowledge him as a 'musical master from the south who now lives in the north'. The US producer of Khaled's 1992 self-titled album, Don Was, talks of his 'charisma', comparing him to other artists he has worked with such as Bob Dylan, Bonnie Raitt and Elton John, and playing down the language barrier as a source of difficulty in understanding his music. The album *Khaled* was recorded in Los Angeles, with a mixture of Algerian and US rock musicians, with Khaled playing accordion and *oud*. A couple of songs have French titles, but all are in Arabic (and the words printed in Arabic on the album cover with no explanatory notes!). The opening track, 'Didi', with its dominant drum-machine patterns, had some success in Europe as a dance single, and was made into a live performance music video, but the subject of the predominantly up-tempo songs on the album remain a mystery to non-Arabic-speaking listeners. Khaled justifies his continued exile, describing himself as both an 'ambassador' and a 'nomad', but most Western listeners have little more than sounds and rhythms and his extraordinary vocalizations to respond to in his music.[57] Khaled is responsible for much of the increasing international popularity of rai, but appears to have substituted his local fan base for an émigré audience in the process. His charisma, charm and energy were evident in a concert I saw him perform to a frenzied, ecstatic émigré audience in London in 1992, beaming while he almost continually signed autographs for young male fans, many sitting on friends' shoulders, who approached him with pen and paper through the swarming throngs of dancing fans. As one of the only Westerners in the audience, it seemed to me that considerations about whether Khaled was performing music for Westerners were purely academic. The sinuous, eroticized forms of dancing engendered by his music seemed quite remote from the more angular, frantically narcissistic dancing that takes place in most Western discotheques.

The Algerian journalist Bouziane Kodla has contextualized rai music and its moral dilemmas as follows:

> Although it is true that rai is about alcohol and sex, adultery and carnal pleasure, life and death, good and bad, it really is only expressing genuine and deeply held frustrations. It doesn't preach about sin, it only throws light on it. It attempts to heal the pain of a generation which is in search of the truth about itself. It stems apathy and says yes to life. ... We condemn the fact that such a part of our national heritage is censored by those who only want to dampen the ultimate Thursday night fever: rai.[58]

This conflict, so reminiscent of the moral dilemmas caused by rock and roll in the West in the 1950s, is barely acknowledged in the marketing of rai on the world music circuit. The cover of Cheb Mami's album *The Prince of Rai*, for example, released on the independent American Shanachie label in 1989, features a wizened Arabic woman shrouded in a veil and the head and neck profile of a camel foregrounded against a photo of the Tamanrassat desert. The recording is categorized as 'Worldbeat Ethnopop', which makes doubly certain the fetishized, exoticized nature of the sleeve's contents. In contrast, the reverse side of the record sleeve features Mami in a tuxedo, surrounded by a group of decidedly Western-looking young men and women. This kind of cross-cultural contrast of imagery and aspiration is a recurring feature in world music.

Although it is increasingly becoming established in Paris with Khaled and others, rai represents one of the few non-western 'other' musics which can boast its own local production system independent of European remixing or technological remastering. Many rai recordings are produced by Rachid and Fethi Baba Ahmed, eccentric brothers who record the vocal tracks of songs with an electronic rhythm played to the singer through headphones, and then add tracks of guitar, bass, percussion, synthesizer and accordion played by Rachid. Sometimes duets are constructed from versions of songs recorded by male and female singers as many as five years apart. The results of this cottage recording industry, based in Oran, are distinctive and sophisticated enough to compete with Western dance music.

'New sounds for a bored culture'

The more extreme forms of exoticization in world music recordings and videos position the viewer and listener as privy to a synthetic form of imaginary global travel similar to that indulged in by Des Esseintes, the protagonist of J. K. Huysmans's nineteenth-century novel *A Rebours* (Against Nature). Huysmans's indolent, aristocratic hero could 'travel' from Paris to London without discomfort by having a typical English dish of roast beef and Yorkshire pudding prepared for him and by immersing himself in a novel by Dickens. World music's inherent invitation to the listener to become lost in an imagined exotic adventure is perhaps most evident in the mass music chart success of the Franco-Spanish group the Gipsy Kings, whose brand of middle-of-the-road flamenco rock caused Jeremy Chunn, a reviewer in the Sydney-based music weekly *On the Street*, to dub them 'Barry Manilow's Gypsy counterparts ... something for the stockbroker's coffee table'.[59] A Gipsy Kings' song was used in Australia for a television commercial for the glossy monthly *New Woman* magazine, enhancing a corporate image of their music as one of the accoutrements of success associated with bourgeois 'femocracy'. Similarly, the success of

Kaoma's rendition of the Brazilian Lambada on their album *World Beat* represents the exoticized corporate commercial face of world music, which requires less extreme shifts in listening patterns than most African music. Even the more adventurous examples of world music are seen by some as a relatively superficial passing trend reflecting a poverty of ideas in current Anglo-American pop and rock music. Joe Boyd of the London-based Hannibal Records, who produce a number of African and Eastern European recordings, has described the British market for world music in rather cynical terms:

> It's providing new sounds for a bored culture. ... Now there is a clearly perceivable market for African music and that market is inescapably *Guardian* and *Independent* readers. White middle class culture has run out of inspiration. The normal sources to plunder are exhausted and white middle class culture is incapable of inventing anything. When this has happened before they tended to adopt working class culture and the biggest source of that musically, American R&B and country, has been plundered dry.[60]

Like Des Esseintes's speculative travel, most of the predominantly sensory products of world music involve translocation from Paris, the major production centre, to London, traditionally the major trading centre of the music industry. Consequently traditionally problematic Anglo-French trade and power relations are involved at the source of the music's global exchange network. As Frith has commented:

> African music ... reaches us almost exclusively via France, via French studios, French engineers, and French producers, via, most importantly, French audiences whom the musicians have learnt to please. The appeal of African music in Britain is as much a triumph of French as African pop values, as any glimpse of French pop TV (and the 1988 success of Mory Kante's 'Yeke Yeke') makes clear.[61]

Many of the African strands of world music originated in Paris in the early 1980s as a strategy to assert a French challenge to the Anglo-American dominance of global popular music. This would occur through the dissemination of the music of the numerous African musicians based in Paris who had built up a strong émigré and Parisian following. The traffic of African music from Paris to London began in 1982 when the jangling guitar-based ju-ju music of Nigerian singer 'King' Sunny Ade and the electric-organ-based Afrobeat of Fela Kuti were exposed to English audiences. Fela Kuti, a political dissident who was imprisoned in Nigeria, often sang highly political lyrics in English. However, promoters misjudged initial interest in him and when a follow-up tour by the singer flopped, English enthusiasm for Nigerian music was dampened. In the same year Peter Gabriel launched WOMAD (The World of Music, Arts and Dance), an international organization whose principal aim was to promote the music of Third World and non-Anglo-American countries through annual concerts. The first WOMAD festival in Shepton Mallet, which featured the relatively obscure Burundi Drummers and Nigerian guitarist Prince Nico, lost money, and Gabriel had to re-form his old rock group Genesis for a tour in order to pay off the deficit. By 1994 WOMAD concerts of 'worldwide music' had been held in Spain, Germany, Italy, Denmark, Finland, Canada, Japan and Australia. Gabriel also set up Real World, a recording label with a vast network specializing in world music which has greatly extended the map of world musicians to include countries such as Egypt, Cambodia, Lapland, Russia, Georgia, China, Madagascar and Morocco. Real World releases are colour-coded into nine areas which cover the globe: Africa, North America, South America, Asia 1, Asia 2, Oceania, Caribbean, Europe and the Indian subcontinent, and by 1995 the label had released more than fifty recordings.

In the late 1970s other Anglo-American musicians and producers like David Byrne, Brian Eno and Jon Hassell (producers of *Possible Music*, an album of 'Fourth World' music which combined ambient music with Burundi drumming and the music of African griots as early as 1980) and Malcolm McLaren (who purloined an LP full of Soweto street music called *Duck Rock*) also began exploring interfaces between their own Anglo-American music and that of the Third World. One reason for this appropriation of 'other' musics by rock and pop musicians was a frustration with the limitations of Anglo-American forms, which, having evolved over three decades from rock and roll to guitar and synthesizer-based rock, appeared to have stagnated by the beginning of the 1980s. David Byrne explained his interest in African music in the late 1970s as 'a way out of the dead end, the one-sided philosophical binder, that Western culture has gotten itself into'.[62]

Sampling, jungle, deracination and exile

More than ever world music is providing raw material for the increasingly diversified and complex mix of musics tapped into by the widespread use of digital sampling. M/A/R/R/S, who produced 'Pump Up the Volume' – a controversial 1987 hit on the British and international charts which sampled no fewer than thirty records – produced an 'Acid Mix' version of 'Yeke Yeke' by Mory Kante, a Malian griot and former musical colleague of Salif Keita. This remix placed a British production stamp on what had been a hit on the French and German charts. It set a precedent for releases such as Bristol-based reggae-dub sound system Massive Attack's remix of 'Musst Musst', a devotional song by one of the most unlikely Third World musicians to cross over into Western European popular music, the Pakistani qawwali singer Nusrat Fateh Ali Khan – a song which subsequently became a huge hit in India in a Hindi pop version in 1994.

The ensuing mix, which incorporated echo, drum-machines, samples and other techno-dance additions, involved a delicate process of cutting, shifting and pasting the melodic phrases and scales of the song without disrupting the devotional meaning of the lyrics.

With the advent of British rave culture and techno music in the 1990s, randomly sampled and often unidentified exotic 'other' sounds were combined with the high-powered, high-frequency, repetitive beats-per-minute ratios of dance music or the ambient electronic effects of trance music to generate purely physical forms of music which appear to rely heavily on the effects of drugs like Ecstasy for their impact. The underground musical economy known as jungle which emerged from British rave culture in 1994, combining reggae, hip hop rhythms and techno, suggested a hybrid Africanizing influence capable of providing an antidote to the soulless European repetitive beats of techno.[63] According to 'Mr. Push and Mr. Bush' in the monthly rave culture magazine *Muzik*, 'junglist' is 'Jamaican patois for a resident of Trenchtown', but the term 'jungle' is said to have originated from London racists referring to fast breakbeat music as 'jungle bunny records'. The term was then adopted by the black musical community in London and given a positive meaning.[64] The sixteen 'jungle and dubhouse tracks' on the 1994 compilation *Downbeat in the Jungle*, which include UK Apachi, General Levy, Zion Train, Slam Collective and M. C. Olive among others, suggest a colourless and largely monotonous recombination of bass and drum-dominated house beats and reggae toasting with few rewards for the listener away from the club dancefloor. While General Levy claimed a diversification of jungle's economy into ragga jungle, soul jungle, trance jungle and techno jungle, Ian McCann identified it in the *NME* in 1994 as a 'music forged as an antidote to whiteboy techno' with a 'black birthright' deriving from reggae roots. McCann also suggested a racist backlash was operating within the contestations taking place within jungle's economy, where white adepts were attempting to obscure its roots in Jamaican reggae, while the dilemmas of sexism and homophobia it shares with hip hop continued to be a feature of the music.[65] These contestations were the subject of an editorial in *The Wire* in June 1995 by Tony Herrington, who argued that concerns by white music critics, that jungle music was moving away from its African-American and Afro-Caribbean roots towards more 'refined', serene and upwardly mobile European musical influences, were 'partly predicated on sensibilities that still regard black music as exotic, dark, mysterious, pulsing with a febrile sense of otherness'. In this context, Herrington argued, notions of 'black' music tended to be imposed by white critics, whose often exotic expectations of black music, which were never applied to white musicians, amounted to 'cultural tourists' insisting on how the visited culture should behave.[66] Similar concerns about musical deracination have been continually circulating in world music and in different forms of 'black' music throughout the world.

Some African and world music deals directly with the implications of its deracinated status on the pan-global market. This deracination is due to both the technological exigencies of the popular music global economy and the migrant status of many of its musicians. The title song of Youssou N'Dour's 1984 album *Emigrés*, which was re-released on the Anglo-American Virgin Earthworks label after his participation in the 1988 Amnesty International rock music tour, addresses Senegal migrants in Paris. The song suggests that they would return to their homeland sooner or later because they belong in Senegal, and the people in their host countries did not understand or know them because of cultural differences. According to a profile of N'Dour in Tower Records' *Pulse!* magazine, this song has become 'the enduring anthem of New York's army of Senegalese sidewalk vendors',[67] but the dilemma of cultural misunderstanding it describes is one which he himself has been largely able to escape, partly owing to the assistance he has gained from his British patron, Peter Gabriel. Lucy Duran has traced N'Dour's career from the strong Western rock and Cuban *pachanga* dance music influences of his early music in the 1970s, through a shift away from European cultural models with his Super Etoile band, back to the traditional percussive rhythms of the Senegambian-based *mbalax* music featuring the *tama* (talking drum), to an international presentation style cross-fertilized by his collaboration with Peter Gabriel:

Working with Peter Gabriel has had an immeasurable impact on Youssou. This is the most obvious in his new style of stage presentation. Most excitingly, Youssou has proved the old rumours that he 'can't dance' are far from true – in fact, he dances exceptionally well, with great charm and impeccable sense of timing. None of the band stands still any more; their movements are subtly choreographed, with considerable wit, to reflect the subject of the song.[68]

N'Dour is one of the few African musicians on the world music circuit who is able to spend a lot of his time in his home country, where he enjoys the status of both a griot and a superstar, and has even become self-sufficient enough to leave Virgin Records and set up his own record label in Africa. With his 1992 album *Eyes Open*, released through Spike Lee's 40 Acres and a Mule Musicworks Company, attempts were made to market 'Senegalese soul' in the USA. The album opens with 'New Africa', a song about African unity, and closes with a rap about the importance of reading between the lines in cross-cultural interpretations, 'Things Unspoken'. But its disjunctive heterogeneity, with four songs in English, one in French, one in Fulani, one in Serer and the rest in Wolof, in styles ranging from Western ballads to traditional *mbalax*, together with its predominantly African concerns, demanded too much from US audiences. The album failed to make much impact in the USA, partly because it lacked a marketable song to release as a single. His 1994 album *The Guide (Wommat)*, which included a top ten single, a collaboration with Neneh

Cherry, 'Seven Seconds', and a powerful version (sung, like much of the album, in a mixture of English, French and Wolof) of Bob Dylan's 'Chimes of Freedom', was, like its predecessor, recorded and mixed by N'Dour and two of the Super Etoile, at N'Dour's Xippi Studios in Dakar (with the exception of 'Seven Seconds', recorded in New York). Aimed more successfully at the world music market, it contained some of his most assured music, a consummate fusion of Senegalese and European musical influences, and its production qualities are virtually indistinguishable from world music products of studios in New York, London or Paris.

Some of the dilemmas of Peter Gabriel's musical collaboration with N'Dour are highlighted on a song released by both artists in 1989 entitled 'Shakin' the Tree'. With lyrics in both English and Wolof, this song is about the defiance of oppressive traditions by African women. It appeared on solo albums by both Gabriel and N'Dour, and a music video of it was aired on MTV. The video embodies some of the problems of cultural collaborations between English and African musicians, as well as possible Anglo-French cultural tensions. Gabriel's dominant appearance in an exoticized African beach setting opens him to charges of neo-colonialist appropriation, while the reduction of the strong and athletic African women in the video to a role of background colour and objects of desire in a song which claims to be celebrating their liberation seems ironically contradictory. Similar problems of cultural identity and relations between First World and Third World can be identified frequently in world music videos, suggesting that readings which aim primarily to demarcate power relations and cultural configurations may be less fruitful than interpretations which seek to identify the sources of pleasure, play and musical collaboration. While music video is an important vehicle of performance and cultural imagery in world music, it can be misleading if seen as a marker of authenticity or circumstances of production of the music.

The Paris-based Zairean singer and keyboard player Ray Lema, whom Ibrahima Sylla cited as an example of a 'de-naturized' musician, occupies a much more deracinated and less privileged position in world music than N'Dour. Lema, a former musical director of the National Ballet of Zaire and an ethnographer of traditional folkloric Zairean music, is a political refugee from Zaire, and has lived in Paris for more than ten years. He has a wide following and gets considerable media coverage in France, but his music, an electro-fusion of Afro-jazz, rock and funk, is virtually unheard of in Africa. His 1990 album *Gaia*, however, which begins with a song called 'Made in France', opening with a few bars of the 'Internationale', has shifted to a more consciously 'African' techno-fusion. In an interview with Chris Stapleton, Ray Lema commented on some of the benefits of his status as an African musician in France:

> Since 1982 things have changed quickly in Paris. French people are now far
> more aware of our presence. The government supports us because they feel

that the French language is receding in the world and that French artists are unable to carry the language overseas. The Africans are the people who can do this – suddenly they are pushing us.[69]

This use of French-based African musicians to promulgate notions of French national musical culture was also reflected in 1989 in the French Revolution bicentennial celebrations, which featured African musicians prominently. In 1991 Lema toured West Africa, promoted by Radio France International. This seven-day, six-country, five-star-hotel African tour, whose audiences consisted of a disproportionate number of diplomatic official parties, was to have included Zaire, but fears that Lema would not be allowed out of the country caused this idea to be dropped. As Charles Martel commented:

Ray and his band were treated with interest and kindness, even if his music left some of the audiences bemused. But local musicians are treated with much more respect than in the past. Music is omnipresent in Africa, and the concept of the 'professional' musician very recent. . . . The idea that you have to come to Paris to make a decent record is slowly sliding into the past . . . I suspect that soon West Africa will no longer have to export its great artists. It will only have to send us great records.[70]

Lema's cross-cultural dilemma illustrates a displaced pan-Africanism shared by the bizarre SAPEUR – the Society for Ambienceurs and Persons of Elegance – founded by Paris-based Zairean singer Papa Wemba, a more extreme example of an exiled cultural practice. The SAPEUR movement, which has spread from Zaire to Paris, Brussels and London, is dedicated to *kitende*, or cloth, and its followers worship the fashion designer Jean-Paul Gaultier, and think nothing of spending up to five thousand dollars on a new suit of clothes. To a certain extent basing their habits and wardrobes on the Zairean president Mobutu, SAPEURs are jet-setting playboys and poseurs, aristocrats of fashion devoted to cleanliness and style. The cult has its own ten commandments, and delineates eight different ways of walking. As the Kinshasa-based musician Emine explained in the BBC television programme *Under African Skies*: 'A SAPEUR is someone who stands out. So those who aren't SAPEURs are those who stay seated . . . people we call Survivors Who are Condemned to Death'.[71]

Originating as it does in a country ravaged by poverty and AIDS, the SAPEURs' fetish for clean lines and elegance seems a perverse adoption of Western styles and values. But it blends bizarrely with a socialist, humanist concern with human rights activism and the colonial exploitation of Africa, as is illustrated in Papa Wemba's most famous song 'Esclave' (Slave) which he sings in *Under African Skies* wearing a hat studded with jewels. 'Esclave' portrays the African diaspora of slavery, invoking Martin Luther King, Bessie Smith, Bob Marley, Nelson

Mandela, Desmond Tutu, Sister Maria Teresa and all those who 'struggled for the cause and the freedom of the black man' in the USA, South Africa, Guadeloupe, Martinique, New Caledonia and the Antilles. Wemba's musical roots were a combination of traditional Zairean rhythms, Afro-Cuban music, US rhythm and blues and rock influences, incorporating electric guitars, keyboards and drum kits as a result of trade routes from Belgium. But his group Zaiko Langa Langa was also affected by President Mabuto's official imposition of 'authenticity' on Zairean culture in the 1960s, reverting to traditional music and banning all foreign influences. The SAPEURs' fetishization of the bourgeois luxuries of the cloth, their ritualizations of the promenade and their seemingly gratuitous concern with decoration is a symbolic appropriation of formerly colonialist bourgeois practices as liberating acts of defiance. Like a number of black musicians in the USA and Britain who wear ostentatiously opulent clothes and gold chains, they are expressing a ritualized commodity fetishism in which, in Paul Gilroy's words, 'consumption becomes an active, celebratory process'.[72]

While the Western consumer of world music maintains an aesthetic distance from the harsh social realities of the Third World, its performers are often involved in practices which disrupt the comfort of this distance and generate a contradictory aesthetic. Papa Wemba's 1995 album *Emotion*, which was produced by Stephen Hague, known for his work with British techno-pop groups the Pet Shop Boys, New Order and Erasure, reveals some of these contradictions in its rather bland Western pop and dance orientation, with Wemba singing in English as well as his native Lingala, covering Otis Redding's 'Sad Song' and incorporating a salsa beat on one track. In an interview in the liner notes to the album, Wemba states that he works with two different and quite separate groups of musicians, one to produce music for his Zairean fans, who expect 'typical African sounds', and the other for an international audience.

Lasers in the jungle: *Graceland* and other appropriations

Ambivalences and contradictions tend to proliferate in Western interventions in the production of world music. Rather than an acknowledgement of the African roots of Anglo-American rock, much of the renewed interest in African music in the West reflects a desire for the exotic in a familiar context, and a quest for new popular musical idioms capable of regenerating repetitive rock music forms, and, in some cases, reviving flagging careers. This latter tendency was particularly evident in the release in 1986 of Paul Simon's contentious Grammy Award-winning *Graceland* album, which sold more than seven million copies. This was an event which placed world music definitively on the map of Western popular music, and which involved widespread accusations against Simon of exploitation of local black South African musicians, as well as breaking a UNESCO cultural boycott of performances in South Africa. In an exhaustive study of the production and reception of *Graceland* in South Africa, Louise Meintjes accounts for conflicting responses to it in terms of arguments for musical transcendence as opposed to cultural specificity, and the use of black South African traditional musical forms for stylistic revitalization as opposed to their appropriation. She identifies two principal responses to a project which many saw as a rupture of the cultural boycott and a cynical exploitation of black South African music:

> *Graceland* has alerted South Africans to the richness and currency of Black South African expression. Interest in other local music not mediated by Simon seems to have followed interest in *Graceland*. On the one hand, this opens up opportunities on the local market for Blacks, since most record companies, major record outlets, and performance venues are owned by Whites. On the other hand, *Graceland* encourages the appropriation of Black Music by White South Africa as a means of establishing a White African (as opposed to colonial) identity.[73]

But, as Neil Lazarus has pointed out, this interest in the 'richness and currency of Black South African expression' led to record companies exerting pressure on black musicians to reproduce the types of music found on *Graceland*, a process which involved returning to styles of music they had abandoned twenty years ago. So, rather than opening opportunities for black musicians, this led to what he describes as the 'underdevelopment' of their music.[74]

Such attempts to induce Third World musicians to avoid innovative hybridizations and return to traditional forms they often have little interest in tends to recur throughout many formations of world music. The most conspicuous of the local black South African musicians who performed in and benefited from the *Graceland* project was the *a cappella* choral group Ladysmith Black Mambazo, who enjoyed considerable success outside South Africa, toured internationally and secured a recording contract with a major international label, Warner Brothers. In an article which points out that *Graceland* was supported and promoted by the pro-apartheid government and white supremacist groups in South Africa as an example of worldwide acceptance and popularity of apartheid, Charles Hamm also explains that Ladysmith Black Mambazo's music had previously been used by the South African Broadcast Corporation to maintain apartheid by promoting Zulu tribal identity and dividing the black population in South Africa.[75] Ladysmith's 1988 album *Journey of Dreams* featured songs sung mainly in English, and was marketed in Australia with a sticker signalling 'As featured in the Nescafé ad'. This Nescafé commercial was broadcast on Australian commercial television for a number of years, and features the group's choral harmonies as an aural backdrop to harvesting scenes on a Kenyan coffee plantation. It extends tendencies which can be found in some of Simon's music videos from *Graceland*, which Meintjes does not consider, but which, when they feature Ladysmith Black Mambazo at all, feature them as a backing group to Simon, performing stylized movements reminiscent of Negro plantation workers in Hollywood 'race' movies. Ladysmith have thus been contextualized in an international context of appropriation which casts them as colonial black stereotypes. But, as Homi Bhabha points out, there is an inherent ambivalence in such stereotypes, which are a fetishized representation of otherness: 'the stereotype ... is a form of knowledge and identification that vacillates between what is always 'in place', already known, and something that must be anxiously repeated ... as if the essential duplicity of the Asiatic or the bestial sexual license of the African that needs no proof, can never really, in discourse, be proved'.[76] While the undeniable power of Ladysmith's often religious vocal music is evident on the group's own recordings, marketing strategies they have been subjected to, and their association with Simon, have tended to reinforce black African stereotypes in a way which affirm a white colonial power and eliminate any possible threat of subversion of white supremacy. The music videos produced from *Graceland* either feature Simon alone (one pairs him with comic actor Chevy Chase miming the hit song 'You Can Call Me Al', about how Pierre Boulez got Simon's name wrong) or foreground him against Ladysmith Black Mambazo. This visually parallels the way black South African musicians on the recording are mixed into a background aural tapestry on which Simon's vocals and largely trivial and apolitical personalized songs are woven. Steven Feld has described the multi-layered aural mix of Graceland as follows:

> 'These are the days of lasers in the jungle,' sings Paul Simon; 'this is a long-distance-call.' These 'connecting'/'us and them' images in the opening song on the *Graceland* record are part of the gestalt of a postmodern African/Afro-American/American musical synthesis that overdubs quirky 1960's Long island/Brill Building Simon lyrics, pedal steel guitar riffs from a Nigerian juju band via Nashville recordings, vocals from Senegalese Youssou N'Dour on a break from recording projects with British pop star Peter Gabriel, and everything else from Synclavier samplers and drum machines to the Everly Brothers and Linda Rondstadt – all over the voices and instruments of South Africa's best known township musicians – bands like Stimela, Boyoyo Boys, General M. D. Shirinda and the Gaza Sisters, and the best known *a cappella* chorus, Ladysmith Black Mambazo. What makes it all fit together? Simon tells us in the record liner notes and in interviews ... that when he heard South African township music 'it sounded like very early rock and roll to me, black urban, mid-fifties rock and roll'. ... Of course, the reason it sounded that way had much to do with the steady stream of Afro-American rhythm and blues records that circulated widely in South Africa, and the way South African pop styles emerged in the larger context of a record industry with very strong links to the American jazz, blues, gospel and soul markets.[77]

Visually and aurally, Simon appears as the white master who exerts a benign rule over his black subjects. Even though he paid his musicians three times the going union rate (which, Feld indicates, still puts them 'in the role of wage labourers'[78]) and top royalties, and gave them co-writing credits, he maintained exclusive copyright ownership of the entire project. As Garofalo points out:

> If his purpose was to showcase black South African music, one has to wonder why he named the project after the estate of the white North American who captured the rock 'n' roll crown by employing – some would say imitating – African-American musical styles. He also added insult to his own injurious violation of the cultural boycott by using as a backup vocalist on the album Linda Ronstadt, who made front page headlines for performing at Sun City and refusing to apologise.[79]

Although the live tour of *Graceland* included exiled black anti-apartheid South African singers Miriam Makeba and Hugh Masakela (whom, Garofalo states, Simon was 'forced to add ... under considerable international pressure'), which suggests that Simon's silence about apartheid may not have told the full story, the colonialist implications of the project are hard to ignore. *Graceland* may have brought international benefits to Soweto township music (although the Azanian National Liberation Army bomb which blew up the offices of the promoter of Simon's 1992 South African tour indicates that not all were grateful), but the benefits it brought to Simon's career were far greater. Nor was it merely South African musicians Simon exploited: both the zydeco musician Rockin' Dopsie and the Los-Angeles-based Chicano band Los Lobos contributed to two tracks on the album which were credited solely to Simon, without any acknowledgement of the contribution of either.[80] The *Graceland* case demonstrates that the issue of appropriation is a wide-ranging and highly complex one, as Feld suggests:

> All of these forms and processes of appropriation – some more direct, some more subtle; some more overtly arrogant and linked to control over the means of production, others more complex and contradictory due to the way they suit both parties, or even strike us as fair tradeoffs – could be detailed song by song, and style by style for this record. Recent recordings by other major international pop stars (for example Peter Gabriel's *So*; Talking Heads' *Naked*) can be approached in the same way – through a kind of archaeological stylistic stratigraphy showing layers and varieties of appropriation, circulation and traffic in musical grooves, and concomitant embeddings, solidifications, and encrustings in the pop rock of musical ownership.[81]

By extension, a corollary 'stratigraphy' could also be applied to non-Western musicians' use of Western forms in a form of reverse appropriation, although the power relations involved would, of course, also be reversed.

In his discussion of *Graceland* in his book *Dangerous Crossroads*, George Lipsitz exonerates Simon from the charge that he deliberately 'depoliticize[d] and decontextualize[d] the music of oppressed people while celebrating his own openness', arguing that his intentions were to promote racial and musical harmony in the interests of 'a global fusion culture that transcends national, racial and ethnic lines'.[82] But in the display of superior power and control as a white American artist superimposing what Lipsitz rather generously describes as Simon's 'lyrics about cosmopolitan postmodern angst over songs previously situated within the lives and struggles of aggrieved Black communities',[83] Lipsitz argues that Simon failed to acknowledge the inequality and consequences of the project.

Lipsitz goes on to compare *Graceland* with David Byrne's 1989 salsa album *Rei Momo*, which he chastises because, like *Graceland*, it did not effectively illumine the power relations between Western artists and their sources of inspiration from the Third World. Lipsitz's main example of the imbalance and inequality he sees in *Rei Momo* is Byrne's use of salsa singer Celia Cruz singing Yoruba lyrics, which he is told evoke memories of slavery and racism, in the salsa/reggae song 'Loco de Amor', where Byrne sings of love as being 'like a pizza in the rain'. This Lipsitz regards as 'primitivism, exoticism, orientalism; [Cruz] is an all-purpose "other" summoned up to symbolize Byrne's delight in musical difference on the west side of Manhattan'.[84] The Manhattan location of Byrne's project, and the fact that the well-known salsa musicians like Cruz, Willie Colon and Johnny Pacheco he collaborated with in *Rei Momo* are also based in New York and have highly successful musical careers there as well as enjoying huge followings in Central and South America, surely differentiate it from *Graceland*'s musical tourism in South Africa. While Byrne's lyrics, which have a far greater claim to be called 'postmodern' than the trivial pop songs which make up most of *Graceland*, may not deal directly with political issues of Third World exploitation, they display a wit, dexterity and intelligence which makes *Rei Momo* a far more successful, challenging and equal musical collaboration, at least to this listener, than the bland, innocuous and forgettable songs of *Graceland*. There are limits to the 'cultural imperialism' thesis: while I would apply it to *Graceland*'s Western pop homogenization of South African mbaqanga, kwela and mbube styles, albeit with some minor reservations, it seems to me excessive to apply it equally to *Rei Momo*'s use of cumbia, orisa, merengue, mapeye, bomba, cha cha cha, samba, rumba and other Latin American styles, many of which were already embedded in American jazz and dance music.

Commodity fetishism, imaginary geography and locality

World music continues to reconstruct itself as an open-ended, all-embracing term: Rob Brookman, the artistic director of the Womadelaide festival in Australia, has suggested that rather than being a music it is 'an attitude towards listening and what you are prepared to accept; i.e., being as open to as many styles, influences and cultures as possible'.[85] One of its indisputably positive factors is the way it has exposed Western listeners to the Third World musical forms (particularly African and Latin American idioms) which have been appropriated by rock and pop music, and revealed in their hybrid, cross-fertilized nature that notions of musical purity and authenticity are often expressions of idealistic forms of colonialist nostalgia. Another factor is that the music itself needs to be differentiated from the marketing economy which has sold it, and which Rick Glanvill has described in terms which are hard to contest.

> At the risk of over-simplifying the nature of the relationship between the West and 'world musicians', it is too often reminiscent of colonial trade patterns. In a very real sense, the music of South America, Africa and Asia is being mined as a raw resource. ... Locally-recorded albums are pressed and packaged abroad, then exported back as the 'refined' product in much the same way as the Gambia, a major exporter of ground nuts, imports tubs of peanut butter.[86]

Commodity fetishism and consumption has always been an essential component of the popular music industry, from ownership of records, cassettes and CDs to fanzines, T-shirts and other artefacts and ephemeral objects related to groups, genres and subcultures. And, as Paul Gilroy has pointed out, this consumption can take on oppositional, liberational signifiers in relation to what he regards as a black musical diaspora extending from Africa through the Caribbean to Britain, Europe and the USA. The Utopian, pan-African aspects of world music could be seen as parallel to what Gilroy has identified as:

> an overarching 'Afro-centrism' which can be read as inventing its own totalising conception of black culture. This new ethnicity is all the more powerful because it corresponds to no actually-existing black communities. Its radical utopianism, often anchored in the ethical bedrock provided by the history of the Nile valley civilizations, transcends the parochialism of Caribbean memories in favour of a heavily mythologised Africanity.[87]

But, to the white Western listener, world music may often be an entirely synthetic sonic experience of surface impacts, like those described in Simon Reynolds's celebration of house music (with which it has been combined successfully by groups such as Trans-Global Underground):

> Above all, this music is shallow, an array of surfaces and forces that engage the listener through fascination (what was that sound?!): there's no depth, no

human truth or social concern to be divined, no atmosphere even, just an
illegible, arbitrary alteration of torques, vectors, gradients, whose opacity is
endlessly resistant to the attempts of white rock critics to read anything into
it.[88]

The harnessing of Third World musics to First World production
technologies and marketing economies may fetishize their exotic properties into physical, surface pleasures, but it also reproduces celebratory and
ritual aspects of their origins in the oppositional cultures of oppressed
racial minorities. In a context of heterogeneous, polyphonic ritual
celebration and dance, world music, like the equally ambivalent and
problematized black British and American musics Gilroy celebrates, can
'become central to the regulation of collective memory, perception and
experience in the present, to the construction of community by symbolic
and ritual means in dances, clubs, parties and discos'.[89]

The hybridized ritual and symbolic construction of community that
often occurs in diasporic African music is powerfully illustrated by
Wakafrica, a collective album of pan-African music released in 1994 by
Cameroonian jazz musician Manu Dibango, who described the project as
follows:

> Music has no frontiers, no generations, music is still music. The challenge
> was this; if you have the album, you can see that on the back is a small bus.
> This bus we call Wakafrica. Let's say we take this bus, and let's just say I'm
> the driver, taking you on a musical safari. So we go to Senegal, we pick up
> Youssou N'Dour, to Mali to say hello to Salif Keita, we go to Benin to say
> hello to Angelique Kidjo, all the way to Cape Town with Ladysmith Black
> Mambazo, you see. It's a kind of musical journey. ... The ambition was to
> put all these people together, to play each other's songs. It's old material, but
> we share a different way. People in Africa have stopped talking and started to
> put projects like this together.[90]

Dibango's musical journey also included King Sunny Ade, Ray Lema,
Geoffrey Oryema, Toure Kounda and Papa Wemba, as well as Peter
Gabriel and Sinéad O'Connor. They perform a repertoire of popular
African songs including Dibango's own 1970s hit 'Soul Makossa' and two
other songs by him, including the title track, Miriam Makeba's 'Pata
Pata', Fela Kuti's 'Lady', 'Wimoweh', and 'Jingo', a Nigerian song
popularized by 1970s rock group Santana. The album also includes
Gabriel's 'Biko' and 'Homeless', the only politically oriented song
featured on Paul Simon's *Graceland* album, originally written in
collaboration with Ladysmith Black Mambazo; it is performed on
Wakafrica by Ray Lema. The CD cover features Dibango twisting his
body into the shape of Africa, illustrating his Utopian aspirations towards
a musical fusion that is representative of the entire continent. His idea of
what constitutes African music is one which acknowledges the dictates of

the popular music industry: 'My music is open, it's not closed. ... We Africans like Western music sometimes, and vice versa, there's no exclusivity like that .... that's show business, and this is a jungle. This is really a jungle.'[91]

The musical safari through the jungle of Africa and the music industry which *Wakafrica* offers is surprisingly homogenized, despite the diversity of styles and nationalities of the performers. What binds the album together is the distinctive, growling jazz-funk style of Dibango, who arranged and played saxophone and keyboards on all the songs, and his band the Soul Makossa Gang, and the overall production of George Acogny. It was recorded in Paris, London and New York, and mixed in Los Angeles (during the January 1994 earthquake, as the liner notes state). Apart from Ladysmith Black Mambazo, Youssou N'Dour and King Sunny Ade, all the performers are based in Paris, the USA or the UK, emphasizing the prevailing sense of deterritorialization of the project. *Wakafrica*'s musical journey through the African continent is a purely imaginary one, dreamed up from a position of exile. As such it expresses what Appadurai has called

> the French idea of the imaginary (*imaginaire*), as a constructed landscape of collective aspirations ... mediated through the complex prism of modern media. ... The locality (both in the sense of the local factory or site of production and in the extended sense of the nation-state) becomes a fetish which disguises the globally dispersed forces that actually drive the production process.[92]

This fetishizing of localities, which is endemic to the concept of world music, is a process which involves all musical styles, genres and sub-genres which are anchored to a place of origin. In the USA, blues styles have been associated with Mississippi or Texas, following a migratory path to Chicago, Memphis or Detroit, while more recently 'grunge' rock has been irrevocably linked to Seattle. In the UK, the 'Liverpool sound' was associated with the Beatles and related 'Merseyside' groups in the early 1960s, and the 'Manchester sound' became a phenomenon in British rock and dance music in the late 1980s, although it did not involve all groups who came from Manchester or necessarily exclude groups from outside that city. All these styles were subsequently adopted, appropriated, transformed and blended with other local styles by musicians remote from these localities.

Most of the dominant localities which have emerged in pop and rock are American or English, and projects like *Coast to Coast*, an account of a pilgrimage by British journalist Andy Bull to the localities where the music of American rock legends like Buddy Holly, Elvis Presley, Roy Orbison, Bob Dylan, and REM was produced, serve to illustrate a history of fetishization of geography in popular music. Bull claims his 'rock fan's US tour' was an attempt to cover uncharted territory:

It had struck me that pop music and the landscape of America – its dreams, aspirations and the love of travel – were inseparable. In pop culture the car and the popular song go hand in hand, but the pop landscape of America is largely unmapped. This seemed curious, when you think of the huge fame of some of the people and the fascinating places that inspired their music. Novelists get a blue plaque and a museum dedicated to them. What has Bob Dylan been awarded? Nothing. My aim in this book would be to go out and find those places, find the people, draw the pop-music map of America in the pages of this book.[93]

Bull's rather literal and ingenuously anecdotal adventure in American musical geography does not take into account the inscription of American rock music in the history of famous rock venues like the Whisky A Go Go in Los Angeles and CBGBs in New York, in local fanzines and the music press, and the appeal of a predominantly 'imaginative geography', to use Edward Said's term in a positive sense,[94] to music fans who lack the wherewithal or desire to visit the locations where the music they revere originated. Bull's book appeared in the same year as a remarkably similar anecdotal mapping of a journey through American popular music by another English journalist, Mick Brown, whose *American Heartbeat: Travels from Woodstock to San Jose by Song Title*, followed an itinerary based on song titles, including 'Chattanooga Choo-Choo', 'Memphis Tennessee', 'Meet Me in St Louis', 'Twenty-four Hours from Tulsa', etc. Brown announces the premise of his book as follows: 'Pop music is a language of hidden codes and meanings. It speaks to those who have ears to listen. It draws maps of emotional landscapes, and sometimes geographical ones too. It plants ideas, dreams, to incubate in the imagination, to be tested and proved. I drew a map of America from songs, came to it like a blind man reading Braille.'[95] Brown is almost continually horrified by the social disintegration, consumerism, cynicism, poverty, disillusionment, and absence of honesty and integrity he witnesses in the USA. Nonetheless, his book concludes on a positive note in Nashville with an account of a festival of Christmas carols involving a mariachi band, country and Western harpist Lloyd Lindroth and an angel chorus, which he celebrates as a healing unification of myths, desires and dreams through music.

Both Bull's and Brown's musical cartographies of the USA illustrate the rhetorical importance and resonance of locality as a marker of popular music, an issue analysed by John Street in an article entitled 'Dislocated? Rhetoric, Politics, Meaning and the Locality'. Street describes how rock music writers connect localities with audiences, musicians, industry and infrastructure, and make ideological judgements of places, their politics and the music associated with them. He compares the place-consciousness of rock and rap music to the importance of roots in blues, and indicates how place often provides a source of identity for musicians and audiences. He breaks locality down into six main indicators of musical identity:

industrial base, social experience, aesthetic perspective, political experience, community and scene. The production of the Motown sound in
Detroit, rock and roll in Memphis and country music in Nashville account
for the rhetorical significance of those cities as industrial centres of
popular music, while Bruce Springsteen's reference to his social roots in
Asbury Park, New Jersey, could be seen as an example of location as a
realistic source of authenticity. Street argues that place can also provide an
aesthetic of escapism or alienation, as in the suburban origins of groups
such as Blur or Hüsker Dü. On the other hand, sites of political struggle
like Zimbabwe, most Eastern European countries, or the ghetto bases of
rap music provide a polemical motive for music as a form of revolt against
oppression. Locality can also be seen as a community which provides 'the
receptacle of the shared values and perspectives that shape the artists' and
give musics what George Lewis has described as 'symbolic anchors in
regions, as signs of community, belonging, and a shared past'. The
widespread notion of the scene connotes a more amorphous local network
of production and consumption of music, combining institutions and
industry with distinctive regional experiences. Street relates these different
notions of locality to shifting national, transnational and global factors in
popular music with which they interact, concluding that there is no clear
or direct link between music and locality, except as a rather nebulous
indicator of identity and difference.[96] But this link, nebulous though it may
be, is a vital one, which serves as an increasingly important means of
describing popular music produced outside the dominant Anglo-American
modes and trade routes with which Street is mainly concerned.

One of the important by-products of world music has been to put
remote and often exotically regarded places like Oran, Kinshasa or
Harare on the map of popular music as sites where the different aspects of
locality defined by Street – industrial base, social experience, aesthetic
perspective, political experience, community and scene – come together,
as well as interacting with national, transnational and global factors. This
has served also to challenge the fixed textual inscriptions of locality and
ethnicity which are often involved in notions of authenticity in music, and
spurious arguments about the origins of musical forms. The importance
of locality in music is the subject of the rest of this book, which examines
popular music produced in countries in Europe and Oceania which lie
outside the prevalent international grids and trade routes of both the
popular music industry and world music. By examining music-making
and its representations in local contexts, the importance of local and
nationally defined cultural and political practices as indicators of musical
meaning is emphasized.

Notes

1. J. Tunstall (1977) *The Media Are American* (London, Constable), p. 57.
2. J. Tomlinson (1991) *Cultural Imperialism* (London, Pinter), pp. 175, 178.
3. D. Robinson *et al.* (eds) (1991) *Music at the Margins* (London: Sage Publications), p. 3.
4. *Ibid.*, pp. 284–7.
5. R. Shuker (1995) *Understanding Popular Music* (London, Routledge), p. 62.
6. A. Appadurai (1990) 'Disjuncture and Difference in the Global Cultural Economy', *Public Culture*, vol. 2, no. 2 (spring), p. 6.
7. R. Garofalo (ed.) (1992) *Rockin' the Boat: Mass Music & Mass Movements* (Boston, South End Press), p. 4.
8. A. Goodwin and J. Gore (1990) 'World Music and the Cultural Imperialism Debate', *Socialist Review*, vol. 20, no. 3 (July–September), p. 73.
9. S. Feld (1991) 'Voices of the Rainforest', *Public Culture*, vol. 4, no. 1 (fall), p. 134.
10. R. Glanvill (1989) 'World Music Mining: The International Trade in New Music', in F. Hanly and T. May (eds) *Rhythms of the World* (London: BBC Books), p. 58.
11. Feld (1991), p. 134.
12. Appadurai (1990), p. 5.
13. Ali Farka Toure and Ry Cooder, *Talking Timbuktu*, World Circuit, 1994.
14. Feld (1991), p. 134.
15. *Ibid.*, p. 134.
16. *Deep Forest*, Colombia, 1992.
17. *Sacred Spirit: Chants and Dances of the Native Americans*, Virgin, 1994.
18. B. Elder (1994) 'Geoffrey Oryema Beats the Border', *Rhythms* (Melbourne), no. 33 (December), p. 34.
19. Ray Lema, *Gaia*, Island/Mango, 1990.
20. P. Sweeney (1991) *The Virgin Directory of World Music* (London, Virgin Books), p. ix.
21. S. Frith (ed.) (1989a) *World Music, Politics and Social Change: Papers from the International Association for the Study of Popular Music* (Manchester University Press), p. 2.
22. J. Collins and P. Richards (1981) 'Popular Music in West Africa (1981)', in Frith (1989a), p. 13.
23. J. Collins (1992) 'Some Anti-Hegemoic Aspects of African Popular Music', in Garofalo (1992), pp. 185, 190.
24. P. Gilroy (1991) 'Sounds Authentic: Black Music, Ethnicity and the Challenge of a *Changing* Same', *Black Music Research Journal*, vol. 10, no. 2, p. 123.
25. A. Martin (1994) 'Young, Gifted and in Trouble', *The Observer* (30 January).
26. *Ibid.*
27. B. Elder (1993) 'Dancing Down the Barriers', *Sydney Morning Herald* (13 September), p. 15.
28. In *The Soul of Mbira*, Finnish Television documentary, 1993.
29. Elder (1993), p. 15.
30. P. Jackson (1989) *Maps of Meaning: An Introduction to Cultural Geography*

(London, Unwin Hyman), p. 6.

31. *Ibid.*, p. 147.
32. *East 2 West: Bhangra for the Masses*, Music Collection International, 1993.
33. S. Banerji (1988) 'Ghazals to Bhangra in Great Britain', *Popular Music*, vol. 7, no. 2.
34. S. Broughton, M. Ellingham, D. Muddyman and R. Trillo (eds) (1994) *World Music: The Rough Guide* (London, Penguin).
35. S. Wells (1993) 'Big Bhangra Theory', *New Musical Express* (23 January), pp. 11–12.
36. A. Sweeting (1995) 'Messianic Reggae Figure Existing in a Mystical Dream-time', *Sydney Morning Herald* (6 February) (reprinted from *The Guardian*).
37. D. Simpson (1993) 'Fant-Asia!' *Melody Maker* (13 February), pp. 42–3.
38. D. Stansfield (1994) 'More Labels Bang Drum for Euro-Asian Bhangra Beat', *Billboard* (1 October), pp. 1, 20, 36.
39. D. Hesmondhalgh (1995) 'Nation and Primitivism: A Small Record Company and its Performance Strategies', unpublished paper, IASPM Conference, University of Strathclyde, Glasgow.
40. R. Morton (1993) 'Mahatma We're All Crazy Now', *New Musical Express* (7 August), p. 26.
41. Apache Indian, *Chok There*, Island Records, 1993.
42. N. Dinnen (1995) 'Making Headway', *On the Street* (28 February), p. 46.
43. I. McCann (1994) 'Welcome to the Junglists', *New Musical Express* (15 October), p. 28.
44. G. Lipsitz (1994) *Dangerous Crossroads: Popular Music, Postmodernism and the Poetics of Place* (London, Verso), pp. 94, 130–1.
45. K. Edshun (1993) Review of Apache Indian, 'Arranged Marriage', *The Wire* (March), p. 71.
46. Quoted in *Drum Media*, Sydney (24 January 1995), p. 44.
47. Sub Bass Snarl (1995) 'Fun-Da-Mental: A Revolution of the Consciousness', *3D* (30 January), p. 16.
48. S. Sweet (1993) 'Fear and Loathing in Pakistan', *Melody Maker* (13 November), pp. 8–9.
49. S. Wells (1995) 'Bummer Holiday', *New Musical Express* (8 July), p. 31.
50. L. Grenier and J. Guibault (1990) ' "Authority" Revisited: The "Other" in Anthropology and Popular Music Studies', *Ethnomusicology*, vol. 34, no. 3, p. 393.
51. In Lois Darlington (1991) 'A Blind Date with Sylla', *World Beat* (June), p. 31.
52. In S. Broughton *et al.*, (eds) (1994), p. 232.
53. V. Perna (1994) 'Intorno alla musica che gira intorno', *IASPM Vox Popular*, no. 2, Bologna, p. 4 (author's translation).
54. In L. Meintjes (1990) 'Paul Simon's *Graceland*, South Africa, and the Mediation of Musical Meaning', *Ethnomusicology* vol. 34, no. 1, pp. 48–9.
55. E. Said (1978) *Orientalism* (New York, Pantheon Books).
56. In *Sydney Morning Herald* (30 July 1988).
57. Jean-Paul Guirado, *Khaled*, French Television documentary, 1993.
58. In A. Morgan (1991) 'Thursday Night Fever: The Story of Rai', *World Beat* (June), p. 46.
59. J. Chunn (1991) 'Singles', *On the Street* (31 July), p. 50.
60. In A. Kershaw and C. Stapleton (1988) 'Back in the High Life', *Q* (September), pp. 64, 67.

61. S. Frith (1989b) 'Europop', *Cultural Studies*, vol. 3, no. 2, p. 171.
62. In *Rolling Stone* (June 1988), p. 56.
63. S. Danielsen (1995) 'British "Blacks" Regain their Musical Heritage', *Sydney Morning Herald* (7 January).
64. Mr Push and Mr Bush (1995) 'Word to the Wise', *Muzik*, no. 3 (August), p. 90.
65. McCann (1994), pp. 28–9.
66. T. Herrington (1995) 'Editor's Idea', *The Wire*, no. 136 (June), p. 4.
67. L. Birnbaum (1992) 'Senegalese Soulman', *Pulse!* (June), p. 41.
68. L. Duran (1989) 'Key to N'Dour: Roots of the Senegalese Star', *Popular Music*, vol. 8, no. 3 (October).
69. C. Stapleton (1989) 'Paris, Africa', in *Rhythms of the World* (London, BBC), p. 21.
70. C. Martel (1991) 'A Trail of Six Cities', *World Beat* (April), p. 44.
71. *Under African Skies: Zaire*, BBC documentary, 1989.
72. P. Gilroy (1987) *There Ain't No Black in the Union Jack* (London, Hutchinson), p. 211.
73. Meintjes (1990), p. 67.
74. N. Lazarus (1994) 'Unsystematic Fingers at the Conditions of the Times: "Afropop" and the Paradoxes of Imperialism', in Jonathan White (ed.) *Recasting the World: Writing after Colonialism* (London, Johns Hopkins University Press), p. 142.
75. C. Hamm (1989) 'Graceland Revisited', *Popular Music*, vol. 8, no. 3 (October).
76. H. Bhabha (1983) 'The Other Question: The Stereotype and Colonial Discourse', *Screen*, vol. 24, no. 6, p. 18.
77. S. Feld (1988) 'Notes on World Beat', *Public Culture Bulletin*, vol. 1, no. 1 (fall), p. 33.
78. *Ibid.*, p. 34.
79. Garofalo (1992), p. 4.
80. Feld (1991), pp. 34–5.
81. Feld (1988), pp. 35–6.
82. Lipsitz (1994), p. 60.
83. *Ibid.*, p. 57.
84. *Ibid.*, p. 61.
85. In L. Barber (1995) 'World Beaters', *The Australian* (28–29 January).
86. Glanvill (1989), p. 64.
87. Gilroy (1991), p. 9.
88. S. Reynolds (1990) *Blissed Out: The Raptures of Rock* (London, Serpent's Tail), p. 174.
89. Gilroy (1987), p. 211.
90. M. D'Sousa (1994) 'Manu Dibango: A Ride through Africa', *3D* (8 August).
91. *Ibid*.
92. Appadurai (1990), pp. 5, 16.
93. A. Bull (1993) *Coast to Coast: A Rock Fan's U.S. Tour* (London, Black Swan), p. 14.
94. Said (1978), p. 71.
95. M. Brown (1993) *American Heartbeat: Travels from Woodstock to San Jose by Song Title* (London, Penguin), p. 5.

96. J. Street (1995) '(Dis)located? Rhetoric, Politics, Meaning and the Locality', in W. Straw, S. Johnson, R. Sullivan and P. Friedlander (eds) *Popular Music – Style and Identity*, (Montreal, IASPM, Centre for Research on Canadian Cultural Industries and Institutions), pp. 255–64.

Discography

Natacha Atlas, *Diaspora*, Nation Records, 1995.
Apache Indian, *Make Way for the Indian*, Island, 1995.
—*No Reservations*, Island, 1993.
—*Chok There (w/Movin' On)*, Island, 1993.
—*Movin' On* (Special), Island, 1993.
The Bhundu Boys, *Shabini*, Discafrique, 1986.
—*True Jit*, WEA, 1987.
—*Pamberi!*, WEA, 1989.
—*Absolute Jit! Live at King Tut's Wah Wah House*, Discafrique, 1990.
—*Friends on the Road*, Cooking Vinyl, 1993.
David Byrne, *Rei Momo*, Sire/Warner Brothers, 1989.
Coldcut/Eric B. and Rakim, *Paid in Full*, Island/Festival, 12-inch, 1987.
Deep Forest, *Deep Forest*, Colombia, 1992.
Detrimental, *Babylon*, Dept Records/Cooking Vinyl, 1995.
—*Living on the Edge*, (w/'Countryman'), Cooking Vinyl, 1995.
Manu Dibango, *Wakafrica*, Giant Records/Warner Brothers, 1994.
Fun^Da^Mental, *With Intent to Pervert the Course of Injustice!*, Nation Records, 1995.
—*Seize the Time*, Nation Records/Beggars Banquet, 1994.
—*Countryman/Tribal Revolution*, Nation Records, 1993.
Jon Hassell and Brian Eno, *Fourth World Vol. 1: Possible Music*, Editions EG, 1980.
Kaoma, *World Beat*, CBS, 1989.
Salif Keita, *Soro*, Sterns Africa, 1987.
—*Amen*, Island/Mango, 1991.
Khaled, *Khaled*, Barclay, Virgin Musique, 1992.
Nusrat Fateh Ali Khan, *Musst Musst*, Real World, 1991.
Angelique Kidjo Aye, Island Records, 1994.
Ladysmith Black Mambazo, *Journey of Dreams*, Warner Brothers, 1988.
Ray Lema, *Gaia*, Island/Mango, 1990.
Loop Guru, *Dunija: The Intrinsic Passion of Mysterious Joy*, Nation Records, 1994.
Cheb Mami, *Prince of Rai*, Shanachie, 1989.
Thomas Mapfumo, *Corruption*, Island/Mango, 1989.
Youssou N'Dour, *Emigrés*, Earthworks/Virgin, 1988.
—*The Lion*, Virgin, 1989.
—*Eyes Open*, Columbia 1992.
—*The Guide (Wommat)*, Chaos/Columbia, 1994.
Geoffrey Oryema, *Exile*, Real World, 1990.
—*Beat the Border*, Real World, 1993.
Sacred Spirit, *Chants and Dances of the Native Americans*, Virgin, 1994.

Paul Simon, *Graceland*, Warner Brothers, 1986.
—*Rhythm of the Saints*, Warner Brothers, 1990.
Malkit Singh (Golden Star UK), *Ragga Muffin Mix 1991*, Oriental Star Records, 1991.
Biggie Tembo, *Out of Africa*, Cooking Vinyl, 1992.
Ali Farka Toure and Ry Cooder, *Talking Timbuktu*, World Circuit, 1994.
Trans-Global Underground, *Dream of 100 Nations*, Nation Records, 1994.
—International Times, Nation Records, 1995.
Various, *Brazil Classics 1: Beleza Tropical* (compiled by David Byrne), Fly/EMI, 1989.
—*Brazil Classics 2: Samba* (compiled by David Byrne), Luaka Bop/Sire, 1989.
—*Downbeat in the Jungle*, WEA/Warner Music Germany, 1994.
—*East 2 West: Bhangra for the Masses*, Music Collection International, 1993.
—*Jit – The Movie Plus Other Big Hits*, Virgin Earthworks, 1991.
—*Red, Hot and Blue: A Benefit for AIDS Research and Relief*, BMG, 1990.
—*Zimbabwe Frontline*, vols 1 and 2, Earthworks/Virgin, 1990.
Papa Wemba, *Papa Wemba*, Sterns Africa, 1989.
—*Emotion*, Real World, 1995.

3

Mixing Pop and Politics? Rock Music in the Czech Republic

The politics of bloc rock

Rock and pop music in the USSR and Eastern Europe became an area of increasing interest to both the Western mass media and Cultural Studies commentators at the end of the 1980s after glasnost, perestroika, the collapse of the Eastern bloc Communist regimes and the constitution of new Western-styled democratic governments. This was largely because rock music represented what was probably the most widespread vehicle of youth rebellion, resistance and independence behind the Iron Curtain, both in terms of providing an enhanced political context for the often banned sounds of British and American rock, and in the development of home-grown musics built on Western foundations but resonating within their own highly charged political contexts. This led to suppositions about Eastern Europe and the former USSR as potent sites of rock music as a form of political resistance, owing to its suppression by the Communist regimes as a form of youth rebellion and the adoption of Western lifestyles. Prior to the collapse of the Communist regimes, this was in some cases true, as rock music acted as a vehicle of social and cultural dissidence which often had political overtones. As the East German critic Peter Wicke claimed in 1991, 'Because of the intrinsic characteristics of the circumstances within which rock music is produced and consumed, this cultural medium became, in the GDR, the most suitable vehicle for forms of cultural and political resistance that could not be controlled by the state'.[1]

Wicke goes on to claim that the strategies of resistance devised by rock musicians in the GDR eventually had a direct impact on the political changes which took place there, and similar claims can be made for the Czech Republic. In the first book-length study in English of rock music in the USSR and Eastern Europe, *Rock around the Bloc*, the US critic Timothy W. Ryback portrays the rise of rock and roll over three generations in the USSR and Eastern Europe as a process of resistance which eventually forced the authorities to accept rock music as a reality rather than a decadent cultural product of Western capitalism. *Rock around the Bloc* is a largely descriptive chronicle of three decades of government suppression of rock music in the USSR and Eastern Europe, and amounts to a social history of the ongoing struggles of Eastern bloc youth against petty Communist bureaucracies rather than an attempt to describe the music itself – although politically significant lyrics are frequently quoted – and its reception by Eastern bloc youth. Regarding the Eastern bloc almost exclusively as a locality of political experience in the production of rock music, Ryback relegates the importance of locality as industrial base, social experience, aesthetic perspective, community and scene to relatively minor concerns. Written in early 1989, before the collapse of the Eastern bloc Communist regimes, Ryback's concluding chapter, rhetorically entitled 'Shattering the Iron Curtain', claimed:

> In a very real sense, the triumph of rock and roll in Eastern Europe and the Soviet Union has been the realisation of a democratic process. Three generations of Soviet-bloc youths have compelled governments to accept step by step a cultural phenomenon long decried as an outgrowth of Western capitalism. In the course of thirty years, rock bands have stormed every bastion of official resistance and forced both party and government to accept rock-and-roll music as part of life in the Marxist–Leninist state.
>
> In the coming years, Soviet-bloc rock faces one final obstacle, perhaps the most difficult one it has yet faced: to make itself heard in the West. . . . As the sounds of rock and roll begin to resonate from East to West, this music which shaped the perceptions and lives of countless millions in the Soviet bloc will hopefully transform the way we in the West view the past and present of our counterparts in the East.[2]

From the perspective of 1995, there is, however, little or no evidence that the 'triumph' of rock music in the former Eastern bloc has been durable, or that any transformation of Western views of Eastern Europe mediated by former Soviet bloc rock music has taken place, and little evidence that any Eastern European rock music is even being heard in the West. A short-lived boom in 1989 saw the release in the West of albums sung in English by Russian rockers Boris Grebenshikov, Gorky Park and Apostrophe, and in Russian by the more avant-garde and satirical cabaret-rock groups Zvuki Mu and Avia, but these had little or no impact on Western listening tastes and ended up in record shop bargain bins. After two Russian independent rock groups had performed at the 1989 Glasgow New Beginnings Festival, Simon Frith reached a relatively pessimistic conclusion about the post-glasnost progress of Russian rock, suggesting that any international resonances were unlikely:

> Far from a continuing surge of post-glasnost energy, there has been a rapid satiation, a quick awareness of audience boredom. The local Soviet live scenes

have collapsed (no longer focuses for other sorts of protest); there are no resources to build a music-making structure independent of either the state or the mafia ... it's clear already that the most interesting Soviet rock is going to reflect nationalist rather than international concerns.[3]

In her 1994 essay 'Did Rock Smash the Wall?' Jolanta Pekacz portrays Western rock music analysts' claims for the political significance of rock music in East Central Europe as exaggerated forms of idealism which she regards as 'incomprehensible on intellectual grounds' and perpetuating a 'self-serving ... mythology'. Such arguments, Pekacz claims, rely on 'fallacious' equations of 'real socialism' and totalitarianism, assumptions that rock exerted pressure 'from below' and helped to bring about the sudden collapse of Communism, rather than being incidental to 'the outcome of a long process that had begun in 1956', and false assumptions that 'rock in the Soviet bloc was in a continuous conflict with the regime'. Pekacz's arguments tend to homogenize the political situations in all Eastern European countries (most of her examples are drawn from Poland), and she assumes that Western assumptions of 'the totalitarian character of socialist reality' are ideologically motivated. Her thesis also relies on equating punk rock in Eastern Europe with 'neo-fascist groups of youth', simplifying ideological expressions by rock musicians into 'us-and-them' oppositions, and a remarkably low estimation of the intelligence of youth in post-Communist countries:

> Estrangement and passivity as confused reactions, radicalism of opinions without radical activity, aggression (criminal and fascist) and auto-aggression, poor understanding of social reality and of the political and economic changes, passivity in professional or entrepreneurial performance, little cultural and social activity and participation in community life and initiatives ('depressive-withdrawing syndrome') and pro-authoritarian attitudes are characteristic of the present attitudes of youth in post-Communist countries. ... Such a background favours certain types of behaviour and activity characteristic of the generation of the 'fall of Communism'.[4]

Since Pekacz's gloomy pronouncements about rock music and politics seem more ideologically coloured than those she condemns, it is worth invoking Lawrence Grossberg's notion of the 'affective' nature of rock music, which he claims cannot be described sufficiently in sociological or ideological terms. The political contexts of rock music involve the complex functioning of what he calls the 'rock and roll apparatus', involving a wide range of extra-musical factors, practices and mediations:

> Rock and roll practice is a form of resistance for generations with no faith in revolution. Rock and roll's resistance – its politics – is neither a direct rejection of the dominant culture nor a utopian negation (fantasy) of the structures of power. It plays with the very practice that the dominant culture uses to resist its resistance: incorporation and excorporation in a continuous dialectic that

reproduces the very boundaries of existence. Because its resistance remains, however, within the political and economic space of the dominant culture, its revolution is only a 'simulacrum'. Its politics emerge only at that moment when political consciousness is no longer possible.[5]

This definition of the simulated resistance of rock music is equally applicable both to the US capitalist context in which Grossberg writes and to the Communist realities of pre-1989 East Central Europe. While it is foolish to argue that rock music 'smashed the wall' or 'tore down the iron curtain', it is clear that extra-musical factors relating to the Czech group the Plastic People of the Universe, a self-avowedly 'non-political' band, had a direct impact on the 'Velvet Revolution' in the Czech Republic, and that rock music generally functioned as an important oppositional practice of resistance in pre-1989 Eastern and Central Europe. This was acknowledged by the President of the Czech Republic, Václav Havel, in a 1991 interview: 'In our former conditions, rock music acquired a special social function. And that's connected with the fact that culture and the arts in general fulfil a different role in our country than they do in the Western world. Under a totalitarian regime, politics as such are eliminated and the resistance has to find substitute outlets of expression. One of those substitute channels was rock music'.[6]

But Havel's acknowledgement of rock as a surrogate medium for political resistance is quite different from the hollow, melodramatic rhetoric employed by Sabrina Petra Ramet in her 1994 book on rock music and politics in Eastern Europe and Russia, *Rocking the State*, which caricatures the political impact of rock music: 'The archetypal rock star became, symbolically, the muse of revolution. The decaying communist regimes (in Bulgaria, Czechoslovakia, and Romania especially) seemed to fear the electric guitar more than bombs or rifles.'[7] Such a view trivializes and crassly misrepresents the often subtle, simulated and affective modes of resistance attached to rock music. Ramet's collectively authored book claims to be 'the first scholarly attempt to treat systematically all the countries and regions of the Western USSR and Eastern Europe',[8] but her chapter on rock music in the Czech Republic and Slovakia concentrates almost exclusively on the lyrics of selected rock songs, attempting to turn them into political tracts. Some of her comments on musical aspects of Czech and Slovakian rock music, like Ryback's before her, are erroneous and misleading. She claims, for example, that there is 'no rockabilly to be found in either republic' despite audible and visible evidence to the contrary, and ignores the astonishingly widespread country and bluegrass music movement to be found there, which Vesa Kurkela has commented on.[9] She also asserts that 'fusion is not popular', although Civic Forum politician Michael Kocáb's prominent and long-standing jazz-rock fusion group Pražský Výběr (Prague Selection), which she mistakenly categorizes as a punk rock group, reproducing Ryback's list of Czech punk groups,[10] is living evidence to the contrary, along with Stromboli and other groups, including the Plastic People of the Universe, who played a form of jazz-rock fusion. The simplistic impression Ramet conveys of Czech rock music as a form of open protest against the Communist regime does not begin to consider the complexities of cultural practice, musical influence, hybridity, appropriation and globalization involved.[11] *Rocking the State* certainly disappoints the expectations articulated by the Hungarian rock music critic Anna Szemere, in a review of the book, that 'five years after the fall of the Berlin Wall, [we] will be provoked with an adequately complex cultural analysis of the ways in which politics and music, state and markets, local and global musical currents intersect and participate in major societal change'.[12]

Any sympathetic appraisal of the state of rock and pop in the USSR and Central and Eastern Europe needs to consider the political and cultural context of deprivation, censorship, enforced clandestinity and isolation in which the music has been forced to operate, but without completely subjugating the music to the political factors involved in its production. Practices such as the use of X-ray plates for making bootleg records in the 1960s, the function of rock groups as 'live jukeboxes' playing banned Western rock music, and the circulation of illegal *magnizidat* tapes of 'unofficial' bands are important to consider, but are often seen by Western commentators as indicators of an abject celebration of the superiority of Western values. Much rock in the Eastern bloc was often forced to function as political statement, even when the main concerns of the musicians were, as the Leningrad group Kino claimed in 1985 on a French television programme *Rock around the Kremlin*, merely to make fashion statements. The Russian rock critic Artemy Troitsky's claim in 1989 that 'Most of the Soviet rock acts were ordinary-looking and ordinary-sounding, but singing something very meaningful in their native language'[13] applies also to rock music in Eastern European countries, and the Czech Republic in particular. What follows is an attempt to approach meanings relating to the production and reception of rock music in the Czech Republic, focusing on Prague as the capital of the Czech music scene, in so far as this is possible without a knowledge of the Czech language, and relying predominantly on source material in English.

The 'Rock 'n' Roll President', the Velvet Underground and the Velvet Revolution

Peter Wicke has commented that the tendency of the Communist authorities In East Germany to read political meanings into the most innocuous of pop songs influenced audiences, who likewise read political dimensions into songs where often none was intended.[14] In a situation where authorities exert political pressure on music, often the very absence of political statement can be seen as a political expression of notions of freedom, desire or pleasure, which are associated with the values of Western capitalism. In the Czech Republic popular music had had this type of entanglement with politics since the 1940s, and continued to do so in the post-1989 climate of liberal social humanism presided over by Václav Havel, himself an unashamed rock music fan.

The close connection between rock music and politics in Czechoslovakia is demonstrated in Havel's essay 'The Power of the Powerless', where he states that the Charter 77 movement might not have been formed were it not for a campaign which he and others launched against the trial and imprisonment of the underground rock group, the Plastic People of the Universe:

> Unknown young people who wanted no more than to be able to live within the truth, to play the music they enjoyed, to sing songs that were relevant to their lives, and to live freely in dignity and partnership. ... Everyone understood that an attack on the Czech musical underground was an attack on an elementary and important thing, something that in fact bound everyone together: it was an attack on the very notion of 'living within the truth', on the real aims of life. The freedom to play rock music was understood as a human freedom and thus as essentially the same as the freedom to engage in philosophical and political reflection, the freedom to write, the freedom to express and defend the various social and political interests of society. ... Who could have foreseen that the prosecution of one or two obscure rock groups would have such far-reaching consequences?[15]

Far more than a merely symbolic representation of freedom of expression, the Plastic People, although not political militants, were an embodiment of Havel's philosophy of 'living in truth'. The group borrowed its name from a song by Frank Zappa about phoneys and hypocrites which also lampooned the President of the USA, but their unconcern with being identified with the song's targets is indicative of the strong musical influence which Zappa exerted on avant-garde and underground rock throughout the Eastern bloc. In 1990 Havel, a long-standing fan of Zappa and Captain Beefheart's 1975 album *Bongo Fury*, appointed Zappa as a special adviser on trade, culture and tourism to the Czech government, causing some embarrassment to the American ambassador to Prague, Shirley Temple. The appointment was not so much a theatrical impulse by the playwright Havel which matched the theatricality of politics in the USA, as evidence of Havel's commitment to redressing the cultural deprivation of Czech youth. Zappa's appointment drew sympathetic comment from *The Economist*'s Prague correspondent, who commented on the proliferation of pop musicians and disc jockeys in the Civic Forum administration, and on the centrality of rock music to Czech politics, in a way which reproduced traditional arguments about generational conflict and rebellion against officialdom:

In Czechoslovakia's peculiar circumstances, this is not as ridiculous as it seems. Rock first began to gather power in the mid-1970s, when Czechoslovak society had settled into the apathy from which no one, least of all the people themselves, ever thought it would emerge. A new crop of rebellious young, wanting to annoy their elders, found rock music the ideal means. It was not part of the official culture; it was not aired on radio or television. ... All sorts of people who might, in other circumstances, have devoted their creative energies to other things gave themselves to rock as an island of independent expression. Even the musically disinterested were drawn to these secret gigs for the same reasons the government so disapproved of them – because they were there. Among these people was a playwright who is now a president.[16]

This rather cynical portrayal of Czech rock as a substitute form of counter-cultural dissident activity compensating for the lack of other outlets for oppositional political activity, while close to Havel's own portrayal of rock as surrogate resistance, underestimates the passion with which rock music had been pursued as a cultural practice in its own right by young people in Eastern Europe. When Havel sponsored a free concert by the Rolling Stones in August 1990 at Prague's Spartakiadni Stadium, filling it to its capacity of 250,000, *The Economist*'s correspondent became even more censorious. A photo of Havel with Mick Jagger, captioned 'It's only rock 'n' roll, but Havel likes it', set the tone of the report: 'His fondness for skateboards and the Rolling Stones may not be enough to carry Czechoslovakia through the tough economic times ahead, particularly if Mr Havel continues to let his own doubts about capitalism hamper his country's reforms.'[17]

In terms of the hard-line economic *realpolitik* many Western observers and advisers were attempting to impose on Eastern European countries, Havel's cultural policy of compensating for the historic lack of access by Czech youth to significant aspects of Western pop music history was seen as an irresponsible frivolity on a par with his rumoured habit of travelling around the interior of Prague castle on a skateboard. (In fact it was a scooter, which had been given to him by a group called the Committee for a Merrier Presence.) But some of the Czech youth who flocked to see the Rolling Stones were no longer very young, and their gratitude was immense, if the testimony of the forty-three-year-old drummer of the Czech band who supported the Stones is any indication: 'It's a dream come true, something I never hoped to see in my life.'[18]

Havel also invited Lou Reed to give a concert in Prague in 1990, in acknowledgement of the influence Reed's band of the late 1960s, the Velvet Underground, had on the Plastic People and the Czech rock scene as a whole. Reed reciprocated by interviewing Havel for *Rolling Stone* (although the magazine spiked the interview) and was surprised by the impact of his music: 'I found out how much the Velvet Underground has meant to those people in Eastern Europe all those years ago. They were out there listening to us, only we just didn't know it.'[19] Havel has described how Reed was almost moved to tears when he heard a Czech group called the Velvet Underground Revival, 'a band that knew his old songs better than he did',[20] play Velvet Underground songs and show him *samizdat* editions of his music. My own experience confirmed this when I saw the Velvet Underground Revival play in June 1995 at the Junior Club in Prague, a modest church-hall-like venue outside the centre of Prague, with a proscenium stage, a very small PA system and the band's amplifiers placed on chairs, enabling them to produce feedback from them from time to time. A group of five extremely dedicated young men in their thirties and older, with no concern for rockist imagery or iconography, they performed for nearly three hours, covering virtually every Velvet Underground track that has been recorded. They augmented their line-up with a woman vocalist who sang the songs originally recorded by Nico and Maureen Tucker, and a woman violinist who covered the viola solos of John Cale. The bearded keyboard player occasionally had to read the English lyrics from sheets of paper, but they were always rendered clearly and phonetically to an audience predominantly in their twenties who danced, drank beer, smoked a little marijuana and generally enjoyed the music. While the atmosphere was reminiscent of 1960s rock concerts in the West, the music was an exciting, accurate simulation of the lost, early days of the Velvet Underground.

1989/1968

One of the main symbols of the Velvet Revolution in Czechoslovakia was the inversion of the year 1989 into 1968, evoking the Prague Spring and a return to the democratic principles of the Dubček government. Re-creating the output of a suppressed past where freedom of expression was possible became the main sustaining force of post-1989 Czech culture: theatres were full of formerly banned plays by Havel and other dissident playwrights, while art galleries exhibited previously censored artists and political cartoonists. Pop musicians performed Beatles and Rolling Stones songs on the streets, and a flourishing bluegrass and country and Western subculture was revealed, with an estimated two hundred bands in Prague alone, and an estimated six hundred to a thousand amateur bands throughout the Czech Republic. According to Joseph Vunhal, the manager of a new country music club in Prague: 'Part of the reason for its popularity is that it was seen as a form of protest music. It is not political, but because it is American, just listening to it and dressing in country and music gear was a form of protest'.[21]

This Czech country music movement, in which songs are sung mainly in Czech, manifests itself in village dances which are attended by young people dressed in cowboy gear, and which often include lasso roping, whip-cracking and beauty contests. These 'cowboy evenings' are seen by

Vesa Kurkela as 'a good example of "nostalgia without memory"' and 'surely an important part of local culture and identity. Czech country music is no doubt local music. At the same time, it is global and transnational.'[22] This type of appropriation and reconstitution of American culture as a form of cultural freedom of expression was also acknowledged and endorsed by President Havel in relation to US culture of the 1960s: 'There are numerous parallels between the '60s in America and Czechoslovakia in the '80s. I could illustrate with hundreds of cases, but I feel the soul of the '60s is being revived by us here today.'[23] Havel cited as evidence the impact of a Joan Baez concert in Bratislava in August 1989, when Baez hid him from police in her hotel room after the authorities had turned the power off when she tried to introduce a Czech dissident singer. 'We Shall Overcome' was still a potent protest anthem in Prague, as British agit-pop troubadour Billy Bragg discovered on his tour of Eastern Europe in May 1990:

> Sometimes it looks like Czechoslovak pop culture went into deep freeze when the tanks came in 1968. It was the year of 'Yellow Submarine', Apple Corp and the politics of psychedelic optimism. ... Instead of the 'Internationale' I sing the song they sang on all their demonstrations, 'We Shall Overcome'. When I finish, the audience rises and sings a verse in Czech. A wonderful moment.[24]

One indication of the endurance of this 1960s spirit of 'psychedelic optimism' was the continuing adulation of John Lennon, whose death in 1980 had arguably more impact in Czechoslovakia than it did in the West. Havel reportedly has a picture of Lennon on the wall of his presidential office, and the 'Wailing Wall' in the Mala Strana on which the youth of Prague painted slogans, pictures and quotations from Lennon's lyrics, defying attempts by the authorities to erase them, continues to exist and is regularly visited by pilgrims. Havel's interpretation of Lennon's death in his *Letters to Olga* had political dimensions few in the West would entertain:

> his death so compellingly reaches out beyond itself, as though there were latent in it more tragic connections, problems and aspects pointing to the present world crisis than in any other event. It might even be called 'the death of the century' (perhaps more so than the deaths of Kennedy and King). ... And you can't help feeling that the shot was fired by the reality of the 80s at one of the departing dreams – the dream of the sixties for peace, freedom and brotherhood, the dream of the flower children, the communes, the LSD trips and 'making love not war', a shot as it were in the face of that existential revolution of the 'third consciousness' and 'the greening of America'.[25]

A 1990 French compilation record of Soviet punk rock was entitled *From Lenin to Lennon*, and, just as 'Let it Be' was used as a political anthem in post-revolutionary Romania, Beatles' songs were regarded in the Czech

Republic as expressions of political freedom and community. 'Lennon Lives' can still be seen in Prague as a slogan on the T-shirts of people too young to have heard the Beatles the first time around.

The Velvet Revolution also reinstated banned Czech folk singers of the 1960s: records by Marta Kubisová and Karel Kryl were sold by students in Prague from street stalls, along with books by Havel and Josef Škvorecký. Kubisová, the most famous 'silenced singer' of the 1960s, enjoyed a comeback at the age of fifty, and her most famous song, 'Modlitba pro Martu' (Prayer for Marta), an anthem for peace and freedom used as the signature tune for a clandestine programme broadcast on Czech television in the autumn of 1968, was once again popular. Kubisová performed to a crowd of 200,000 in Wenceslas Square and her 1969 album *Songy a balady* was re-released eighteen years later. Another of her songs, 'Ring-o-Ding', which invokes the sound of the ringing of bells of freedom and the end of oppression, became an anthem of the Velvet Revolution, accompanied by the jangling of keys by crowds, simulating the sound of bells.

Kubisová sang both these songs at a concert organized by the French anti-racist group SOS Rassismus, which was held in the Staroměstská náměstí (Old Town Square) in Prague on the eve of the June 1990 elections. These were the first free elections held in Czechoslovakia for almost fifty years, and brought a landslide victory for the Civic Forum Coalition party headed by Havel. For the Prague audience at this concert, however, the main drawcard was Michael Kocáb. A member of Havel's administration, Kocáb was responsible for negotiating the withdrawal of Soviet troops from Czechoslovakia, but he was also the most popular rock musician in the country. (His 1991 live album celebrating the withdrawal of Soviet troops featured a guest appearance by Frank Zappa, who played a guitar solo and exhorted a cheering audience to 'keep your country unique' in its 'new future'.) The volume of the roar with which the audience acknowledged Kocáb's appearance, immediately after the V-signs and key and flag-waving which concluded Marta Kubisová's set, prompted her to reappear under the mistaken impression that she was being called back for a special encore. Kocáb then announced a 'surprise appearance' by an exhausted President Havel, who had been carefully informing foreign media that he was not engaged in any form of campaign for Civic Forum. Havel gave a brief and very hoarse denunciation of racism before announcing another surprise guest, Paul Simon, who performed 'The Boxer', 'Bridge over Troubled Water' and 'Sounds of Silence' to a delighted crowd, accompanying himself on acoustic guitar. Havel's 'gift' to the audience probably surpassed any direct political statement about the elections which he might have made. As an advertisement for the uncensored cultural politics of Civic Forum, the concert, which concluded with a long set by Kocáb, was made more effective politically by its lack of any reference to the election, demonstrating a humanist cultural policy where political concerns no longer needed to be foregrounded. As Wicke has commented:

> The aesthetic nature of rock music is of far-reaching importance for any political involvement with it. It is not only that behind this music lie very contradictory and socially conflicting cultural processes, but the music itself is also not to be taken as a textual embodiment of ideology, an ideological text, however deeply it is linked to contexts which determine the apparatus of the production of ideology.[26]

The SOS Rassismus concert, with its absence of skinheads or punks, its Hare Krishna stall selling vegetarian food, and despite its anti-racist rationale and the ideologically charged appearances of Marta Kubisová and Michael Kocáb, representing the old 1968 Prague Spring and the new democracy of the Velvet Revolution respectively, was a celebration of a newly won democratic freedom in which popular music could at last assume a non-ideological role. This freedom was, of course, predicated on a long history of enforced politicization and political suppression of popular music.

Jazz, pop and rock in Czechoslovakia: a brief history

In August 1947 the Australian jazz pianist Graeme Bell and his Dixieland Jazz Band performed to audiences of more than five thousand people at a World Youth Festival in Prague and helped to generate the first Czech Dixieland jazz movement. This set a precedent for the entry and acculturation of other American-derived forms of popular music in Czechoslovakia. As Josef Škvorecký recalls in the preface to his novella *The Bass Saxophone*:

> although the bishops of Stalinist obscurantism damned the 'music of the cannibals', they had one problem. Its name was Dixieland. A type of the cannibal-music with roots so patently folkloristic and often (the blues) so downright proletarian that even the most Orwellian falsifier of facts would be hard put to deny them. Initiates had already encountered isolated recordings of Dixieland during the war, and after it ended a group of youths heard the Graeme Bell Dixieland Band.[27]

Bell's band was prevailed upon to stay for a four-month tour of Czechoslovakia, and recorded a series of 78s of jazz standards for the state record label Ultraphon, as well as two original compositions, 'Czechoslovak Journey' and 'Walking Wenceslaus Square' (reissued in Australia in 1982 on an LP entitled *Czechoslovak Journey 1947*). Bell has described the thirst for jazz in Czechoslovakia at the time:

We were told that we were the first jazz band to come to Prague; the Czechs were starved of jazz. There was not one American record of any description for sale there. If one somehow got hold of a record, one was obliged to let every collector in Prague hear it. Reaction to the straight-out commercialism of the local bands brought about the formation of three or four groups who were trying to play jazz at home. These came to hear us each night.[28]

Bell was an important influence on the jazz pianist Jiří Šlitř, who with Jiří Suchý, the 'Czech Elvis', founded the Semafor Theatre in Prague in 1959, and initiated a series of satirical cabarets and concerts which were enormously popular, drawing audiences of a million people in the theatre's first five years – a number equal to the population of Prague.[29] Bell returned to Prague for the first time since 1947 to give a concert in 1993, but was disappointed by the touristic developments that had taken place in the city. The kind of resistance that his traditional jazz had represented in 1947 had long been surpassed, although according to Bruce Johnson's study of Bell's musical influence in Europe, he was 'rapturously received, including by contemporary youth, as the father of the Czech jazz movement'.[30] The mixture of starvation and passion with which the freedom of expression of jazz and later rock and roll was pursued in Eastern Europe in the 1950s was obstructed by what Anna Szemere has described as 'the view ... according to which almost all Afro-American popular genres, whether jazz or rock 'n' roll or the twist, were considered nothing but the cultural trash of decadent imperialism'.[31] In *The Bass Saxophone*, Škvorecký describes ten restrictions imposed by Nazi authorities on dance orchestras in Eastern Europe, against fox-trots, minor keys, blues tempos, syncopation, trumpet mutes and other appendages, drum solos, plucked double-basses, pizzicatos, scat singing and saxophones. He comments that almost identical restrictions were imposed under Stalinism, which has consequently ensured that an underground popular music culture has existed in Eastern Europe since the Second World War.[32] In his essay 'Hipness at Noon' he outlines the activities of the Jazz Section of the Czech Musicians' Union. Through an administrative loophole, this union managed to operate as a vital clandestine cultural force from its formation in 1971 to its banning in 1983. As well as assisting rock groups and publishing books on popular music (including a history of Western punk rock) it published works by banned Czech novelists and poets, providing proof of an absence of differentiation between popular music and products of high culture.[33]

Havel has indicated that the advent of rock and roll in the Czech Republic was as culturally significant as the jazz era. In his nostalgic description of concerts he attended by the Akord Klub at the Reduta Theatre in Prague in 1956 and 1957, he writes:

It was in fact the first – or, rather, the first well-known – rock band in Czechoslovakia, and it was an enormously interesting and important phenomenon. . . . At their late-night concerts in Reduta they played famous rock-and-roll tunes for which they had written their own lyrics, and they played their own compositions as well. . . . The room would only hold sixty people, but all of Prague, if I can put it that way, was jammed in . . . it didn't take much expertise to understand that what they were playing and singing here was fundamentally different from 'Kristynka' or 'Prague Is a Golden Ship'. The novelty was not only in the music, in the rhythms of rock and roll, which was something new here then, but above all in the lyrics . . . they reminded no one of the banal lyricism of the official hits. The atmosphere in Reduta was marvellous, and what was born in those sessions was that very special, conspiratorial sense of togetherness that to me is what makes theatre.[34]

Havel compares the songs of the Akord Klub's bass player, Jiří Suchý, to the satirical cabaret of the Liberated Theatre of Voskovec and Werich between the wars, and Suchý went on to team up with Jiří Šlitr in 'East Europe's most brilliant songwriting and stage team',[35] performing satirical revues and musical comedies. This highlights what is a particularly common feature of much rock music in Russia and Eastern Europe: a tendency towards satirical cabaret and rock and roll pastiche, which is evident in Russian groups like Zvuki Mu, Avia and the Secrets, the Hungarian group Committee, and post-punk Slovenian groups like Borghesia and Laibach, who even released their own version of the Beatles' album *Let it Be*. In the mid-1980s, this satirical tendency manifested itself more directly in a form of 'pop Stalinism' which parodied Communist slogans and social engineering programmes. Alenka Barber-Kersovan has described 'pop Stalinism' as an 'ironical identification with the regime where the affirmation of Stalinist ideology collapses into its own opposition', giving the example of the 'new primitivist' Slovenian group Agropop, who 'composed a vulgar chaos of what the Slovenian listeners were daily exposed to through the media in [an] ironical crosscut thought the Slovenian soundscape'.[36] The group's 1986 album, for example, was entitled *For the Homeland with Agropop Forward*, a parody of the slogan 'For the Homeland with Tito Forward'. Similarly, in 1991 the Czech group Pravda, named after the chief organ of the Soviet Union Communist Party, and using the red star with a hammer and sickle inside as their symbol, released *Lidé bděte!* (People Awake). In tracks like 'Pravda Stalinská', this album mixed house music beats, female cries of ecstasy, Communist slogans and sound effects like a rooster crowing with a choir singing Communist songs. The Slovakian group I Kidnaped [sic] a Plane also combined 'pop Stalinism' with techno, incorporating samplings of traditional Romanian flute and accordion music into repetitive, militaristic house music in 'Securitate Beat'. Paul Berman, writing on American cultural influences on Czechoslovakia in the *Village Voice*, found such Eastern European intellectual and satirical manifestations in rock music questionable:

The relations between American and European rock may be murkier than is sometimes supposed. It is my impression that Euro-rockers get on stage with the proper instruments and the right look, but with ideas that are often as not geared for cabaret more than dancing. They show too much interest in poetry and theatre, not enough in African-derived rhythmic sophistication; too much profundity, not enough groove. Melancholy cynicism, the European disease, oozes from the amplifiers.[37]

Havel's impressions of the Akord Club reflect a close connection between Czech pop music and theatre. This suggests an intellectual, artistic orientation in popular music derived from an appropriation of Western musical forms and styles which are detached from their social and cultural origins, and pastiched and redirected into a more self-conscious cultural context. When this new cultural context came under threat of censorship, the music took on a social and political dimension often quite different from that of its root forms. Berman's misgivings about European rock stem from a dislocation between rock music's Western origins and its Eastern European relocation. But in the case of punk rock, there was frequently a direct link between the anger, alienation and political protest inherent in its 'dole queue rock' context in London in 1977 (disregarding its art school fashion dimensions) and its relocation and appropriation in Eastern Europe. Ryback, for example, suggests that the explosion of punk rock in Poland in the early 1980s was a direct result of General Jaruzelski's imposition of martial law in 1981,[38] and the sense of 'no future' which prevailed in the initial manifestations of punk rock in the UK and the USA certainly had little difficulty in finding co-relations among Eastern European youth. As one Prague punk told Anna Kashia Natya of the French magazine Photo in 1990, 'Being a punk in Prague ... is more authentic than anywhere else in Europe, because here there is really "no future" '.[39]

The artistic director of the Plastic People of the Universe, Ivan Jirouš, whose notion of a 'parallel' or alternative underground culture was referred to by Havel in his writings, and who became a member of the Havel administration, placed the Plastic People in what he called the 'third Czech musical revival', which he located in 1973. While the first phase covered rock and roll, he placed the second musical revival in the late 1960s, when the Beatles-influenced 'bigbit' (big beat) boom occurred, and there were several hundred rock groups in Prague alone.[40] This coincided with the 'bigbit' boom elsewhere in Eastern Europe and in the USSR, which Artemy Troitsky has described in his book *Back in the USSR*; the first rock music concert in the Soviet Union took place in 1966 at the Ministry of Foreign Affairs. Troitsky records that the first Czechoslovakian 'bigbit' festival was in November 1967, and describes the popular music scene in Prague at the time in terms of predominant English and US blues and rock influences: 'In Prague everything was simple. There were several clubs in the centre of the city (Sunshine, F-club, Olympic), and every week there were concerts by beat groups. The Matadors played like the Yardbirds, The Rebels played West Coast, Framus-5 played r 'n' b and the Olympics sang in Czech in Beatle style.'[41] Olympic's name coincided with that of one of the venues where they played, the Club Olympik in the centre of Prague, which was closed by authorities in 1970 under the normalization programme of the Communist regime (although Aleš Opekar has claimed that 'similarity with the group's name is incidental').[42] The band had been formed in 1962, and was led by Petr Janda, the bourgeois son of a Prague lawyer and concert violinist. They have proved to be the most durable Czech rock group, surviving what Ramet has broadly identified as four principal phases of Eastern European rock music over the past three decades: an initial imitative phase, when Anglo-American models were copied directly; the emergence of original rock compositions, usually sung in English; a switch to native language lyrics and the development of more locally oriented musical styles; and the appropriation of 'local and exotic folk idioms' and, in some cases, a return to the use of English language vocals in a 'quest for a world market'.[43] In 1995 Olympic proved their continuing popularity over a thirty-three-year period when they gave an unannounced performance at the Prince Music Festival in Prague, and were received ecstatically by an audience of more than two thousand people, most of whom sang along with every song the band performed.

Initially performing mainly Czech versions of Beatles songs, and even – like their Hungarian counterparts Illes – dressing up in military uniforms in imitation of the Beatles in *Sergeant Pepper's Lonely Hearts Club Band* in 1967, they were also influenced by psychedelic English groups like Pink Floyd and the Soft Machine. But they performed their own compositions as well as Beatles songs, impressing Allen Ginsberg when he visited Prague in 1965, and touring Northern Poland with the British rhythm and blues band the Animals in 1966. Olympic's first album *Zelva* (Tortoise) was released on the state label Supraphon in 1968, and this is generally considered to be the first 'official' recording of Czech rock music. Aleš Opekar has described it as an important document of the 'period of the first real attempts to adapt rock music to the Czech environment', although it consists of songs from the band's repertoire of 1966, released at a time when they were more strongly influenced by hippie psychedelia.[44] Also influenced by English rhythm and blues and the Mersey Beat, which had become accessible to Czech rock fans through Radio Luxembourg, Olympic incorporated aspects of accordion-based Czech folk music. The lyrics of the songs on *Zelva* – the tortoise of the title is a 'symbol of peace and resistance against unfavourable influences from outside' – expressed what Opekar describes as 'a spontaneous, free and easy attitude to the world. The topics are taken from everyday life and seasoned with a number of miscellaneous, bizarre and grotesque ideas, resulting in odd associations.' But Opekar concludes that 'the songs are not burdened with deep thoughts and they definitely do not reflect the essence of the struggle of ideas or the principal social conflicts of their time.'[45] Fourteen of Olympic's thirty albums had been released on CD by Supraphon by 1989, a testimony to the group's successful compromises with the post-1968 Husak regime, which allowed them to tour extensively both within and outside the Eastern bloc. Voted the most popular Czech rock group in polls throughout the 1960s and 1970s, they appeared on West German and Austrian television, but not on Czech television, and their albums, despite being high in the pop charts, were often difficult to find in Czech record shops. By the 1970s Olympic had modified its sound into an anthemic, synthesizer-based form of symphonic stadium rock, with heavy metal guitar flourishes and often lengthy solos by Janda, and continued to sing their repertoire in Czech. They were again voted the most popular Czech group in 1983, consolidating their official status as the acceptable sound of the Communist regime, and represented Czechoslovakia at Communist youth festivals in the Soviet bloc and in Cuba.[46] As Ramet has pointed out, they still managed to deal with ideologically contentious themes such as saving the environment (in the 1979 album *Holiday on Earth*) and mechanization and the dehumanization of repetitive work (in their 1984 album *Laboratory*).[47]

In 1992 the leading Czech independent recording label Monitor released *Dej Mi Víc ... Olympik* ('More Action from Olympic', a reference to their song 'More Action in Love'), a thirtieth anniversary tribute album of thirteen Olympic songs – at least two of them from *Zelva* – performed by popular post-punk, heavy metal and blues rock groups such as Alkehol, Plexis, Mercedes, Hagen Banden and Žlutý Pes (Yellow Dog). There was even a track performed by Rapmasters, one of the two prominent rap groups in Prague, indicating that Olympic are greatly appreciated by subsequent generations of Czech rock musicians as pioneers of Czech rock. The group's compromises with the Communist regimes' restrictions on rock music enabled them to perform their music over three decades and provide audiences with a much-needed degree of continuity which makes them the most important rock group in the Czech Republic. Petr Janda also runs a recording studio, where a number of younger bands record, and in 1995 he formed a citizens' group called the Initiative to Protect the Czech Music Market, proposing a quota of forty per cent radio air time in the Czech Republic for Czech music.[48] This was in response to the relatively small amount of Czech music played on Czech commercial rock stations like Radio 1, Evropa 2, City Radio, Frekvence 1, Fun Radio, Radio Profil, Radio Puklicum, Radio Dragon, Hellax Radio and others which have proliferated, playing predominantly US and English rock music, since Czech airwaves in the 1990s opened up to a free market economy. Ironically, the leader of a group sometimes accused of 'selling out' and collaborating with the Communist regime has assumed a political role in struggling to assert the identity of Czech music against the saturation of the local market by US and English music.

The Plastic People of the Universe

In contrast to Olympic, the reputation of the Plastic People of the Universe, who are probably the most well-known Czech rock group outside of the Czech Republic, is based predominantly on their political dissidence in the 1970s and 1980s, rather than their often atonal, dissonant and avant-garde music, which is sometimes difficult to listen to. The group's artistic director, Ivan Jirouš, has claimed the group never had any political intentions, and has described their emergence in the clandestine, underground rock scene in Prague in the late 1960s. The first and for a while only leading musical figure of this scene was the psychedelic rock band the Primitives Group, who played covers of songs by Jimi Hendrix, the Animals, the Grateful Dead, the Doors, Zappa's Mothers of Invention and the Fugs, among others, as well as their own compositions. Jirouš states that the Primitives Group knew little more about the 'psychedelic' music they produced than the meaning of the word, but that 'through their music they tried to create in the listeners a particular mental state which, temporarily at least, liberated them' and that their particular form of underground music was 'emotionally and instinctively, rather than consciously, understood'.[49] A silent 8-millimetre film of a live performance by the Primitives, shot by an amateur East German film-maker, is the only extant visual record of the group, which English titles in the film describe as 'the only underground rock group in Eastern Europe'. The group cavort ritualistically, stripped to the waist, wearing masks, make-up and shoulder-length hair, surrounded by flaming torches, in a demonic performance style reminiscent of 1960s 'gothic' rockers like the Crazy World of Arthur Brown. Ryback records that the group usually tried to incorporate one of the four elements – air, earth, fire and water – into their performances, and specialized in avant-garde happenings at a Prague theatre called the F-Club. One of these was a Fish Feast, when they poured water over the audience and threw fish at them, and a Bird Feast, in which band and audience were buried in feathers, and the lead singer appeared nude.[50]

When the Primitives Group split up in 1969, the Plastic People of the Universe, who had been formed in 1968 by Milan Hlavsa, inherited their role as chief representatives of the underground rock scene, and early photos of the group feature them performing at the F-Club in Prague in 1969 dressed in togas and wearing make-up, with trees and plastic tubes as a backdrop, and posing nude in make-up in a forest. The Plastic People also used fire in their performances, and, according to Jirouš, 'reflected a kind of cosmology of the underground ... understood in mythological terms as an alternative mental world different from the mental world of people living in the establishment'.[51]

Later the avant-garde group DG307 – named after the official Czech government medical classification for the mentally insane, which was often invoked to remove political dissidents – was founded by singer Pavel Zajicek with the Plastic People's bass player and lead vocalist Milan Hlavsa as a sister group to the Plastic People. DG307 tended to produce formless, atonal and predominantly percussive improvizations which sometimes set out to be acoustically disruptive. A film of them performing at Milan Hlavsa's wedding in 1975 shows a group of long-haired, long-bearded hippies playing violin, saxophone and a series of bizarre home-made percussion instruments such as hacksaws, ritualistically chanting, burning paper, blowing up balloons and blowing through hose pipes. An album of live recordings from 1973 to 1975 by DG307 released by Globus International in 1990 confirms a sense of sonic rebelliousness, revealing a group even more tortured, anguished and uncompromisingly dissonant than the Plastic People. Starting with the monotonous, minimalist twelve-minute track, 'Anti', the album continues with a series of tracks entitled 'Horrors', 'Purge', 'Degeneration', 'Lament' and 'New Partisans', all of which contribute to an overwhelming sense of gothic ominousness, with piercing vocals and repetitive percussion occasionally augmented by a subdued guitar, dirge-like organ, screeching saxophone and mock-gipsy violin. In the same year Globus International also released a similarly atonal avant-garde rock album, with lyrics in German, by another prominent member of the Czech musical underground, guitarist, saxophonist and vocalist Mikoláš Chadima, who was a Charter 77 signatory and leader of The Rock & Jokes Extempore Band from 1978 to 1981, later forming the MCH Band. Another similarly avant-garde rock group of the time was Aktuál, who also produced formless, repetitive, incantatory music featuring chants and prominent percussion.

The Plastic People were granted professional status until 1970, but, when the authorities prohibited English band-names and repertoires in the early 1970s, the band lost this status and went underground. From 1970 to 1972 their lead vocalist was Paul Wilson, a Canadian English teacher working in Prague who subsequently translated much of the work of Havel, Škvorecký and other prominent Czech authors into English. Although he sings (in Czech) on only two tracks of the group's recorded output, Wilson sang lead vocals in a concert of songs by the Velvet Underground which the Plastic People performed at the F-Club in Prague in February 1971 in homage to US pop artist Andy Warhol (who was of Czech origin). A 'low-fi' mono tape recording of this event, made by Binny Laney, reveals him as a slightly shaky and perfunctory vocalist, and the band's renditions of the songs are accurate but lacking in vitality. Only one song – the spoken-word story 'The Gift' – is performed in Czech, and the concert is introduced by a speech by Jirouš – who never played with the group, but acted as their artistic director – about Warhol's cultural significance.

After the Plastic People were effectively forbidden to play in public by being denied professional status, they were forced to play at private parties at venues such as Havel's farmhouse in northern Bohemia (where they later recorded their album *Passion Play*). They persevered with their utopian, libertarian inclinations in clandestinity, playing songs (in English) based on poems by Blake, Spenser and the Czech romantic poet Jiří Kolar (in Czech). This use of poetry by the group, according to Jirouš, 'drew people's attention to the fact that contemporary rock music was not completely cut off from the Western cultural heritage of which we are a part.' Unable to give state-approved public concerts, which were vetted by cultural commissars of the Union of Composers, they had to resign themselves to playing illegal gigs for groups of friends. While many unofficial groups capitulated to state demands and began playing mainstream 'Europop', or sought work in the USSR, the Plastic People resolved, in Jirouš's words, that 'it is better not to play at all than to play music that does not flow from one's convictions. It is better not to play at all than to play what the establishment demands.'[52]

By 1973, when official pressure had eased somewhat, the Czech underground rock scene began to re-emerge, and the Plastic People played at exhibitions and parties, appearing with DG307 at the First Festival of Underground Culture in 1974. During this period the Plastic People performed songs by the banned poet Egon Bondy, who belonged to an older generation than the musicians but whose work contained an abrasive, scatological edge. As Martin Machovek has noted, Bondy's works were 'renowned for their outspokenness, sincerity, aggression and the inclusion of taboo subjects, which has always been highly appreciated in the Czechoslovak cultural underground'.[53] Both Bondy and Jirouš were part of a delegation of Czech writers who attended a conference on Czechoslovakian Literature and Culture at New York University in April 1990 – a further indication of the important role rock music plays in official post-Velvet-Revolution Czech culture.

Despite Bondy's often abrasive and scatological lyrics, none of the Plastic People's material was overtly political, however, nor did they intend to pursue a strategy of political opposition, as their saxophonist Vratislav Brabenec has explained: 'We were involved in an unequal fight, but that was never our intention. We never liked singing protest songs. The conflict was artificially engineered by the police and the state apparatus. ... As regards being romantic heroes, I saw us more as madmen. We certainly experienced more fear than romance.'[54] In his introduction to a book of essays, poems, stories and plays by Czech dissident writers and musicians (including Jirouš and Havel, and an essay by the Charter 77 philosopher Jan Patocka on the Plastic People and DG307) published in London in 1978, Paul Wilson rejected the characterization of the Plastic People and other bands in the Czech underground as 'dissident'. He argued that dissidence implied a 'critical dialogue' with the regime, whereas the Czech underground realized that such a dialogue was impossible and simply turned their backs, pursuing their own concerns:

> In this sense, without actually being 'political', the underground was far more radical than the so-called unofficial opposition because it turned its energies to what could actually be done, in the present. Instead of trying to work out political alternatives, they created a cultural alternative that fulfilled their own needs now; instead of asking the regime to give them more freedom, they behaved as if they were free already.[55]

This notion of 'living as if', which was also articulated by Havel in relation to the idea of creating a 'parallel culture' (Jirouš's term) to that of the regime, represents a form of non-political, underground opposition that avoids any direct confrontation with the regime. In this way, the Plastic People and other groups created their own alternative, clandestine cultural circuit and avoided any overtly political behaviour. None the less, this did not protect them from harassment, suppression and banning by the regime.

The Plastic People's first album to appear in the West was given the ironic title (in English) *Egon Bondy's Lonely Hearts Club Banned*. This was produced in London without their knowledge from tapes made in 1973 and 1974, and consists entirely of songs with lyrics by Bondy. The liner notes, probably written by Paul Wilson, provide clues to the group's musical background:

> The Plastic People's musical mentors were Frank Zappa, Captain Beefheart, the Fugs and the Velvet Underground and something of these influences can be heard in their music. But they've never tried, as so many groups in Eastern Europe do, simply to import Western rock into an alien scene. Over the years they have developed a mature and original style of their own. Their music and Bondy's lyrics are saturated with the atmosphere of Prague, a city where the music and the mundane, the absurd and the real, mingle in everyday life. This record is not a cry of protest. It's a deliberate statement of what is possible in what seems to be an impossible situation.[56]

The album begins with a song entitled '20', in which guitar, violin and saxophone play in unison a dirge-like sequence, while Hlavsa intones Bondy's lyrics in an angst-ridden howl. For those born in the 1950s, like the Plastic People's generation, the song suggests, the Prague Spring had provided the only glimmer of a life outside the grey, state-imposed conformity of totalitarianism. Those of Bondy's generation, having borne witness to the Nazi era and the Soviet invasion of Hungary, have an even bleaker heritage. Those old enough to have lived through the foundation of modern Czechoslovakia in 1918 and the brief period of democracy between the wars under Tomas Masarýk, the song implies, have long given up hope of alternatives to a Stalinist regime. Far from being a protest song, '20' expresses a philosophical bleakness, and a sense of no future for young people which anticipate the nihilist anger of punk, but hint at a desire for social and cultural change similar to that described by Peter Wicke in rock music in the GDR: 'It was the almost total lack of an attractive and stimulating cultural life within the mainstream of everyday experience for the majority of the population that constituted the concrete impetus for radical and fundamental social change'.[57]

The album contains songs with titles like 'Constipation', 'Toxic', and 'Look at You, All Sound Asleep' which express a despair and disgust reflected in the obsessively repetitive, Velvet-Underground-like rhythms of the music, the wailing saxophone and Hlavsa's raucous, snarling, even coughing, vocals. But a more hippie-like, magical and optimistic streak emerges in songs like 'The Wondrous Mandarin' and 'Magic Nights'. The rather literary lyricism of the lyrics combines with free-flowing, echoing saxophone and violin solos which recall 1970s 'progressive rock' groups like the Fugs or the Flock, as well as a free jazz influence, along with residues of Bohemian folk music, while the 'dirty' but intricate guitar solos are similar to those of Frank Zappa.

The Plastic People's second album to appear in the West, *Passion Play*, was released in Canada in 1980, and is even less musically accessible than the first, its anger and anguish even more pronounced. It is a 'concept album' which follows the format of Christ's passion, with lyrics based on the Old Testament. It may even be an allegorical expression of the group's own persecution, as well as reflecting the widespread impact and influence which *Jesus Christ Superstar* had all over Eastern Europe and in the USSR. *Passion Play* was composed by saxophonist Vratislav Brabenec, and first performed live at Václav Havel's farm in Hradecek, where it was also recorded in 1978. The Canadian Broadcasting Corporation broadcast it as *The Hradecek Passion* in March 1980, probably owing to the influence of Paul Wilson, whose translations of the Czech lyrics are printed on the record's inner sleeve. Ten musicians are credited as taking part in the recording and performance. The often atonal, avant-garde jazz-rock style, which uses sax, electric piano, viola, violin, bass viol and percussion, is reminiscent of 1970s British and European jazz-rock fusion groups like Henry Cow, Slapp Happy and Faust, while the Zappa and Captain Beefheart influences are still discernible, especially in Milan Hlavsa's growling, anguished vocals. The lyrics of the songs contain few, if any, direct political references, and any sense of dissent is detectable only in the general scatological, angry and occasionally religious tone of the songs.

Havel's response to the Plastic People and DG307 in 1976 relates their music's anguished formlessness, repetition, experimentation and ritualistic obsessiveness to a sense of aesthetic and philosophical resistance to oppression:

> Although I'm no expert on rock music, I immediately felt that there was something rather special radiating from these performances, that they were not just deliberately oddball or dilettantish attempts to be outlandish at any price, as what I had heard about them might have suggested: the music was a profoundly authentic expression of the sense of life amongst these people, battered as they were by the misery of the world. There was disturbing magic in the music, and a kind of inner warning.[58]

In February 1976 the Plastic People took part in what was the largest illegal underground rock event in Czechoslovakia, in the village of Bojanovice outside Prague. The occasion was Ivan Jirous's wedding, and more than a dozen groups performed for over four hundred people. As a result, at least twenty-seven musicians from five groups were arrested, and musical equipment, tapes, films and photos were confiscated by the police. The musicians were charged with 'creating public disturbances' and 'singing indecent songs'. The indictment against the Plastic People referred to lyrics 'of extreme vulgarity with an anti-socialist and anti-social impact, most of them extolling nihilism, decadence and clerical-ism'.[59] Seven of the musicians received prison sentences, including Jirouš, who was jailed for eighteen months, and Paul Wilson was expelled from Czechoslovakia. A previous official attack on the Plastic People had taken place in 1974, when police attacked and beat up hundreds of young people waiting for a concert at which the Plastic People were to appear, and the Hermanice farmhouse where the group rehearsed had been bulldozed to the ground. Ivan Jirous was arrested and sentenced for the fourth time in 1982, and in 1984 police set fire to the house in Rychnov where the group performed. By this time the Plastic People had effectively been put out of action, Brabenec decided to emigrate, and the group split up.

The Plastic People's importance in Czech public memory is clear from the release by Globus International of *Bez Ohňú je Underground* (Straight from the Underground) a recording of a concert at the Roxy Club in Prague by a re-formed Plastic People in December 1992, performing versions of the Doors' 'Light My Fire', the Velvet Underground's 'Waiting for the Man', the Fugs' 'Garden is Open' in Hlavsa's heavily accented English, along with three of the Plastic People's most well-known tracks, 'Modrý Autobus' (Blue Bus), 'Podivuhodný Mandarín' (The Wonderful Mandarin), and 'Magické Nocii' (Magic Nights). Globus International also released an eight CD/vinyl LP boxed set of the Plastic People's complete recorded output in 1993, much of it live material recorded on rather 'low-fi' equipment. *Francovka* and *Eliášův Oheň* (Fire of Elias) contained assorted, mainly live and often raucous material from 1974 to 1979, featuring some lengthy violin and guitar improvizations, while *Egon Bondy's Lonely Hearts Club Banned* and *Passion Play* were followed by *Slavná Nemesis* (Famous Nemesis) from 1979, *Leading Horses* from 1981, *Hovězí Porážka* (Slaughtered Cattle) from 1983–84, and *Midnight Mouse* from 1984. The later music is slightly mellower, and often more melodic and rhythmic than the 1970s music, indicating a less angry and angst-ridden approach, but maintaining the group's distinctive jazz-rock-folkloric blend of keyboards, saxophone and violin. A boxed set of material by DG307 was also released in 1992, along with a new album, *Artificially Flavoured*, featuring Hlavsa, Pavel Zajicek's gothic-sounding organ and female singer Micaela Němcová's mysterious vocalizations in material that was structured relatively accessibly for this group, although sudden irruptions of silence and tearing sounds lend an avant-garde flavour. This re-formed version of DG307 gave what was announced as their last ever concert at the Prague Roxy Club in 1994, and were described by Lorrayne Anthony as

> somewhere between early Peter Gabriel and the Velvet Underground, the essence of pre-'88 Czech rock: loud, spoken poetry with a tiny soprano vocal wafting in and out of the mix, barely audible over sad strings and relentless percussion. ... old-timers like DG307 continue to strike awe into new audiences ... moving people's minds more than their feet, yet the number of teenagers at the gig indicates that people remember that, even in the new free market Czech Republic, rock 'n' roll can still be rebellious.[60]

After the break-up of the Plastic People, Milan Hlavsa and Ivo Popisil, who had been associated with the Plastic People, became involved in Garáz in 1984. Garáz played a relatively 'straight ahead', up-tempo, jazz and funk-oriented rock repertoire until it disbanded in 1988. A 'Best of Garáz' compilation was released by Globus International in 1990.

Hlavsa then formed Půlnoc (Midnight),with two other former members of the Plastic People, guitarist Jiří Kabes and keyboard player Josef Janíček, but without the approval of Plastic People founder Jirouš. Půlnoc were invited by Lou Reed to play at the Cartier Foundation festival for Andy Warhol near Paris in June 1990, having previously played in the USA in April 1989. This tour, which included dates in New York, San Francisco and Seattle, did not create much impact, although Richard C. Walls claims it was 'a critical success, though not having any American label affiliation kept them a cult item'.[61] Even under Reed's tutelage, they were upstaged at the Andy Warhol event by a dramatic and apparently spontaneous ten-minute reunion of the Velvet Underground for the first time in twenty years in a performance of their most famous song, 'Heroin'. Ellen Willis of the *Village Voice* was unimpressed by Půlnoc's performance: 'the Velvets have informed [Půlnoc's] revolutionary zeal, but not, apparently, their music, which doesn't make it'.[62] This echoed numerous other dismissals of Eastern bloc rock in the Western popular music press, where little attempt was made to consider its history of technological and information deprivation.

Nonetheless, Půlnoc persevered with their attempts to cross over into the West, and toured the USA again in 1990, managing to secure a contract with Arista. In an interview with Richard C. Walls, Hlvasa stated that any connection between Půlnoc and 'political opposition' was a misconception, preferring to let the group's music speak for itself.[63] The album they released on Arista, *City of Hysteria*, which was produced in New York by Robert Musso, included re-recordings of a number of tracks from their 1991 self-titled Globus International album. Track titles were in English, although most of the songs were sung in Czech, with English translations of the lyrics in the liner notes. The album also included a version (in English) of the Velvet Underground and Nico's songs 'All Tomorrow's Parties' and a 'Song for Nico'. The liner notes played up the group's connections with the Plastic People, reproducing a 1994 essay by Havel describing their predecessors' spiritual basis in the 'ethnically, culturally and historically diverse focus of European history' which occurs in Prague, a battleground of European struggles which 'end up as something worldwide'. But Havel emphasizes the particularity of the group's Central European orientation:

> Even if they had the technical means at their disposal, the Plastics will probably never end up on the world hit-parade (nor is that their aim). Their music may never strike a close chord with millions of rock fans from San Francisco to Tokyo, and yet, encoded within it is an important warning, some highly specific information about the existential fine tuning of people who find themselves in a place where the knots of history are tied and untied.[64]

This almost exclusively local sphere of operation proved to be even truer for Půlnoc than for the Plastic People, despite some positive responses from the New York *Village Voice*, where Milo Miles explained *City of Hysteria*'s indifferent reception in the US:

> the pop audience here has responded to Půlnoc with the same cursory attention granted the political turnover in Eastern Europe. Slow sales point up how much *City of Hysteria* suffers from the deadly perception that it's both incomprehensibly foreign and tainted with old-fashioned influences. Most fans are not connected to the brooding, furtive 'existential fine tuning' of Prague that Václav Havel praises.[65]

Criticizing the group's excessive mournfulness and absence of funk, Miles went on to praise Půlnoc's female vocalist Michaela Němcová and lead guitarist Tádeaš Věrčák's feedback-driven post-punk pyrotechnics, suggesting that when these cohered with the cello, keyboards and drums the band became 'the first East European rockers Western adepts should imiate with relish'. Robert Christgau was similarly impressed, placing *City of Hysteria* at number eleven in his *Village Voice* top sixty albums for 1991 (between Ice-T and Nirvana), and even adding the Globus

International album at number thirty-six.[66] But these encouragements did not translate into any degree of US success for the band, who eventually split up in 1993. Hlavsa went on to form Fiction with another female vocalist, Jitka Charvátová, releasing in 1994 a self-titled album, which included a version of the Velvet Underground's 'Venus in Furs'. Song lyrics were printed in both Czech and English, and one track, 'Poets of Silence', is performed in both Czech and English, indicating a perseverance by Hlavsa in attempting to reach anglophone listeners, although the album was not released outside the Czech Republic. The translated lyrics reveal a poetic, by turns apocalyptic and lugubrious concern with dreams, visions, distant voices and mirrors. The music is mellow, melodic and dominated by keyboard washes and samplers, similar to Půlnoc's but without its prominent lead guitar. The Velvet Underground influence is still discernible, but there is a distinctive Czech rock lineage stretching back to the Plastic People. Hlavsa continues to be a major figure in a local music scene which has produced only two internationally successful musicians: the jazz double-bass player Miroslav Vitous, formerly of Weather Report, and now permanently based in the USA, and rock guitarist Ivan Kral, who played lead guitar in Patti Smith's group in the later 1970s, and later backed Iggy Pop, eventually forming his own group, Native, a Czech–US hybrid.

'Eccentrics on the Ground Floor'

In 1989 Aleš Opekar and Josef Viček published *Excentrici v Přízemí* (Eccentrics on the Ground Floor), a book which profiled forty-eight Czech rock groups whom the authors considered not to be part of the Czech musical underground but who were too experimental and uncompromising to be part of the Czech musical mainstream.[67] Most of the 'ground floor' groups profiled – like Garáz, the OK Band, Pražský výbér, and VZ – have ceased to exist, but the book included five groups who have continued to occupy prominent places in the Czech musical scene in the 1990s: Babalet, Iva Bittová and Pavel Fajt, E, Laura a její tygři, and the YoYo Band. Babalet and the YoYo band represent one pole of Czech musical eccentricity: a small but durable Czech reggae scene. This also includes Švihadlo, led by Vincent Richards, a Jamaican-born musician, and Hypnotix, who have a Senegalese vocalist who sings in English and in 1995 recorded an album mixed by the British On U Sound System. The YoYo Band, who have existed since 1982, are an all-Czech group whose distinctive 'white reggae' includes funk, Latin, jazz, African and calypso elements sung in Czech and played on keyboards, timbales, conga, trumpet and saxophone. There is only one guitar, and the group do not feature the 'chicken scratch' guitar sound normally associated with reggae, or express any Rastafarian philosophy. In performance, they incorporate cabaret-like antics, with the brass section employing elaborate hand gestures, but they stop short of parody, producing infectiously danceable music. Babalet, in contrast, feature an African singer and conga player, Martin Tankwey, although the rest of the group are Czech and their songs, which have an orthodox Rastafarian orientation, are in Czech, with a folk rock and reggae beat and calypso inflections. A song entitled 'Africa, Europa' on their 1994 album *Kytkový Reggae* indicates the group's attempt to forge links between a Czech folk tradition and a broad African musical diaspora. In an Eastern European context, having a black African musician in a reggae group is clearly read as an indicator of musical authenticity, although the YoYo Band's success without one is notable – even if it could be argued that the music they produce is hardly reggae at all.

The appropriation of Jamaican reggae in the Czech music scene has a much stronger counterpart in Poland, as Wojciech Marchlewski has indicated. In 1986, a Polish reggae festival attracted some forty reggae groups, and a Rastafarian movement had developed alongside them, adopting dreadlocks and red, yellow and green clothing, and cultivating marijuana. As Marchlewski comments: 'In the later years [of the 1980s] Polish rasta [followers] started to search for their own, Polish "roots". This search made them quit towns and move to the countryside where they hoped to find the "roots" in the slavic folk tradition. This, in its turn, led to the creation of the native genre of Polish, folk-based reggae intertwined with West Indian motifs.'[68] A similar combination of Slavic folk elements and reggae can be found in the music of the small but distinctive Czech reggae scene.

Also included among the 'Eccentrics on the Ground Floor' are a group considered to be the first Czech rap group, Manželé, whose name means 'Married Couple'. Initially a folk music duo, their self-titled album was originally recorded on 'low-fi' home equipment in 1984 with guitar, synthesizers, bass and drum-machine, and released on a cassette. Re-released on CD in 1991, it features songs like '(Down with) Jizák', about a newly constructed town south of Prague, and 'UFO', both of which use rap to express political ideology, placing emphasis on the rhythmic use of spoken word, with only the endings of words rhyming, over sometimes deliberately sparse mechanical beats which have an automaton-like quality. Partly owing to the difficulty of adapting the intricacies of the Czech language to the rhymes and rhythms of rap, there are only two other prominent rap groups in Prague, Rapmasters and JAR (whose name refers to the Republic of South Africa), both of whom released two albums between 1992 and 1995. Rapmasters often sound like a Czech version of white US rappers the Beastie Boys, and while their first album, *Skandal*, has an abrasive, aggressive techno sound in songs like 'Prezident' and 'Slzkej had' (Slimy Snake'), their second, *3 Na 3* (3 on 3) produced a single which went to the top of the Czech hit parade in June 1995.

Featuring a strongly repetitive techno-pulse beat, disco-styled choruses and lyrics consisting of rhyming couplets, Rapmasters's music is more aligned with disco, techno and house music than hip hop. Although the group members' names, J. Bell, Mr George and M. C. Young, and visual appearance (goatee beards, gold chain, Raiders baseball cap and beanie) indicate a prominent US hard-core hip hop influence, their music consists predominantly of electronically produced, repetitive house and dance beats.

Both Rapmasters and JAR are included on a 1993 Monitor compilation album entitled *Techno-Rap-Dance*, along with groups such as Techno-boys, Rave Model, Imrich Tekkknofactory, Morphotronic and Pravda, which indicates how their particular brand of rap music is sandwiched between techno and dance music, with little distinction being drawn between the three different forms. JAR also sound similar to the Beastie Boys, but are musically more adventurous and eclectic than Rapmasters, incorporating rock guitar (one of their tracks samples Jimi Hendrix), acid jazz, funk and heavy metal influences, as well as English language tracks like 'No Money' and 'Johannesburg' on their first album. JAR's musical playfulness indicates that, along with Rapmasters, their concerns are more with enjoyment than polemics, and neither group appears to take itself entirely seriously. While Rapmasters do not adopt any black American or Afrocentric musical influences, JAR's name and song titles like 'Johannesburg' and the brief *a cappella* 'Peoples of Africa' on their first album do suggest a rhetorical alignment with South Africa, but this seems the subject of parody rather than solidarity. African elements are absent from their second album, which celebrates 'Funky Alcohol', among other subjects, and features the group in eccentric costumes and poses on the cover, suggesting a rap equivalent of the mock-punk antics of Czech punk group Tři Sestry. This tendency towards self-parody has been noted by Simon Frith in East German rock groups prior to the collapse of the Berlin Wall, where he observed 'an edge of self-mockery, a slightly dismayed feeling that they'd never really know if they were any good'.[69] While there is free access to English and US music in Eastern Europe in the 1990s, and Prague in particular has a steady stream of concerts by groups and musicians from the West, there is still a sense of isolation and parochialism due partly to the inaccessibility of the Czech language, which restricts musicians to a relatively small local audience. This audience is often familiar with the Western models which groups like Rapmasters, JAR and Tři Sestry are drawing on, which perhaps explains the sense of self-consciousness and eccentricity these groups display.

Other notable 'eccentrics' who have survived into the Czech musical scene of the 1990s include Laura a její tigři (Laura and her Tigers – the name derives from a short story by William Saroyan), a slick, 'pop Stalinist'-style jazz-cabaret group whose spectacular live performances feature up to nine male performers dressed identically in white shirts, sunglasses and 1950s-style thin black ties, and two women singers in sunglasses and night club attire. E, a Brno-based avant-garde minimalist heavy metal group led by the visual artist Vladimír Kokolia, also continue to record and perform. Brno-based singer and violinist Iva Bittová's avant-garde gipsy-influenced music and free-form scat-like vocalizations, sometimes performed with her husband, drummer Pavel Fajt, is sometimes compared to Laurie Anderson's music by Western observers. The couple were featured along with Bill Laswell's quartet Last Exit and others on a 1990 US compilation of live performances at the New York avant-garde jazz club the Knitting Factory. The liner notes to the compilation describe the Knitting Factory as 'the most challenging, surprising, and innovative new music club in New York' where 'jazz, classical and rock all come together ... [to] point the direction music will be taking in coming years'. All these groups produce highly idiosyncratic, Czech-language music which is close to avant-garde notions of musical fusion, restricting them to a cult following, although Laura a její tigři's populist cabaret performance style made them a highlight of the 1995 Prince Music Festival.

The Prague music scene in the 1990s

Despite the euphoria of the first free elections for almost half a century, Prague in June 1990 appeared to offer few amusements for young people, many of whom hung about on street corners, some with ghetto blasters playing Western rock or rap. Even the apparently spontaneous music events on the streets were subject to curfews, and records and tapes by English and American rock groups in the record shops seemed unaffordable when they were available. (In 1990 locally produced records and cassettes cost about 65 korunas – or less than one pound – but imported records could cost anything up to ten times that amount, and by 1992 local CDs were retailing for 150 korunas. This price had more than doubled by 1995, with imported CDs costing up to 600 korunas, or £14.50, roughly equivalent to CD prices in the UK.) Discos operated on Wenceslaus Square mainly for tourists, there were posters for a few sporadic rock and jazz events, and a number of folk and rock bands played in the streets, but the atmosphere remained subdued in comparison to Western European cities in summer. This was possibly due to a statement that one T-shirt slogan (in English) made about the plight of young people in Prague: 'Franz Kafka didn't have much fun here either'.

A 1990 article in the monthly pop culture magazine *i-D* by Yugoslav journalist Vanja Balogh unearthed signs of life among young pop and rock fans which were not apparent to the casual tourist. At the student-run 007 Club near Prague Castle, music by groups such as Public Enemy and the Pogues could be heard, and the skateboarders frequenting the courtyard opposite the Prague National Theatre – where Havel's first play, *The Garden Party*, was playing – expressed enthusiasm about the Beastie Boys and Run DMC, but told her: 'The only place to go out at nights is the 007 but that is only on Saturdays. So we usually end up coming here after cruising the city. Prague is boring. The thing to do these days is go home and paint your jeans. Music-wise there is very little information about what is going on outside, but we know about acid house and rap.'[70]

When I visited Prague in the summer of 1992 for a conference on Central European popular music, the mood still seemed sober, a sobriety indicated by the glimpse we caught of a pensive Havel driving out of Prague Castle on the day he had tendered his resignation and the split between the Czech Republic and Slovakia had become a certainty. But in this two-year period Prague had changed immensely: prices had almost doubled since 1990; it now had the biggest tourist boom of any European city and was being marketed as a kind of second Salzburg, as the city where Mozart conducted the premiere of *Don Giovanni*. Kafka had been resurrected as an unlikely cultural hero, along with Andy Warhol, whose Czech origins had been exhumed, and there were even postcards available of the John Lennon wall. The theatres were no longer dominated by Havel's plays and the work of banned writers from the late 1960s, and audiences were smaller. Ticket agencies advertised *Les Misérables*, the Laterna Magika and puppet shows about the Beatles and the life of Kafka. The empty shells of Supraphon record shops that had closed down seemed to be all over the city, while new private recording labels proliferated. The business of making revenue out of tourism had given Prague the atmosphere of a prosperous Western European city without the actual prosperity, while economic realities appeared to have forced many inhabitants into an austerity as pronounced as the days of the Communist regime.

By 1992 a number of rock clubs had become established around Prague, including the Rock Cafe, which had opened at the beginning of 1991, next door to the long-standing Reduta jazz club on Národní, near the National Theatre. The Rock Cafe, which hosted both local and foreign rock groups, is run by a company called Novy Horizont, who also operate a record label, and includes two music venues, a record shop, boutique, art gallery, musical instrument bazaar and video viewing lounge. Other Prague rock clubs listed in the Prague-based fortnightly English-language newspaper *Prognosis* in 1992 were the Malostranská beseda, which also has a record shop and art gallery, the Borat, the Belmondo Revival, the RC Bunkr, the Delta, the Klub Prosek, the Mamma Klub and the Junior Klub. By 1995 the number of jazz, rock and folk music venues advertised in the *Prague Post*, which assumed the function of *Prognosis* after the latter went bankrupt at the end of 1994, had swollen to more than twenty. Újezd, which also ran a record label, was a prominent addition, along with Alterna Komotovka, Subway, Klub Rotonda, Delta and Roxy.

Punk lives

Punk rock clearly continued to fulfil an important function in Prague in the 1990s. The Civic Forum coalition government quickly took steps to legitimize it, and separate it from the right-wing, racist skinhead phenomenon that was spreading among disaffected youth in post-Communist Eastern Europe. The first 'official' punk rock concert in Prague was held in the Palace of Culture in January 1990, and the first-ever punk convention took place in April 1990, but, as a Czech photographer told Balogh: 'There were hundreds of punks with outrageous hairstyles and dirty clothes. ... Punks still can't walk the streets in their full anarchist gear, but they have survived and sometimes you can see them in certain spots in the city.'[71]

When punk rock and heavy metal first reached Czechoslovakia in the early 1980s, they had been subjected to intensive government suppression. In 1983 records by the heavy metal group Kiss were banned, reportedly because the double 's' in the group's name was seen as an SS logo. In the same year, the music critic of the Communist Party newspaper *Tribuna*, Jan Kryzl, wrote an angry attack on both heavy metal and punk rock, denouncing them as 'primitive', 'hideous', 'provocative' and 'obscene', and as a result numerous Czech rock groups lost their licences:

> It is no coincidence that so-called punk and new wave has been disseminated in our republic by Western radio stations and other means ... the aim being pursued by foreign intelligence agencies is two-fold: Firstly to introduce our young people to this musical trash, and secondly to then form bands here suggesting that this is part of a new 'wave' sweeping the world. These bands are meant to produce music which is antithetical to all aesthetic and moral norms.[72]

This condemnation of foreign musical influences, which was reprinted in the Communist Party newspaper *Rude pravo* and publicly criticized by the Czech Jazz Section for nurturing 'hate and distrust in thousands of young people',[73] led to an official crackdown on Czech rock groups, and a number of violent clashes between Czech authorities and rock fans in Bohemia between 1983 and 1986.

In April 1990 Monitor, a new independent record label run by Vladimír Kočanderle and Josef Přib, former musicians with the new wave OK Band, who had survived by compromising with the demands of the Communist regime, released *Rebelie*. This was the first-ever 'official' compilation of Czech 'punk and oi' music, featuring seven groups: Tři Sestry (Three Sisters), Fabrika, Orlík, Šandy, Našrot, Do Řady! (To Order!) and the once-banned Plexis, whose original name, Plexis PM, Ryback points out, was an anagram of 'Sex Pistols' and 'Exploited'.[74] Plexis were also featured on two other punk rock compilations in 1991, AG Kult's *Action Punk*, which also featured Do Řady! and others, and

Epidemic. But, according to Petr Bergmann in a report on a lively, diverse and evolving Czech punk scene in the US magazine *Maximum Rocknroll*, Plexis had left the scene 'for money, popularity and for girls'.[75] By 1992, with their album *White Killer*, which included a Czech version of the Beatles' 'Back in the USSR', Plexis had completely gravitated away from punk to heavy metal.

A few tracks on *Rebelie* stand out for their energy and intuition, above a general tendency towards Sex Pistols and John Lydon derivations and heavy metal riffs. Orlík, who went on to release *Demise!* an album on Monitor in 1991, produce a distinctively 'grungy', dirty guitar sound in three songs, which denounce skinheads, celebrate the Žižkov area of Prague and satirize mainstream pop singer Karel Gott, while Tři Sestry (an all-male band well known for their beer-drinking, despite their name, and one of whose members is called Nikotin) incorporate a piano accordion into the standard punk line-up of guitars and drums to produce the most idiosyncratically Czech-tavern-like sounds on the recording – a distinctively local variant of what has become a global idiom. The use of the accordion, which Czech emigrants in the US contributed to zydeco music, was considered synonymous with stuffy, traditional folk music in the 1960s by rock groups like Olympic, who used it in parody. But Tři Sestry appear to have revitalized the instrument to generate a sound similar to that of Irish punk-folklore group the Pogues. On their 1991 album *Alkáč je největší kocour* (Alcohol is the Best Tomcat), the accordion is used in mostly up-tempo, danceable punk numbers, which include a Czech version of a song by British punk group Sham 69, and feature a surprise guest appearance by Olympic's Petr Janda, in whose studio the album was recorded. The album also 'quotes' from the Dead Kennedys' 'California über Alles', and 'Saturday Night Fever', includes snoring and belching sound effects, and ends with a short burst of Mozart, as well as incorporating a banjo on two tracks, indicating a satiric cabaret-style approach which links it to more mainstream Czech rock music.

By 1995, Tři Sestry and their leader, Lou Fanánek Hagen, who also runs a side project, Hagen Baden, had become sufficiently mainstream to be featured on the cover of the long-standing 'official' Czech pop music monthly *Melodie*, which was started in 1963. But Tři Sestry's 1993 album, *Svedska Trojka* (Three Swedes), is as abrasive as the group's earlier albums, continuing their blend of traditional accordion tavern music and up-tempo punk, including a Sid Vicious-style punk parody of Bob Dylan's 'Knocking on Heaven's Door', a Czech–English parody of Paul Anka's 'I'm a Lonely Boy' ('Omelouny boj'), a nod to German punk rock group Die Toten Hosen, and a dedication to Karel Gott, 'because he likes punk'.

Rebelie was followed in 1991 by a companion compilation of thirty tracks of Czech hard-core punk, featuring groups such as Serious Music, Director, MOR, Czechcore SRK, Sebastian, Subverted and others, with a cover featuring a skinhead emerging from a manhole into the middle of a street. Most of the music matched this image, expressing a series of raw, often anguished, disgusted and hard-edged forays into guitar-generated noise and strangled vocals.

Some of the reasons for punk rock continuing to survive into the 1990s in the Czech Republic are indicated by Simon Frith in his description in 1988 of the group VZ, which he sees as an illustration of the 'different rhythms' of Eastern and Western European rock histories: 'the best, most driven punk band I've seen since 1977. Talking to the group afterward I found them to be in their late twenties, weary, wary men whose energy is eaten up keeping going. In a country that has heavily policed "protest" for a decade, a rock career has a different pace, a different determination than in Britain or the USA.'[76] The resilience and durability of punk rock as a vehicle of social and political opposition in the Czech Republic is illustrated by a news item in the *New Musical Express* of 30 April 1994, which reports the first live public appearance in nearly two years by former Clash member Joe Strummer at the Repre Klub in Prague with a local group called Dirty Pictures, playing a collection of old Clash numbers.[77] The event, at which at least twenty-five Czech groups played, was a charity benefit called 'Rock for Refugees' for OPU, an organization aiding refugees from Bosnia, and was attended by over a thousand people. Dirty Pictures are a Czech–American group, whose lead songwriter, vocalist and guitarist, 'Huckleberry Dirt', is an American resident in Prague. Their 1993 album, *Escape from Sloppy Lake*, which is available only in the Czech Republic, sounds similar to the Clash of the late 1970s, and there are very few Czech references in any of the songs, some of which refer directly to a US context – one track is entitled 'Stupid American'. An abrasive, apolitical punk ethos prevails, even expressing boredom at the conflict in Bosnia, while the song 'Unlonely' is one of the few with any Czech frame of reference. Dirty Pictures' hope that Joe Strummer would return the favour and introduce the band to London audiences indicates the restrictions of the Czech musical market and continuing perceptions by groups in other countries of the USA and the UK as markers of real musical success.

'Slacker City'

Lack of up-to-date music technology was initially a major problem inhibiting the development of Czech rock and pop music. Lack of access to samplers, sequencers, and other digital equipment taken for granted in Western popular music production, meant there was little chance of getting a hearing on the global circuit. Interest in Czech rock and pop music seems to be confined to a political context which attracts intellectuals but does not shift many units, as Půlnoc's experience in the USA in 1992 proved. Lorrayne Anthony's observations about DG307's

1994 Prague concert indicate that the pre-1989 dissident bands were still capable of producing a strong mixture of curiosity and nostalgia for the clandestinity of the 1970s underground in Prague, but that a new local music scene following contemporary Western models was evolving:

> the feeling today when watching any of the pre-revolution bands is similar to the tension and excitement of the old days. Most of the audience is made up of people who remember those times; the others are intrigued by the sounds of an era that was so isolated from Western rock. However, in the newly capitalist Czech Republic, the dissident music of the past is now being mixed with more modern influences from the West. The result is an eclectic music scene in a city that rivals Paris when it comes to beauty and romance – or to sex and drugs and rock 'n' roll, for that matter.[78]

As examples of new, Western-influenced Czech music, Anthony cites the YoYo Band and the Latin and African-influenced jazz-folk group Sum Svistu. She describes other prominent Czech rock groups in Western terms: Support Lesbiens are 'Prague's answer to Seattle grunge', while The Ecstasy of Saint Theresa are 'Prague's answer to the Orb'. This implies a form of conversation, or call-and-response antiphony, between Western and Eastern Europe; although it is likely that very few Westerners are listening to these responses, or even aware that there is any dialogue. In the case of the Ecstasy of Saint Theresa, there are no distinctively Czech features in the group's 1992 album *Sussurate*, with its almost parodic 'dreampop' English song-titles ('pistacchioplaces', 'swoony', 'toalison', 'icecreamstar', etc.), incomprehensible vocals, 'low-fi' wash of swirling guitar noise and feedback. The influence of English 'shoegazer' guitar bands like My Bloody Valentine predominates, and the album's blurred electronic sheets of sound are an example of what Simon Reynolds has called the 'oceanic rock' of late 1980s English bands like the Cocteau Twins and A. R. Kane. Reynolds describes 'oceanic rock' as an apolitical, escapist music which 'wants to liberate itself from the confines of the self, time and the "real" world. This rock is an attempt to discover lost innocence and peace. It's hypnotic, or narcotic, a fall back into the blissful continuum of unconsciousness.'[79] The implicit connection with drugs is confirmed by Anthony's description of The Ecstasy of Saint Theresa in concert: 'their ambient soundscape of echoed guitars and industrial electronics produces a psychedelic experience which, combined with the Republic's very liberal drug laws (everything is legal for personal use only; selling, buying and passing to a friend is punishable by law) results in a fuzzed-out, appreciative audience.'[80] The group's 1994 album of rather anodyne, ambient-trance instrumental music, *Free D (original Soundtrack)*, which was recorded over a month-long period in London, with additional sessions in Prague and Brno, reveals that the group is made up of eleven members, at least four of whom are English. Apart from cello, ocarina, flute, voice, guitar, keyboard, percussion and samples, the group also produce what are described as '3-D silence, sound space oscillation', 'colour rhythm sound' and 'heavenly bells', resulting in an amorphously universal musical drift with little connection with a Czech musical context or any other distinctive features.

According to an article in the English style magazine *The Face*, Prague in 1994 was showing signs of becoming a libertarian mecca for Western youth similar to the 'hippie haven' of sex, drugs and music in Amsterdam in the 1970s. In a year in which an estimated seventy-nine million tourists came to Prague, *The Face* designated it as 'Slacker city', profiling some of the estimated thirty thousand Americans who populate the city, enjoying 'a revitalised bohemia where the clubs, drugs, drink and living is easy and Americans are everywhere'.[81] Only an 'upscale native Czech audience' appeared able to appreciate the local American newspapers and Metropolis English-language radio station, but not even they could afford the foreign-owned boutiques, restaurants, clubs and bars which cater for foreign tourists. The drug Ecstasy had been on the scene for some time, and drug abuse was starting to take its toll among Czech youth. The article, by Charles Gant, characterizes the predominantly American expatriate 'slacker' scene in Prague as 'a bunch of privileged nouveau hippies, slumming it in a city that's sufficiently poor to treat them like kings, yet sufficiently Western to offer them many of the comforts of home'.[82] It begins and ends with an Aerosmith concert at the Strahov Stadium – tickets for which cost the equivalent of £10 – using Aerosmith's thanks to its Prague audience 'for letting us rock your world. ... And ... rocking ours' as a metaphor for the unequal cultural exchange taking place between Czechs and Americans.

World music and the Czech Republic

Despite its rich folk musical heritage, and the existence of Czech groups like Točkolotoč and Věra Bilá's Romany band Kale, both of whom have been compared to the Gipsy Kings, the Czech Republic continues to remain outside the world music circuit. It is completely absent from *World Music: The Rough Guide*, and Philip Sweeney's *Virgin Directory of World Music* devotes half a page to Czechoslovakia, noting that 'all of the countries in the [Eastern European] region are avid consumers of Euro-American mainstream pop-rock, and also have groups creating their own versions of it'.[83] Only Olympic, Marta Kubisová, Karel Kryl and Karel Gott are cited, along with 'apolitical rock-pop' groups like Elan and Stromboli – whose often contentious English-language lyrics in songs like 'Back in the Castle' on the 1990 album *Meltdown*, as Ramet has observed,[84] surely make them far from 'apolitical'. US beat poet Allen Ginsberg's influence on the music scene of the 1960s is given more prominence than most of the Czech musicians cited.

Other Eastern and Central European countries continue to make few inroads on to the world music map, and when they do, as in the case of the highly successful *Mystères des Voix Bulgares* of the Trio Bulgarka and Balkana, or the Transylvanian folk and Hungarian 'house' music of Marta Sebestyen and the group Muziskas, it is for the relative exoticism of traditional regional folk music. As Petr Dorůžka has commented, 'more than ninety per cent of the world musical production does not reach European listeners at all ... the European influences that penetrate ... best are those that are the farthest ones from the "centre" '.[85] Despite the European Broadcasting Union's establishment of the World Music Workshop in 1987 and the distribution of a monthly World Music ratings list by a panel of thirty-three disc jockeys from seventeen European countries since 1991, world music is still a foreign concept in much of Central and Eastern Europe. In rock and pop spheres, an Anglo-American linguistic and distributional hegemony continues, as Vesa Kurkela has noted:

> When listening to popular music in the post-communist societies like [the Czech Republic], Poland and Hungary we very soon start to ask if there is any reason to speak about national music any more. The musical environment in private and public places sounds similar, no matter which town or village we are passing by. The best indicator of this cultural grey-out is music of the mass media, especially local music radios, where we are no longer able to distinguish national features according to music broadcast. To put it more precisely, we find only one transnational music language, which consists of various styles of Afro-American music.[86]

Although it could be argued that house and dance music became less Anglocentric in the late 1980s with Italian, Belgian, Swiss and German variations on a predominantly Anglo-American genre, these variations expressed little if nothing of their native European musical cultures. It is only in world music and the restricted international subculture of avant-garde popular music that European national barriers seem to have little importance. As the Australian critic Philip Brophy has indicated: 'the problems of differentiating avant-garde rock along nationality lines lie in the way that this stream of rock music connects with the broad historical references and sources more than with localised social and cultural environments'.[87]

The recognition of Iva Bittová and Pavel Fajt's avant-garde blend of folk, jazz and experimental rock music in Western Europe and the USA is one example of this 'broad historical' connection occurring in the Czech Republic, although it may also involve a loss of any sense of national identity in the process.

Progress in Prague

The political function which rock music assumed in the former Soviet bloc up to 1989, often as a repository for oppositional activity denied other outlets by authoritarian regimes, reflects a valorization of rock as both an expression and symbol of the freedom of young people perceived as existing in the West. But this perception did not dominate the way in which rock music in Eastern European countries defined itself. What Artemy Troitsky said of rock in the USSR is also true of the Czech Republic and other Eastern European countries:

> the definitive Soviet rock bands were not about dance, entertainment, or artistic innovations, but about telling people the truth. Under Brezhnev, rock was the only truly informal and uncontrollable art form, and whereas dissident samizdat books and magazines were only accessible to tiny circles of intellectuals, rock songs, thanks to a gigantic underground taping industry, knew no boundaries. The social and political role of rock was nothing if not colossal: in those deceitful days, this was the only way for millions of kids to identify with the truth and to learn about State hypocrisy and corruption, and to find out about the alternative way of life.[88]

With increased opportunities for realization of this alternative, critical, Western-styled way of life and the attendant economic and social hardships of a free market economy, deregulation and privatization, the political role of rock in Eastern Europe has become less prominent. The introduction of MTV Europe in Prague in 1990, and its establishment on the international rock touring circuit, meant there is virtually open access to Western rock music. In the summer of 1995 Prague was included on the international touring circuit of groups and performers like the Rolling Stones, REM, Faith No More, Sinéad O'Connor and Soul Asylum, as well as more 'left field' artists like the Young Gods, dEUS and Laurie Anderson. (Ticket prices ranged from 250 koruna, or £6, for dEUS to 585 koruna, or £14, for Laurie Anderson.) The former dissident millionaire Martin Kratochvíl, a jazz pianist who is also president of the entertainment conglomerate Bonton, which owns thirty-two music outlets, and two radio stations, film production studios and 90 per cent of the Czech Republic's music publishing industry, has emerged as a Richard Branson-like figure symbolizing the free-market orientation of the Czech music industry in the 1990s.

In an article published in English in 1994, former dissident Czech novelist Ivan Klíma, who had been forced to work as a street-sweeper under the Husak regime, takes stock of 'progress in Prague' since the Velvet Revolution. He recounts how, before 1989, cultural events were financially accessible to all, well-patronized, and willingly accepted by many despite being subject to totalitarian state control and censorship:

Books were published, television programmes were made, art was exhibited and the theatres were full. It is true that bookshops stocked a rather limited range of titles, and the repertoire of the theatres and cinemas was a little thin. Television was often monotonous, with current affairs programmes tending towards the mendacious. ... On the other hand, books and tickets to cultural events of all kinds were cheap because the state subsidised all it permitted. While censorship denied everything that was new and disturbing, it also blocked the worst trash – for instance, the pornographic and violent videos and magazines that have swamped free countries had to be smuggled in small quantities across our borders and so never invaded the mass media.[89]

Immediately after the Velvet Revolution, Klíma states, there was considerable demand for the formerly banned cultural products of dissidents and experimentalists, but also for 'foreign trash', which began to dominate Czech culture once the dissident demand subsided, and Beckett was replaced in the theatres by *Les Misèrables*. In a context where censorship and state patronage were immediately replaced by the dictates of the marketplace, he recalls a conversation with a famous protest singer of the 1960s, who had been idolized by young audiences under the Communist regime but now plays to audiences of thirty people. He proceeds to chronicle a dying-off of previously vital Czech cultural forms such as animation, puppetry, publishing, cinema and theatre, which have been replaced by an import culture of 'Disneyesque megakitsch', 'dumb comedy', pornography and 'rubbish'. It is a bleak and disillusioned report which portrays an intelligentsia, who had vainly hoped that the government would continue to subsidize creative expression, totally unprepared for the 'invasion of mass culture from the free part of Europe'. Klíma concludes with the hope that 'at least a part of the Czech cultural public ... will continue to keep our culture alive' since 'small countries need their own culture far more than large countries do'.[90] While his concern with the influx of 'foreign trash' into the Czech Republic almost evokes echoes of pre-1989 Communist Party's rhetorical attacks on the influx of foreign rock music, it also expresses a disturbing nostalgia for aspects of a regime which denied him his livelihood as a writer.

Egon Bondy expressed similar reservations about the Velvet Revolution in a satirical poem written in July 1990, describing the subsequent euphoria as lasting three weeks, and 'anti-communist rant' surviving for six months before the elections. He satirizes the stream of memoirs, eulogies, collages and cartoons which were produced by former dissident artists in 1990, and describes a sober new generation for whom the past forty years have no meaning, and who face a future which Bondy sees as a turbulent one, 'tied to the shambles of a world divided' between winners who cannot find what they have won, and the people who have always borne the cost of social changes.

The cultural malaise Klíma and Bondy diagnose has had some impact on Czech rock music, possibly contributing to the demise of Půlnoc and leading to a number of groups and performers such as the Ecstasy of Saint Theresa, Dirty Pictures, Support Lesbiens, Bunch of No Hopers, Macbeth and others preferring to abandon any sense of a Czech musical tradition and identity and sing in English and play in Anglo-American idioms in the hope of appealing to an international market. On the other hand, the proliferation of rock music venues and independent recording labels like Panton, the former state-run youth recording label operational since the 1980s, Monitor, Bonton, Popron, Reflex, Globus International, Art Production, Nový Horizont, Opus, Orion, Alexim and others indicates that Czech rock and pop music appear to have negotiated the free market economy of the 1990s better than most areas of high culture. And while Havel's sympathy and understanding for rock music and the presence of rock and jazz musicians like Michael Kocáb, Pavel Kantor (head of protocol) and Jarda Koran (Mayor of Prague) as prominent political figures clearly had an impact on the survival of rock music in the Czech Republic, this is frequently over-emphasized and trivialized. (An Australian Broadcasting Corporation 'Foreign Correspondent' news programme about Havel prior to his 1995 trade visit to Australia, for example, portrayed him as 'the rock and roll president' and seemed more concerned with prying into his lifestyle and giving him CDs by Australian rock groups than in discussing his politics.)

But as an expression of the importance of the transnational language of rock music in the local, indigenous culture of small countries, Czech rock, as manifested by groups such as Fiction, Laura a její tigři, the YoYo Band, Tři Sestry, JAR and others, and musicians like Iva Bittová and Pavel Fajt, shows signs of having absorbed its Anglo-American influences and drawn on the cultural heritage of the Plastic People of the Universe and the Czech musical underground to create something unmistakably its own. Freed of the inextricable link between popular music and politics for three decades, Czech musicians of the 1990s are enjoying a period of relative local prosperity, even if their international profiles are still very low.

Notes

1. P. Wicke (1991) 'The Role of Rock Music in Processes of Political Change in the GDR', in J. Lull (ed.) *Popular Music and Communication* (Beverly Hills, Sage Publications), p. 1.
2. T. Ryback (1990) *Rock around the Bloc: A History of Rock Music in Eastern Europe and the Soviet Union* (Oxford University Press), pp. 233–4.
3. S. Frith (1989) 'Independent's Day', *Village Voice* (19 December), p. 77.
4. J. Pekacz (1994) 'Did Rock Smash the Wall? The Role of Rock in Political Transition', *Popular Music*, vol. 13, no. 1, pp. 41–9.
5. L. Grossberg (1984) 'Another Boring Day in Paradise: Rock and Roll and the Empowerment of Everyday Life', in R. Middleton and D. Horn (eds) *Popular Music: Performers and Audiences* (Cambridge University Press), p. 232.

6. In S. Schiff (1991) 'Havel's Choice', *Vanity Fair* (August), p. 123.

7. S. Ramet (ed.) (1994) *Rocking the State: Rock Music and Politics in Eastern Europe and Russia* (Oxford, Westview Press), p. 2.

8. *Ibid.*, p. ix.

9. V. Kurkela (1994) 'Music Culture as Collage: The End of National Musics?' in A. Opekar (ed.) *Central European Popular Music: Proceedings from the international conference Prague 15–17 July 1992* (Prague, IASPM), pp. 110–12.

10. Ryback (1990), p. 199.

11. In Ramet (1994), pp. 55–72.

12. A. Szemere (1995) Review of *Rocking the State, Popular Music*, vol. 14, no. 2 (May), p. 273.

13. A. Troitsky (1989) 'Simply Red', *The Listener* (25 May), p. 6.

14. Wicke (1991), p. 12.

15. In J. Vladislav (ed.) (1989) *Václav Havel or Living in Truth* (London, Faber), pp. 63–5.

16. Unattributed (1990) 'Rock Around the Revolution', *The Economist* (3 February), p. 91.

17. Unattributed (1990) 'Havelling Through', *The Economist* (8 September), p. 63.

18. Unattributed (1990) 'Stones: A Dream Come True', *The Sun-Herald*, Sydney (19 August).

19. In *New Musical Express* (5 May 1990).

20. In Schiff (1991), p. 123.

21. Unattributed (1991) 'Leather Boots, Czech Shirts, 'n' Stetsons', *The European* (March).

22. Kurkela (1994), p. 112.

23. In *Village Voice* (16 January 1990), p. 74.

24. B. Bragg (1990) 'On the Road', *New Statesman and Society* (22 June), p. 46.

25. V. Havel (1989) *Letters to Olga* (London, Faber), pp. 149, 167.

26. P. Wicke (1990) *Rock Music: Culture Aesthetics and Sociology* (Cambridge University Press), p. 182.

27. J. Škvorecký (1980) *The Bass Saxophone* (London, Picador), p. 16.

28. G. Bell (1988) *Australian Jazzman* (Sydney, Child & Associates), p. 89

29. Ryback (1990), pp. 37–8.

30. B. Johnson (1995) 'Australian Jazz in Post-War Europe – A Case Study in Musical Displacement', *Perfect Beat*, vol. 2, no. 3 (July), p. 54.

31. A. Szemere (1983). 'Some Institutional Aspects of Pop and Rock in Hungary', in R. Middleton and D. Horn (eds) *Popular Music: 3* (Cambridge University Press), p. 122.

32. J. Škvorecký (1980) pp. 10–11.

33. J. Škvorecký (1984) 'Hipness at Noon', *The New Republic* (17 December).

34. V. Havel (1990) *Disturbing the Peace* (London, Faber), pp. 42–3.

35. Ryback (1990), pp. 25, 38.

36. A. Barber-Kersovan (1994) 'What is "Slovenian" in Slovenian Rock Music?', in Opekar (1994), p. 30.

37. P. Berman (1990) 'Stars, Stripes, and Czechs: World Revolution and the American Idea', *Village Voice* (20 November), p. 48.

38. Ryback (1990), pp. 181ff.

39. A. Natys and C. Kazor (1990) 'Ils ont 20 Ans à Prague', *Photo*, Paris, no. 269 (February), p. 56 (author's translation).
40. I. Jirouš (1983) 'Underground Culture', *Index On Censorship*, vol. 3, p. 32.
41. A. Troitsky (1987) *Back in the USSR: The True Story of Rock in Russia* (London, Virgin Books), p. 22.
42. A. Opekar (1994a) 'Towards the History of Czech Rock Music: Turtle – The First LP by a Czech Rock Group', in Opekar (1994) p. 70.
43. Ramet (1994), p. 3
44. Opekar (1994), p. 66.
45. *Ibid.* pp. 69, 71.
46. Ryback (1990), pp. 57, 67, 76, 77, 199.
47. Ramet (1994), p. 65.
48. A. Renahan (1995) 'Czechs Face the Music', *Prague Post* (14–20 June), p. 11a.
49. Jirouš (1983), p. 32.
50. Ryback (1990), pp. 76–7.
51. Jirouš (1983), p. 33.
52. *Ibid.*, p. 34.
53. M. Machovec (1992) 'Introduction', in *Yazzyk Magazine* (summer), p. 17.
54. V. Brabenec (1983) 'Heroes or Madmen?', *Index on Censorship*, vol. 1, pp. 31–2.
55. P. Wilson (1978) Liner Notes, Plastic People of the Universe Boxed Set, Globus International, 1992.
56. Unattributed (1974) Liner Notes, *Egon Bondy's Lonely Hearts Club Banned*, London.
57. Wicke (1991), p. 2.
58. Havel (1990), p. 126.
59. In Berman (1990), pp. 49, 170.
60. L. Anthony (1994) 'Prague's Rock Underground', *i-D*, no. 129 (June), p. 82.
61. R. Walls (1991) 'Půlnoc: Dissidents Just Wanna have Fun!', *InMusic* (February–March), p. 7.
62 E. Willis (1990) 'And Then?', *Village Voice* (3 July), p. 74.
63. Walls (1991), p. 7.
64. V. Havel, Liner Notes, Půlnoc, *City of Hysteria*, Arista, 1991.
65. M. Miles (1991) 'Prague Rock', *Village Voice* (17 December), p. 84.
66. R. Christgau (1991) 'Albums', *Village Voice* (17 December).
67. A. Opekar and J. Vicek (eds) (1989) *Excentrici v přízemí* (Prague, Impuls).
68. W. Marchlewski (1992), 'Modernity and Tradition: Americanisation and Tradition in Polish Popular Music', unpublished paper.
69. S. Frith (1989) 'Propaganda Pop', *Village Voice* (17 January), p. 77.
70. V. Balogh (1990) 'Power to the People: A Prague Diary', *i-D*, no. 82 (July), p. 51.
71. *Ibid.*, p. 49.
72. A. Casey (1984) 'Jailhouse Rock!' *Sun-Herald*, Sydney (26 August).
73. Ryback (1990), p. 200.
74. *Ibid.*, p. 202.
75. P. Bergmann (1991) 'Scene report: Czechoslovakia', *Maximum Rocknroll*, no. 96 (May).
76. Frith (1989), p. 77.

77. In *New Musical Express* (30 April 1994), p. 5.
78. L. Anthony (1994), p. 82.
79. S. Reynolds (1990) *Blissed Out: The Raptures of Rock* (London, Serpent's Tail), p. 127.
80. Anthony (1994), p. 82.
81. C. Gant (1994), 'Prague: Slacker City', *The Face*, no. 70 (July), p. 89.
82. *Ibid.*, p. 92.
83. P. Sweeney (1971) *The Virgin Directory of World Music* (London, Virgin Books), p. 109.
84. Ramet (1994), p. 67.
85. P. Dorůžka (1994) 'World Music: Subjective View from Prague', in Opekar (1994) p. 54.
86. V. Kurkela (1994), p. 54.
87. P. Brophy (1987) 'Avant-garde Rock: History in the Making', in M. Breen (ed.) *Missing in Action: Australian Popular Music* (Melbourne, Verbal Graphics Pty), p. 40.
88. A. Troitsky (1989), p. 6.
89. I. Klíma (1994) 'Progress in Prague', *Granta*, no. 47 (spring), p. 250.
90. *Ibid.* , p. 255.

Discography

Graeme Bell's Dixieland Jazz Band, *Czechoslovak Journey 1947*, Swaggie, 1982.
Babalet, *Kytkový Reggae*, Popron, 1994.
Iva Bittová, *Dunaj*, Panton, 1989.
Iva Bittová and Pavel Fajt, *Bittova and Fajt*, Panton, 1991.
DG307 (*1973–5*), Globus International, 1990.
—*Uměle Ochuceno/Artificially Flavoured*, Ujezd, 1992.
Dirty Pictures, *Escape from Sloppy Lake*, Bengal Records/Panton, 1993.
Ecstasy of Saint Theresa, *Sussurate*, Reflex Records, 1992.
—*Free-D (Original Soundtrack)*, Aion/Free Records, 1994.
Fiction, *Fiction*, Popron, 1994.
Garáz, *The Best of Garáz*, Globus International, 1990.
I Kidnaped (*sic*) a Plane, *I Kidnaped a Plane*, Slovart, 1991.
JAR, *Frtka*, Monitor, 1992.
—*Mydli-to!*, BMG/Ariola, 1994.
Laura a její tygři, *Best of Laura a její tigři*, Bonton, 1994.
Manželé, *Manželé*, Bonton, 1991.
Marta Kubisová, *Songy a Balady*, Supraphon, 1990.
MCH Band, *Es Reut Mich F . . .*, Globus International, 1990.
Ocean, *Pyramida Snu*, Opus, 1991.
Olympic, *Zelva*, Supraphon, 1989.
—*Kdyz Ti Sviti Zelena*, Supraphon, 1989.
Orlík, *Demise!*, Monitor, 1991.
The Plastic People of the Universe, Boxed Set, Globus International, 1992:
—*Francovka*, 1975–9.
—*Eliásuv Ohen* (Fire of Elias), 1972–4.
—*Egon Bondy's Lonely Hearts Club Banned*, London, Invisible Record, SCOPA,

    1978.
—*Passion Play*, Bozi Mlyn Productions, Station 'L', Toronto, 1978.
—*Slavná Nemesis*, (Famous Nemesis), 1979.
—*Leading Horses*, 1981.
—*Hovezí Porázka* (Slaughtered Cattle), 1983–4.
—*Midnight Mouse*, 1984.
—*Live 1992, Bez Ohnu Je Underground* (Straight from the Underground), Globus
    International, 1992.
Plexis, *White Killer*, Reflex, 1992.
Pravda, *Lidé Bdete!* (People Arise), Alexim, 1991.
Pražský Výběr, *Live – Adieu CA*, Art Production K, 1991.
Půlnoc, *Půlnoc*, Globus International, 1991.
—*City of Hysteria*, Arista, 1991.
Stromboli, *Shutdown*, Panton, 1990.
Tři Sestry, *Alkac je nejvetsi kocour* (Alcohol is the Best Tomcat), Reflex, 1991.
—*Svédská Trojka* (Three Swedes), Monitor, 1993.
Various, *Dej Mi Víc . . . Olympic* (More Action from Olympic), Monitor, 1992.
—*Live at the Knitting Factory*, Volume 4, A&M, 1990.
—*Rebelie: Punk 'n' Oi!* Monitor, 1990.
—*Rebelie II: Hardcore*, Monitor, 1991.
—*Techno-Rap-Dance*, Monitor, 1993.
YoYo Band, *Lehkou Chůzí* (Strolling), Monitor, 1992.

4

Questions of Style: The Italian Posses and their Social Contexts

Crossovers, novelties and parodies

In August 1989 *New Musical Express* writer Paolo Hewitt announced the arrival of Italian House music on the Anglo-American dance music scene with this caution: 'If our view of European music has been conditioned in the past by a stream of novelty singles and crass Euro disco workouts then it is time to think again.' Hewitt claimed that Italo House, as it became labelled, was more substantial than the gimmicky and pornographic frivolity of Belgian New Beat, which had briefly entertained English dance music enthusiasts in 1988, and was a fortuitous answer to a slump in the 'phenomenally quick turnover of musical styles dance music generates' which had DJs 'anxiously looking around for the "Next Big Thing"'. It also seemed to offer an escape from Anglo-American ethical and copyright dilemmas of digital sampling in offering 'quality dance music, fresh in its simplicity and almost nescient of its roots. ... There is very little debate about the ethics of sampling or whether white boys can play the blues.'[1] The skills of Italian DJ crews Black Box, the DFC Crew and Gino Latino with their rootless rearrangements of American rhythm and blues samples over house music beats were gratefully accepted as a new dance music phenomenon which offered a suitable substitute for what was perceived as an absence of new ideas in the British market, but its launching in the UK also acknowledged the probability of its rapid obsolescence.

Primarily Italo House was accepted in the UK because there seemed to be nothing recognizably Italian about it, despite its origins in Ital Disco, as house music as a genre relies to a considerable extent on erasing origins. The screeching voice of 1970s American disco singer Loleatta Holloway in Black Box's hit 'Ride on Time', which was the highest-selling single in Britain in 1989 – the first Italian 'song' to have such international success since Domenico Modugno's 'Volare' in the 1950s – became emblematic of the Italo House sound. But neither 'Ride on Time'

nor Black Box's follow-up single, 'Everybody Everybody', which topped
US dance charts in 1990, had any recognizable Italian features. Nor did
any other examples of Italo House, despite DJ Andrea Gemelotto's
claims that examples of Italo House such as the DFC Crew's 'Sueno
Latino' had distinctive keyboard motifs and a way of organizing samples
which expressed a 'kind of melodic sound which is typically Italian'.[2] In
the case of 'Ride on Time', Hollaway demanded instant compensation
from Black Box for their uncredited sampling of her vocals, and, as Ross
Harley has pointed out, Black Box were as surprised as she was to
discover the identity of their anonymous vocalist, since they had simply
sampled her voice from an unlabelled bootleg album called 'DJs
Essentials Inc.'.[3] As Simon Reynolds has indicated, deracination and
anonymity are endemic to house music: 'It's difficult to imagine a genre
more place-less or hostile to an infusion of ethnicity. Although it comes
from a place (Chicago) it does not draw anything from its environment.
House departs from the old organic language of music – roots, cross-
pollination, hybridisation.'[4] Writing before the Italo House phenomenon
had occurred, Reynolds concluded that the popularity of house music in
the UK proved the irrelevance of questions of nationality and location in
pop music, and the advent of Italo House merely provided support for his
argument. A displacement and loss of identity often perceived as
postmodern was also a feature of house music. As Harley has indicated,
the over-hyped Italo House phenomenon was largely the work of a small
number of Milan-based producers and remixers like the Groove Groove
Melody production team who operated under more than a dozen
different English names, such as Black Box, Starlight Sensation and the
Mixmaster, and sampled mainly 1970s US soul recording artists singing
in English. The Mixmaster's 'Grand Piano', for example, involved
copyright negotiations with nine US and UK record companies and
included samples of Joe Tex, Coldcut, Tyree and Loleatta Holloway.[5]
But, according to the Italian sociologist Felice Liperi's rather rhetorical
interpretation, the success of Italo House as an international dance music
label was largely due to a discovery of the importance of marketing in a
musical genre that relied on its 'anonymous and indefinable form':

> The discovery of the commercial viability of a musical product that was 'made
> in Italy' was paradoxically a form of liberation from the cultural conformity of
> the terrible decade of the 1980s, because suddenly the creative and innovative
> elements inherent in consumer products were discovered. ... The protagonists
> of Italian rock music had never considered the idea of success in these terms. In
> the past they had attempted simply to present their musical products as they
> were, without changing a comma. The techno-dance scene completely
> overturned this logic: the emphasis was on imitation and conformity as a
> means of communication and making money. While these 'vulgar' objectives
> were being achieved, a new generation was equipping itself for the use and
> conquest of the means of production of ... success.[6]

This tendency toward anonymity and consumerist reproducibility also characterizes Italian acid jazz, if the 1993 compilation *Totally Wired Italia Vibrazioni* is any indication. Produced in Milan by Fred Ventura and Stefano Comazzi, four of the nine tracks on this compilation feature the two producers and others under the names Nu Perspective (on two tracks, called 'Jazzitivity' and 'Hip Hop Beat'), Groove Instinct and Basic Hip, while Enrico Colombo also appears under two different sobriquets, Next Generation and Deep Code. One track, by Straight Beat, is called 'Over and Over' and consists of a female voice singing the title repeatedly over repetitive dance beats. The album conveys an overwhelming impression of totally characterless, anonymous and mechanical dance muzak constructed by numbers, which could have been produced anywhere and sounds like it comes from nowhere. In musical terms, Italo House and acid jazz DJs and producers do not express anything remotely identifiable as Italian, functioning as what Harley described as 'poor soul imitators, despite emerging as a force to be reckoned with on the international dance floors'.[7]

The exponents of Italo House were distinguished mostly by the fact that they mixed records faster than their British counterparts, letting a record play for little more than a minute before mixing in another one, reflecting a widespread restlessness and impatience echoed in Italian pop music listening practices. Hewitt remarked on Gino Latino's habit of rapping constantly over the records he played, in a non-stop stream of verbal diarrhoea also regularly to be found issuing from many of the disco, pop and rock music disc jockeys on an estimated four thousand private radio stations throughout Italy.[8]

In a special 'International Spotlight' feature on the Italian popular music industry in 1992, the US music industry magazine *Billboard* portrayed an industry where a strong local revival appeared to be taking place. An economic analysis showed an industry hard-hit by CD and cassette piracy, which cost more than an estimated $80 million a year. (A survey published in the *European* in June 1995 placed Italy eighth in the world's top ten CD and cassette piracy territories, and third in Europe, behind Russia and Poland, with more than 35 per cent of album sales coming from pirated products.[9]) Piracy is encouraged by the high price of CDs, which retail for up to 35,000 lire (about £14), and cassettes, which cost up to 22,000 lire (about £9). *Billboard* also reported that sales of local Italian recording artists for 1991 accounted for 46 per cent of the national market, international artists for 45.4 per cent and classical music for 8.6 per cent, with figures for the first quarter of 1992 rising to 51 per cent for local artists.[10]

Three separate articles by David Stanfield in *Billboard* in 1992 profiled Italian dance music as 'rul[ing] the international dance floors with imported talent', the rise of dialect bands and a 'roots recovery' as a reflection of a decline in interest for Anglo-American music and a preference for local music, and a mainstream pop market struggling for international recognition of Italian performers. Italy's dance and techno music sector was portrayed as relying exclusively on vocal talent from the USA or UK in order to facilitate exportation to those countries, a curious international exchange economy relying on seemingly anonymous Italian mixers. As one recording executive stated, international success was a prerequisite to domestic success in dance music, which relied on disguising a record's Italian origins: 'There's no local interest until a release is presented as an import. Then they fall on their knees to take it.'[11]

The Naples-based Flying Records, one of Italy's most prominent international dance labels, was portrayed in *Billboard* as relying heavily on its priority artist Digital Boy, described as 'one of the few Italian techno artists who can perform in concert'.[12] Digital Boy is Luca Pretolesi, a composer, producer and mixer based in Melazzo, in the region of Alessio, near the popular song capital San Remo in the far north-west of Italy. His 1993 album, *Digital Beat by Digital Boy*, was a series of remixes of tracks by Italian composers disguised under generic names like the Moab (whose 'Didjeridu Trance' features the Australian Aboriginal instrument along with an Arab-sounding vocal and monotonous dance beats), New York, the End, and POW (a military beat dance version of the 'River Kwai March (Whistle Song)'). Only one composition was by Digital Boy himself, a trance-like electronic drone over a repetitive throbbing pulse, and the album's overall impression is of an almost mind-numbing banality and monotony. His 1995 *Ten Steps to the Rise*, recorded on his own label, D-Boy Records, features all his own compositions, a slight acid jazz influence, English lyrics by Ronnie Lee, and raps by Ronny Money, an African-American also featured on the previous album. Other guests include Acid Smurf (a disco singer who repeats the words 'Cross it Over' ad nauseam), Asia (credited with 'females [sic] vocals and soul vibrations') and M. D. Cool (another US rapper). Pretolesi's father also plays acid rock guitar on one track, and although *Ten Steps to the Rise* is stylistically more consistent than the previous Digital Boy album, with a wider range of electronic and studio effects, the portentous banality of Ronny Money's and M. D. Cool's raps, most of which simply promote Digital Boy, and the general monotony of the music, make it something of an ordeal for the listener. (In the case of a track called 'Mental Attack', which repeats the phrase 'See ya muthafucka' over particularly brutal beats, it becomes almost physically painful.) As Acid Smurf spells out repetitively, the album's overwhelming US flavour is aimed at a crossover into the US market, but it is difficult to regard it as anything but an unconscious parody of US and UK rap, acid jazz, trance and techno posturings.

In another *Billboard* profile of Italy in July 1995, correspondent Mark Dezzani reported a music industry 'rising above political and economic uncertainty' with a 5 per cent growth rate in 1994 (offset by 4 per cent inflation) and a 'deep talent pool and thriving dance scene strengthening the business'. The fall of the Berlusconi government at the end of 1994 was seen as forcing a 'change from a system of comfortable, informal cartels to the roller-coaster of free market competition', portraying the Italian music industry almost in the same economic terms as post-Communist Eastern Europe. A major review of traditional marketing practices was reported to be in progress, after the major labels in Italy (Polydor, Virgin–EMI, RCA, CGD/East West, Ricordi/BMG, Sony and MCA) recorded a poor year for local artists in 1994, although the annual San Remo Song Festival, traditionally a major source of revenue for the major labels, had record audiences in 1995. Despite this apparent slump, mainstream recording artist Laura Pausini, a former San Remo winner, received the World Music Award in Monte Carlo in 1994 for her album *Solitudine*, which sold four million copies, the highest of any Italian singer. The continuing success of the Italian dance music scene was again portrayed as dominated by independent record companies such as Flying Records, described as 'the smallest major and the biggest independent' by its managing director Angelo Tardio, while independent rap and dance label Vox Pop was also featured in the article as an example of the strength of local niche markets.[13]

The *NME*'s perception of Italian pop music as 'novelty singles' and 'crass disco' reflects predominant perceptions of Italian popular music in the UK and the English-speaking world. Historically, Italian popular music has never fared well in the international arena, and crossover hits have been few and far between. Ever since Modugno's (and Dean Martin's) international success with 'Volare' – which Franco Fabbri has described as 'the last great celebration of the traditional song, a modern version of "O sole mio" '[14] – commercial success outside Italy for Italian recording artists has usually been confined to a novelty or curiosity context, often attached to traditional Italian musical stereotypes. The blues-rock star Zucchero's brief international crossover success in the early 1990s relied on him composing and singing mostly in English, particularly when he was assisted by Eric Clapton on guitar, and the support of London Records in the UK, who 'adopted him as one of its own'.[15] His collaborative song 'Miserere' relied heavily on the pop success of Luciano Pavarotti, who himself is a case of Italian opera crossing over into pop charts and sports stadiums, reinscribing 'O sole mio' as an Italian tourist cliché in the process. Often parody is involved in the novelty value of Italian pop: 'Pippero', a bad-taste disco pastiche in which members of the Bulgarian female folk group le Mystére des Voix Bulgares are forced to sing nonsensical disco music lyrics in Italian, was a minor crossover hit in the English-speaking world in 1992. It was created by the Frank Zappa-influenced Milanese cabaret group Elio e le Storie Tese, who work in a burlesque idiom of self-consciously banal, parodic pop gimmickry and have gained a cult following in Italy.

Umberto Fiori has noted that a strong sense of parody is a recurrent feature in Italian popular music, as in the case of Renato Carosone's 1960s satirical Neapolitan cabaret-style parodies of American rock songs and Italian tear-jerking ballads. This element of parody often became unconscious in Italian rock music in the 1970s:

> The way in which they did this was to play, as it were, in inverted commas. As in a cabaret number, rock was displayed rather than played ... parody – that is to say that relation between words and music characteristically highly mediated – together with intertextuality and transcodification, seems inevitable in a music of such mixed origins, and in fact it was mainly in these terms that the aesthetic problems presented themselves to the Italian musicians who wanted to play rock.[16]

Fiori extends this argument to all European rock music, and indeed all popular music in general. According to Franco Fabbri's interpretation – or parody? – of Fiori, 'all popular song is based, more or less consciously, on parody: that is, parody intended as the reproposal, in a different context, and in a simplified form together with a sung text, of material and musical styles elaborated elsewhere'.[17] While this implies that the roots and origins of popular music are always 'elsewhere', and that local or even national popular music has disappeared, it also suggests the possibility that reproposals of foreign musical styles can still express local cultural practices and concerns, as has often been the case in Italian popular music.

Stansfield's *Billboard* profile also suggests that mainstream Italian pop music has tended to rely on an almost parodic exaggeration of stereotyped, generic 'Latin looks' and romantic qualities for promotion outside Italy. This has made it difficult for Italian popular music to be taken seriously abroad, as a rather embittered promotions director of Dischi Ricordi, Maurizio Miretti, admits:

> Italy is a country where ridiculous things happen even at the government level, and I'm afraid that other territories don't take us seriously. We're stereotyped as a loud and noisy nation of killers because of the Mafia and Camorra ... we have large numbers of greatly talented artists who should be able to compete on the European market. But there are few actual prospects because we as a nation lack credibility and respect.[18]

Nonetheless, Eros Ramazzotti managed to sell 3.2 million copies of his 1990 album *In ogni senso* (In any sense) worldwide, and achieve the status of an international superstar, while Zucchero and the female rock singer Gianna Nannini have also achieved significant sales outside Italy, although less notably in the English-speaking world. But *Billboard* noted that mainstream Italian pop had lost ground domestically in the 1990s, as had Anglo-Saxon influences, in favour of more 'roots'-based, local forms of music which employ local dialect, regional traditions and Mediterranean ethnic musical influences. Stansfield signals this 'roots revival' with the release in 1992 of a new album, *Medina*, after a ten-year absence by the dialect-based Neapolitan folk group Nuova Compagnia Di Canto Popolare, who had been at the forefront of an often politically oppositional movement of locally based Italian singer-songwriters and musicians in the 1970s.[19] The Nuova Compagnia, together with *cantautori* (singer-songwriters) of the 1970s like Francesco de Gregori, Lucio Dalla, Paolo Conte, Francesco Guccini, Pino Daniele (who sings in Neapolitan dialect) and Fabrizio De Andre (who sings in Genovese and other dialects) along with a number of others, had instituted a distinctively national form of locally directed, politically conscious music which became popular amongst the Italian left. Some of these *cantautori* have survived a pop crossover into the 1990s, with Dalla becoming a mainstream pop figure, occasionally teaming up with Pavarotti, and De Gregori also moving into the pop genre of *musica leggera* (literally 'light music', and the title of one of his albums). Daniele topped the charts in 1995 with his album of lightweight self-penned Neapolitan love songs, *Non calpestare i fiori nel deserto* (Don't trample on the flowers in the desert), which includes a rap track, 'Stress', involving chart-topping pop-rapper Jovanotti, while De Andre's son, Luca, emerged as a pop star in the 1990s.

Like Italian cinema, Italian popular music suffered a severe recession in the 1980s. In his article 'Rock music and politics in Italy', Fiori uses the example of an open-air concert in Tirrenia in the province of Pisa by Genesis, promoted in the summer of 1982 by the Italian Communist Party (PCI) as part of its annual Feste dell'Unita, to illustrate the depoliticizing of the consumption and production of rock music in Italy, and the institutionalization of the oppositional, dissenting aspects of rock music that had previously been so potent throughout the 1970s. To Fiori, the Genesis concert represented

> an unmistakable step forward in the slow process of the 'normalisation' of the relationship between rock and politics in Italy. Explosive material until a few years before, rock music in the 1980s seems to have returned to being a commodity like any other, even in Italy. The songs are once again simply songs, the public is the public. The musicians are only interested in their work, and the organizers make their expected profits. If they happen to be a political party, so much the better: they can also profit in terms of public image and perhaps even votes. ... Italy now learnt how to institutionalise deviation and transgression. An 'acceptable' gap was re-established between fiction and reality, desire and action, and music and political practice.[20]

Exactly a decade later, while the Feste dell'Unita, now run by the 'de-Stalinised' PDS (Partito Democratico della Sinistra), had moved on to promoting concerts by touring British and American heavy metal groups, the summer of 1992 in Italy signalled the emergence of the distinctively local, repoliticized and decentralized 'Italian posses', a term appropriated from Jamaican reggae sound systems. This new form of 'explosive material' constituted a largely home-grown movement of regionally based Italian rap, ragga and ska musicians and performers. It is arguably one of the most important phenomena in the ongoing history of the often vexed relationship between music, politics and the appropriation of US and other foreign influences in Italian popular music. The Italian posses signalled a renewal of oppositional, transgressive and even deviant political practices in Italian popular music and youth culture which again closed gaps between fiction and reality, desire and action. In its sincere and direct attention towards local political and social problems, its creation of a distinctive youth subculture, and its recourse to dialect and Mediterranean folk music sources, Italian hip hop echoed the attempts to create a 'national popular culture' (to use Gramsci's often-quoted term) by some Italian rock groups like PFM and Area in the 1970s. If, as Zygmunt Baranski has suggested, Italian distinctions between popular and mass culture originated in 'the need to differentiate between what was felt to be popular and "genuinely" indigenous, and what was seen as popular but "foreign", or rather "transatlantic"',[21] Italian hip hop could be said to have originated in the latter but progressed towards the former. Borrowing the term *rispetto* (respect) from Jamaican reggae, it used the imported US and Afro-Caribbean musical styles of mixing, scratching, rapping and graffiti to express the posses' regionally indigenous political and cultural concerns.

The hip hop nation takes Cisternino

By 1992, Italian hip hop had become a resolutely local manifestation, with each posse tending to identify itself strongly in terms of its city of origin, but linking up on a more national network through festivals and rap music events, where the strongly regional and local concerns of most of the posses were respected and shared. One example of this local and national link-up occurred in Cisternino, a small, relatively remote village in Apulia roughly half-way between Bari and Brindisi, in the traditionally underprivileged, neglected 'peasant south' of Italy. Usually overlooked by tourists intent on getting down to Brindisi and over to Greece, its principal attraction is the thousands of medieval beehive-shaped stone dome houses called *trulli* which dot the flat countryside of the Valle d'Itria around it and are concentrated in the nearby town of Alberobello. The *trulli* were originally occupied by *contadini* (peasants), many of whom have sold up to *stranieri* (foreigners) and moved into town. Work is hard to find in the area, and the youth of the town have been unwilling and disinclined to continue the traditions of the *contadini*, so unemployment is high, along with emigration to the industrial north of Italy, or Switzerland

and Germany. As Apulian rapper Papa Ricky's self-titled 1995 debut album begins:

> The south is an ancient, wise and generous land
> Where bread tastes like bread and oranges are abundant
> But the people's smiles hide the bitter tears
> Of those who are stuck in the shit and those forced to emigrate[22]

Like a lot of small towns in the south of Italy, there is a lot of hanging around on streets by young and old, and little or nothing in the way of entertainment. Not a great deal happens in Cisternino, except in the summer, when hordes of holidaymakers swarm down from the north to the beaches. That is its attraction: I ended up living there for a year in 1977, a watershed year of Italian student protest and radical left activity, and I go back there periodically to observe how slowly it changes.

My last visit, in the summer of 1992, coincided with the emergence of the Italian posses. To my surprise, I had an opportunity to witness the phenomenon at close range in Cisternino. Every summer the local variation of the Festa dell'Unita, the Alter Festa, is organized by the local branch of ARCI, the cultural wing of the former Communist Party. In 1992 this featured an evening of jazz with trumpet maestro Enrico Rava, 'New Acustic Shag Music' (*sic*) with Miro, a London group (who in the event failed to turn up), 'Psychobilly Crossover' with the Rome-based group Cyclone and 'Post Punk Raggamuffin' with the French group Raymonde et les Blancs Becs. The Circolo ARCI of Cisternino was not afraid to mix and mess with its musical genres and import cultures; it was a far cry both geographically and musically from the Rifondazione Communista (Communist Refoundation) festival I later went to in Venice, which featured a local rock group with an undistinguished African vocalist along with one of the stalwarts of the long and honourable postwar tradition of Italian political song, Ivan della Mea, performing his mostly Marxist material from the 1960s and 1970s.

The Cisternino festival also had a rap night, and the 'buzz' it gave off was immediate and local. The line-up featured the nationally celebrated Italian posse Isola Posse All Stars, featuring Papa Ricky, who is from Lecce, capital of the nearby Salento region, although based in Bologna. Papa Ricky was one of the protagonists of the Italian hip hop scene, having started his musical career in a psychobilly band in Lecce, and then switched to reggae with the Ganja Prophets in Bologna, singing in a combination of Italian and Salento dialect, and absorbing the influence of English dub poet Linton Kwesi Johnson and bhangramuffin rapper Apache Indian. The Isola Posse had a hit in 1992 with 'Stop al panico' (Stop the Panic), a hard-core rap with ragga inflections about the murder of three *carabinieri* in Bologna. The video clip of the song, which was featured regularly on the national music channel Videomusic, uses newspaper headlines and newsreel footage about mafia and racket killings together with street scenes in which the group rap, American gangsta-style, and crowd scenes which emphasize a community orientation. The prominent Lecce-based Salento Posse was also in the Cisternino line-up, along with lesser-known local formations like the Bari-based Suono Mudu and Zona 45, both of whom featured female rappers, something of a rarity on the Italian scene, and Rappers Terronist (a play on 'terrorist' and *terrone* (peasant), a deprecating expression for southern Italians) from Brindisi. The festival programme notes to the rap night describe the national posse phenomenon with a local inflection in telegraphic bursts of bold print, telling a familiar story of urgency, militancy and opposition in a polemical rhetoric reminiscent of the 1970s:

> There are lots of posses all over Italy and they're growing all the time: in Rome, Bologna, Milan, but also in Messina, Iglesias, Teramo, Cosenza, Naples, Lecce. Some make fleeting appearances at a festival at some social centre, others are still getting their acts together: *but all of them are trying to re-invent a language of radical politics from scratch.* What has happened is very different from the explosion of punk and rock groups in the early 80s: *rap doesn't care about clubs, apprenticeships or contests for beginners: it is and has always been the sound of the social centres, of festivals in remote provincial towns, of programmes on tiny private radio stations.*
>
> *It is a public, collective, noisy language of social commitment, which needs to unravel itself in real time, in full view of everyone.*
>
> Rap in Italian, or (better still) in dialect: a fascination for the most extreme language of Afro-American culture has transformed itself into a powerful medium through which people's eyes can be opened to our own situation. It is an important choice of activity, because it has been developed in the face of the immense superficiality that almost the entire range of Italian mass media has displayed towards the rap phenomenon for years.
>
> In a time of zombie-like adulation of the Far West, Italian rap is not holding back. It is telling the story of an authoritarian country which is cracking down and splitting up in two, in four, in eight: Mafia, evictions from social centres, drug laws, leagues, racism, cartels, Gladio, corruption, state secrets and mysteries.
>
> *It does this the only way it can: exaggerating, provoking, fighting. Jumping straight to conclusions: before someone else makes them for everyone.*[23]

The overwhelming impression of the Cisternino rap night was of a musical *comizio* (rally), generating productive, creative chaos made up of a multiplicity of voices interrupting the flow of music to address the audience, often at the same time, about a variety of different but mostly political subjects, including the mafia, the increase of racketeering in the region, the historical neglect of southern Italy by the government, marijuana legislation and corruption in the hospital and health system. Despite a poor sound system, the unmistakable beats and rhythms of rap and ragga came through strongly. Often the stage was occupied by a bewilderingly large number of performers, all clamouring to be heard, but the sense of collective urgency was evident, along with the display of Afro-American rap and Jamaican ragga styles in both music and dress. This was particularly evident with the Isola Posse All Stars, who were the most popular of the groups performing, using a great deal of call and response with the audience. (Examples were 'Five hundred years of exploitation!' and 'How many bastards are there? – Too many!'.) The Isola Posse also borrowed the distinctive ragga bass line from the Salento-based Sud Sound System's single 'Fuecu' (Fire), confirming the solidarity that exists among the local posse. Something was happening, even in Cisternino, where nothing much ever seemed to happen. To confirm this Sud Sound System, who call their Salento dialect reggae 'tarantamuffin' to connect it with the origins of the tarantella, a dance based on the panicked reactions of a woman bitten by a tarantula spider, turned up for a gig a couple of weeks later in the nearby beach resort of Rosamarina.

In 1994 *Salento Showcase*, an album featuring the southern Italian sounds of thirteen Apulian hip hop posses and rappers, was released by Ritmo Vitale records, based in Lecce, which took its name from the chorus of Sud Sound System's 'Fuecu'. Along with prominent figures like the Salento Posse, who incorporate the traditional southern Italian sounds of a piano accordion into their ragga-style dialect rap, Sud Sound System's 'international reggae' and Nandu Popu's freestyle ragga toasting were female rappers Lady Ninja, Marilena and Mad Sabrina and others, in a collective representation of the ragga-rap of this southern Italian region. Despite the compilation's rather homogenized, minimalist and low-fi, percussion and bass-dominated sound production, local storytelling styles and musical motifs are unmistakably present amongst the loping ragga rhythms, giving the album a distinctive Salento flavour. One strong theme uniting the album, besides the fact that all tracks are credited to the same composer, A. Petrarchi, and selected by DJ War of Sud Sound System, is references to fire and the heat of the sun – a feature which also aligns Italian ragga with its Jamaican counterpart. This connection with the sun is acknowledged by Italy's longest-standing reggae group, Africa Unite, who originated near Turin in 1985, and whose 1995 album is entitled *Un sole che brucia* (A burning sun):

> Italy has a heritage of popular music, and this has had a positive influence on [Italian] reggae groups, along with an awareness of belonging to a growing musical scene. ... Reggae is popular music that is more simple and melodic than rock. It originated in Jamaica but has had a smooth passage into Italy. The sun burns in the south of Italy the same as it does in Jamaica ... A burning sun is intended as the symbol of the strength of music, and its power to communicate.[24]

The emergence of a distinctive southern Italian ragga-rap scene was acknowledged by the Academy Award-winning Italian film maker

Gabriele Salvatores in his 1993 film *Sud* (South), which used Papa Ricky's ragga version of 'O sole mio' – which he interprets as 'not just a song for Southern Italians, since the sun heats up all the land' – along with cuts by Nando Popu and the Neapolitan rappers Possessione, Bisca and 99 Posse on its soundtrack.

Italian rap, the *centri sociali* and a culture of antagonism

The speed with which the Italian posses became a social and musical phenomenon is notable. In an article in the Italian rock music magazine *L'Urlo* (The Cry), Fabio De Luca notes that the first Italian hip hop festival took place in Padua in June 1991, but between then and the summer of 1992 there had been a rapid shift from the largely English-language efforts of 'a first/second generation ... born from the encounter between Italian DJs and native-speaking (of English, obviously) rappers' – such as Power MCs, Radical Stuff, MC Fresh, South Force, Sergio Messina, Casino Royale, etc. – to a 'third generation' of Italian-language posses.[25] As Ernesto Assante has commented, many of this third generation of posses began to use regional dialects, after exploring the limitation of US rap derivations:

> rap is spoken language par excellence, and as long as [Italian] rappers tried to adapt Italian to the stylemes of Afro-American hip hop, the results they achieved were ridiculous. As soon as they made use of the possibilities offered by Italian, dialects, and everyday spoken language, they gave a real shake-up to the lyrics used by the *cantautori*, which were poetic but often remote from everyday life.[26]

A distinctive musical hybridity also emerged among the Italian posses, pushing out the parameters of hip hop, which more often than not became fused with raggamuffin reggae, dance hall and ska influences, leading to the coinage of the term 'rappamuffin' in a 1992 Flying Records compilation of Italian rap and ragga entitled *Italian Posse: Rappamuffin d'Azione*. A whole network of ragga-rap groups stretching from Sicily to Bergamo, who often collaborated in joint concerts and jams in *centri sociali* such as the Leoncavallo in Milan, became established. The principal Italian-language rap groups who had released independent recordings by 1992 were Assalti Frontali (Rome), Articolo 31 (Milan), AK 47 (Rome), Comitato (Milan), Il Generale (Florence), Lion Horse Posse (Milan), 99 Posse (Naples), Nuovi Briganti (Messina) and Possessione (Naples). The more ragga-oriented and ska-inflected groups included Africa Unite (Turin), who in 1992 dropped the 'd' off Africa United, a name based on a track by Bob Marley, and changed the language of their songs from English to Italian, as did the Rome-based rapper Sergio Messina and the Milan-based ragga-rock rappers Casino Royale. Other ragga and ska groups who emerged in 1992, many of whom were associated with the Bologna-based independent record label Century Vox and the Milan-based Vox Pop, included Devastatin' Posse (Turin), Dissociata Posse (Ivrea), Fratelli di Soledad (Turin), Fuckin' Camels' n' Effect (Bologna), Isola Posse All Stars (Bologna), Loschi Dezi and their off-shoots Mau Mau (Turin), OTR (Varese), Strike (Ferrara), Sud Sound System (Salento), and La To.sse (Turin). Rather than reproducing the traditional rivalry between Rome and Milan as cultural capitals, the Italian posses tended to emerge around Turin and Naples, which represented focal points for hip hop scenes in northern and southern Italy respectively. While a number of Neapolitan and southern Italian groups mixed Neapolitan and southern dialects and musical influences with ragga and rap, the Mediterranean migratory patterns from the south of Italy, Africa and the Middle East which converged in Turin also produced a number of ethnic influences in that city's hip hop scene. As Raiss, the vocalist with the Neapolitan ragga group Almamegretta, stated:

> Turin and Naples are the two poles of Italian music in the 1990s: the periphery of the world begins at Naples, which is the port that opens to the South and filters through all its problems. Turin, on the other hand, is the port which opens to the North, but it is also the most Italian city in Italy, the place where the ethnic mixture between races, and between North and South, is most pronounced: it's a kind of laboratory. The Turin groups are the result of those processes: Africa Unite mix music of the South and cultures of the North, and Mau Mau do likewise, as well as having a Senegalese member, Nsongan.[27]

While none of the Italian posses made an impression in the English-speaking world, they represented a diversified 'national popular' musical movement as widespread and important as the protest-inflected *cantautori nuovi* (new singer-songwriters) of the late 1970s. These *cantautori* had risen to prominence during a period of isolation when most English and American rock singers avoided Italy owing to its reputation for violent and disruptive behaviour at rock concerts, and Franco Fabbri has described them as able to strike a chord with their predominantly student, left-wing audiences, and 'fill a gap, maintaining something of the political meeting and integrating it with the rituals of a rock concert'.[28] After this political function of Italian popular music had almost disappeared in the 1980s, the Italian posses emerged as the prevailing soundtrack to the disruptions and dislocations of the 1990s, the era of the right-wing, Berlusconi-driven 'second republic'. This turbulent era was the result of the *mani puliti* (clean hands) judicial investigations of the widespread corruption scandals which began in Milan, referred to as *tangentopoli* (kickback city), the growing success of the fight against the Mafia, and the decimation of the former ruling Christian Democrat party and the Socialist Party owing to corruption. It also saw a resurgence of Fascism, the rise of the northern Italian provincial nationalism of the Lega

Nord (Northern League) and the radical realignment of the various parties of the left.

Most of the politicized Italian hip hop posses came from the community-based origins of the *centri sociali occupati* (occupied social centres), and some, like 99 Posse, Lion Horse Posse, Isola Posse All Stars and others, named themselves after *centri*. (Lion Horse Posse took their name from probably the most celebrated *centro sociale*, the Milan-based Leoncavallo, which was founded in 1972, and closed down in 1994 amid considerable controversy.) The *centri sociali* emerged all over Italy in the mid 1980s, in the wake of the *riflusso* (recession and resignation) of 1970s left-wing militant students and disaffected young people, as semi-illegal, alternative, self-organized activity centres. Self-organized groups occupied and refurbished disused buildings, often in the outer suburbs of the large Italian cities. The centres were run along collective and co-operative lines which were sometimes similar in organization to the defunct Communist Party community centres, the Case del Popolo (literally 'People's Houses'). They developed into underground drop-in centres, youth clubs, drug rehabilitation centres, and even recording studios, cinemas, video and post-industrial art galleries and cyberpunk computer centres for '*hackeraggio*' (hacking) in some cases, as well as providing rehearsal rooms and concert venues for punk rock groups, eventually transforming into hip hop music and graffiti art centres. In some cases there was a direct line of continuity between the politically committed wing of the Italian punk rock scene of the 1980s and the hip hop movement of the 1990s. The Florentine rapper Il Generale, for example, began as a punk rocker, as did Papa Ricky.

A 1992 book about the Italian Posses, *Posse italiane*, lists ninety-three *centri sociali* which have existed in thirty-three Italian cities from the 1980s to 1992. The list includes twenty-six in Rome, thirteen in Milan, five in both Florence and Bologna, three in Naples and two in Turin.[29] It was here that the Italian posses cut their teeth and often their first recordings, although a number of the *centri sociali* were subsequently closed down and cleared out by local councils. In his study of the cultural and political significance of the *centri sociali*, Alba Solaro takes an orthodox left-wing view in regarding their development as sites for the growth of an Italian hip hop movement as a 'post-political' phenomenon:

> In these *centri sociali occupati* there were as many veterans of the political experiences of the previous decade as there were of the younger generation who had hardly been affected by the parabola of the movement, and were generally not interested in militancy and the old ideologies. It was a post-political generation who responded to the collapse of political languages with music.[30]

But it was also a subcultural movement which discovered a new rhetoric of political militancy of its own, using rap music to criticize political corruption, the mafia, homelessness, unemployment, racism, the mass media, the unions, wage restrictions and a whole range of social and political ills which the *posse* attributed to an increasingly visibly corrupt Christian Democrat government. As Luca De Gennaro, host of 'Planet Rock', a radio show on RAI (Radio e televisione italiana), the Italian national radio, and a prominent producer and writer on Italian rap music, stated in 1993:

> Over the past two years, rap has become the real political voice of the young, anti-government population. The roots of this movement can be traced to the anti-government student demonstrations two years ago. As was the case with America, they initially saw rap as the simplest form of musical expression, but Italian hip hop now has its own distinctive styles.[31]

Rap music could even be seen as one of the main cultural catalysts of a political renaissance of oppositional Italian youth movements, and became the accompaniment of a new upsurge of political demonstrations against the Christian Democrat government in the early 1990s, while rappers like Frankie Hi-NRG, the 99 Posse and Fratelli Soledad gave performances in support of the left-wing alliance of *progressisti* in the 1994 elections. Although some rappers, like Speaker Dee Mo' of the Isola Posse All Stars, publicly dissociated themselves from Communism, Paolo Ferrari has identified a 'radical wing' of Italian rappers. This includes Sa Razza, a ragga group from Iglesias, a small inland region of Sardinia, who rap in Sardinian dialect, and Assalti Frontali and AK47, who both emerged from the Rome-based Onda Rossa Posse, one of the earliest Italian groups to use Italian. The name of this group emphasizes the connection between Italian rappers and 1970s left-wing political activity, deriving from an extreme left-wing pirate radio station of the 1970s, which also formed a *centro sociale* in Rome. Onda Rossa Posse, AK47 and Assalti Frontali claim to express the 'collective point of view of the *centri sociali*, and squatters'[32] and refuse to be involved with any recording label. In Ferrari's view, they

> represent a number of things: the courage to rap in Italian, the claim to belong to a history of Italian insurrection, from the resistance of the Communist groups of the 1960s ... to 1977 and the experience of the Autonomia Operaia in Rome. It is not a heritage that is easy to work with, even from within, but their activity has in itself the essence of a magnificent daily challenge. .... *The Commitments* starts with the premise that the Irish are the 'blacks of Europe'; what if Communists were the 'blacks of Italy'?[33]

Liperi concludes his 1993 study of the impact of techno, cyberpunk, splatter and hip hop on Italian youth culture with a rather portentous claim for the significance of Onda Rossa Posse's EP *Batti il tuo tempo* (Beat Your Own Time) and Assalti Frontale's 1991 album *Terra di Nessuno* (No Man's Land), which, he asserts:

immediately emerged as the most advanced example(s) of Italian rap. No other group had previously succeeded in bringing to public attention such a fully developed musical statement or such a coherent militant discourse. With *Terra di Nessuno* we are confronted with an album that synthesizes a phase of our recent political and cultural history. This is not just a result of its technical professionalism, but due to its intrinsic qualities; again the language of rap has proved to be an excellent means of describing and narrating protest and opposition in rhyme. ... It is a major work constructed out of rhyme and 'talk over' in raggamuffin style which completes a phase in the evolution of hip hop in Italy, and signals a landmark in the evolution of the relation between politics and culture in Italy on the threshold of the third millennium.[34]

Although rather rough-edged in their production qualities (both albums are emphatically and defiantly self-produced), the Onda Rossa Posse and Assalti Frontali albums do express a strong degree of anger and militant eloquence in the hard-core style of Public Enemy and NWA, which has rarely been surpassed in Italian rap, although they no doubt have more appeal to the 1968 generation of political militants than to the youth of the 1990s. Employing what Liperi refers to as 'combat rap',[35] Onda Rossa Posse combine hard-line political lyrics with dramatic orchestral samples, thumping bass lines, scratching, a mournful flute solo and a saxophone break embroidering the saxophone refrain from Kid Frost's 'La Raza'. *Batti il tuo tempo*, with its refrain 'batti il tuo tempo per fottere il potere' ('beat your own time and fuck up those in power') is an emotional, but clearly telegraphed, call to action and rebellion against the 'criminal bastards' who represent all forms of political, institutional and mafia-controlled power in Italy. Dropping expletives into their discourse and attacking drug dealers in the style of US gangsta rappers like NWA, sampling national television news reports and police sirens, celebrating the courage of political prisoners and chronicling examples of police violence against civilians, Onda Rossa Posse present an emotive, rhetorical view of a 'fucked up country' riddled with violence, injustice and greed.

Assalti Frontali's album begins with a grinding rock riff as rapper Castro X announces 'a frontal assault ... with another bomb in my hand, ready to explode commonplaces and break down doors', commencing a stream of verbal free association which leads into the album's title track, set in Rome's graffiti-covered Nomentano station, where rapper Militant A reflects on past brushes with the police and the courts, and resolves to keep smiling. '00199' is the postal code of the working class Forte Prenestino district of Rome, but also a graffiti tag for the group's two female rappers, Breezy G and Cheecky P, who express the history of the district in 'signals of colour straight from the heart', to the sounds of rattling spray cans. Subsequent tracks attack businessmen, Vatican officials and industrialists with mobile phones on commuter trains between Rome and Milan, television news, the Northern League, the leader of the PDS, Occhetto (with help from the Lion Horse Posse) and the futile death of an Italian pilot in the Gulf War. The final track, 'Drops of Sun', proclaims that 'music is important, it gives colour to life, the soundtrack of the street beat ... like the graffiti written on a heart by a ray of sun as beautiful as spring'. The album is also distinguished by the participation of an elderly militant Communist, Sante Notarnicola, who contributes a track entitled 'Nostalgia and Memory', looking back over the postwar activities of the Resistance, workers' struggles in the 1950s, student revolts in the 1960s, strikes and the squalor of the working-class districts of Rome, and stigma of being labelled as a 'terrone'. Notarnicola's perspective gives the album a local historical background which links it to what he describes as 'the ever-present red tradition which links generations and their shared journeys, experiences, struggles, feelings and proletarian memory'.[36]

This sense of continuity with an indigenous tradition of oppositional militancy going back to the partisans of the Resistance, which is expressed by the 'combat rap' of Assalti Frontali and others, is also embodied in *Materiale Resistente*, a compilation album by Italian posses and rock groups released in 1995 by the Consorzio Prodotti Indipendenti, a left-wing co-operative. Devised as an alternative celebration of the fiftieth anniversary of the liberation of Italy at the end of the Second World War, this compilation involves eighteen contemporary groups performing radical re-interpretations of Italian partisan songs like 'Bella Ciao', 'I ribelli della montagna', 'The Partisan's Lament' and others. The combination of traditional folk elements like the piano accordion and often radically reworked atonal rock riffs is sometimes jarring, but most of the results are intriguing. Africa Unite contribute one of the few original compositions in a ragga song entitled 'Il partigiano John', which contrasts sharply with the general tenor of the album, while the Torinese posse Mau Mau show that their style of folkloric ragga is more directly linked to the Mediterranean peasant tradition of the partisan songs. The hybrid Italo-Irish group Modena City Ramblers, who sing in both English and Italian and produce a folkloric-punk sound highly reminiscent of Irish group the Pogues, produce a convincing version of 'Bella Ciao', and other groups have varying degrees of success in re-interpreting traditional songs of militancy.

A defining epithet of militant Italian rap is 'antagonistic', indicating a culture of opposition which during the 1980s had lost the means of articulating itself. As Liperi explains:

if, on the one hand, antagonism in Italy has continued to accumulate not only political connotations but also social and territorial ones (such as the renaissance of the *centri sociali*) on the other, it had not succeeded in giving expression to any identifiable culture. The linguistic forms of hip hop culture offered an immediate connection with the world of social opposition because it was the immediate, direct result of it. If rap in its crudest form can be considered as a means of making political speeches [*comiziare*] through music, this is one of the main reasons that it offered the most direct vehicle of expressing anger against corruption, organized crime and social upheaval.[37]

One prominent example of this use of rap as a rhetoric of political opposition was the 1994 tour by the Neapolitan 99 Posse in tandem with their offshoot Bisca, whose often punning discourse represents a form of *rappresaglia* (reprisal) – the title of one of their tracks. Performing nearly sixty concerts over five months at a series of locations between Bergamo, Naples and Sardinia, a selection from Bisca 99 Posse's 'Incredible Opposition Tour' was subsequently released as a live double album. Performing mostly in Neapolitan dialect over a ragga beat with saxophone and rock guitar embellishments, the group dealt with subjects ranging from Naples, 'a city that has been forgotten, exploited, abandoned and despised by everyone except [Fiat boss] Agnelli' (a chant-like song performed with Arab music and a piano accordion), the Gulf War, guaranteed salaries for the self-employed, 'two thousand years of exploitation' of immigrants, illegal employment, unemployment, 'an intelligent bomb', hatred, the 'idiocy' of the mass media and politicians, and a revival of anti-Fascism. Few of Bisca 99 Posse's songs deal with anything other than political subjects, and run the risk of browbeating their audiences to the point of exhaustion, as do some of the other 'combat' rappers, many of whose political subject matter, critical targets and musical frames of reference overlap.

Jovanotti and pop-rap

The strong sense of militancy and antagonism in Italian rap aligned to the *centri sociali* has also had an impact on more mainstream examples of Italian hip hop. The most popular Italian rapper in terms of record sales and chart hits is Jovanotti, whose real name is Lorenzo Cherubini, and who entitled two of his top-selling albums *Lorenzo 1992* and *Lorenzo 1994*. (Jovanotti means 'young men'.) As a television and disco star in the late 1980s, he was famous for a teenage pop hit entitled 'Sei come la mia moto' (You're like my Lambretta), and the journalist Paolo Zanuttini described him as 'straddling the hedonistic idiocy of the late 1980s with commercial dexterity'.[38]

As a successful pop star, Jovanotti has been the target of satirical barbs. The Venice-based reggae group Pitura Freska, whose symbol is the lion of Venice smoking a joint, and who perform cheeky songs about sex and political scandals in Venetian dialect, mercilessly lampooned 'La mia moto' and Jovanotti's appeal to teenage girls on their 1992 album *Na bruta banda* (An Ugly Mob). Pitura Freska parodied 'La mia moto' in 'So mato per la mona (La Mia Moto)' (I'm cunt-struck by my Lambretta), and their parody was directed at Jovanotti's sudden discovery of an ideological commitment of sorts in the 1990s, and his campaign against AIDS. A member of Pitura Freska defended the group from charges of anti-feminism frequently levied against them by saying 'it's Jovanotti whose anti-feminist: now he's playing at political commitment so he can recycle himself, and talking about safe sex, but in my view he's only making the chickens laugh.'[39] At the other extreme, the young Calabrese disc jockey and fledgling pop star DJ Flash released a disco-styled rap hit song in 1994 entitled 'Un Lorenzo c'è già' (There's already a Lorenzo), apparently designed to displace Jovanotti as a pop icon.

Jovanotti's political commitment surfaced in 1992, when he voted PDS in the elections, after composing an election rap called 'Ho perso la direzione' (I've lost the drift), also composing an 'instant song' called 'Cuore' (Heart) about the death of the anti-mafia magistrate Giovanni Falcone. Although he continues to represent the flippant, commercial pop face of Italian rap, an idiom which had begun to be incorporated into the most conventional of Italian *musica leggera*, Jovanotti showed that even this idiom could incorporate ideological gestures.

In June 1994, the first – and to date last – Italian rap single to be released in Australia and the English-speaking world was Jovanotti's up-tempo 'Penso positivo' (I Think Positive). This CD single included three other cuts from *Lorenzo 1994*, and incorporated acid jazz-like brass, disco whoops, shouts, grunts and backing vocals, and plenty of scratching into its mix. A review in *On the Street*, a free weekly Sydney music paper, welcomed it into the local dance music scene without even commenting on its Italian language vocals, suggesting there might be a niche for it in anglophone dance music culture (although this did not prove to be the case). *On the Street* praised the unusualness, tempo, contemporaneity, construction, sound quality, tone and sex appeal of 'Penso Positivo': 'This is the feelgood release of the week and one for the Soho bar or downstairs at Zoom. It's something like you've never heard before, up and vibrant, rooted in jazz but with a precise contemporary feel, cruisy but methodical, clean and celebratory. . . . Plus, as the cover proves, Mr Jovanotti is a huge spunk!'[40] 'Penso positivo' avoids any ideological subjects in celebrating the achievements of Italian and international imagination in activities ranging from mathematics to music to revolution. Its release in the English-speaking world, although in the tradition of Italian novelty singles, was a step closer to a recognition of some forms of indigenous Italian popular music, even if it also signalled a continuing chasm between the dictates of the international popular music market and the activities of the Italian posses.

Jovanotti achieved a considerable degree of popularity outside Italy, joining Eros Ramazzotti and Laura Pausini as the most internationally successful Italian pop stars of the mid-1990s. According to Liperi, he was invited to host a BBC programme for young people in 1989, when his brand of teenage 'party music' was at its peak, and later appeared on *Yo! MTV Raps* in the USA.[41] In 1994 he headlined a series of fifteen concerts in Germany, Switzerland, Slovenia, Holland, Belgium, Portugal and France with Eros Ramazzotti, as well as playing a twenty-five-date European tour of his own. In 1995 he was the only Italian artist at the Montreux jazz festival, and was the first Western musician to break the economic and cultural embargo against Cuba, performing at his own expense in Havana to an audience of twenty thousand people, many of whom were familiar enough with his music to sing along.

Rap spread quickly into *musica leggera*. Even 'dinosaurs' of popular song like Adriano Celentano, a rather moralistic Roman ballad singer who came to prominence in the late 1950s, adapted spoken-word raps into his repertoire in an attempt to keep up with contemporary musical idioms. In his 1992 song 'Il re degli ignoranti' (The King of Dunces), which could have been addressed to his son's generation, he used a spoken-word, rap-like idiom to explore his responses to the boredom and lack of responsibility of contemporary youth. Celentano's daughter was Jovanotti's partner for a time, and Jovanotti described him as 'a very important influence ... almost an idol'.[42] On his 1994 album *Quel punto* (At that Point), the fifty-seven-year-old Celentano included a track called 'Il seme dello rap' (The Seed of Rap), which claimed he was the originator of Italian rap. In an interview he dismissed Italian rap groups of the 1990s as *quattro mocciosi* (an insignificant bunch of snotty-nosed kids) – with the exception of Jovanotti. These statements drew mostly contemptuous response from Italian rappers, who described Celentano as an irrelevant anachronism in the Italian music scene, who was simply seeking publicity.[43]

In the wake of Jovanotti's success, *rap leggera* has become a commercially successful category in Italy, its main protagonists including Articolo 31, Alta Tensione, Ottiero and Radiotitolati. Even the *a cappella* group Neri per Caso (Black by Chance), one of the winners of the 1995 Festival of San Remo, whom *Billboard* described as crossing 'the harmonising of the Manhattan Transfer with the vocal instrumentation of Bobby McFerrin',[44] could be regarded as representatives of the commercial face of Italian rap. Their cover versions of classic Italian pop songs on their double-platinum (200,000 units) 1995 album *Le ragazze* (Girls) incorporated ragga and rap trimmings. Articolo 31, also featured in *Billboard*'s 1995 Italian survey, produced a successful chart-scoring album in 1994, selling more than 70,000 copies.[45] The group's 1994 single, 'Ohi Maria', is a lightweight rap panegyric to marijuana that announces itself as a tongue-in-cheek, Latin-style love song 'in the style of the *cantautori*' and ends with a plea to 'legalize it', quoting from Peter Tosh's reggae anthem, and showing the influence of Cypress Hill. It received considerable radio airplay in 1995, and was included on a giveaway Flying Records cassette with the Berlusconi-owned television weekly magazine

Tutto Musica & Spettacolo in July 1995. This was despite complaints against the song by the 'Mamme contro il rock' (Mothers Against Rock) – an Italian equivalent of the US Parental Music Advisory organization. Articolo 31, who along with the Varese group Sottotono have provided rap soundtracks for television commercials, are one of a number of rap groups on the Crime Squad label, an offshoot of Flying Records, which has emerged as one of the main independent labels promulgating the more pop-oriented Italian posses, like Alta Tensione, DJ Flash, Frankie Hi-NRG MC, OTR, Radiotitolati and others, who are included on a 1994 Crime Squad compilation, *Nati per rappare* (Born to Rap). In this context, as Piombo a Tempo, who had their origins in the Lion Horse Posse, have indicated, '[Italian] hip hop today is what "Saturday Night Fever" was twenty years ago'.[46]

Questions of style: 'street credibility' versus 'funky sensibility'

While the recorded output of Jovanotti and other Italian pop-rappers displays unmistakable traces of parody, unconscious or otherwise, some of their more politically oriented rap recordings could be seen to operate as 'edutainment', designed to educate young people about drugs, safe sex, violence, political corruption and other social issues. In this they share the influence of LA rappers Boogie Down Productions with what is probably the most well-known and often-compiled Italian rap track, Frankie Hi-NRG's 'Fight da faida' (Fight the Feud), which first appeared in 1991. This hardcore-styled rap sold more than 15,000 copies for the small Bologna-based dance and acid jazz label Irma, and many Italian ten- and eleven-year-olds are said to have learned it by heart and understood it. It calls for a halt to the family blood feud practices of the camorra and the mafia as one of the fundamental cause of Italy's social and political evils. As Frankie Hi-NRG MC has indicated, it is a small but important protest: 'when you speak about the mafia, you have to make sure that you're small enough for them not to worry about you. From this point of view, I don't have any problems.'[47]

The main focus of 'Fight da faida' is its text, as is emphasized in the video clip of the song in which the lyrics run continuously across the images, in the style of Prince's 'Sign of the Times'. The musical arrangement employs only a jew's harp and drum-machine, along with samples from Sly and the Family Stone and the Jungle Brothers, and a saxophone break reminiscent of 'La Raza' by Kid Frost, with whom Frankie performed in Rome in 1992, in a freestyle session along with other Italian rappers. Built around the English refrain 'you gotta fight', it uses standard Italian to give maximum comprehensibility to its message, although it includes a segment in which a child's voice raps in Sicilian dialect. The extended 'diss' of the Mafia is expressed through a rapid-fire proliferation of internal rhymes which De Luca has called 'a bit too kissed for the subject in question',[48] and which cannot be rendered in English. It begins:

> Father against father, brother against brother, / born in a grave like butcher's meat; / men with minds / as sharp as blades, / cutting like crime / angry beyond any limits, / heroes without land / fighting a war / between the mafia and the camorra, Sodom and Gomorrah / Naples and Palermo / Regions of hell / devoured by hell flames for eternity, / and by a tumour of crime / while the world watches / dumbly, without intervening. / Enough of this war between families / fomented by desire / for a wife with a dowry / who gives life to sons today / and takes it away tomorrow, / branches stripped of their leaves / cut down like straw / and no one picks them up: / on the verge of a revolution / to the voice of the Godfather, / but Don Corleone is much closer to home today: / he sits in Parliament. It's time to unleash / a terminal, decisive, radical, destructive offensive / united we stand, all together, now more than ever before, / against the clans, the smokescreens, the shady practices maintained by taxes, / lubricated by pockets: / all it takes is a bribe in the right pocket / in this obscene Italy .../ ... you gotta FIGHT THE FEUD!!![49]

A former disc jockey who was influenced by Afrika Bambaataa and the Sugarhill Gang, Frankie Hi-NRG used Grandmaster Flash's 'The Message' and Public Enemy's 'Fight the Power' as models for 'Fight da faida'. Of Sicilian origin, but born in Turin and based in Perugia, he lived for thirteen years in Caserta, near Naples, where the liner notes of the *Italian Posse* compilation claim 'he shared the anger of young people who were rejecting the stigma South = Camorra'. His second single, the disco-oriented and totally rhyme-driven 'Faccio la mia cosa' (I Do my Own Thing, 1993), which was released in six different mixes, indicated a shift away from political concerns, its refrain 'faccio la mia cosa nella casa' (I do my own thing in the house) appearing to reply to his critics by associating himself with a freestyle, isolationist and non-community-oriented position. It was followed by the musically more adventurous 'Libri di sangue' (Books of Blood, 1993), a generalized criticism of political corruption and violence by the strong against the weak and innocent, which refers to the beating of Rodney King by Los Angeles police in 1992 but not to any specific Italian events. In 1994 he released 'Potere alla parola' (Power to the Word) and a successful first album, but neither made as much impact as 'Fight da faida'.

The Sicilian rap group Nuovi Briganti, who made their first recordings and performances at the Fata Morgana *centro sociale* in Messina, were one of a number of militant rappers who have accused Frankie Hi-NRG of betraying the independent, alternative principles of the Italian hip hop movement represented by the *centri sociali*: 'The impression is that he attempts to exploit the phenomenon, and talks about the mafia without really knowing the situation. A radio hit like *Fight da faida* runs the risk of giving the mass general public, who are a long way from the underground, an image of hip hop that has very little to do with antagonism.'[50]

In an interview published in 1992, Frankie Hi-NRG MC was eloquent in his own defence of his position as a propagator of rap as 'pure information' to a discotheque clientele, invoking the criteria of autonomy and authenticity as indicators of his sincerity in the face of the 'disses' of his colleagues:

> What counts in rap is content and message, not rivalry and jealousy. I don't believe that someone who has something to say can necessarily only go to a social centre or a squat. There's no such thing as a privileged audience, at least as far as I'm concerned, and I think rap has a duty to get across to people who go to discos, people who until now never thought it was possible to dance to a text like *Fight da faida*. The important thing about being part of the scene is sharing the essential co-ordinates that make hip hop into a philosophy of life. ... I want to make use of all the doors and windows that are available to me, as long as my total autonomy is guaranteed. In a nutshell, I see rap as a rhythmically sung newspaper, and I appreciate all the posses who have authentic motivations, from the Nuovi Briganti in Messina to the Devastatin' Posse in Turin.[51]

In a widely diffused cover story entitled 'Rissa nelle posse' (Riot in the Posses), a special summer 1992 issue of the Italian music monthly magazine *Fare Musica* (Making Music) set Frankie Hi-NRG MC up in opposition to Papa Ricky. The story, by Paolo Ferrari, was described as 'an encounter/conflict between two Italian ragga-rappers who appear to be antagonists', and contrasted Ricky's 'street credibility', which came from the 'collective and political hip hop of the *centri sociali*' with Frankie's 'funky sensibility', which was ascribed to the 'free hip hop of the *homeboy* who gets his act together at home to break the silence, without any fixed reference points in the outside world'.[52] (Italian interpretations of the US term 'homeboy' sometimes give it a literal interpretation.) Papa Ricky was reported to have refused to be photographed with Frankie or to speak with him, and expressed his concern about the inevitable commercial exploitation of the posses in the form of major-label compilations like *Italian Posse*, which in his view included groups who had 'nothing to do with the Italian hip hop and ragamuffin scene'. In the view of Ricky's Isola Posse colleague Speaker Dee Mo', this exclusion also applied to Frankie HI-NRG MC, who 'is not a protagonist of the Italian hip hop scene, he's part of the dance scene; the basis of his disco music is dance, which means he's got nothing to do with us'.[53]

The *centri sociali* rappers' appropriation of claims to a monopoly over authentic hip hop practices and their strategies of exclusion of those who had not 'paid their dues' in the *centri sociali* could alternatively be regarded as the posturings of a self-defining, politically correct orthodoxy.

Ideological and territorial conflicts over claims of authenticity versus fashion and opportunism are common in popular music scenes everywhere. What they illustrate most is the heterogeneity of local music scenes, to which Italian rap is no exception. This is affirmed by Ferrari, who invokes Gramsci's concept of hegemony in distinguishing the diversity and multiplicity of the Italian rap scene from 'homogenous nuclei who run the risk of becoming sectarian in their need to defend themselves against business and banality. Italian hip hop follows a lot of different paths, and has a lot of schools: it is important that each individual works within their own course, as hegemonic claims don't help anyone.' [54]

The somewhat manufactured conflict between Papa Ricky and Frankie Hi-NRG MC was largely concerned with issues of hip hop credentials, which became conflated in Italian rap parlance into notions of style. Speaker Dee Mo's single 'Questione di stile' (A Matter of Style) expresses the philosophy of the in-group of politically committed, *centri-sociali*-based network of ragga rappers, who have adapted Jamaican and African-American idioms, roots and street-cred claims into an indigenously Italian context of *maximum rispetto*. Most of this group record on the Century Vox label, and are mentioned by name in a roll-call which concludes the song. Papa Ricky reinvoked this sense of style in relation to sense of a 'second family' he gets from the Century Vox label: 'When we talk about "style", that's what I mean, it's not a way of rapping: style is the human side of the business.'[55] But by the time Papa Ricky's debut album eventually appeared in 1995, he had left Century Vox for Virgin Records, and included Frankie Hi-NRG amongst the list of acknowledgments and thanks on the album.

'Questione di stile' also has a more general sphere of application in exhorting its listeners: 'Don't give your time to those / who don't have respect / who are false and vile / and don't have style.' Fabio De Luca has elaborated on this interpretation of style in a review of Speaker Dee Mo's single in a way that applies to the entire Italian hip hop scene in its rejection of accusations of US cultural imperialism:

> Rap, hip-hop, ragamuffin. ... It's a question of stylistic strategy, talking loud and strong, and listening up. Hybrid languages which are infinitely practical (do-it-yourself), which come across right in your face in a way that hasn't happened for millennia. ... 'Questione di stile' is exactly that: words in rhyme, messages in style, the art of 'passing on' ideas and the usual old bullshit of 'being appropriated by a foreign culture.'[56]

Antonio Santirocco's review of Jovanotti's *Lorenzo 1992* represents a noteworthy attack on the *centri sociali* adherents' tendencies to monopolize claims of 'credibility and legitimization', exposing their political rhetoric as another form of fashionable stylistic appropriation:

Italian rappers with their grim faces who hate Jovanotti more than anyone else are more interested in cultivating their own little art form than listening to what someone else has to say, even though he's been saying it long before they were. On one side you've got the snobs from the social centres who dress up in hip hop gear to show their mothers or their wives how trendy they are ... on the other there's this little braggart born in the jungle who grew up on the fringes of the yuppie scene and claims to be the wet-nurse of Italian rap. Which do you believe?[57]

Another feature of the *centri-sociali*-based hip hop movement that Santirocco's view underlines is a lack of humour or irony. Groups like AK 47, for instance, sometimes produce little more than a series of simplistic oppositional slogans, as in their song 'Vip (Vipaganoipadroni)' (VIPs – the Bosses Pay You), which repeatedly accuses the Italian trade unions of being financed by the bosses. This lack of a sense of irony is reaffirmed by Pierfrancesco Pagoda in relation to the graffiti practices of the Italian hip hop movement, which are influenced as much by the Italian militant political graffiti of the 1970s as by its American models:

the slogans (because that is basically what they are) are unmistakably influenced by the experiences of 1977 (and therefore there is a left-wing connection), but the new hip hop generation is so far lacking in the ability (or the desire) to use the complex weapon of irony, which was an essential component of the cultural and political production in 1977. It's also true that the average age of the rappers is extremely young, and thus they still have infinite possibilities ahead of them in the development of their lyrics.[58]

The ongoing conflict between views of Italian hip hop as a playful, fashion-oriented (and potentially ironic and parodic) pop lifestyle on the one hand, and an exclusive vehicle for authentic oppositional political statement on the other, is illustrated by the Neapolitan group Possessione. In their rap track 'Appeso a un filo' (Attached to a String), which pronounces that 'Those who follow fashion are attached to a string', they address the issue of Italian hip hop's dependency on American imported fashion on the one hand, and its total politicization of rap music on the other:

There are those who consider you to be a rapper if you wear Jordan shoes and hold you in contempt if you don't wear Raiders bomber jackets and those who make an exclusively political issue out of it and spit on those they don't consider to be 'militants', often ignoring everything that has gone before, and why a brother has got into hip hop.[59]

In the title track of their 1993 EP *Il posto dove vivo* (The Place Where I Live), which contains a cover photo of an ugly back street in Naples full of depressed apartment blocks with washing hanging from balconies, Possessione announce their own exclusively local concerns, which connect them to a global hip hop culture. The title track expresses disgust at the squalor, violence, prostitution, drug abuse and corruption of Naples, a city famed for the camorra and *l'arte di arrangiarsi* (the art of getting by):

> The place where I live is like an enormous sewer / Where nothing is recycled, just soaked up like a sponge / So the land is pregnant with the shame and the stink / Of those who nurture this disgusting filth
>   The place where I live is like a jungle / People are killing one another and no one tries to stop it / No pity no love no law / And no one to enforce justice
>   The place where I live is a den of iniquity / Where sex is sold at the going market price / A dog that is beaten can vent its frustration / But here mongrels get rich on faking love
>   The place where I live is riddled with corruption / The mafia is in league with the jurisdiction / The only way to get a job is to pay a bribe
>   The place where I live is totally boring / And everyone wants to get away from the paranoia / Some shoot up, some smoke dope, some snort speed / You can bet anyone who says they're doing all right is bluffing ...[60]

The litany-like catalogue of this 'picture of shame fired in the faces of those who govern' is highlighted by a spare backing track, consisting of scratching, a sound like a police siren, and drums. As a portrayal of the sense of outrage, frustration and helplessness of life in the ghettos of Naples, it may rely on stylistic traits of an idiom imported from the US, but it expresses social concerns that are unequivocally Italian.

The Italian roots of rap

The Italian posses' appropriation of Jamaican and black American styles saw words like *rappare, scratchare* and *ragga* enter the Italian language, and *rispetto* and *nella casa* (in the house) take on new meanings. It is also worth recalling that the term 'ghetto' is Italian, and was first used to refer to the Jewish quarter in Venice. The word is from the Italian *gettare*, which means to cast, referring to the traditional employment of Jews in metal foundries, but also taking on the meaning of 'to cast aside'. The disparaging hip hop appellation 'bitch' also unfortunately found its way into Italian, in the pop-rap group Sottotono's track 'Biccia', albeit without the more extreme misogynist connotations given it by Afro-American gangasta rappers. ('Rap' also became a marketing label in Italy for a brand of motor scooter exhausts.)

But there are a number of home-grown historical and traditional precedents to some of the styles and idioms of Italian rap. In a review of Vincenzo Perna's Italian translation of David Toop's study of US rap, *The Rap Attack*, Loredana Lipperini argues that the ritual insults and verbal jousting endemic to rap can be traced to the calls of washerwomen portrayed in Baroque madrigals as well as in the 'dozens' of the US black ghettos.[61] The popular Roman dialect tradition of exchanging sung ritualized insults is also illustrated in the opening scene of Pier Paolo Pasolini's 1962 film *Mamma Roma*, in which Anna Magnani as the title character exchanges improvised strophes with her former pimp (Franco Citti) and his new bride. 'Signifying' 'sounding' or 'flyting', as Joan and William Magretta have indicated, is a strong feature of many cultures throughout the world, and Italian popular culture has its own particular carnivalesque variation, which is reflected in the exchanges of abuse in the films of Lina Wertmuller. The most forceful example of this kind of verbal duelling is the exchange of insults between the working-class Neapolitan deckhand Gennarino (Giancarlo Giannini) and his blonde Milanese boss Raffaella (Mariangela Melato), who are stranded on a desert island in Wertmuller's *Swept Away*.

Many of Wertmuller's films upset feminist orthodoxies in the 1970s in the same way as hardcore and gangsta rap in the USA have been taken to task for their misogyny in the 1990s. Italian rap continues to be almost exclusively male-dominated, as is illustrated by the range of groups covered in both the standard textbook on the subject, *Posse italiane*, and the 1992 film *Suoni dalla città*, a survey of the rap and ragga scene in Turin, which, apart from showing two brief glimpses of subsidiary women rappers performing with La To.sse and Assalti Frontali, has an entirely male focus.[62] Two rare examples of female rappers, apart from those involved in Assalti Frontali, are Carrie D, who is from Turin and part of the Century Vox crew, and Sardinian rapper Clara Murtas, who has used traditional Sardinian lullabies as a basis for rap, while AK 47, the Salento Posse, Suono Mudu and the Bari-based Zona 45 include female rappers in their line-ups. Despite this male domination, most of the *posse* tend to avoid misogyny, although Pitura Freska have angered Italian feminists with graphically lecherous songs like 'Biennial', which uses the tune of Harry Belafonte's 'Banana Boat Song' to celebrate the volume of female flesh at the Venice Biennale.

Most of the ritual insults used in Italian hip hop are directed at right-wing political parties like the Lega del Nord (Northern League), which has been the subject of both 'Legala' (Put them in a Straitjacket) by La To.sse, and 'Slega la lega' (Smash the League) by Fuckin' Camels 'n' Effect. Other rappers 'diss' judges, industrialists and mafiosi; sometimes all together, as in Pitura Freska's 'Na bruta banda' (An Ugly Mob), which launches a generalized attack on all 'those who command'.

Lipperini argues that Italian rap music could be said to have dual origins in the oral traditions of the griots of Africa and in the *recitativo* used in early Italian operas in Florence in the sixteenth century, with their *imitar con canto chi parla* (imitating in song a person speaking).[63] In his book *Opera*, published in 1949, Edward J. Dent traces the origins of Italian opera, which throughout the seventeenth century was a form of recited music drama in which vocal declamation was made to music which was focused around a figured bass line: 'what the promoters aimed at more than anything else was the declamation of the words. If there was anything like a complicated orchestral accompaniment, the words would not be heard.'[64] This led to the development of lyrical refrains to break the monotony of the declamation, and these in turn evolved into arias. As a way of keeping the narrative in opera moving, early Italian opera developed *recitativo secco* (dry recitative), which was 'accompanied merely by a bass viol holding the bass in slow notes, and a harpsichord filling up the minimum of harmony'.[65] The musicality of opera required the words to be metrical, and one had to be able to beat time to the music, which meant that the speech patterns were both melodic and rhythmical. With the development of commercial opera in Venice, songs and dances were interpolated into operas, along with 'the interplay between voice and instruments in the course of a song'.[66] By the time of Gluck, audiences had grown weary of the single voice in operas, and the duet form was borrowed from comic opera, which enabled two characters to 'quarrel and call each other names'.[67] This device was developed into 'concerted finales' in which several characters could engage in conversation. One of the features of Italian rap is what is referred to as the *microfono rotante* (rotating microphone) in which a large number of rappers swap verses of a song. This multiplicity of voices, in which random elements are often incorporated, is sometimes extended into *microfono aperto* (open microphone), when audience members are invited to improvize raps. As Sud Sound System has claimed: 'The microphone is open to anybody: in our concerts there is no difference between who's on stage and who's on the dance floor.'[68]

A number of the Italian *posse* incorporate elements of traditional regional Italian music, from the Apulian peasant shouts and chants used by Suono Mudu to the Neapolitan shepherd's horn used by 99 Posse. The *fisarmonica* (piano accordion), violin, *djembe* (an African drum), *requinto* (Mexican guitar), tub bass, balalaika and other arcane instruments used by Mau Mau represent a more hybridized combination of traditional instruments. Mau Mau, whose name means 'tramp' or 'vagabond' in Piedmontese dialect, as well as referring to both the Kenyan revolutionary group and a deprecating Torinese term for southern Italian immigrant Fiat workers, call themselves an *acustica tribu* (acoustic tribe) because they play only acoustic instruments when they perform live. The group's ragga-inflected music, which sounds very much like an Italian version of the Algerian rai and Celtic-influenced French groups Les Negresses Vertes and Mano Negra, is a syncretic mixture of Mediterranean, African and Jamaican influences. The singer and main composer of Mau Mau, Luca Morino, has stressed that the group does not play traditional music and is not part of the Italian *posse* movement – although they are continually identified with it by critics, commentators and other musical groups – quoting Senegalese musician Baaba Maal to indicate that they are more concerned with a universal music.[69] The fact that both the group's albums have been mixed at the Real World studios in Bath and that the second, *Bass Paradis* (1994), was issued on EMI with English translations of the Piedmontese lyrics, indicates Mau Mau's connections with world music. These are shared by other Italian groups like Kunsertu and Sensaciou, both of which produce Middle Eastern musical inflections, and record on the Anagrumba label.

Also on the Anagrumba label are Almamegretta, a Neapolitan group who combine traditional Neapolitan music with rap, rock, Algerian rai, ragga and dub in what is evidence of a distinctively original musical and ideological direction in Italian rap. 'Almamegretta' is Neapolitan dialect for *Anima migrante*, (migrant soul), the title of the group's debut 1993 album, which was produced by Ben Young, an associate of the Bristol-based Massive Attack, and displays the range of the group's combination of 'roots' music with migratory musical 'routes'. In their song 'Figli di Annibale' (Sons of Hannibal) they explore rhetorical notions of African roots in Italy. The song claims that when Hannibal, the 'great black general', brought 90,000 African men across the Alps along with his famous elephants, there was considerable cross-breeding during the fifteen to twenty years he remained in Italy after his defeat of the Romans. This explains 'why so many Italians have dark skin ... dark hair ... dark eyes ... a trace of Hannibal's blood has remained in all their veins'. (It is also worth noting that southern Italians are referred to derogatively in Piedmont as 'moru' – Moorish, African or Saracen.) The song also suggests that during the Second World War a large number of African-Americans 'filled Europe with black babies', both sources having a particularly strong impact in the south of Italy.[70] The journalist and critic Goffredo Fofi has commented on the distinctive impression the group had in live performance at the *centri sociali* Officina 99 in Naples:

> 'Alma Megretta' play a strange and original mixture of different influences: Neapolitan and Arab, with some traces of the rock of the past and a hint of Latin American music along with more than a pinch of ragga. One of their songs, *Figli di Annibale*, which is perhaps their best achievement to date, is charged with a strong claim for the 'African' part of Italian and southern European culture, and will certainly cause discussion. It is not always the case, but with songs like this one feels in this ex-warehouse the sense of a new development of a new culture.[71]

Almamegretta's second album, *Sanacore 1995*, combined traditional Neapolitan songs with a strong, driving ragga and dub beat, producing a surprisingly harmonious hybrid which was mixed by Adrian Sherwood and Andy Montgomery of the London-based On U Sound System. According to *Billboard*, 'The industry phrase "musical contamination" fits this band's blend of electronic ambient music and traditional Neapolitan roots, spiced with flavours from the Casbah quarter of

Naples'.[72] As the group's vocalist, Raiss, explained, the hybridity of the group's sound is seamless and spontaneous:

> I like exploring with my voice the melodic aspects that arise from playing Neapolitan reggae. If we sketched out an experiment in associating Naples with reggae in *Anima migrante*, in *Sanacore* we took it much further, to the extent that you can no longer tell if our music is more reggae or more Neapolitan: the amalgamation of the two elements was created naturally, in a spontaneous way. It's almost as if we pretended that reggae was Neapolitan music. ... Reggae is melancholy and languid music played in minor chords, like melodic Neapolitan music, which is why it is the closest of all other styles of music to our sensibility. This also explains why the Italian language is more adaptable to reggae than to rock, punk or other forms: reggae is music that allows one to communicate in a relaxed way.[73]

In the summer of 1995 Almamegretta performed on tour with the traditional Neapolitan actor and singer Peppe Barra, who specializes in performing the Neapolitan *commedia dell'arte* character Pulcinella, as well as having sung in the traditional music group Nuova Compagnia Di Canto Popolare. Performing both separately and together, the two presented an evening of Neapolitan song which showed how harmoniously Almamegretta's *centri sociali* and ragga orientations could blend in with traditional Neapolitan culture. Almamegretta also appeared in a spectacular televised concert in the Piazza Plebiscita in Naples dedicated to the memory of opera singer Enrico Caruso, performing with Lucio Dalla, Caetano Veloso, Joan Armatrading, Neri per Caso and others, taking notions of musical hybridity to new heights.

The use of regional dialects by a large number of other Italian posses also attempts to build 'a new culture' out of Italian hip hop, drawing on rap and ragga in conjunction with local popular folkloric traditions, frequently using peasant songs as a basis, along with dance forms like the tarantella. In 'In Sa La' (The Road), Sa Razza use Sardinian dialect to express the dilemma of being forced on to the 'road' of emigration to the mainland, owing to growing unemployment and economic hardship, and to express pride in their Sardinian heritage: 'We prefer Sardinian rap slang / And to boast about being Sardinian, brother, you've got to defend yourself, / This is the cause we're rapping for / This is the only hope for my people / To survive − survive on the road!'[74] Sud Sound System's 'tarantamuffin' uses samples of traditional southern Italian instruments, and the group has discovered in reggae a vehicle for exploring their own southern Italian dialect and musical traditions:

> Reggae, like jazz and blues, has a value as universal protest, because it has an immediate application to the listener's private, intimate spheres, rather than to external antagonist attitudes. At first we were attracted by reggae's rhythmic hypnosis, which we found able to express the musicality of our dialect. Then

we noticed that in these Jamaican texts there was an infinite sense of southern culture. There is the same attachment to roots, the desire to sing about love and sentimentality, intolerance for the oppression of school and military service. But above all we liked reggae's desire to fight against human malaise. It's an interior music.[75]

Such is the importance of the use of traditional regional dialects and musical elements by Italian rap and ragga groups that the Milan-based Istituto De Martino, which carries out research into traditional popular music forms such as work songs and ritual chants, has made contact with a number of rap groups, seeing Italian rap as 'a genre which has analogies (but also a lot of differences) with popular improvisation'.[76]

Far from being subject to accusations of cultural imperialism for its use of African-American and Jamaican models, the Italian posses passed quickly through an initial phase of imitating outside models into an acculturation of rap which created its own distinctive and diverse musical culture with its own boasts, taunts, tensions and ideological conflicts. As Possessione stated in their song 'Appeso ad un filo' (Attached to a String) in 1992:

Now the dream has come true here in Italy 'rep' has been born, the movement has been created and articulated in Italian. Our own 'rep' has developed and become Italian rap, rappin', never again will pseudo American be the rule, the trend, the fashion. Now there are those who look like they're in uniform 'in the house' and go up to the microphone with their heads held high, but all they know how to say is 'Get on up'. This tribe who can dance, but can't think or act, tries to compete with those who really rage, and don't need to make up their stories, and don't fake the anger in the things they have to say.[77]

By 1995 the more politically overt aspects of the Italian posses had declined in popularity, and a new Italian rock revival, led by groups like Negrita, YoYo Mundi, La Crus, Massimo Volume, Ustmamò, CSI and others – many of whom featured on a 1995 Polydor compilation, *La musica che cambia* (The Music that Changes) – appeared to be under way. According to Luca De Gennaro, writing in the Italian rock music monthly *Rock Star*, the Italian posses had become the much-discussed subject of 'politically correct' magazines, television programmes, books and doctoral theses, but by 1995 the phenomenon had burned itself out, at least as far as media interest was concerned. Like the 'Italian new wave' phenomenon in rock music in the 1980s, De Gennaro argued, it was time to re-evaluate the posses in terms of quality, and sift out the survivors. Mau Mau and Almamegretta were designated as 'destined for a brilliant future', while question marks were placed over Frankie Hi-NRG MC, Papa Ricky, Casino Royale, Africa Unite and Bisca 99 Posse, although new exponents of militant rap like Sangue Misto and Piombo a Tempo provided some indications of the genre's likely durability, with the more commercial pop-rap exponents like Articolo 31 also showing signs of security.[78] This view seemed to be shared by Mada of Africa Unite, who saw little of durable value in the 'Mediterranean reggae' scene, which appeared to have been 'a trend which burned itself out very quickly'. He saw the main exception as Sangue Misto, whose 1994 jazz-oriented album 'provided the basis for new experiments'. Mada described the posse phenomenon as 'characterized by a slogan-oriented approach, which had huge problems in terms of musical expression ... [which] involves making music, not populist political rallies'.[79] Raiss of Almamegretta, on the other hand, saw a need to continue with ideologically committed musical projects, employing a metaphor reminiscent of the collapse of the Berlin Wall:

> The posses demolished a wall: at that time there was nothing left, rock was finished, while now the new rock scene is about transformation and crossover. The posses broke through the wall of the 1980s, which was a wall of non-communication erected by the cult of [Socialist Party leader and ex-Prime-Minister] Craxi and yuppies, but the fact is that those who break down walls run the risk of being buried in the rubble. This is a crucial time for Italian music: we need to produce more committed projects like Bisca and 99 Posse's, which is what we are trying to do with our new album.[80]

Both Mada's and Raiss's comments suggest that the perceived crisis point in Italian popular music in 1995 had affinities with Eastern European disillusionment with rock music as a vehicle for the expression of politically oppositional viewpoints. While the post-Berlusconi, post-*tangentopoli* 'second republic' of Italy has few other affinities with post-Communist Eastern Europe, there seemed to be common ongoing debates about the relations between rock, rap, reggae and politics.

De Gennaro's article prefaced a three-part survey of new emerging Italian musicians and recording labels, referred to as 'Generazione I'. Many of the rock groups profiled, however, showed few, if any, signs of distinctive re-appropriations of the different aspects of the particular genre they drew on, while the new Italian acid jazz and dance music scene also outlined seemed doomed to oblivion outside the strict and anonymously transnational parameters of the dance music scene.[81] Almamegretta and Mau Mau may well prove to be, and deserve to be, the most important 'survivors' of the Italian posse scene. The entire Italian posse phenomenon, however, both politically and musically, in its blending of Afro-Caribbean and African-American musical traits with traditional Mediterranean forms, and its connection with traditional Italian left-wing political concerns, continues to represent the most vitally distinctive manifestation of a heterogeneous national popular music traditionally besieged by parodies and novelties.

Notes

1. P. Hewitt (1989) 'The Boot's on the Other Foot', *New Musical Express* (19 August), p. 26.
2. *Ibid.*, p. 26.
3. R. Harley (1993) 'Beat in the System', in T. Bennett *et al.* (eds) *Rock and Popular Music: Politics, Policies, Institutions* (London, Routledge), p. 216.
4. S. Reynolds (1990) *Blissed Out*, (London, Serpent's Tail), p. 174.
5. Harley (1993), pp. 220, 229.
6. F. Liperi (1993) 'L'Italia s'è desta. Tecno-splatter e posse in rivolta', in M. Canevacci *et al.* (eds) *Ragazzi senza tempo: Immagini, musica, conflitti delle culture giovanili* (Genova, Costa & Nolan), pp. 167–8. (All quotations from Italian sources are the author's translation.)
7. Harley (1993), p. 215.
8. Hewitt (1989), p. 27.
9. Unattributed (1995) 'Russian Music Pirates Lead the World', *The European* (16–22 June).
10. M. Hennessey (1992) '91 vs. '90: Overall Sales Up, but Unit Sales Down as Recession, Piracy and Rentals Gnaw at Profits', *Billboard* (4 July), pp. I–2, I–14.
11. D. Stansfield (1992a) 'Italy Rules the International Dance Floors with Imported Talent and Fast-breaking Trends', *Billboard* (4 July), p. I–15.
12. *Ibid.*, p. I–5.
13. M.Dezzani (1995) 'Italy's Music Industry Rises above Political and Economic Uncertainty', *Billboard* (1 July), p. 71.
14. F. Fabbri (1989) 'The System of *Canzone* in Italy Today' (1981), in S. Frith (ed) *World Music, Politics and Social Change* (Manchester University Press), p. 135.
15. D. Stansfield (1992b) ' "Latin Looks" Help, but Hard Work a Bigger Factor in Enabling Italian Acts to Get Over Away from Home', *Billboard* (4 July), p. I–10.
16. U. Fiori (1984). 'Rock Music and Politics in Italy', in R. Middleton, and D. Horne (eds) *Popular Music 4: Performance and Audiences* (Cambridge University Press), pp. 271–2.
17. F. Fabbri (1983) 'What Kind of Music?' in R. Middleton and D. Horne (eds) *Popular Music 2* (Cambridge University Press), p. 138.
18. Stansfield (1992b), pp. 1–10.
19. D. Stansfield (1992c) 'Italians Tired of "Anglo-Saxon Music" Reach for the Local Aesthetic', *Billboard* (4 July), p. I–6.
20. Fiori (1984), pp. 261–2.
21. Z. Baranski (1990) 'Turbulent Transitions: An Introduction', in Z. Baranski and R. Lumley (eds) *Culture and Conflict in Postwar Italy: Essays on Mass and Popular Culture* (London, Macmillian), p. 11.
22. Papa Ricky, *Lu Papa Ricky*, Virgin Music Italy, 1995.
23. Unattributed (1992) Alter Festa, Cisternino, Programme Note.
24. In A. Campo (1995a) 'Nel nome di Marley ecco gli Africa unite', *La Repubblica* (*Supplemento Musica* no. 12) (7 June), p. 17.
25. F. De Luca (1992) 'Italian Rap Attack' and 'Singoli-Speciale Rap', *L'Urlo*, vol. 2 (March–April), p. 43.

26. E. Assante (1995) 'La lingua della strada diventa rap', *La Repubblica* (*Supplemento Musica* no. 12) (7 June), p. 6.
27. In A. Campo (1995b) 'Reggae Mediterraneo: Almamegretta', *Rumore*, no. 41 (June), p. 53.
28. Fabbri (1989), p. 141.
29. In Carlo Branzaglia, Pierfrancesco Pacoda and Alba Solaro (1993) *Posse italiane: Centri sociali, underground musicale e cultura giovanile degli anni '90 in Italia* (Florence, Editoriale Tosca), pp. 141–2.
30. A. Solaro (1993) 'Il cerchio e la saetta: Centrali sociali occupati in Italia', in Branzaglia *et al.* (1993), p. 19.
31. In L. Harpin (1993) 'One Continent under a Groove', *i-D*, no. 116 (May), p. 60
32. In Liperi (1993), p. 197.
33. P. Ferrari (1992) 'Rissa nelle posse', *Fare Musica,* no. 135 (summer supplement), p. 15.
34. Liperi (1993), pp. 203–4.
35. Ibid., p. 203.
36. Assalti Frontali, *Terra di nessuno*, Self Produced, 1991.
37. Liperi (1993), p. 199.
38. P. Zanuttini (1992) 'Non e qui la festa', *Il Venerdi* (28 August), p. 77.
39. D. Bignardi (1992) 'Freskonate', *Panorama* (23 August), p. 108.
40. Unattributed (1994) in *On the Street*, Sydney (28 June).
41. Liperi (1993), p. 170.
42. In Zanuttini (1992), p. 77.
43. In *La Repubblica*, (30 June, 31 June 1994).
44. Dezzani (1995), p. 74.
45. *Ibid.*, p. 75.
46. F. Bianchini *et al.* (1995) 'Generazione I', *Rock Star* (April), p. 42.
47. In Harpin (1993), p. 60.
48. De Luca (1992), p. 46.
49. In Branzaglia *et al.* (1993), p. 109.
50. *Ibid.*, p. 100.
51. *Ibid.*, pp. 102–3.
52. Ferrari (1992), p. 11.
53. *Ibid.*, p. 15.
54. *Ibid.*, p. 11.
55. *Ibid.*, p. 14.
56. De Luca (1992), p. 46.
57. A. Santirocco (1992) 'Ma tu da che parte stai?', *Fare Musica*, no. 135, (summer), p. 115.
58. P. Pacoda (1993) 'L'antagonismo in musica: Posse in azione', in Branzaglia *et al.* (1993), p. 88.
59. Possessione, *Il posto dove vivo*, San Isidro, 1993.
60. *Ibid.*
61. L. Lipperini (1992) 'Se sei un ladro dillo col rap', *La Repubblica* (22 August), p. 25.
62. Cooperativa Zenit-Arti Audiovisivi (1992), *Suoni dalla città* (Turin).
63. Lipperini (1992), p. 25.
64. E. Dent (1949) *Opera*, (London, Penguin), p. 102.

65. *Ibid.*, p. 103.
66. *Ibid.*, p. 104.
67. *Ibid.*, p. 105.
68. In Lipperini (1992), p. 25.
69. K. Laing (1994) 'The Europeans', Radio National, Australian Broadcasting Corporation (14 August).
70. Almamegretta, *Figli di Annibale*, Anagrumba, 1993.
71. G. Fofi (1993) 'Prefazione', in Branzaglia *et al.* (1993, p. 8.
72. M. Dezzani (1995c) 'Italian Acts to Follow', *Billboard* (1 July), p. 74.
73. In Campo (1995b), p. 53.
74. In Branzaglia *et al.* (1993), pp. 105–6.
75. *Ibid.*, p. 97.
76. In *La Repubblica* (28 August 1992).
77. Possessione, *Il posto dove vivo*.
78. L. De Gennaro (1995) 'Lo stato delle cose', *Rock Star* (April), p. 36.
79. In D. Amenta (1995) 'Africa Unite: Un sole che brucia', *Mucchio selvaggio*, no. 209 (June), p. 40.
80. In Campo (1995b), p. 53.
81. De Gennaro (1995), p. 36.

Discography

Africa Unite, *People Pie*, Newtone records, 1991.
—*Babilonia e poesia*, Vox Pop/Flying Records, 1993.
—*Un sole che brucia*, Vox Pop/Flying Records, 1995.
AK 47, *0516490572*, self-produced, 1992.
Almamegretta, *Anima migrante*, Anagumbra/BMG, 1993.
—*Figli di Annibale*, Anagumbra, 1993.
—*Sanacore 1995*, Anagumbra, 1995.
Articolo 31, *Messa di vespiri*, Flying Records, 1994.
Assalti Frontali, *Terra di Nessuno*, self-produced, 1991.
Bisca 99 Posse, *Incredibile Opposizione Tour*, Io/Flying records, 1994.
Black Box, *Ride on Time*, Deconstruction Records/RCA, 1989.
Casino Royale, *Dainamaita*, Blackout/Polygram, 1993.
Pino Daniele, *Non calpestare i fiori nel deserto*, CGD, 1995.
Digital Boy, *Digital Beat by Digital Boy*, Flying Records, 1993.
—*Ten Steps to the Rise*, D-Boy, 1995.
Frankie Hi-NRG MC, *Faccio la mia cosa*, RCA/BMG, 1993.
—*Libri di sangue*, RCA/BMG, 1993.
Fratelli di Soledad, *Barzelette e massacri*, X Records, 1992.
Jovanotti, *Penso Positivo*, Soleluna/Ploygram Italia, 1994.
LHP (Lion Horse Posse), *Vivi e diretti*, self-produced, 1992.
Mau Mau, *Sauta Rabel*, Vox Pop/EMI Italiana, 1992.
—*Bass Paradis*, Vox Pop/EMI Italiana, 1994.
99 Posse, *Curre curre guaglio*, Esodo/Flying Records, 1993.
Onda Rossa Posse, *Batti il tuo tempo*, self-produced, 1990.
Papa Ricky, *Lu Papa Ricky*, Virgin Records, 1995.
Piombo a Tempo, *Cattivi maestri*, Crime Squad, 1995.

Possessione, *Il posto dove vivo*, San Isidro, 1993.

Sangue Misto, *SXM*, Crime Squad/Flying Records, 1994.

Various, *Fondamentale*, Century Vox/Sony, 1992 (includes Isola Posse Allstars, Sud Sound System, Sa Razza, Speaker Dee Mo', Devastatin' Posse, OTR, Papa Ricky, Fuckin' Camels 'n' Effect).

—Italian Posse: Rappamuffin d'Azione, Flying Records, 1992 (includes Sud Sound System, Frankie Hi-NRG MC, Comitato, Possessione, La To.sse, 99 Posse, Il Generale).

—*Materiale resistente*, Consorzio Produttori Indipendenti/Polygram, 1995.

—*La musica che cambia*, Polydor, 1995.

—*Nati per rappare*, Crime Squad/Flying Records, 1994.

—*Salento Showcase* 1994, Ritmo Vitale, 1994.

—*Sud*, San Isidro, 1993.

—*Totally Wired Italia Vibrazioni*, Acid Jazz, 1993.

5

Real Wild Child: Australian Popular Music and National Identity

Australia Day

In Sydney on 26 January 1995, the Australia Day national holiday, three conflicting configurations of national identity in popular music took place. At the Sydney Showgrounds, an estimated 34,000 people attended The Big Day Out, a rock festival involving more than fifty local and international rock groups and eighteen DJs on six different stages. Modelled on a similarly named event held in Scotland, the success of the Sydney Big Day Out had escalated to such an extent that in 1995 it sold out three weeks beforehand. (Two nights prior to Australia Day, a concert at Sydney's Entertainment centre featuring three of the most popular Australasian bands of the past ten years, Midnight Oil, Crowded House and Hunters and Collectors, had failed to sell out, suggesting that The Big Day Out was a higher priority for the majority of local rock music punters.[1]) As well as music, The Big Day Out involves a series of 'alternative' carnivalesque entertainments including skating, 3D cinema, a hot rod display, computers, clothing and CD stalls, Green and pro-Republican political campaigners and a host of other attractions. Initiated in 1992, by 1995 the event had become what Jon Casimir described as

> a festival of the counter culture, a gathering of the tribes, of all those teen and twentysomethings ... who see themselves as somehow spiritually or philosophically outside the mainstream – pretty much all of them/us these days. Inner-city types rub shoulders with kids from the suburbs and nightclubbers mosh next to grunge rockers. Everywhere you look there are people with nothing in common other than questionable dress sense and the wish not to be identified as Classic Hits radio listeners.[2]

Something of an apotheosis of this 'gathering of the tribes' occurred at The Big Day Out in 1993, which culminated in US punk and grunge bands Iggy Pop, Sonic Youth and Mudhoney joining forces with Australian gothic-punk group Nick Cave and the Bad Seeds in a chaotic version of Iggy Pop's punk anthem 'I Wanna be your Dog'. Iggy Pop was carried onstage, stripped to waist (he had previously exposed himself to the audience during his set) by Nick Cave, and they and the other male musicians proceeded to stagger about and fall over one another in a prolonged mêlée. This event was later reverentially recorded in the local music press as the climax of what even the middle-aged *Sydney Morning Herald* music critic Bruce Elder described as 'a great tribal offering ... a day of genuine celebration and joy'.[3]

The predominant musical language of The Big Day Out is 'white trash' hard rock and grunge, with usually no more than one black American or Aboriginal group on the bill. This is largely because on the same day a few kilometres away at the Yarra Bay Oval on Aboriginal Land in La Perouse, a slightly smaller event with far less media coverage called Survival Day occurs. Also a day-long event, Survival Day features a line-up of Aboriginal and Torres Strait Islander musicians celebrating what they refer to as Invasion Day with an audience of Aboriginal Australians, Australians of non-English-speaking background and Anglo-Australian sympathizers. There is little overlap between The Big Day Out and Survival Day, and no overseas performers in the latter event. In 1995 the line-up included Archie Roach, Ruby Hunter, Tiddas, Brenda Webb, Mixed Relations, Kev Carmody and the Warumpi Band, to nominate only those performers who have achieved some degree of attention in the Australian media and music industry, performing to an audience estimated at eighteen to twenty thousand, nearly 50 per cent of whom were non-Aboriginal.[4]

Notable for their absence from the bill of Survival '95 were Yothu Yindi, the Yolngu group from North-East Arnhem Land in the Northern Territory of Australia, who have become the most successful Aboriginal rock band, both locally and internationally, in Australian history. Yothu Yindi, who perform rock music with *yidaki* (didjeridu) and *bilma* (clap sticks) augmenting guitars and drums, and feature traditional dancers in tribal dress and bodypaint, were involved in a third, more mainstream, Australia Day event, the Qantas Australia Day Concert in the Sydney Domain. Attended by a significantly larger audience than both The Big Day Out and Survival Day, the Australia Day Concert was also televised nationally on the Kerry Packer-owned Channel Nine. Hosted by blond compere Richard Wilkins, a former MTV veejay who at one point sang 'Happy Birthday' to celebrate Australia Day with the crowd, this event prominently featured the Australian flag, along with numerous references to its national airline sponsor. The televised version of the concert concluded with a rock guitar rendition of 'Waltzing Matilda', reminiscent of Jimi Hendrix's version of 'The Star-Spangled Banner'. Performers included guitarist Tommy Emmanuel, who played a duet with didjeridu player Alan Dargin, and Kate Ceberano, a jazz-cabaret-styled singer of

Filipino origin, who commented on the mixed ethnicity of the audience: 'Look at you, all the multinationals out there ... I'm a mixed breed myself.' Yothu Yindi performed 'Baywara', a song about the Yolngu creator of the land and its song lines, and 'Djapana', or 'Sunset Dreaming', but not 'Mabo', their song celebrating the Torres Strait Islander who overturned the colonial notion of *terra nullius* and brought about legal recognition of Australia as a post-colonial, Aboriginal-owned country in 1992. Yothu Yindi were also induced to join with the other performers in a finale rendition of expatriate singer Peter Allen's song 'I Still Call Australia Home', which is also the theme song in Qantas television advertisements. The concert's jingoistic affirmations of Australianness ('You can't get more Australian than that', commented Wilkins, a New Zealander, after Yothu Yindi's performance), illustrated the complexities and sensitivities involved in constructions of an Australian national identity which has been forced to expand its 'traditional' Anglocentricity to incorporate acknowledgement of the rights of both Aborigines and people of non-English-speaking backgrounds.

The ethnic configurations and community celebrations of the Australia Day Concert, and its supplementation by the alternative 'tribal gatherings' of The Big Day Out and Survival '95, illustrate the conflicts, contradictions and contestations involved in musical representations of an increasingly hyphenated and hybridized Australian national identity. The use of Yothu Yindi in particular as an index of Australian national cultural identity has been debated by a number of writers as, alternatively, representing an illustration of 'a classic symptom of systemic racism',[5] 'the flagship for Aboriginal Australia' (as the group's manager described them)[6] and 'the perfect example of the kind of national cultural expression we should be celebrating now'.[7]

Yothu Yindi and Aboriginal popular music

Largely as a result of a history of genocide, dispersion and appropriation of land in Australia by European convicts and settlers since 1788, Aborigines number about a quarter of a million, which represents about 1.3 per cent of the population of Australia. There are still almost two hundred different Aboriginal language groups spread throughout the country, and Torres Strait Islanders, from the island situated between Queensland and New Guinea, are also a small but significant presence in Australia. Music has played a particularly strong role in traditional Aboriginal belief systems, with the entire continent being linked by a network of song lines which combine the ancestral totems of the Aboriginal Dreamtime. Historically, Aboriginal popular music in Australia has appropriated prevalent white Anglo-American influences such as gospel – influenced by European missionaries – country and Western, rock and reggae, which have been combined with traditional Aboriginal musical instruments such as the didjeridu and *bilma* (clap sticks). The country and Western singer Jimmy Little was the first Aboriginal singer to have a number one single in Australia in 1970 with the gospel song 'Royal Telephone', but it was not until the early 1980s that Aboriginal rock and reggae music began to emerge. Coloured Stone, formed by singer-songwriter Buna Lawrie in South Australia in 1978, were the first Aboriginal rock group to record and are still an important presence in the Australian music scene. Bob Marley's 1979 tour of Australia was an important influence, inspiring a number of Aboriginal bands, including No Fixed Address and Us Mob, who were featured in the 1981 film *Wrong Side of the Road*. As George Lipsitz has commented:

> by taking on Marley's pan-African vision, indigenous Australians transformed themselves from a tiny national minority into part of the global majority of 'non white' people. Like the Maoris in neighbouring New Zealand ... indigenous people in Australia found that the Jamaican's genius for situating 'Blackness' in Caribbean, African, European and North American contexts helped them understand what it meant to be 'Black' in former British colonies in the South Pacific.[8]

But far from being recognized as part of an international pan-African diaspora, *Wrong Side of the Road* showed that Aboriginal rock musicians were an isolated and unrecognized minority going against the grain in their own country, despite a sense of solidarity with black musicians throughout the world. Groups like No Fixed Address and Us Mob faced entrenched barriers of racism in their struggles to make an impact on the local music industry, and No Fixed Address's song 'We Shall Survive (in the white man's world)' became an anthem for Aboriginal struggles. As Marcus Breen has indicated, *Wrong Side of the Road* 'marked the beginning of a public recognition of music as a tool in the fight to communicate the Aboriginal story'.[9]

In 1980 CAAMA (Central Australian Aboriginal Media Association) began broadcasting in Alice Springs, and its studio was used to record Aboriginal groups such as the Warumpi Band, who were the first mixed Aboriginal and white band, and whose 1983 single 'Jailanguru Pakarnu' (Out from Jail) was the first rock song to be recorded in an Aboriginal language. The Warumpi band subsequently released 'My Island Home', which became another Aboriginal anthem, although it was written by the white musician Neil Murray. CAAMA has since grown into a major radio and TV broadcaster covering the 'red centre' of Australia, as well as running a twenty-four track recording studio, record label and music publishing company. Its recorded output – mainly on cassettes – reflects the diversity of Aboriginal popular music – from a country rock compilation of songs warning against the dangers of AIDS, *How Could*

I Know? featuring groups such as the Areyonga Desert Tigers, the Amunda Band and the Tableland Drifters, to educational songs from the radio series *Bushfire Radio*, Aboriginal choirs from Central Australia, a country music album by Trevor Adamson, and an album by the Western Arnhem Land rock, reggae and funk group Black Bela Mujik, who feature Aboriginal vocal inflections, didjeridu and *bilma*.[10]

Owing to the fact that Aborigines continue to be the poorest, least healthy, least educated, most unemployed and most imprisoned people of Australia, most Aboriginal musicians find themselves engaged, directly or indirectly, in political struggles for the recognition of Aboriginal sovereignty and land rights in Australia through their music. As Jimmy Little stated: 'the very fact that an Aboriginal performer gets on stage and sings is a political act.'[11]

Many Aboriginal rock groups also use the didjeridu, which, owing to its immediate sonic association with Aboriginality, is a distinctive marker of indigenous identity. The use of the didjeridu often has a strong cultural function as what Karl Neuenfeldt has referred to as a 'reclamation and revitalisation of ... indigenous heritage'.[12] Its use in an electric rock format also takes on a polemical function, Neuenfeldt argues, in creating 'a "space" in the soundscape of the dominant culture and in that sense [it] has the potential to be resistive to its ideology while simultaneously accommodating, adopting and adapting its technology.'[13] The didjeridu has also been widely sampled (and sometimes played) in world music and European dance music contexts, where its function as what Neuenfeldt has called 'an aural icon of Aboriginality'[14] loses its immediate local context. This occurs despite occasional acknowledgements by English and European musicians who use the instrument as a sign of their respect for Aboriginal people, which often merely conveys essentialistic associations with vague notions of Aboriginal spirituality. In these contexts, the didjeridu's sonic connotations are blurred into indicators of the exotic, or it becomes what Veena Virdi described in *Melody Maker* in 1995 as 'last year's "in" instrument ... subjected to ethnotrance overkill.'[15] These appropriations increase the importance of its use by Aboriginal musicians as a direct expression of Aboriginal culture. In Aboriginal rock music, the didjeridu often acts as an 'earth', supplementing the bass guitar, and sometimes standing in for rhythm or even lead guitar. As Graeme Turner has commented in relation to Yothu Yindi's use of the *yidaki* (didjeridu):

> The effect of the didjeridu is to provide a richer but slacker tone, to complicate or suffuse the beat, meanwhile releasing all the resonances of the exotic, of World Music, of constructions of the 'primitive'. Band members see the didjeridu's expansive sound wave operating so as to tie the lower register of the band's sound together and to give a variety to the bottom end no other instrument can give: as drummer Hughie Benjamin puts it: 'the bottom end of the didj is fantastic, it rattles your ancestors.'[16]

Turner also notes that the didjeridu's modal and melodic effect is particularly suited to more up-tempo 'thrash' rock songs. A particularly strong example of this occurs in one of Yothu Yindi's oddest recordings: a version of Australian heavy metal group AC/DC's song 'Jailbreak' on a 1995 AC/DC tribute compilation album. Yothu Yindi's version of the song incorporates *bilma* as an arrestingly 'primitive' rhythm pulse from the beginning, but it is not until the vibrant circular pulse of the didjeridu comes in more than half way through the song that its deep, earthy 'grungy' resonance under singer Mandawuy Yunupingu's growling vocals supplies an ominous, 'gothic' sonic quality which outdoes AC/DC's original aggressive, nightmarish use of 'dirty' power chords. The song also takes on added political resonances in Yothu Yindi's hands as its narrative of an escape from jail resonates in the context of the high incidence of Aboriginal deaths in custody, with the sonic associations of the didjeridu complementing an oppositional polemical 'attitude'.

It was not until the emergence of Yothu Yindi in the late 1980s that rock music by Aboriginal bands gained any degree of mainstream recognition in Australia, and this was strongly influenced by its increasing recognition overseas as a distinctively Australian form of music. The use of the didjeridu and *bilma* by Anglo-Australian rock groups like Midnight Oil and Gondwanaland had to some degree prepared the way for this recognition, but a series of events in the early 1990s provided consolidation. The Australia-wide success of Jimmy Chi's 1960s-style musical *Bran Nue Day*, based on an anti-mining protest song written in 1978 and set in the Aboriginal-dominated town of Broome, Western Australia, was due in large part to the show's highly benign, non-politically-threatening nature. Treating European missionaries as amiable buffoons and inviting the audience to join in the final chorus 'There is nothing I would rather be / Than to be an Aborigine / And watch you take my precious land away',[17] *Bran Nue Day* featured the Chinese-Aboriginal country music group Kuckles. Kuckles' music attracted the attention of white Australians to other Aboriginal musicians like the Broome-based rock group Scrap Metal, whose members – of Aboriginal, French, Filipino, Japanese and Indonesian descent – also include members of Kuckles. Similarly, the Cairns-based Tjapukai Dance Company's show *Proud to be an Aborigine* proved to have a strong appeal to overseas audiences, and this popularity was eventually reflected in Australia by sales of more than twenty thousand copies of the CD of songs from the show.

Other prominent Aboriginal performers include Kev Carmody, whose poetic protest songs against missionaries, genocide, poverty and numerous other topics invited comparisons with Bob Dylan's early work, and Archie Roach, whose song 'Took the Children Away', about his own experience as a child of being forcibly separated from his family, like 10 per cent of Aborigines, became something of an Aboriginal anthem. By the early

1990s, Aboriginal music was becoming increasingly difficult to ignore, despite continuing reluctance by mainstream radio stations, most of them committed to an Anglo-American and white Australian 'heritage rock' format,[18] to play it. New Aboriginal women groups and performers like Roach's wife Ruby Hunter, Toni Janke and Brenda Webb, 1994 ARIA award winners Tiddas (Sisters), rock group Mixed Relations (formed by ex-No Fixed Address singer and drummer Bart Willoughby) and the Torres Strait Islander singer Christine Anu extended the range of hybrid musical forms played and sung by indigenous musicians from country, rock and reggae to folk, a cappella, pop and dance music. In a prominent feature article on Aboriginal music in 1992 in the *Sydney Morning Herald*, Bruce Elder claimed: 'over the past six months Aboriginal music has suddenly asserted its right to be heard ... after 200 years of neglect the music of Aborigines, and the feelings of Aborigines as expressed through their musical culture, are reaching out to a larger audience.'[19] While Elder attributed this increase in the profile of Aboriginal music in Australia to 'the growing awareness of white Australians', it must also be attributed to a gradual erosion of prejudice by recording companies, radio stations and the Australian music industry in general against indigenous Australian music, which was largely due to increased interest in Aboriginal music overseas.

Yothu Yindi, who include white as well as Aboriginal musicians in their line-up, were at the forefront of a significant hybridisation of traditional Aboriginal music, rock and dance technologies, playing and singing a blend of traditional *djatpangarri* music of the Gumatj and Rirratjingu clans of North-East Arnhem Land and 'pub rock', with reggae and even calypso influences. The name Yothu Yindi means 'mother and child', with a broader signification of family and tribe, and group leader Mandawuy Yunupingu emphasizes their educational concerns with increasing cultural understanding between Aboriginal people and Balanda (white Australians), based on the cross-cultural notion of *ganma*, the place where fresh river water meets the salt water of the sea.[20] As Yunupingu, who is also the headmaster of a country school in Arnhem Land, told the *New Musical Express*: 'our sole purpose as a band is that we're trying to develop and create impact for our culture, involve people from Western civilisation in our world view. And music has a universal language that can convey that.'[21]

Yothu Yindi released their debut album *Homeland Movement* in 1988, the year in which the bicentenary of the arrival of white settlers in Australia was celebrated. The album's rather stark use of predominantly traditional Aboriginal music on one side of the album, and driving rock on the other, immediately attracted attention. The single 'Living in the Mainstream' expressed an Aboriginal notion of 'mainstream' as 'a literal stream, a stream that carries knowledge'[22] which was rather different from the Western idea of mainstream culture, but nonetheless illustrated the group's desire to negotiate with Western ways. A tour of America in the same year as support group to Midnight Oil, in which Native American rap artist John Trudell was also featured, was filmed and screened by the Australian Broadcasting Corporation (ABC) and released commercially as a video, helping to bring attention to Yothu Yindi both locally and internationally. The role of Midnight Oil in promoting Aboriginal bands like Yothu Yindi, the Warumpi Band, Scrap Metal and Coloured Stone by offering them supports in their highly politicized hard rock concerts, which are attended by a high proportion of white urban male working-class audiences, is important in that it has engendered as much indifference to these groups as attention. As John Castles has stated in an account of Aboriginal music which is exemplary in engaging in the complexities of the subject:

> Midnight Oil seem to preside over a field of meaning which has 'no place' for urban Aboriginal bands ... the stagescape Midnight Oil dominates also tends to keep tribal bands 'in place' along the collective past/individual future divide. Until recently Midnight Oil's supports have exhibited the shy, retiring qualities that have come to signify the 'real' outback Aborigine, attributes which do much for Midnight Oil's authenticity by association but little for the support band's chances of commercial success.[23]

In 1991 Yothu Yindi released 'Treaty', a song advocating the realization of a formal pact between black and white Australians promised by former Prime Minister Bob Hawke, which was written collaboratively by Mandawuy Yunupingu with Midnight Oil's singer Peter Garrett and folk-rock artist Paul Kelly. A European-style dance music remix of 'Treaty' by a Melbourne-based sound system calling itself Filthy Lucre became the first single by an Aboriginal artist to feature in the Australian top twenty charts for sixteen years. It went on to become the first single by an Aboriginal artist since Jimmy Little to top the charts in Australia when it went to number one on the Adelaide radio charts in September 1991, although it peaked at number eleven on the national charts. The original recording of 'Treaty' featured a strong dance beat, and the video clip of the song incorporated documentary footage which included former Prime Minister Bob Hawke throwing an Aboriginal spear and Aboriginal Affairs minister Robert Tickner, accentuating the song's address to an unfulfilled promise by Hawke in 1988, to establish a treaty between white and Aboriginal Australia which would protect Aboriginal land rights. The lyrics of the song combined English and Yolngumatha, and the English lyrics of the song begin:

> Well I heard it on the radio – And I saw it on the television – back in 1988, all those talking politicians – Words are easy, words are cheap – Much cheaper than our priceless land – But promises can disappear – Just like writing in the sand – Treaty Yeh Treaty Now Treaty Yeh Treaty Now ... This land was

never given up – This land was never bought and sold – The planting of the Union Jack – Never changed our law at all[24]

Only the first three phrases of these lyrics are retained in the Filthy Lucre remix, in apparent emulation of the English sound system Massive Attack's remix of Pakistani qawwali singer Nusrat Fateh Ali Khan's 'Musst Musst'. Filthy Lucre never met Yothu Yindi, but their remix met with the band's approval, and in a live concerts the band tended to perform the song in its original version with the addition of taped samples of the Filthy Lucre remix. The remix begins with an English voice shouting 'Clap your hands and dance!' followed by an electric organ riff recalling British blues-rock group Spencer Davis's 1960s hit 'Gimme Some Lovin''. Synthesizer and bass, drum-machines, echo and samples are foregrounded, while the Aboriginal lyrics, sampled didjeridu solos and clap sticks are more prominent than in the original version, suggesting an emphasis on the more exotic, Aboriginal features of the song at the expense of its political sentiments. Designed for the dance floor, the Filthy Lucre remix met with Yunupingu's approval, and was described in reverential terms by local music critics. Scott Pullen of the music weekly 3D saw it as 'guaranteed to put Yothu Yindi on the world map and get you on the dancefloor. A contender for the finest dance track ever produced in this country',[25] while Lynden Barber described it as 'one of the brighter spots in this year's radio playlists, the ancient and the modern fusing around a dance pulse owing much to '70s disco aristocrat Hamilton Bohannon'.[26] Rumours even circulated in the Australian music press that copies of the Filthy Lucre *Remix of Treaty* were exchanging hands in British dance clubs for £20 each, indicating an overseas recognition which legitimized the recording's cultural credentials.

Filthy Lucre's techno-based erosion of the political message of the original 'Treaty' was parallelled by a much more fragmented and fast-moving video re-release of the 'Treaty' remix, filmed by Stephen Johnson, the Darwin-based director of the video clip which accompanied the original release of Treaty. This second video version of 'Treaty' featured jerky camera movements and a picture-frame effect, highlighting Aboriginal young people dancing and enjoying the band's performance, and editing out the Bob Hawke sequence, which was seen as potentially confusing to overseas viewers, along with sequences of an Aboriginal painting depicting the treaty. The result conveys a far more anonymously homogenized impression of Aboriginality combined with a fast-paced European techno dance beat, while Aboriginal land rights and other local political imagery, such as brief inserts of Aboriginal street protests, was also removed.

The remixed 'Treaty' single and video became the subject of considerable debate, involving notions of Yothu Yindi as representations of an authentic form of Aboriginal culture and their appropriation by media and industrial interests in a way which echoed arguments about the exoticization of world music. While some saw the remixes as little more than examples of political censorship enabling the song to achieve mainstream media acceptance, others, like Lisa Nicol, argued that 'Rather than simply representing Aboriginal politics in a simplistic and visually obtrusive way, the *process of production* of the videos is paramount, and its procedures faithful, and even submissive to, Yolngu ways and philosophy'.[27] This process of production involved the director's induction into the Gumatj tribe and learning its language, and a collective decision made with tribal elders to focus on what he described as a 'positive, healthy and strong side of Aboriginal culture'. Critics of the video of the remix, Nicol argues, were imposing their own political convictions on Yothu Yindi's musical output and expecting a political commitment which 'seems to deny them the artistic freedoms that Anglo-Celtic musicians enjoy'.[28] On the other hand, as Philip Hayward argued, ' "Treaty" is not just any old song or video, it's a new highwater mark for Aboriginal culture's access to the popular culture mainstream',[29] and as such needed to be considered in the broader context of its political and cultural significance as a statement of relations between Aborigines and white Australia. Mandawuy Yunupingu also expressed his perspective on the Filthy Lucre remix of 'Treaty', indicating that what appeared as 'selling out' to some was rather an involvement in compromise in the interests of promoting of racial harmony:

> at first I didn't know what a dance mix was – someone had to take me aside and explain. But we gave them the go ahead as long as they kept the Yolngu side, the Aboriginal side, intact so that it doesn't lose the magic that we've got. They respected that and when I heard it I thought it was really good ... these days we're doing more compromising in terms of cultural situations, and you've got to do it because you're dealing with the commercial aspects of the industry. As long as our values, beliefs and principles remain intact then I think that's the way to go – and I think we've got the strength to do that. ... We don't want to be a museum piece. We aim to make people aware that we have a unique culture that can co-exist with Western culture.[30]

While the loss of the original version of the song's elaboration of an Aboriginal view of the British invasion of Australia is an important factor to consider, the way in which groups of young Aboriginals adopted the remixed version of the song and danced to it on street corners offered a legitimation of Yunupingu's openness to a hybridization of Aboriginal culture and white Western music technology. As Yunupingu explained, the melody of 'Treaty' is derived from popular Aboriginal dance music in the same way as catchphrases are used in Balanda music, so that 'the dance mix to "Treaty" seems perfect. It corresponds in both cultures every which way'.[31] But in the view of Michael Gudinski, head of the label Yothu Yindi record on, Mushroom Records, the largest and longest-standing independent label in Australia, it was a question of political compromise: 'Sometimes you've got to back the message off a little, otherwise the message doesn't get through to the majority. The way the song works now, so many more people would have been exposed to it'.[32] The cultural reciprocity Yunupingu speaks of is not matched by Gudinski's view of the 'Treaty' remix, which sounds more like standard music industry rhetoric of crossover used to market the song successfully in the Australian musical mainstream.

In 1992 a 'UK Remix' of 'Treaty' by William Orbit was released in Britain and the USA, which transformed the original song into an ambient-house music track, giving added prominence to the exotic sonic qualities of the didjeridu, adding electronic effects and a techno dance beat and effectively removing all the lyrics of the song with the exception of the refrain 'Treaty' here, treaty now' and some of the Yolngumatha phrases. It was difficult to see this UK remix, despite its inclusion of the complete text of the song on the record sleeve (in the UK but not the USA), as anything more than an exercise in musical 'colonial discourse'. The song's political statement was entirely removed, leaving only bland, ambient-styled evocations of the Australian outback within a rigid and repetitive techno dance beat. But, in an interview in the English monthly fashion magazine *The Face*, Yunupingu welcomed the UK remix, 'as long as they don't give us pommy accents'.[33]

In the 1992 ARIA (Australian Recording Industry Association) awards, which were broadcast live on Channel 9 as well as to an estimated twenty million viewers outside Australia, Yothu Yindi won more awards than any other artist: Australian Song of the Year and Best Australian Single for 'Treaty', Best Indigenous Record for their LP *Tribal Voice* and Best Album Cover Artwork award, while Filthy Lucre won the Best Engineer of the Year award for their 'Treaty' remix. 'Treaty' also won a Human Rights Commission's award for Songwriting and the APRA (Australian Performing Rights Association) award for Song of the Year, and the video of the song won MTV and Australian Music Awards. The remixed 'Treaty' single and the album *Tribal Voice* both achieved gold record status in Australia, selling more than 35,000 copies. Yothu Yindi's success in the ARIA awards was marred somewhat by group leader Mandawuy Yunupingu being refused service in a Melbourne pub the night before he received the awards (ostensibly because he was wearing jeans), but Yunupingu did not mention this incident in his acceptance speech, part of which was delivered in the Yolngumatha language. In an article which Yunupingu was commissioned to write for the Australian edition of *Rolling Stone* after the incident (which was eventually settled amicably after an apology by the publican) he stressed the need to overcome racism and discrimination and claimed that 'today's society required Aboriginal people to be part of the white system', reiterating the notion of *ganma* as the meeting of fresh water and salt water.[34]

On the evening after the ARIA awards, Richard Wilkins presented edited 'highlights' from the ceremony on the local version of MTV in a way which illustrated the 'white system' at work. The programme included extracts from the acceptance speeches and live performances by most of the Anglo-Australian award winners: Baby Animals (who have been described as 'the last gasp of pub rock',[35] won three awards, and had three songs aired on the programme), the internationally successful INXS, fronted by British migrant Michael Hutchence, Scottish-born rock 'dinosaur' Jimmy Barnes, 'indie' rock group Underground Lovers, Deborah Conway, and mainstream guitarist Tommy Emmanuel. Only then was there a live performance of Yothu Yindi's song 'Djapana', misspelt 'Dajapana' in MTV's subtitles and mispronounced 'Dja-pán-a' in Wilkins's back-announcement, suggesting that he had not even listened to the song. This was shown without any introduction or even an extract from Yunupingu's ARIA Awards acceptance speech. Yothu Yindi were also preceded by performances by Aotearoa/New Zealand singer Jenny Morris and Canadian émigré Wendy Matthews, both of whom had performed at the ARIA event but not won awards. The reduction of Yothu Yindi's dominance of the ARIA awards to a minor presence in this MTV recapitulation clearly signalled the 'otherness' Yothu Yindi represented in the context of an Anglo-Australian music industry whose 'salt water' continued to swamp the 'fresh water' of Aboriginal culture.

But in contrast to MTV's cultural ineptitude, there was widespread active promotion of Yunupingu and Yothu Yindi by Australian media and politicians as cultural ambassadors and symbols of Aboriginality, both at home and abroad, after the ARIA successes. This promotion relied on an image of Yothu Yindi as politically non-threatening, ethnically colourful and 'media-friendly', which was facilitated by the remixed 'Treaty' video. The degree of this promotion became particularly evident in 1993, the Year of Indigenous People, when Yunupingu was nominated 'Australian of the Year'. (The same award had gone in the bicentennial year of 1988 to the blond, British migrant, middle-of-the-road singer John Farnham, indicating the importance both music and ethnicity have assumed in the award.) Yunupingu's honour was welcomed by Aboriginal and Torres Strait Islander Affairs minister Robert Tickner as 'speaking volumes to people throughout the world about Australia's dedication to change', and Tickner described Yunupingu as 'an outstanding ambassador for Aboriginal people and their achievements and for Australia as a whole'.[36] Yothu Yindi subsequently performed at the Sydney Opera House – a symbol of their acceptance by mainstream Australian culture – and toured Europe, playing at the Royal Festival Hall in London as part of Corroboree, a three-week festival at London's South Bank which also featured Archie Roach, Kev Carmody, Tiddas and Aboriginal films, dance and visual arts. This venture into Europe was seen by Yunupingu as 'tapping into the global beat',[37] although songs like 'Mabo', which proclaims 'Terra Nullius is dead and gone / We were right and you were wrong', on their new album *Freedom*, indicated unambiguously where their concerns lay. ('You were wrong' was later changed to 'they were wrong' in order to ensure radio airplay.[38]) Yothu Yindi's concerts in London were widely reported in Australia, and a film of one of them shown on Australian television, in what seemed like a concerted attempt to portray the group as a symbol that any residues of British colonialism in Australia had been put to rest. But the new album failed to match the success of 'Treaty' and *Tribal Voice*, suggesting a novelty aspect to Yothu Yindi's appeal which had begun to wear off.

In an enthusiastic feature review in the November 1993 issue of the Australian *Rolling Stone* of the Festival Hall concert entitled 'The Velvet Revolution', Michael Dwyer proclaimed: 'You can cut loose to Midnight Oil without listening to a word; you can wiggle your butt to Sting without having heard of the Amazon; but at the end of a Yothu Yindi gig, there's not the slightest chance that a single gyrating bod has failed to grasp The Message'.[39] The 'message' that Yothu Yindi's Aboriginality was perceived by many Australians as expressing outside Australia was a post-colonial assertion of Australia's commitment to Aboriginal rights and sovereignty, but in view of the living conditions of the majority of Aborigines in Australia it contained a degree of hypocrisy that was difficult to overlook. But the local implications of Yunupingu's elevation to ambassador status were of greater importance. In the November 1993 issue of Australian *Rolling Stone*'s rival monthly music magazine, *Juice*, Andrew McMillan (author of *Strict Rules*, a book about Midnight Oil's contentious 1986 'Blackfella-Whitefella' tour of remote Aboriginal communities in the Northern Territory with the Warumpi Band) chronicled a tour by Yothu Yindi of the Northern Territory. Accompanied by Australian country music veteran Slim Dusty, this was a three-week campaign to combat alcoholism in Aboriginal communities. Called the *Raypirri* tour, a term for discipline and self-control used in North-East Arnhem Land, it was funded by the federal government's Drug Offensive. In an area where dancing and overt responses are considered shameful, the tour received a predominantly restrained and subdued response from often quite small local Aboriginal audiences in what Yunupingu described as 'a Typical Yolngu reaction. Quiet appreciation', and the success of its message was difficult to gauge. McMillan's conclusions about the positive national impact of Yothu Yindi reflected by the tour emphasizes that, rather than being Australian national icons, they represent a culture which is not so much exotic as completely foreign to most urban Australians:

By breaking through, Yothu Yindi have been embraced by everyone from the Prime Minister to the Australia Day Council to the Drug Offensive and the Australian Tourism Commission. On a national level they've enhanced our perceptions of Aboriginal people, taken the pop medium to expose their culture, their language, their dance and their art, to say Yolngu culture is alive and well and happy to share aspects of its culture. Mandawuy's songs are like postcards from another culture, studies, glimpses of a foreign lifestyle.[40]

This foreignness is aptly illustrated by Yunupingu's tendency to shout 'Yo!' at the conclusion of a song, an expression which, as Philip Keir has pointed out, 'is not an American rap affectation; "*yo*" quite simply means yes in the local Yolngu or Aboriginal language'.[41] As Philip Hayward has argued, the prevailing media portrayal of Yothu Yindi in Australia as 'safe, exotic and somewhere else' 'conveniently serves to elide all that's troubling to white culture' about Aborigines.[42] This was illustrated by the use of the group by the Australian Tourism Commission and Qantas in a highly successful $75 million campaign involving television, cinema, radio, newspaper, magazine and billboard commercials promoting Australian tourism in Japan.

Yothu Yindi's rise to prominence as national symbols and Aboriginal rock stars contrasts with the continuing lack of recognition of other Aboriginal performers and rock groups. In 1991 Coloured Stone, the longest surviving Aboriginal rock group, who had moved away from politicized reggae forms towards more generalized, not ethnically specific rock influences, released a CD entitled *Inma Juju – Dance Music*. The title suggests an alignment with both world music and techno-dance music, evoking the Nigerian guitar-based ju-ju dance music popularized by King Sunny Ade, while addressing itself to the urban dance club circuit. This release, which included dance-oriented remixes of three tracks from Coloured Stone's 1986 album release *Human Love* (an ARIA award winner in 1987), was an apparent attempt to emulate the dance-pop crossover chart success achieved by Yothu Yindi, but went relatively unnoticed. The album's lack of publicity or accompanying video release may have been due to what John Castles described as Coloured Stone's 'increasing suspicion of the constraints imposed by an automatic linking of their music with their Aboriginality'.[43]

Prevalent images of Aboriginality also became an indicator of Aboriginal musicians' alliance with concepts of world music, especially as a marketing strategy in the USA. A review of Yothu Yindi's *Tribal Voice* in the pop section of *Billboard* in May 1992 suggested that the album 'could strike a responsive chord here in both world music and alternative and modern rock outlets' and praised the album's 'fresh feel that should delight the politically correct as well as music fans who value something different'. In the same issue of *Billboard*, Archie Roach's album *Charcoal Lane*, which had sold little more than 2,000 copies in Australia, despite winning an ARIA award, was reviewed even more enthusiastically in the world music section as 'A unique and frequently moving album [which] heralds the arrival of a stunning talent'.[44] While there is little evidence that either album sold particularly well in the USA, these reviews indicate US attraction to the indigenous novelty of Aboriginal rock music. This attraction was framed in terms of Hollywood stereotypes of prehistoric cultures when 'Treaty' was included on the soundtrack and in a video sequence in *Encino Man*, a 1992 American comedy film about a prehistoric cave dweller who emerges in modern-day Los Angeles. The Los Angeles entertainment weekly *Drama-Logue* tagged Yothu Yindi's 1992 US tour to the theme of the film:

> Following in [Encino Man's] ground-breaking footsteps is the Yolngu Aboriginal band Yothu Yindi, whose members have ventured from their native Australia – with their eclectic and electric combination of sights, sounds and stirring sociopolitical themes intact – to thunder across the rest of civilisation ... Yothu Yindi's music presents to the modern world the songs, dances and attitudes of the band's 60,000-year-old ancestors and modern contemporaries.[45]

This portrayal of Yothu Yindi manages to encapsulate their 'socio-political' concerns as a black ethnic minority into a characterization of the band as a package-tour-like index of the sights and sounds of prehistoric Australia, reflecting the more exotic aspects of world music.

The homogenization of the many different forms of music in Africa which is endemic to the notion of world music is paralleled by a similar reduction of diverse Aboriginal cultures and languages in Australia into a single pan-Aboriginal music. As Castles notes, 'Aboriginal musicians must steer a course between the cliffs of essentialization on one side and assimilation on the other'[46] in their negotiations with Anglo-Australian mainstream culture. While Yothu Yindi managed to negotiate this course with admirable success, they continue to remain the exception that proves the rule as far as the national and international promotion of Aboriginal musicians is concerned. As Kev Carmody stated in 1992:

> Yothu Yindi deserve to be congratulated for putting black back on the musical agenda in this country for the first time in years. Yet bands like Coloured Stone, Warumpi Band, No Fixed Address, Joey Geia and even Roger Knox have been at it for years. They've all put out classic stuff, which has been ignored. To get airplay on mainstream radio is almost a fluke, you get it by accident. That's why I don't see the floodgates opening for Aboriginal music, I really don't. There seems to be a structural resistance in the industry.[47]

This view of Yothu Yindi as exceptions to the rule elevated into icons of Aboriginality has been put forward by Adam Shoemaker in his study of the politics of the marketing of Yothu Yindi, and the inscription of Mandawuy Yunupingu as 'the first certified black Australian pop star' (despite the prior existence of Jimmy Little).[48] Shoemaker argues that the stigmatizing of Yunupingu as a prime Aboriginal achiever and an ambassador for Australian culture as a whole (he has also been characterized as the first Arnhem Land Aborigine to graduate with a university degree in education and to become a school headmaster) illustrates 'the non-Aboriginal obsession with black Australian ground-breakers ... [as] both a catalyst for, and the product of, a racist ideology'.[49] Shoemaker portrays the marketing of Yothu Yindi as an example of commercial and political appropriation which subjects Aboriginal culture to a 'souvenir mentality', and provides evidence that the conditions of 'cultural reciprocity' which Yunupingu advocates do not yet exist in Australia. It is difficult to disagree with this argument: while Yothu Yindi remains a highly desirable image of Australian national cultural identity which the mass media, and the music, advertising and tourist industries are only too willing to exploit, this image cannot be separated from the statistics of Aboriginal health, mortality, employment, housing, imprisonment and education.

The obverse side of Yothu Yindi's elevation to icon status was aptly illustrated by the 1995 ARIA awards, which were loudly heralded in the mass media as signalling the injection of new blood into the Australian music industry. Instead of the usual nominations of figures such as John Farnham, Jimmy Barnes, INXS, Midnight Oil, Wendy Matthews, Kate Ceberano and other members of the 'old guard' of the Australian music industry, the awards were dominated by teenage grunge group Silverchair and mainstream US-styled soul singer and former child star Tina Arena, whose album *Don't Ask* had sold over 250,000 copies. With Yothu Yindi having faded somewhat from the public eye, and few other Aboriginal artists having released recent material, the only indigenous artist to win any award was Christine Anu, who was nominated in a number of categories, but won only the Best Aboriginal/Islander award for her album *Stylin' Up*. This award was not even included in the televised section of the awards, but she was nonetheless made the object of a joke about her name in the most abject bad taste by the presenter of the awards, television talk show host Richard Stubbs.

World music in Australia

Debates about appropriation of indigenous music have occurred in Australia in relation to *Tabaran*, a record produced in Papua New Guinea in 1989 by the Melbourne ambient music group Not Drowning Waving, but not released until 1991. Featuring Papua New Guinea musicians Telek, the Moab Stringband and others, this album was nominated for a 1992 ARIA award in the Best Indigenous Record category, along with Yothu Yindi, Archie Roach and Kev Carmody. In their sleeve notes to the album, Not Drowning Waving claim: '*Tabaran* is not a representative album of Papua New Guinean music nor is it anthropological. It is merely the result of a six week "get together" between six musicians from

Melbourne and a variety of musicians who reside in or near Rabaul on the northwest tip of New Britain island.'[50]

This downplaying of any ethnomusicological claims for the cross-cultural collaboration, in apparent acknowledgement of the controversy surrounding Paul Simon's albums, has been challenged by ethnomusicologist Michael Webb, who argues that there are a number of parallels between *Tabaran* and contemporary ethnomusicology: both involved collaborative fieldwork and make use of field recordings, as well as being works of 'cultural and political advocacy'. *Tabaran* also refers to Papua New Guinea musical styles and political and social events in its lyrics and liner notes, and 'offers a glimpse of musical life in and around Rabaul', although this is more in the nature of what Webb calls 'elements of travelogue'.[51] In its musical exoticism, Webb claims in his rather dry analysis of *Tabaran*, the album extends what Gage Averill has referred to as 'the "Paul Simon cargo cult" network': it is clearly marketed as a Not Drowning Waving album, and the band was in control of the production process.[52] (Although, as Tiffany Hutton has pointed out, the Papua New Guinea musicians were paid for their time, given a percentage of the album's profits and a publishing advance and credited in all publicity, while Pacific Gold studios in Rabaul, where the album was recorded, retained the rights to its release in Papua New Guinea on cassette.[53]) Webb none the less describes the result as 'an innovative soundscape, rich in surprises and contrasts', and through Not Drowning Waving's subsequent collaboration in performance with Papua New Guinea musicians, argues that they approached 'the half way mark' in musical collaboration which put them above merely reinforcing Pacific stereotypes.[54]

After the album was released, the band returned to Papua New Guinea to play live concerts with some of the musicians they recorded with, and subsequently toured Australia with Telek and others, who performed in traditional head-dress and costumes, accompanied by a series of slides of Papua New Guinea. Although the musical adventurousness and openness of the concerts was exhilarating, charges of appropriation and exploitation of Papua New Guinea music were levelled against the group. An expatriate Australian resident in Port Moresby wrote an indignant letter to the Sydney weekly music paper *On the Street* after attending Not Drowning Waving's concert in the Papua New Guinea capital, during which a fight broke out, and accused the group of 'all purpose ethnic indicators', 'rehearsed pidgin phrases' and 'neo-leftie rhetoric. ... Suffice it to say they lack a little in the "cred" department'.[55] But, as Hutton points out, the group's reluctance to market the album as world music, and the decision by the group's recording label, Warner-Reprise, not to release the album outside Australia, meant that any world-music-type debates about appropriation and cultural imperialism were restricted to a purely local context. Hutton also argues that *Tabaran* suffered commercially from its own ambiguity and lack of 'sexiness' in world music terms:

> The African and South American influences prevalent in world music have always been perceived as having a distinctively sexual feel to them, the exotically erotic 'jungle beat' appeal, whereas we are perhaps more inclined to think of Papua New Guinea in ethnographic, *National Geographic* terms. Although it is tempting to see world music as a long-overdue acceptance of non-Western musical styles, the range of what finds acceptance remains narrow. The musical styles on *Tabaran* were perhaps too subtle and esoteric to fit: world music as a genre is perhaps not without its own brand of conservatism.[56]

Despite consistently positive reviews in the local music press, and a citation in the Australian edition of *Rolling Stone* that 'Not Drowning Waving are one of the most important bands working in Australia today'[57] *Tabaran* did poorly in commercial terms, selling only 10,000 copies. When the group's 1994 album *Circus* fared little better, group leader David Bridie suspended the group to concentrate on what was initially a side-project, My Friend the Chocolate Cake, which also involved other members of Not Drowning Waving. My Friend the Chocolate Cake won an ARIA award in 1995 for 'Best Adult Contemporary Release', a rather nebulous category which does little to describe the group's distinctive position in the Australian music scene. Elder has described their music as lying 'somewhere between the Penguin Cafe Orchestra, Celtic folk music, the late 1970s styling of bands such as Magazine and the ambient flourishes of Brian Eno'[58] but this topography overlooks the distinctively Australian subject matter of much of their music. Many of the group's songs are set in suburban Melbourne, and evoke a strong local sense of melancholy, blending classical cadences with pop ballad formats.

Not Drowning Waving's *Circus*, which also included Papua New Guinea, Aboriginal and Aotearoa/New Zealand musical elements, was nominated for the Best Indigenous Recording in the 1994 ARIA awards. The eventual winners of the award, Aboriginal–Scottish *a cappella* group Tiddas, rather unfairly took Not Drowning Waving to task for 'not being black' and thus not qualifying for the award. The following year the title of the award category was judiciously changed to Best Aboriginal/Islander Recording. Bridie has also been much in demand as a producer of recordings by Aboriginal and Torres Strait Islander artists such as Archie Roach and Christine Anu, also collaborating with the latter on a number of compositions, and often introducing Celtic musical elements. He was also featured as a producer and performer on the largest-ever compilation of Australian Aboriginal musicians, CAAMA's 1995 *Our Home, Our Land*, a cross-section of contemporary Aboriginal and Torres Strait Islander music which included twenty-eight performers. A composer and performer of film, television and theatre soundtracks, Bridie was also musical director of *South East*, a 1992 multicultural music and dance project which explored links between traditional Asian art forms and popular youth culture. Bridie reworked Vietnamese and Cambodian musical pieces, and remains an important musical figure in his explorations of Oceanic musical forms which serve to locate Australia in the Asia-Pacific region. As with many musical innovators, his recognition has not been widespread.

While groups such as Yothu Yindi and (potentially at least) Not Drowning Waving are seen as examples of world music outside of Australia, locally they are perceived as pre-eminently Australian. But in the 1990s, when groups such as the Bhundu Boys, Mahalthini and the Mahotella Queens and Kanda Bongo Man began to tour Australia, the live impact of world music as a new source of highly enjoyable dance music began to create a significant local market. In the late 1980s, local world music groups like the Okapi Guitar Band, an Afro-Australian group, the Zambian-born reggae artist Larry Maluma and his group Kalimba, and Nakisa, a largely female Anglo-Australian group who played Greek, Turkish and Iranian music, and their *a cappella* offshoot Blindman's Holiday, began to emerge. The first entirely local world music Festival was held in Sydney in August 1989 as part of the annual multicultural Carnivale festival, and from 1993 Womadelaide, a local version of the annual Womad world music festivals in the UK, became a biannual event in Adelaide, attracting audiences of several thousand people.

But many local 'ethnic' music groups remained trapped in local community 'ghettos' partly caused by the rather solemn and tokenistic image inherent in the concept of Australian multiculturalism. Arguments have been put forward in Australia criticizing the government policy of multiculturalism as no more than an appropriation of the cultures of marginal non-Anglo ethnic minorities for the nourishment and enrichment of an entrenched Anglocentric power base. A musical illustration of this tendency occurs in *Port of Call*, a post-bicentennial album released in 1989 by Sirocco, a largely Anglo-Australian instrumental group who combine didjeridus, bagpipes, crumhorns, electric guitars, ouds, bouzoukis, Tibetan bells and a wide range of other oriental, Middle Eastern and Anglo-Celtic instruments. *Port of Call* is in four parts: 'Desert', where the didjeridu evokes desert in the Northern Territory; 'City to City', which 'combines both the Middle Eastern and Western traditions to offer the brash images of the multicultural city; the oud and drum provide a basis for the changing moods of the city, while the sparkling glissandos of the harp-like Kanun add a touch of exotic mystery'; 'Mountain', which uses cheng and recorder to evoke an oriental mountainscape; and the eponymous 'Port of Call' suite, based on the Australian Museum's bicentennial *First Impressions* exhibition, which simulates musically the journey of the tall ships from London to Australia, ending with a triumphant blast of bagpipes.[59] It is difficult to interpret this musical representation of the British invasion of Australia as anything other than a celebration of colonialism, and one which places all the other exotic and multicultural musics Sirocco appropriates in a similarly colonialist context.

World music is generally perceived in Australia as a non-Australian genre, and few local musicians are accorded the status of world music. After Nakisa held a poorly attended series of concerts at Bondi Pavilion in Sydney in 1991, for example, jazz critic Gail Brennan commented: 'World music and jazz suffer a similar climate in Australia. Interest is high, but attendances don't always follow – unless the artists come from somewhere else in the world.'[60] Different constructions of non-Anglo-Australian musicians related to the world music genre are offered by two 1994 compilations involving Australian 'ethnic' musicians. *Tribal Heart*, a compilation by Peter Noble of Aim Records, is a result of what he describes as careful consideration of 'the question of just what does constitute world music styles of Australia and the South Pacific, bearing in mind the migration to Australia of people from many countries, and particularly African and Caribbean nations over the past decade or so'.[61] Beginning with the Aboriginal band Blek Bela Mujik, the compilation features black and brown indigenous reggae musicians from Australia (I Land), Aotearoa/New Zealand (Moana and the Moahunters, Herbs, Willie Hona) and Papua New Guinea (Barike), along with a range of African and Caribbean groups based in Australia (Fon Ton From, Larry Maluma, Musiki Manjaro, etc.). The result is a remarkably consistent and coherent musical statement which says a great deal about the acculturation of Afro-Caribbean and reggae influences in the South Pacific region, while introducing the listener to a wide range of little-known regional exponents of hybrid African, Jamaican and Pacific musical styles. It serves in the process to define a little-known area of world music located in the Oceanic region. On the other hand, *Earthcore*, another compilation album of world music with an Australian focus, serves to illustrate the cultural and musical imbalance between local and global notions of the genre, with the former at best being seen as local derivations of the latter. Presented by Anglo-African radio presenter Jaslyn Hall as a sampler of her world music programme on the national 'youth radio' station JJJ, *Earthcore* attempts to blend Aboriginal and non-Anglo Australian groups and performers with some of the standard, recognized figures of world music. Hall's advocacy of world music is distinguished by her uncritical enthusiasm for any music which can be placed within the broadest parameters of the genre, and this is reflected in the lack of any musical cohesion in the compilation, which she describes as 'my puddle in the middle of an ocean of "world music"'.[62] *Earthcore* offers Aboriginal musicians the Sunrize Band, Kev Carmody and Alan Dargin, the Senegalese-Australian group Bu Baca Diop, Larry Maluma, Anglo-

Australian female *a cappella* group Arrameida and the Mystère-des-Voix-Bulgares-influenced Martinitsa Choir as local echoes of Mory Kante, Nusrat Fateh Ali Khan, Le Mystère des Voix Bulgares (as reinterpreted by Italian group Elio e le Storie Tese), Apache Indian, Lucy Dube, Khaled, Zap Mama, Angelique Kidjo and others. The album expresses a seemingly borderless heterogeneity and diversity in world music in both its local and European configurations, as well as incorporating reggae, a cappella and rock. The musical and cultural discrepancies between the Australian and non-Australian components are pronounced, situating the Australian tracks as humble and aspiring 'poor relations' of the more widely known exponents of world music who are included.

This 'poor relation' status is borne out by the existence of a number of publicly funded folk-oriented musicians and musical groups from non-Anglo ethnic communities in Australia who operate largely outside the parameters of the Australian music industry. These musicians belong to a genre referred to by Marcus Breen as 'community music', which has emerged as the dominant local variant of world music.[63] Linked to a folk music ideology, community music is linked to notions of the social usefulness of music as helping to define local ethnic cultures, with overtones of 'worthiness' which limit its appeal to a wider audience. Prominent musicians in this field are the Anglo-Australian Linsey Pollack, who performs Macedonian bagpipe music in various formats – most notably in a multicultural group called the Paranormal Music Society – and Kavisha Mazella, an Italo-Indian musician who promoted the West Australian Italian women's choir Le Gioie delle Donne (The Joys of the Women), who sing traditional Italian peasant songs. Both these musicians operate in multicultural spheres which blend different ethnic styles of music in distinctive ways, but which tend to operate in 'underground' community subcultures. Occasionally these submerged subcultures emerge into a public attention that does little more than confirm their existence. In mid 1992, for example, 'Stop the War in Croatia', by Croatian-Australian singer Tomislav Ivcic, slipped unnoticed to number one in the ARIA charts, indicating a Croatian presence in the record-buying public which had previously been invisible.

Australian hip hop: kickin' to the undersound

Rap and hip hop in Australia have also been largely relegated to an 'underground' subculture that rarely emerges into the mainstream of the music industry, which has almost continually refused to acknowledge that an Australian hip hop scene exists. What follows owes a great deal to the extensive field work carried on in Sydney hip hop by Ian Maxwell, who has noted that the two rap albums by Australian artists which have had any noticeable impact on the local music scene both contain references to

Australian hip hop's underground status in their titles: Sound Unlimited's *A Postcard from the Edge of the Underside*, released by Columbia/Sony in 1992 and Def Wish Cast's *Knights of the Underground Table*, released on Random Records in 1993.[64] It is also no coincidence that both groups originated in the Western suburbs of Sydney, an area traditionally regarded as working-class, underprivileged and crime-ridden, with a large proportion of immigrant inhabitants and deprived of many of the social and cultural amenities enjoyed by the inner and northern suburbs of the city. As Diane Powell has stated in her book about the Australian mass media's 'demonization' of Sydney's Western suburbs, *Out West*, the area is comparable to a ghetto:

> Ghettos do not exist in discourse about Australian cities. Yet most Australian cities contain areas that are segregated along class, economic, cultural and ethnic lines. Ghetto is not an appropriate word for these low density suburban, rather than high density inner-urban, areas. However, in Australian culture, to live in some suburbs is to suffer an equivalent stigma to that borne by people living in the ghettos of Europe or America.[65]

The Western suburbs have continued to provide the main historic centre of hip hop culture in Sydney, partly owing to the strong concentration of non-Anglo migrant communities such as Greeks, Italians, Lebanese and Vietnamese, whose youth have been attracted by the racially oppositional features of African-American hip hop and adopted its signs and forms as markers of their own otherness. Muggings, killings and heroin dealing attributed to the Vietnamese street gang the 5Ts in the suburb of Cabramatta have also fuelled the mass media with discourses, which are often highly exaggerated about ghetto-styled street wars and migrant criminal subcultures. In their song 'Tales from the Westside', Sound Unlimited reconstruct a history of the Sydney hip-hop scene in the Western suburbs, locating its origins in the suburb of Burwood in 1983. This break-dance scene, initially influenced by Malcolm McLaren's video 'Buffalo Gals', echoes similar phenomena in a number of countries throughout the world. Kode Blue of Sound Unlimited has described the sense of transnational solidarity provided by this international network of the Hip Hop Nation:

> A lot of it is universal, a lot of those themes do carry right across. That's how come we can call ourselves people who are into rap or hip hop, because we can identify with what they're doing. We can never be Public Enemy but we do follow similar types of guidelines, just being human – being kids that grew up in the 80s and 90s, seeing what's wrong with the world ... I think this is the first time that a whole generation of people from all over the world have been able to speak to each other through music.[66]

Sound Unlimited comprised two rappers of Chilean and Filipino extraction, Rosano 'El Assassin' Martinez and his sister, Tina Martinez (T-Na), along with Kode Blue, an Anglo-Australian, and Vlad DJ BTL, who is of Russian extraction. Initially called Sound Unlimited Posse, they emerged from a group called the Westside Posse, who were featured on a compilation album of Australian rap music, *Down Under By Law*, released by Virgin Records in 1988. This album made no impact on the charts and did not sell in significant quantities, but provided evidence of a fledgeling hip hop scene predominantly infatuated by Afro-American gangsta rap. It also featured two female components, Sharline, whose 'Hardcore Love' was in the style of US female rappers like Queen Latifah, M. C. Lyte and Yo Yo, and Fly Girl 3, who took their name from a track by Queen Latifah, and 'dissed' macho behaviour. Apart from Westside Posse and Pest-A-Side, in which Rosano Martinez also featured, there were two other notable Sydney groups on the album: the boasting, disco-oriented Swoop, the longest survivors of the local hip hop scene, and Mighty Big Crime, who were oriented towards funk. Most of these groups adopted the trappings of US hip hop, including, in some cases, its boasting and a bragging, macho attitudes towards women, and a reiteration of gun rhetoric (the opening track, by the Westside Posse, is entitled 'Pull the Trigger'). Despite the Australian accents, few local cultural referents emerged, and the American parlance and inflections of US hip hop models were adopted by most of the groups, who ended up sounding like 'poor relations' of their US counterparts. Apparently minimal production facilities also gave the album a rather amateurish feel, but it did represent an emerging scene, capable of developing distinctive local tendencies with further encouragement. This encouragement was not provided, as Virgin quickly distanced itself from the project, and most of the groups subsequently disbanded.

Sound Unlimited Posse soon developed a localized political perspective, moderating their admiration for Public Enemy, for whom they played as a support group on their Australian tour, receiving encouragement, advice and offers of work from Flavour Flav. Their 1990 debut single, 'Peace by Piece', a relatively 'soft' rap promoting racial tolerance, was followed in 1991 by 'Unity', which advocates universal racial harmony, and 'Paradise Lost', which recognizes the priority of Aboriginal land rights and attacks Australian racist attitudes. The video for 'Unity' closely mirrors the urban ghetto-styled iconography of Public Enemy's Spike Lee-directed clip 'Fight the Power', with a group of young 'hoods' raising clenched fists on a rooftop with a Sydney city skyscape in the background, but the local concerns were also strongly evident.

Sound Unlimited Posse were relatively successful in marketing terms, being the first and only Australian rap group to be signed to a major record label, Sony, and even performed with a group of break dancers at the 1993 ARIA awards. Some of their output shared an affinity with the whimsical, playfully 'soft' rap of De La Soul and other rappers associated with the US 'Native Tongues' movement, making them easier to incorporate into the mainstream. But as the opening track of their album, a portrayal of the music industry entitled 'Sharks and Rodents', indicated, they regarded signing to a major label as a compromise. But Sound Unlimited played the game too well – the album was produced in Boston by Slamm Antunes productions, who also co-authored a number of tracks. The Antunes had previously worked with US teen pop idols New Kids on the Block, and Derek Antunes subsequently joined Sound Unlimited as the group's resident drummer, married Tina Martinez and indirectly triggered the group's break-up. (The Martinez siblings and Antunes reappeared in 1995 as Renegade Funktrain, a decidedly more mainstream, pop-oriented soul group whose first single, 'I Wonder', was a cover of a song by 1970s rock singer Boz Scaggs.) According to Ian Maxwell and Nikki Bambrick, *A Postcard from the Edge of the Underside* was received with 'dismay' by the local hip hop community, and regarded as too 'crossover' and commercial: 'over-produced, over-instrumentalised and altogether too slick'.[67] But the group retains the distinction of being the only Australian rap group to record on a major label, and their status as a mixed-gender, non-Anglo migrant-dominated group related them to universal, collective, multicultural and transnational notions of hip hop. Rosano Martinez's comments in a 1990 interview indicate an embrace of the more peaceable trans-national and community-based aspects of US hip hop:

> I like the idea of a gang in the way that it unifies all individuals. I like that vibe and the idea that people will stick together, even if they don't know each other, because they're on the same wavelength. The Zulu Nation is a real positive thing, and people like De La Soul and the Jungle Brothers are the new generation. In today's society you've got a worldwide instant media and you can't really say you're from a certain country; you can only state the way you think.[68]

The group's 1992 single 'Kickin' to the Undersound', which was introduced by Flavour Flav, addresses itself to this global rap community, but also expresses local concerns, sampling Men at Work's reggae-inflected worldwide 1982 hit single 'Down Under' – which has been described as 'a de-facto national anthem'[69] – and defining the group as an Australian entity in a more hard-core, but dance-oriented style than their previous releases. The group also identified themselves with the colours of the Aboriginal flag, and played on the catchphrases 'underground', 'undersound' and 'down under', locating Australia, rap and non-Anglo-Australian identity as submerged and marginalized. 'Kickin' to the Undersound' remains an important defining moment in Australian hip hop, and, despite the subsequent demise of Sound Unlimited, it locates the local rap scene as 'underground' in terms of both the local music industry and the cartography of global hip hop.

Def Wish Cast also used flag imagery to identify themselves in strongly nationalistic terms in their 1992 debut EP, entitled AUST *Down Under Comin Upper*, which announced the arrival of Australian hip hop in no uncertain terms. The track 'AUST', which Maxwell has described as 'the unrivalled anthem of Australian hip hop',[70] attempts to give Australian hip hop scene equal weight to those of the USA and UK: 'A.U.S.T. ... an island that many never look twice at as being associated with rap – on hip hop charts they come across a new discovery U.S., U.K., U.S., what A.U.S.T. ... Hold up a new flag our own turn for the better / The letters that stand alone not in the shadow of any other country Def Wish Cast from A.U.S.T.'[71] Lead rapper Def Wish's rapid-fire ragga rap, which has been described as 'syllable ballistics', was influenced more extensively by Jamaican rappers from the UK than Afro-American rappers, and is almost incomprehensible at times. The group's use of 'dirty' samples, complete with vinyl scratches and static, from 1970s soul records and kung fu and science fiction movies as well as other non-musical sources, make their rather cluttered sound difficult to listen to. As Maxwell has commented:

With a curious blend of musical styles: an African-American derived hip hop crossed with the Jamaican-dub raggamuffin, delivered in a nasal, vowel-bending Australian accent, presenting itself as somehow defining of an 'Australian-ness' fit to 'hold up a new flag', Def Wish Cast set about a programme of cultural self-definition which itself reassigns 'cultural' value in terms of commitment to acts of appropriation, rather than in terms of adherence to a more directly received, linear 'tradition'.[72]

The import-dominated Australian hip hop culture which Def Wish Cast mythologizes is largely confined to a small and fragile, and almost exclusively male, subculture based around a record shop in central Sydney, the Lounge Room, local fanzines such as *Vapours* and *Head Shots*, a couple of programmes on local community radio stations and sporadic gigs at various clubs (although Miguel D'Souza, host of the weekly programme 'The Mothership Connection' on 2SER, has claimed that the programme attracts up to 10,000 listeners).[73] There is also a small but growing number of locally produced albums, some on cassette only, by groups such as Illegal Substance, 046, White Boys, Easybass (formerly the Urban Poets) and Noble Savages, who featured Blaze, a graffiti artist, owner of the Lounge Room and a key figure in the Sydney hip hop scene. The fragility of the scene is further symptomized by the break-up of Def Wish Cast in 1994, after *Knights of the Underground Table* had made little impact on the national charts, but reportedly reached number two on the independent charts in Norway. As Maxwell has indicated:

This Australian, specifically Sydney-based in this instance, hip hop community is almost obsessively self-reflexive: through the lyrics of the raps, the sources of the samples layered into the backing tracks, the graffiti art layered into the visual background of the railway tracks of suburban Sydney, through the clutch of locally produced and globally distributed hip hop magazines, through the radio and print commentaries produced by the hip hop culture's intellectuals, the hip hop community consistently narrativises the terms of its own possibility as, simultaneously, a specifically Australian, local formation, and as an integral part of a transnational, global formation.[74]

It is in the interests of serving this collective cultural identity, Maxwell argues, that notions of authenticity come into play, specifically in relation to a commitment to 'hard-core' hip hop consisting of what Blaze has described as 'fat beats, dope rhymes'. The hiss and crackle of a sample taken from a vinyl recording is also an important indicator of authenticity illustrating 'truth to the music'.[75] In his analysis of Def Wish Cast's album, Maxwell points to its specific Australian references, locating 'rappin' writin' and breakin'' in the Western suburbs, where such practices fill a cultural void, and noting the group's insistence on Australian accents, to the extent that they dissociated themselves with guest rapper M. C. Kane because they found his style too American.

Maxwell rightly uses Def Wish Cast's hybridity of influences to contest the American cultural imperialism thesis which has frequently been expressed in the Australian mass media, most notably in a prominent feature article in the *Sydney Morning Herald* in 1994 by Richard Guilliatt, entitled 'U.S. eh? Why Young Australia is so Smitten with American Culture'. This article examined widely expressed concerns that Australian youth were not only turning to American basketball and other sporting heroes and clothes and rejecting the previously strong local and national sporting traditions of cricket, swimming and rugby league, but also embracing McDonald's, US cultural icons like James Dean, and television programmes like *The Simpsons* and *Melrose Place*. Guilliatt suggested that Australian youth was being subjected to 'an unstoppable geyser of American pop culture' which threatened to flood a hard-won Australian cultural identity. Interviewing Western Sydney rapper Sean Taylor of the group Voodoo Flavour, he pointed to his use of 'pilfered' US hip hop jargon such as 'phat', 'chill', 'props' and 'kickin'' as an indicator of 'African-American culture as the *sine qua non* of cool for Australian youth', identifying hip hop as 'the dominant youth style'. Statistics provided by an advertising agency survey demonstrated that 90 per cent of Australian young people's favourite programmes were American, 85.1 per cent wore American sports clothes, the favourite sport of 92 per cent was basketball, and 87.31 per cent rented only US videos. But Guilliatt countered his extended dramatization of this widespread US cultural invasion and loss of local identity with the suggestion that US influences had been just as predominant in Australia in the 1960s and 1970s. He concluded with an apparent open-ended ambiguity, opposing a characterization of the global village as Los Angeles with a portrayal of Def Wish Cast's 'broad Strine accents' and association with 'a growing clique of hip hop crews pursuing an Australian identity' as evidence of 'a wave of patriotism' in a youth culture which found strong cultural and social affinities with US cultural forms.[76]

What emerges most strongly from this article is the globalization of these US cultural icons and the universality of local panics about their contaminating influence, and a neglect of the strong local cultural indicators which are expressed even in the adoption of these imported and borrowed forms. While young Australians might easily be mistaken for Americans if regarded solely in terms of their clothes and visual appearance (and photographs accompanying the article served to prove this point), the singularity of Australian speech patterns, social practices and cultural forms of expression is still unmistakable. And since the social realities of life in the urban ghettos of the USA are vastly different from the relative comfort and affluence of Australia, the fetishized American artefacts of hip hop culture take on a strong imaginary quality. As Sound Unlimited discovered when they visited the USA in 1992, Australian social realities pale in comparison to the harshness of life in the urban ghettos of the USA:

> America is totally different to Australia, it opened our eyes to a lot of things. Life is really hard for young kids, particularly for young black kids. ... The hip hop community was similar to here in that we all listened to the same music and came from a similar background. It's just that the whole thing is intensified by the fact that life can get really hard.[77]

Maxwell supplies an indicator of the level of exaggeration in the moral panics about US influences expressed in Guilliatt's article in Illegal Substance's rap track 'Drive-Bye'. This begins with a news report of a brawl between Lebanese and black youths at a dance party in Villawood in Western Sydney which ended in the death of an eighteen-year-old youth. The song compares the brawl to the beating of Rodney King by Los Angeles Police, and suggests that Sydney is becoming as violent as Los Angeles. 'Drive-Bye' works in references to Ice Cube and Ice-T, and samples John Travolta's 'Staying Alive' as well as the sounds of gun shots and squealing car tyres in what is virtually a parody of US hard-core gangsta rap. It expresses what Maxwell describes as 'the media-mythologised space of the Western suburbs as a proto-Los Angeles. Asian gangs in Cabramatta. Rooty Hill as Compton. Werrington as South Central. Watch out! It's happening here too! the ghetto is on its way.'[78] Moral panics about the perceived spread of pernicious social influences related to US hip hop culture are parodied, and 'Drive-Bye' also serves to illustrate the imaginary identification with US hip hop which largely characterizes the local hip hop scene.

The development of a national Australian hip hop scene was given some degree of 'official' recognition by the release by Mushroom's subsidiary label MXL in 1995 of *Home Brews Volume 1*, a compilation of eleven Australian rap tracks by mostly unrecorded and almost exclusively male 'bedroom' hip hop practitioners from Sydney, Canberra, Melbourne and Adelaide. Appearing seven years after *Down Under By Law*, it provided a book-end to a local hip hop 'tradition' still in the process of defining itself. Robert Brailsford's liner notes expressed a prevailing sense of fragility:

> apart from having a hip-hop history, it is a history being built on. The main problem being Australian hip-hop suffers the same fate as English or for that matter Zambian hip-hop. The prevailing attitude is that only American hip-hop is real. ... The main challenge for Australian hip-hop is to discover and consolidate what makes it unique. I don't really think anyone knows what that is, but *Home Brews* should provide some clues.[79]

Unlike *Down Under By Law*, the album's diversity of styles is immediately noticeable, with trip hop, ragga, acid jazz and funk influences predominating. The album's title comes from its opening track, Canberra group Koolism's 'Extraordinary', which refers rather self-consciously to a boomerang and 'true home brew kids', echoing the long-standing 'Aussie kids are Weet-aBix kids' television commercial. Produced by acid jazz exponent Matt Hayward, it includes Melbourne group Mamas Funks, the remnants of Mama's Funkstikools, the Australian representatives on Tommy Boy's *Planet Rap* compilation, a rather odd and monotonous ambient-jungle instrumental by Sydney-based Mouvement Electronique, liberal telephone call samplings from Debt Crew, freestyle rappers Voodoo Flavour, the ragga-oriented Wicked Beat Sound System, a rap about prostitutes by Melbourne-based Merma, a 'diss' of the Australian music industry by Brazilian rapper Bill Almeida of BSK, and Sydney crew Raised by Wolves. As a grouping together of exponents of a virtually invisible underground movement, the album is a valuable indicator of some of the developments in the national hip hop scene.

While hip hop's appeal to Australian youth of non-English-speaking backgrounds as a vehicle for expressing their otherness within Australian culture has often been noted, Maxwell's work portrays the Sydney scene as dominated by middle-class Anglo-Australian rappers. Rap also appears to have made little impact on Aboriginal youth culture, where rock, reggae and country remain the dominant adapted musical forms. But it is notable that the only two Aboriginal rap crews to have performed in Sydney are both female. The duo Blakjustis – Torres Strait Islander Goie Wymarra and Aboriginal Paula Maling – originated at the Eora Aboriginal Centre for Visual and Performing Arts in Sydney, and performed at Survival '94. Influenced by Public Enemy, their repertoire includes 'Motherland', about the European invasion and decimation of Aboriginal Australia, the forcible removal of Aboriginal children from their families, and black deaths in custody. Their song 'Biggest Mob of

Blacks' was written as a celebration of Survival Day, celebrating the survival of Aboriginal people and culture. The group also perform comedy sketches and work separately as DJs on Koori (Aboriginal) Radio, and had a strong impact within the Aboriginal community in Sydney, but are otherwise little known, and have not recorded.[80] Also performing at the Survival '94 concert were the Alice-Springs-based rap-dance trio Arrernte Desert Posse, three teenaged girls who combine traditional Aboriginal music and dance elements, complete with body-paint, *bilma* and didjeridu backing tapes, with more urban aspects of hip hop, donning flannel shirts and beanies in a highly theatrical, choreographed representation of their rap music. Both groups represent an 'underside' to an underground scene struggling to define itself, and clinging to a largely imaginary notion of community. As Blaze has stated, referring to a growing number of young hip hop crews in Sydney such as his own group Noble Savages, Etnik Tribe, Beats-a-Frenik, Sleek the Elite, Easybass, Capital Punishment, Industrial Dispute and Stored Information, the local scene is united by a single-minded dedication and commitment to hip hop culture: 'it's just a bunch of kids, basically, who have the drive and initiative and they just do it in their spare time. They realize Australia's not the kind of country where you're gonna make money from it, and if you do think that way you're doomed to failure.'[81]

Australian dance music: back to *terra nullius*?

The Sydney-centricity reflected in Australian hip hop recurs in local dance music or rave culture, which quickly distanced itself from the local hip hop scene as an inner city phenomenon, and in the late 1980s based itself around a series of dance parties held in the Hordern Pavilion, a venue with a five thousand capacity based in the Sydney showgrounds. (In one notable example of inner-city segregation in 1990, a dance party held at Homebush in the Western suburbs of Sydney contained a separate 'inner city lounge' reserved for patrons buying their $36 tickets in advance.[82]) As Andrew Murphie and Edward Scheer point out in their study of Australian dance parties, Sydney dance culture had few local indicators of its identity, celebrating its internationalism through a scene initially dominated by visiting British and European backpackers, known in local parlance as 'Eurotrash': 'Dance culture has allowed Sydney, somewhat megalomaniacally, to see itself as a music capital of the world.'[83] This megalomania was bolstered by the establishment of Sydney as the gay capital of the Southern Hemisphere, marked by the growing international popularity of the annual Sydney Gay and Lesbian Mardi Gras celebrations, which culminate in an all-night dance party in the Hordern Pavilion, and the annual Sleaze Ball, a predominantly gay event which takes place in the same venue. Sydney's house parties – imported in

concept directly from London via Chicago – were usually legal, unlike
their UK counterparts, but had what Murphie and Scheer describe as a
'feeling of illegality ... to do with the aggregation of sex, fashion and a
participation in a "global culture". These seemed to transcend the so
called "tyranny of distance" and connect Australia with the instantaneity
of fashion and music fashion in the rest of the world.'[84] Initially defined by
a group called the Recreational Art Team (RAT), who held a series of
large New Year's Eve events, priced out of the range of anyone but the
affluent, Sydney dance culture was a simulacrum of rave culture in Europe
and the USA, in which 'a diverse group of designer bodies is involved in
the pseudo-collective process of constructing a "groove" which, in any
event, takes place "somewhere else" in the virtual space shaped by
designer drugs.'[85] Using Meaghan Morris's notion of Australian cultural
activity as a 'radical forgetting of original codes ... a compilation culture
of borrowed fragments, stray reproductions and alien(ated) memories',[86]
Murphie and Scheer portray a scene constructed almost entirely from the
flotsam and jetsam of European and American import cultures. The
weekly 'Madchester' raves dedicated to a celebration of the Manchester
sound, which were held in Sydney in 1990 and 1991, offered 'the seductive
sounds of nostalgia for unreachable origins',[87] while the more than 90 per
cent ratio of imported dance music played at most parties turned the
Australian house and dance party scene into a weightless, featureless *terra
nullius* of simulated and displaced origins.

Nonetheless, an Australian dance music culture with recognizable
properties did emerge with the establishment of the Sydney-based Volition
Records in 1984. Set up by British expatriate Andrew Penhallow, Volition
was inspired by the British dance label Factory, and began releasing
records by local underground techno group Severed Heads, world-
ambient trance group Single Gun Theory and the techno-industrial
Scattered Order. Severed Heads, a sonic collage group who consist largely
of producer and video-maker Tom Ellard, had begun in 1979 as a totally
independent outfit, marketing their own rather avant-garde, industrial
material by mail order before eventually making a deal with Vancouver-
based independent label Nettwerk, which specialized in techno, dance and
industrial music, as well as the London-based label Ink. When the group
also signed up with Volition, it found itself dealing with three labels, a
situation symptomatic of the international focus of the Sydney dance
scene. As Ross Harley has stated in his survey of the Volition label,
Severed Head's three-label connection represented an

> alliance of forces that helped Severed Heads reach the same 'local' market in
> Europe, North America and Australia. This 'axis' also confounds the notion
> that the kind of music Severed Heads and other Volition techno-pop acts
> produce is tied to a specific locality or 'cultural geography'. Although Ellard's
> music does have strong connections to the Australian independent/experi-
> mental scene, he would have long since given up making music were it not for

the number of dispersed localities (recording, production and distribution contexts) he could tap into around the world. The same remains true for other successful Volition acts, Boxcar and Single Gun Theory.[88]

This international focus was consolidated when singles by Severed Heads ('Greater Reward') and Brisbane-based technopop group Boxcar ('Freemason'), whose music was reminiscent of British dance-pop groups like New Order and Dépêche Mode, reached the top ten of the US *Billboard* dance charts in 1987. Both were mixed by Sydney-based producer Robert Racic, whose influence directed Severed Heads into a more commercially oriented, techno and dance music format. Volition concentrated its efforts on promoting Severed Heads, Boxcar, Single Gun Theory and Scattered Order locally and on the international dance music circuit for a number of years before signing a number of new Australian dance music acts who were showcased on the label's 1992 double-CD compilation *High*. This recording announced the consolidation of an Australian dance music and rave culture, featuring sixteen Australian dance acts including Sydney-based South End, Third Eye and Itch-E and Scratch-E, Brisbane-based Sexing the Cherry and Vision 4/5, as well as the label's original quartet of groups. But unlike the first wave of Volition acts, the newer groups on *High* did not make any notable impact outside Australia. Yet, according to Harley, there were important local implications in the 'dynamic mix of ambient, trance, hardcore, humorous, dance, acid and club sounds' on the *High* compilation, which remained in the top five in the ARIA compilation charts for five months:

> this type of music represents a discernible shift in the sonic landscape of Australian music. These new techno sounds have a 'physicality' that mirrors the rhythm and aural dimension of the dance nightclub. The dense electronic drum tracks and swirling synthesiser sounds provide a sonic backdrop which is quite unlike that provided by live rock bands. Although there have been other moments when the Oz rock ethos has been significantly challenged, this represents the first time a wave of heavy techno-based sounds became audible in a variety of different locations simultaneously (and not just in the nightclubs – on radio, in bars, lounge rooms; at small and large parties alike).[89]

Other challenges to the 'Oz rock ethos' were emerging from Melbourne, which had developed its own electronic ambient-dance music scene with groups like Zen Paradox and Soma, among others, but the amorphously anonymous nature of the music meant that there was little to distinguish it from other examples of the genre throughout the world. One exception which proved the rule was South End and Sydney DJ Nik Fish's release in 1994 of 'The Winner Is . . .', a dance single which repeatedly sampled the announcement of Sydney's successful bid for the Olympic Games in the year 2000 over a repetitive pulse of dance beats. A clamorous but contentious event to many opposed to the proliferation of a jingoistic

Australian sports culture and the homogenization and fast-track urban development of Sydney the Olympic games represented, the Sydney-centric patriotism of 'The Winner Is ...' appealed to a certain political conservatism and yuppie-styled complacency within the local dance culture scene. This contrasted with the independent, alternative ethos proudly displayed by the Volition label. Despite Harley's claim that the Australian dance music scene represented ' "local" music fight[ing] for its right to exist internationally through the adoption of and dialogue with a number of synthetic styles, even "histories" ',[90] it could also be seen as merely replacing the stultifying orthodoxy of 'Oz rock' with a soulless *anomie* based on a spurious international self-image. This impression was confirmed by Itch-E and Scratch-E's cheeky acceptance speech for winning Best Dance Music Release at the 1995 ARIA awards, in which they thanked 'the Ecstasy dealers of Australia' for helping them win the award. This remark took on particularly unpleasant overtones a few weeks later with the widely publicized death of a fifteen-year-old girl after taking Ecstasy.

'Oz rock': Australian music's dead centre

> The chief objection to 'Oz Rock' is that it is essentially an anachronism, a reactionary music that looks perpetually over its shoulder to a decaying, less progressive Australia. It breathes the stale air of that sleazy, neurotically masculine world where women were molls or madonnas and the White Australia policy ruled supreme. It is that music blunt enough to force a way through the dull haze of drunkenness.
>
> (Lynden Barber, 'Oz rock, a corporate creation')[91]

Most of the Australian popular music I have considered so far exists largely outside the mainstream parameters of the national music industry, which has historically defined itself through events such as the ARIA awards in terms of the white Anglo-Australian, male-dominated, nationalist tradition of 'Oz Rock'. This tradition can be seen as the dominant narrative of an exhibition entitled *Real Wild Child! Australian Rock Music Then and Now* which was mounted at Sydney's Powerhouse Museum in 1994, where it ran for two years prior to a national tour. Taking its title from US punk rocker Iggy Pop's 1985 reworking of Australian rock and roll star Johnny O'Keefe's 1958 hit 'The Wild One' – the first Australian rock and roll hit record – the exhibition traces four decades of Australian rock music. The title's reference to Iggy Pop's version of 'Wild One' – which is also used as a theme to ABC television's music video programme *Rage* – rather than Johnny O'Keefe's suggests a lingering aspiration for legitimation of Australian music by the US music industry, as well as portraying the local music scene as a wayward child in the shadow of a perceived US cultural imperialism.

The trope of the 'wild child' has recurred in a number of guises since Johnny O'Keefe, from internationally successful vintage thrash metal group AC/DC's lead guitarist Angus Young's perennial school uniform costume to Chrissie Amphlett's impersonation of a nubile schoolgirl in a gymslip in the Melbourne rock band the Divinyls. This gymslip image was recycled by Sydney female metal-thrash group Nitocris, who were too young to play in pub venues in their first year of activity, on the cover of their 1995 EP *Epic Voyage*, which includes a version of AC/DC's 'Dirty Deeds Done Dirt Cheap'. Another variation on the 'wild child' trope occurs in a 1995 Australian television commercial for McDonald's, which pairs fourteen-year-old Australian blues guitarist prodigy Nathan Cavalieri in a recording session with US blues veteran B. B. King, with both addressing each other as 'Mister' and going off for a hamburger. Even within the local music industry, this commercial has been interpreted as symbolizing the fledgeling, dependent status of Australian popular music in relation to the US music industry. The continual press reports of the slow but steady progress up the US charts to number nine in October 1995 of *Frogstomp*, an album by fifteen-year-old schoolboy grunge trio silverchair further illustrates this childlike economic subservience to the US market. (By mid-October 1995 *Frogstomp* had sold 140,000 copies in Australia and 500,000 in the USA.) Described by *Rolling Stone* writer David Fricke as 'Nirvana in pyjamas'[92] after the popular local pre-school children's television show, *Bananas in Pyjamas*, silverchair have been protected from excessive media exposure. Their manager imposed a total media ban on the group after their ARIA awards in 1995, which were accepted on their behalf by the seven-year-old son of the producer of the group's debut album. silverchair's status as the new 'great white hopes' in a continuing lineage of 'Oz rock' was emphasized by their performance at the conclusion of the ARIA awards of 'New Race', a song by Iggy Pop-influenced 1970s Australian punk rockers Radio Birdman (who subsequently reformed for the 1996 Big Day Out). While silverchair and ex-child star Tina Arena's dominance of the ARIA awards were widely read as evidence that a 'new race' had supplanted the established figures of 'Oz rock' of the 1980s such as John Farnham, Jimmy Barnes, Midnight Oil, INXS, Ice House, Kate Ceberano and others, it is important to note that in both musical and industrial terms they merely continue to reproduce an established mainstream musical lineage.

Apart from illustrating the pervasiveness of the 'wild child' lineage, the *Real Wild Child* exhibition charts the 'Oz rock' lineage, absorbing all the 'other' aspects of Australian popular music such as music by women and Aborigines, punk rock, indie music and dance music, into its prevailing monolithic discourse. The exhibition catalogue contains brief historic surveys by prominent local journalists on sub-genres such as women in Australian rock, dance music (incorporating hip hop, represented solely by Sound Unlimited), Aboriginal music and the different music scenes in

Sydney, Melbourne, Brisbane, Adelaide and Perth, while the exhibition itself also absorbs 'Australian' musicians of Aotearoa/New Zealand origin like Split Enz, Crowded House, Dragon, Mi Sex, Jenny Morris and Dinah Lee. Midnight Oil receive a feature interview in the catalogue as an affirmation that 'the Australian records that have fared best internationally are those who are most Australian',[93] and there is a prominent feature on Johnny O'Keefe, the 'once and future wild one'.[94] Pub rock is also surveyed, and characterized as 'unpretentious and hard-edged ... music that got to the point',[95] and a history of Australian rock, charting the shift from being 'fuelled by the latest international fad' in the 1960s to 'local relevance' in the 1990s,[96] presents the exhibition's overall perspective. The exhibition itself consists of 'fetish' objects ranging from two of Johnny O'Keefe's suits to clothing worn by AC/DC, Midnight Oil, INXS, Split Enz and Kylie Minogue, Men at Work's saxophone and Yothu Yindi's didjeridu and guitar, which features the image of the Aboriginal flag, and the *Countdown* music television show host Ian 'Molly' Meldrum's cowboy hat, probably the most potent icon of all in terms of enduring public images of Australian popular music. There are also historic record covers, a video juke box, fanzines, historic posters advertising gigs, and various interactive exhibits devoted to studio recording, Australian music quizzes and virtual reality musical instruments. The heterogeneity of the exhibition's layout is subordinated to the homogeneity of its narrative, and dominated by the all-absorbing 'master narrative' of nationalism.

According to Marcus Breen, more than 80 per cent of recorded popular music sold in Australia is imported,[97] but Peter Garrett has claimed that the remaining 20 per cent of local product still makes Australia the third largest exporter of popular music in the world.[98] The Australian music industry also has more government protection than in most other countries. This was clearly illustrated in 1995, when a five-year enquiry by the Price Surveillance Authority (PSA) into the high prices of CDs in Australia ($31 or £14.80) culminated in a direct intervention by the Prime Minister, Mr Keating. Keating ordained that prices should remain as they were, provided that the 'big six' major multinational recording companies made an unspecified commitment of $270 million over three years to the local music industry. The 'big six' (EMI, Sony, Polygram, Warners, BMG and the Rupert-Murdoch-owned Festival, which has links with the most prominent independent label, Mushroom) thus successfully maintained a highly profitable (55 per cent profits in 1989) monopoly on 90 per cent of recording copyright control in Australia, pegging CD prices at up to 46 per cent higher than in the USA.[99] What particularly rankled the CD-buying public about this situation was that in 1991 twenty-six prominent local musicians, including John Farnham, Neil Finn, Kate Ceberano and Peter Garrett of Midnight Oil, had supported an aggressive campaign by the 'big six' against the PSA to prevent parallel imports and deregulated prices. Garrett and others argued that this was because local musicians' royalties would be threatened by an import system which allowed for the possibility of cheaper releases of their recordings being sold back to Australia from overseas markets. During this campaign, Garrett let slip that he bought most of his CDs outside of Australia, an option not enjoyed by most local consumers.

The besieged atmosphere emanating from the Australian music industry's reaction to the PSA enquiry was amplified in April 1995, when a 'summit' mounted by Australian musicians outside Parliament House in Canberra asked for government support for what was portrayed as an ailing industry: stagnant record sales – further threatened by the absence of music copyright on the Internet – a diminution of the market share of local acts by one-third, virtually no Australian musicians making an impact on overseas markets in the past five years, little airplay on local radio and a live scene dominated by international acts and a plethora of local tribute bands – some of whom played the repertoires of Australian artists. Symptomatic of this slump in the industry was the emigration of Jimmy Barnes to France, leaving an estimated debt of $4.7 million.[100] But these fears were expressed mainly by established recording artists, disguising the fact that most of the diversity and musical appeal in the local music scene lay elsewhere, among more than sixty small independent labels which marketed local music and imported specialist music. In October 1995, for example, a *Sydney Morning Herald* feature profiled Shock Records, which distributes sixty local independent record labels and ninety overseas labels, and had exported recordings worth $9 million in the past financial year to the USA, the UK, Europe, Canada and South-East Asia. Working on the principle of selling two thousand copies of one hundred recordings rather than two hundred thousand copies of one recording, Shock represents 200 Australian bands, and illustrates a market which makes up in diversity for what it lacks in major sales.[101] But as a result of the failure of the PSA enquiry, Shock were forced to remove thousands of items from their import catalogue and raise their import prices in 1995, because they were being charged publishing royalties both in Australia and overseas.[102]

Marcus Breen has characterized the Australian recording industry in terms of native birds, comparing the multinational major labels to lyrebirds, who reproduce the sounds of other birds, while the specialist local labels set up by the majors to supply the local market are compared to magpies, skilled in finding and collecting objects, and local indigenous independent labels are portrayed as flightless emus, who produce a 'guttural, choking sound'.[103] Breen argues that the Australian music industry is Australian only in so far as it is situated inside Australia, consisting of major labels which function as neo-colonialist outposts, marketing Australian artists such as Midnight Oil, INXS, Kylie Minogue, Crowded House and others 'not as Australian bands, but as major international acts, devoid of a national identity'. The local independent labels are 'often the mediators of the emotional and cultural baggage of indigenous popular music',[104] prompting the majors to set up subsidiaries to tap into this 'baggage', a dynamic which, Breen concludes, contains hopeful indications of a collaborative promotion of Australian music. But the increasingly aggressive way in which Australian mainstream recording artists are being marketed by the major labels in the Asia-Pacific region, for example, with no interest in any reciprocal exchange of music, is indicative of an approach in which Australian musical product is often 'dumped' on unsuspecting overseas markets with little regard for its indigenous indicators. Mainstream pop singers such as Tina Arena, Rick Price, Diesel, GF4 (formerly Girlfriend) and Peter Andre, none of whom have any recognizably 'indigenous' Australian features in their music, are being used to take advantage of a demand for foreign music in countries such as Japan, Singapore, Hong Kong and Korea, in an entirely profit-motivated neo-colonialist exercise which reproduces the traditional role of the major labels in Australia.[105]

The question of the absence of any recognizable indicators of national identity in Australian music, especially the music marketed abroad, is one that is addressed by Graeme Turner:

> While there are pockets of musicians doing original things at any one time in the suburbs of Melbourne or Sydney or Perth, it is characteristic of such music that we describe it through reference to genres which come from elsewhere: we talk of new ska bands, or revival/tribute bands, or technopop bands, and so on. To look for 'the Australian' element is to look for a local inflection, the distinctive modification of an already internationally established musical style. It would not be difficult to argue that the work of the Divinyls, or The Church, or The Saints, or even the Black Sorrows, is distinctive but it would be very difficult to describe that distinctiveness, or indeed the stylistic conventions which frame their music, as Australian. One would argue similarly about earlier, 'classic' Australian bands such as Daddy Cool, The Easybeats, or Skyhooks. The American and British dominance of popular musical styles and of the retail music market has been so comprehensive that one cannot really locate an indigenous musical style either in the mainstream or in the 'alternative' fringe of the Australian rock and pop industry.[106]

But as Turner has indicated elsewhere, Yothu Yindi provides a convenient compendium image of a hybrid Australian national musical identity which resolves the problem of defining distinctive Australian features,[107] as well as providing a potent aural and visual expression of indigenous music. As we have seen, Yothu Yindi primarily represents an oppressed indigenous minority which can be appropriated as an indicator of national identity only with considerable difficulty. Turner argues that it is the contexts in which Australian music is produced and consumed which define its Australianness, pointing to Australian radio, television and print media as constructors of popular histories of Australian music. But most of these histories reproduce dubious nationalist narratives of the post-colonialist 'Aussie battler' against US and UK domination and the 'cultural cringe', which saw Australian culture as inherently inferior examples of foreign models. This leads him to consider the importance of live venues, and pubs in particular, as sites of recognition of a 'national character' in Australian music culture. The problem with this, as he acknowledges, is that the often masculinist, racist and reactionary discourses of 'Oz rock' and pub rock become conflated with attempts to 'champion the egalitarian, the unpretentious, the "authentic" – the dominant values of Australian culture'.[108] This is what the *Real Wild Child* exhibition also attempts to do in its construction of a history of Australian popular music.

But Turner also suggests that it is often in 'a middle level of small, quiet, concert-styled venues for the Paul Kellys of the industry'[109] where much stronger indicators of local Australian features can be found. The example of Paul Kelly is a resonant one. If national identity can be defined in the subject matter of songs, Kelly's quiet, unpretentious country-rock style, which has ranged from celebrations of the cricketing prowess of Don Bradman to portrayals of black deaths in custody, represents an unforced expression of one kind of Australian musical identity. This is complemented by the work of David Bridie, the music of a range of Aboriginal and Torres Strait Islander recording artists, Euro-ambient group Gondwanaland's one-armed Anglo-Australian didjeridu player Charlie McMahon, who has been granted access to secret knowledge of the Kintu tribe, Midnight Oil's overt and often self-conscious hard rock expressions of Australianness, with their use of didjeridu and widespread local polemical subject matter, and the less self-conscious output of a number of other, often unheralded musicians who ensure that Australian music is not a *terra nullius* of overseas musical influences but a heterogeneous polyphony of post-colonial local voices.

Notes

1. J. Casimir (1995a) 'Fast and Furious Oils keep Fires Burning', *Sydney Morning Herald* (26 January), p. 19.
2. J. Casimir (1995b) 'Defining Sydney's Youth Culture', *Sydney Morning Herald* (28 January), p. 14A.
3. B. Elder (1993) 'Iggy Carries the Day', *Sydney Morning Herald* (28 January).
4. Unattributed (1995) 'Concert Fee Hampers Aboriginal Turnout' and 'The Big Day Out: The Aftermath', *Drum Media* (31 January), p. 16.
5. A. Shoemaker (1994) 'The Politics of Yothu Yindi', in K. Darian-Smith (ed.) *Working Papers in Australian Studies Nos. 88-96* (Institute of Commonwealth Studies, University of London), p. 23.
6. Quoted in *ibid.*, p. 27.
7. G. Turner (1995) *Making it National* (Sydney, Allen & Unwin), p. 202.

8. G. Lipsitz (1994) *Dangerous Crossroads: Popular Music, Postmodernism and the Poetics of Place* (London, Verso), p. 142.

9. M. Breen (1994) 'I Have a Dreamtime: Aboriginal Music and Black Rights in Australia', in S. Broughton *et al.* (eds) *World Music: The Rough Guide* (London, Rough Guides, 1994), p. 657. See also Breen (1992) 'Desert Dreams, Media, and Interventions in Reality: Australian Aboriginal Music', in R. Garofalo (ed.) *Rockin' the Boat: Mass Music & Mass Movements* (Boston, South End Press), pp. 149–70, and C. Lawe Davies (1993) 'Aboriginal Rock Music: Space and Place', in T. Bennett *et al.* (eds) *Rock and Popular Music: Politics, Policies, Institutions* (London, Routledge), pp. 249–65, for overviews of Aboriginal rock music.

10. D. Simmonds (1990) 'From Motown to Ourtown', *The Bulletin* (9 October), pp. 112–13.

11. In T. Mitchell (1993) 'Tony Mitchell Replies', *Perfect Beat*, vol. 1, no. 2 (January), p. 31.

12. K. Neuenfeldt (1994) 'The Cultural Production and Use of the Didjeridu in World Music', *Perfect Beat*, vol. 2, no. 1 (July), p. 93.

13. K. Neuenfeldt (1993) 'The Didjeridu and the Overdub', *Perfect Beat*, vol. 1, no. 2 (January), p. 75.

14. Neuenfeldt (1994), p. 101.

15. V. Virdi (1995) 'Meandering Stars', *Melody Maker* (18 February), p. 9.

16. Turner (1995), p. 199.

17. Jimmy Chi and Kuckles (1991) *Bran Nue Day: A Musical Journey* (Sydney, Currency Press and Broome, Magabala Books), p. 15.

18. See J. Potts (1992) 'Heritage Rock: Pop Music on Australian Radio', in P. Hayward (ed.) *From Pop to Punk to Postmodernism: Popular Music and Australian Culture from the 1960s to the 1990s* (Sydney, Allen & Unwin), pp. 55–67.

19. B. Elder (1992) 'Black Music Shakes Off the Past', *Sydney Morning Herald* (14 January).

20. J. Stubington and P. Dunbar-Hall (1994) 'Yothu Yindi's "Treaty": Ganma in Music', *Popular Music*, vol. 13, no. 3 (October), pp. 243–60, provide a musicological analysis of 'Treaty' in relation to the cross-cultural concept of *ganma*.

21. In *New Musical Express* (1 February 1992), p. 33.

22. In Shoemaker (1994), p. 35.

23. J. Castles (1992) '*Tjungaringanyi*: Aboriginal Rock', in P. Hayward (1992) p. 19.

24. Yothu Yindi, *Tribal Voice*, Mushroom Records, 1992.

25. S. Pullen (1991) 'On Disc', *3D* (20 June), p. 20.

26. L. Barber (1991) 'Rock', *Sydney Morning Herald* (17 September).

27. L. Nicol (1993) 'Culture, Custom and Collaboration – Yothu Yindi's *Treaty*', *Perfect Beat*, vol. 1, no. 2 (January), p. 30.

28. *Ibid.*, pp. 31, 29.

29. P. Hayward (1993) 'Safe, Exotic and Somewhere Else', *Perfect Beat*, vol. 1, no. 2 (January), p. 40.

30. In S. Hitchings (1991) 'We'll Kick Arse No Worries: Yothu Yindi', *On the Street* (23 December), p. 27.

31. P. Keir (1992) '*Tribal Voices*', *Rolling Stone* (Australian Edition), no. 466 (January), p. 75.

32. In C. Lawe Davies (1993) 'Aboriginal Rock Music: Space and Place', in T. Bennett *et al.* (eds) *Rock and Popular Music: Politics, Policies, Institutions* (London, Routledge), p. 254.

33. In *The Face* (February 1992).

34. M. Yunupingu (1992) 'Black and White', *Rolling Stone* (Australian Edition), no. 471 (June), p. 34.

35. In *Real Wild Child! Australian Rock Music Then and Now* (Sydney, Powerhouse Museum Exhibition Catalogue, 1994), p. 9.

36. In Shoemaker (1994), p. 26.

37. M. Dwyer (1993) 'The Velvet Revolution', *Rolling Stone* (Australian Edition), no. 489 (November), p. 54.

38. In *Juice* (November 1993), p. 46.

39. Dwyer (1993), p. 55.

40. A. McMillan (1993) 'Homeland Movement', *Juice* (November), p. 46.

41. Keir (1992), p. 74.

42. Hayward (1993), p. 41.

43. Castles (1992), p. 32.

44. M. Newman *et al.* (1992) 'Album Reviews', *Billboard* (23 May), p. 43.

45. E. Stimac (1992) 'The *Tribal Voice* of Yothu Yindi On the Edge of Musical Discovery', *Drama-Logue* (25 June–1 July), p. 2.

46. Castles (1992), p. 31.

47. In R. Miller (1992) 'Is this the birth of Koori Cool?', *Songlines*, no. 3, p. 6.

48. In Shoemaker (1994), p. 21.

49. *Ibid.*, p. 23.

50. Liner Notes, Not Drowning Waving and the Musicians of Rabaul, Papua New Guinea, *Tabaran*, WEA, 1990.

51. M. Webb (1993) '*Tabaran* – Intercultural Collaboration', *Perfect Beat*, vol. 1, no. 2 (January), pp. 4, 5.

52. *Ibid.*, p. 6.

53. T. Hutton (1993) 'Uncertain Identities: Marketing *Tabaran*', *Perfect Beat*, vol. 1, no. 2 (January), p. 17.

54. Webb (1993), pp. 11–12.

55. Unattributed (1991) 'Not Drowning Waving', *On the Street* (17 April), p. 31.

56. Hutton (1993), p. 21.

57. *Ibid.*, p. 16.

58. B. Elder (1994) 'Suburbia in Pastel Shades', *Sydney Morning Herald* (26 September).

59. Sirocco, *Port of Call*, Jarra Hill Records, 1989.

60. G. Brennan (1991) 'Nakisa', *Sydney Morning Herald* (29 June).

61. P. Noble (1994) Liner Notes, *Tribal Heart: World Music Styles of Australia, New Zealand and the South Pacific*, Aim Records.

62. J. Hall (1994) Liner Notes, *Triple J Earthcore: A World Music Show Compilation*, ABC Music/EMI.

63. M. Breen (1994) 'Constructing the Popular from Public Funding of Community Music: Notes from Australia', *Popular Music*, vol. 13, no. 3 (October), pp. 313–26.

64. I. Maxwell (1995) 'Steppin Freestylee: Improvised Rap and the Negotiation of Community in the Sydney Hip Hop Scene', unpublished paper, International Association for the Study of Popular Music, University of

Stathclyde, Glasgow, 1995.
65. D. Powell (1994) *Out West: Perceptions of Sydney's Western Suburbs* (Sydney, Allen & Unwin), p. xiv.
66. I. Maxwell and N. Bambrick (1994) 'Discourses of Culture and Nationalism in Sydney Hip Hop', *Perfect Beat*, vol. 2, no. 1 (July), p. 13.
67. *Ibid.*, p. 10.
68. In *On the Street* (15 August 1990), p. 21.
69. *Real Wild Child!* (1994), p. 11.
70. I. Maxwell (1994a) 'Def Wish Cast "Down Under Comin' Upper"': Rapping the Westside', unpublished paper, International Association for the Study of Popular Music, Southern Cross University, Lismore, p. 7.
71. Def Wish Cast, *Knights of the Underground Table*, Random Records, 1993.
72. Maxwell and Bambrick (1994), p. 16.
73. Maxwell (1995).
74. Maxwell (1994a), pp. 2–3.
75. *Ibid.*, pp. 4–6.
76. R. Guilliatt (1994) 'U.S.eh? Why Young Australia is so Smitten with American Culture', *Sydney Morning Herald* (25 June), pp. 1A, 4A.
77. In R. Gow (1992) 'Unlimited!', *On the Street* (28 October), p. 19.
78. I. Maxwell (1994b) 'Busting Rhymes', *Real Time*, no. 3 (October–November), p. 4.
79. R. Brailsford (1995) Liner Notes, *Home Brews Volume 1*, MXL/Mushroom Records.
80. G. Young (1994) 'Blackjustis: Black Justice', *Vertigo*, no. 7, University of Technology, Sydney, pp. 30–1.
81. Unattributed (1995) 'Head Shot: Blaze Hip Hop Yoda + Original Wax Junkie', *Head Shots*, no. 2, p. 18.
82. J. Casimir (1990) 'Dance, But Don't Step into My Lounge', *Sydney Morning Herald* (5 September), p. 3.
83. A. Murphie and E. Scheer (1992) 'Dance Parties: Capital, Culture and Simulation', in Hayward (1992), p. 172.
84. *Ibid.*, p. 175.
85. *Ibid.*, p. 180.
86. *Ibid.*, p. 182.
87. *Ibid.*, p. 183.
88. R. Harley (1995) 'Acts of Volition – Volition Records, Independent Marketing and the Promotion of Australian Techno-Pop', *Perfect Beat*, vol. 2, no. 3 (July), p. 32.
89. *Ibid.*, p. 41.
90. *Ibid.*, p. 46.
91. L. Barber (1987) 'Oz Rock, a Corporate Creation', *Sydney Morning Herald* (29 August), p. 51.
92. In *Rip It Up*, no. 213 (May 1995), p. 4.
93. *Real Wild Child!* (1994), p. 25.
94. *Ibid.*, p. 22.
95. *Ibid.*, p. 14.
96. *Ibid.*, p. 29.
97. M. Breen (1994) 'Introduction', *Popular Music*, Australia/New Zealand issue, vol. 13 no. 3 (October), p. 240.

98. P. Garrett (1991) 'The PSA Would Kill the Music Industry with Cheaper Records', *Sydney Morning Herald* (12 August).
99. A. Ramsey (1995) 'Keating Sings to his Mates' Tune', *Sydney Morning Herald* (29 April), p. 33.
100. R. Guilliatt (1995) 'Pop Music Industry is Singing the Blues', *Sydney Morning Herald* (26 April), pp. 1, 6.
101. J. Casimir (1995) 'Shock Tactics Take Major Music Companies by Storm', *Sydney Morning Herald* (14 October).
102. S. Coupe (1995) 'Shock and CD Prices', *Drum Media* (17 October), p. 30.
103. M. Breen (1992) 'Magpies, Lyrebirds and Emus: Record Labels, Ownership and Orientation', in Hayward (1992), p. 40.
104. *Ibid.*, p. 50.
105. Unattributed (1995) 'Asia Prepares for an Aussie Assault', *Sydney Morning Herald* (5 May).
106. G. Turner (1992) 'Australian Popular Music and its Contexts', in Hayward (1992), p. 13.
107. Turner (1995), pp. 193–202.
108. Turner (1992), p. 21.
109. *Ibid.*, pp. 23–4.

Discography

046, *LIFE*, self-produced, 1995.
Christine Anu, *Stylin' Up*, White/Mushroom Records, 1995.
Tina Arena, *Don't Ask*, Col/Sony, 1995.
Blek Bela Mujik, *Come-N-Dance*, CAAMA, 1993.
Coloured Stone, *Inma Juju – Dance Music*, 1992.
David Bride and John Phillips, *Projects 1983–1993*, White Records, 1994.
Kev Carmody, *Pillars of Society*, Larrikin Records, 1989.
—*Bloodlines*, Festival, 1993.
Def Wish Cast, *Knights of the Underground Table*, Random Records, 1993.
Easybass, *Space Program 1996*, self-produced, 1995.
Gondwanaland, *Wide Skies*, Warner, 1993.
Gondwana, *Travelling*, ABC Music, 1994.
Ruby Hunter, *Thoughts Within*, White Records, 1994.
Illegal Substance, *Off da Back of a Truck*, Illegal records, 1994.
Tomislă Ivcic, *Peace in Croatia*, POS/BMG 1992.
Paul Kelly, *Deeper Water*, White Records, 1995.
My Friend the Chocolate Cake, *Brood*, White Records, 1994.
Nakisa, *Camels in the City*, Sandstock Music, 1991.
Nitocris, *Epic Voyage*, Phantom Records, 1995.
Noble Savages, *Noble Savages*, Hell Tasty Recordings, 1995.
Not Drowning Waving and the Musicinas of Rabaul, Papua New Guinea, *Tabaran*, WEA, 1991.
Not Drowning Waving, *Circus*, White Records, 1993.
The Paranormal Music Society, *Moving On*, Larrikin Records, 1993.
Archie Roach, *Jamu Dreaming*, Aurora/Festival, 1993.
—*Charcoal Road*, Aurora/Festival, 1991.

Sirocco, *Port of Call*, Jarra Hill Records, 1989.
silverchair, *Frogstomp*, Murmur/Sony, 1995.
Soma, *Soma*, Mumbo Jumbo/Polygram, 1994.
Sound Unlimited, *A Postcard from the Edge of the Underside*, Columbia, 1992.
Southend with Nik Fish, *The Winner Is . . .*, Volition Records, 1994.
Tiddas, *Sing about Life*, ID/Phonogram, 1993.
Various, *Aids: How Could I Know?*, CAAMA/Polygram, 1990.
—*Down Under by Law*, Virgin Australia, 1988.
—*From the Bush*, CAAMA/Polygram, 1990.
—*Fusebox: The Alternative Tribute*, Ariola/BMG, 1995.
—*High: A Dance Compilation*, Volition Records, 1992.
—*Home Brews Volume 1*, MXL/Mushroom, 1995.
—*The Joys of the Women (Le Gioie delle Donne)*, ABC Music/Phonogram, 1993.
—*Our Home, Our Land*, CAAMA/Mushroom, 1995.
—*Tribal Heart: World Music Styles of Australia, New Zealand and the South
     Pacific*, Aim Records, 1994.
—*Triple J Earthcore: A World Music Show Compilation*, ABC Music/EMI, 1994.
White Boys, *Westside*, Warlord Records, 1995.
Yothu Yindi, *Homeland Movement*, Mushroom Records, 1988.
—*Tribal Voice*, Mushroom Records, 1991.
—*Treaty (Filthy Lucre Remix)*, Razor Records/Mushroom, 1991.
—*Treaty (William Orbit Remix)*, Mushroom/Hollywood Records, 1992.
—*Freedom*, Mushroom Records, 1993.
Zen Paradox, *Eternal Brainwave*, Psy-Harmonics/Polygram, 1993.

6

The Sounds of Nowhere? Bicultural Music in Aotearoa/New Zealand

A history of appropriations

In a small country of three and a half million people, Aotearoa/New Zealand popular music has affinities with that of the Czech Republic in having little impact on the international music scene, and relying heavily on imported music from the USA and Britain. Historically, Aotearoa/New Zealand popular music has followed other Western countries in absorbing and appropriating Anglo-American trends, although its Maori–Pakeha (European) biculturalism and its geographical isolation has often lent idiosyncratic and eclectic colourings to its adaptations of external forms and models. North American influences were dominant in the early years of Kiwi rock and roll. In 1957, for example, US imports comprised 97 per cent of the Aotearoa/New Zealand top twenty singles chart. Strong residual colonial and cultural ties to Britain, however, meant that British musical trends tended to have a stronger impact on the less commercially oriented sectors of the local music scene. This factor tends to be overlooked by commentators like Geoff Lealand in *A Foreign Egg in Our Nest?*, a book which sets out to prove a cultural imperialist thesis in asserting that Aotearoa/New Zealand film, television, and popular music are overwhelmingly dominated by influences from the USA. In characterizing Aotearoa/New Zealand as 'the end consumers of fashions that have been determined in overseas markets' and 'the furtherest-flung outpost'[1] of Anglo-American global initiatives such as Live Aid, Lealand dismisses locally produced music as irretrievably second-hand: 'Simply put, all Aotearoa/New Zealand music (from classical to country and Western) is derivative. It borrows from abroad; expanding on imported influences, denying them, and then re-embracing them. Styles, themes and sounds are all borrowed; consequently Aotearoa/New Zealand-produced music is governed by universal, or international sounds and rhythms.'[2] But Lealand's argument is rather too 'simply put'. In an attempt to prove his thesis, he reproduces Radio New Zealand statistics of the percentages of North American (36–60 per cent), British (21–55 per cent) and Australian (2–7 per cent) records in the Aotearoa/New Zealand top twenty singles chart from 1966 to 1984, which shows that Aotearoa/New Zealand records have never occupied more than 18 per cent of total chart successes (or less than 4 per cent) in any one year. This becomes evidence that 'popular music in New Zealand has largely been culture "imposed from above" (that is, from the Northern Hemisphere) ... overseas artists have always been the most popular in Aotearoa/New Zealand, with usually at least half of these from the United States'.[3]

But a closer look at these statistics reveals that two peak periods in local musical success, from 1968 to 1973 and 1980 to 1984, are paralleled by a decline in US dominance and an increase in the impact of British music on the charts. This suggests a confluence between Aotearoa/New Zealand and British music which is worth investigating. The list of local records which reached the Aotearoa/New Zealand top twenty from 1966 to 1975 included as an appendix to John Dix's remarkable, encyclopedic study of Aotearoa/New Zealand rock music from 1955 to 1988, *Stranded in Paradise*, reveals a predominance of British mod-styled pop-oriented bands and singers. The influence of the Beatles, the Rolling Stones, the Kinks and other British beat groups was particularly strong, and cover versions of their songs were frequently played by local groups. This was partly a result of a continuing fascination with the British 'Swinging Sixties' boom, and partly because Aotearoa/New Zealand radio and television had begun to provide significant space for local performers and musicians for the first time.

This emergence in the 1960s of a significant body of local pop-oriented performers, who were able to make an impact on the commercial mainstream of local chart-oriented pop music while performing music which appealed to the less commercially oriented tastes of students and rock fans, was relatively short-lived. In New Zealand as elsewhere, the 1970s saw rock music take on an increasingly oppositional, 'counter-cultural' aspect, scorning chart-oriented pop music. One of the main ingredients in the development of the music associated with the Flying Nun label in the 1980s is a 'jangling' pop guitar-oriented mode, strongly influenced by the Velvet Underground, which refers back to this late 1960s local pop boom with a mixture of nostalgia and pragmatic pastiche. In the 1990s, a number of re-releases of albums by local groups of the late 1960s such as Bari and the Breakaways and Tom Thumb, along with compilation albums of 1960s rock groups like the La De Das, the Pleazers and others, and an anthology of more obscure 1960s Kiwi garage bands, *Wild Things*, suggested that this all-but-forgotten period of local music was undergoing a revival of local recognition. Books on the rock music scene in Wellington and Auckland in the 1960s by Roger Watkins, and a magazine, *Social End Product*, dedicated to forgotten local music of the same period, provided further evidence of moves in the 1990s to reclaim the local music scene of the 1960s, which had frequently been dismissed as derivative of the English beat scene.[4]

In dismissing Aotearoa/New Zealand popular music as imitative and derivative, Lealand overlooks the dynamics of a process of cannibalizing and recycling of its own history which characterize post-1970s popular music globally, irrespective of national origin. He also overlooks the positive aspects of the 'tyranny of distance' which enables Aotearoa/New Zealand popular musicians to poach, consume and reconstruct selected fragments from imported musical practices, often reassembling them in new and idiosyncratic combinations.

In his 1995 book *Understanding Popular Music*, Aotearoa/New Zealand writer Roy Shuker finds Lealand's argument still applicable to the country's music scene of the 1990s, citing the fact that 'the multinational record companies continue to supply approximately 90 per cent of the domestic market'[5] in the 1990s as continuing evidence of the lack of a distinctively local or national musical product. Shuker also includes the statistic that in 1985 46 per cent of the top hundred albums in Aotearoa/New Zealand were from the US, and 43 per cent from the UK. Regarding the small-scale but ever-growing success in the USA and Europe of Aotearoa/New Zealand independent music produced by labels such as Flying Nun, Xpressway and IMD as 'label sounds' rather than national sounds, Shuker argues that there is still little evidence of any distinctive national identity in Aotearoa/New Zealand music. Comparing the country unfavourably to Canada, he suggests that, in order to survive, much local music has to imitate and appropriate dominant Anglo-American styles. But Shuker excepts 'certain forms of Maori (indigenous) music' – an exclusion which in itself tends to make his argument inapplicable to all Aotearoa/New Zealand popular music.

As indicators of national musical identity, Shuker posits three interrelated factors: local associations deriving from a band or performer's name or song lyric content; evidence of a local accent in the pronunciation of words of a song; and local musical styles or idioms such as the rather amorphously defined 'Dunedin sound' associated with the Flying Nun label. In all cases, Shuker argues, there is scarce evidence of any distinctively local features in Aotearoa/New Zealand rock and pop music, citing an experiment in which university students were unable to distinguish between a series of local and international hits of the past twenty years unless they already knew the songs. This he attributes to a perceived necessity for local bands to imitate international styles and trends in order to receive radio airplay, which he uses as a preface to an analysis of arguments for and against a local music quota on Aotearoa/New Zealand radio, which has yet to be introduced.[6]

There seems little doubt that any 'national identity test' for rock and pop music would yield similar results to Shuker's in the UK, the US,

Canada, Australia and a number of other countries of the world where there is a predominant output of English-language-based music. (And without knowing in advance the country of origin of the Swedish rap-dance group Lucky People Center, the Dutch rap groups the Urban Dance Squad and S2 Unlimited, or the Belgian rock group dEUS, to take three from a wide range of possible examples of anglophone groups from non-anglophone countries, it would be impossible to locate them.) But, as in the case of the increasing output of music from different countries and regions of Africa within the parameters of world music, familiarity with music of a particular local idiom or from a particular geographical location induces an ability in the listener to identify other music in that idiom or location. While styles such as soukous, merengue, ju ju, high-life etc., are obviously far easier to identify than rock or rap music from Holland, Belgium or Sweden, it is arguable that a familiarity with such musics produces an ability to locate identifiable musical tendencies.

Leaving aside the distinctive features of Maori and Polynesian music, it is arguable that Crowded House's early albums (but not the 1994 *Together Alone*) have few identifiably Aotearoa/New Zealand features, and the country's popular music does not have an immediately identifiable indigenous musical instrument such as the didjeridu. None the less rock groups like the Clean, the Chills, the Bats, Straitjacket Fits, the JPSE and others who emerged on the Flying Nun label in the 1980s share a range of identifiable musical and extra-musical features (melodic guitar 'jangle', often 'low-fi' production, lack of concern with image, lack of political or social comment in lyrics, pop inflections, etc.). These can be related indirectly to their origins in the 'Dunedin sound' (even if the Bats are from Christchurch) and make them recognizable as Aotearoa/New Zealand bands.

Chris Knox, a key figure in Flying Nun since its inception, who has also been described as 'the godfather of New Zealand punk', has recorded a number of songs which make unmistakably local references and represent a strong sense of Aotearoa/New Zealand identity in a socially oppositional context. His 1990 album *Seizure* contained a song entitled 'Statement of Intent' which acrimoniously attacked the local music industry for its reluctance to promote the country's artists, while 'Flying in the Face of Fashion' characterized Aotearoa/New Zealand recording artists as a distinctive group of musicians whose music challenged prevailing US and British musical fads. In the same year, Knox released 'Song for 1990', a satiric attack on the sesquicentenary celebrations of British settlement which took place in that year. In this song, Knox mocked the sesquicentenary and the Commonwealth Games as jingoistic nationalist events, and satirised claims of racial harmony in Aotearoa/New Zealand, 'a nation strong and secure and benign. ... We have no problem keeping our Maoris in line. ... Our race relations are best among all of our peers.' The song also reflected on the absence of Aotearoa/New

Zealand music from radio stations, and mocked the stereotype of the country's national character as 'so humble and so self-effacing, not up ourselves at all'. It is difficult to overlook such a distinctive example of a 'Aotearoa/New Zealand sound', yet Knox's music is also popular in independent music circles in the USA – his 1995 album *Songs of You and Me* went to number one in the US College Music charts. Knox, who is also one half of the eccentric, 'low-fi' rock group Tall Dwarfs, sings with a strong Aotearoa/New Zealand accent, and frequently performs in the beach attire typical of an Aotearoa/New Zealand holidaymaker, and even uses jandals (the local equivalent of the Australian rubber thonged sandals) as a percussion instrument, in the manner of traditional Australian Aboriginal dancers. A major factor in the obfuscation of an Aotearoa/New Zealand identity is its tendency to be confused with an Australian identity, particularly since many Aotearoa/New Zealand musicians take up residence in Australia. None the less the identity expressed by an Aotearoa/New Zealand accent is immediately detectable in Australia.

The corollary of Shuker's argument about signs of Aotearoa/New Zealand identity could perhaps be proved by using the 1995 Flying Nun twelve-track sampler, *The Sound is Out There*, in an 'invisible jukebox' test. Subjects could be asked if they could spot the two US groups, Cul De Sac and Labradford, and the one UK group, Stereolab – recent signings to the label – who are included along with nine Aotearoa/New Zealand artists. But Shuker's three categories of local identification are useful, although he underestimates their manifestation in local music. By excluding the disproportionately rich and strong musical heritage and influence of Maori and Polynesian minorities, he effectively restricts his field of survey to *pakeha* (European settler) musicians, where similarities to and derivations from other English-language music are strongly evident. Even here, as he acknowledges, an Aotearoa/New Zealand accent and idiomatic inflection is still detectable – but perhaps more difficult to identify by nationals to whom it is not immediately noticeable. The growing tendency for Maori and Pacific Islander groups and performers to use their native languages is of course another distinctive linguistic feature. While bands' and performers' names often have only an oblique relation to national identity, again the growing incidence of Maori and Polynesian names is strong evidence. A series of postings on the Kiwi Music Internet news group in 1995 about references to local place names in songs by (almost exclusively *pakeha*) Aotearoa/New Zealand musicians suggests that there are also far more of these than are commonly supposed, with musicians such as the Muttonbirds (a distinctively local name) and their predecessors the Front Lawn being particularly strong in local associations. (A related series of correspondence about non-Aotearoa/New Zealand groups and performers who have recorded cover versions of songs by Aotearoa/New Zealand artists also revealed a surprising number of examples.[7]) It is more difficult to define a local sound, style or genre, although the 'Dunedin sound' is one example, with the growing use of pre-European traditional Maori instruments and vocal chants being another more distinctive example. In what follows, I will be arguing for the distinctiveness of much locally produced music in New Zealand which is often located only obliquely through rhetorical and extramusical associations. This distinctiveness also relates to the particularly idiosyncratic way in which a range of Aotearoa/New Zealand musicians have appropriated and adopted a range of Anglo-American models, styles and influences.

Splitting Enz

The name of the first Aotearoa/New Zealand rock group to achieve any sort of international prominence, Split Enz, despite having been interpreted as 'a deliberate gesture of parochial pride'[8] and a mark of 'the genuine pride we had managed to sustain over the years for the homeland',[9] can also be interpreted as announcing the group's need and desire to leave the country and seek its fortune outside Aotearoa/New Zealand. Both Split Enz and Neil Finn's subsequent band, Crowded House, whose song 'Don't Dream It's Over' was the subject of considerable local pride when it reached number three in the USA in 1987, tend to be regarded outside Aotearoa/New Zealand as Australian groups, if their nationality ever has cause to be identified. Crowded House's 1992 hit 'Weather with You' consolidated the group's international acclaim by reaching the top ten in England, and being the only song by an Australian or Aotearoa/New Zealand group to feature (at number 99) in a 1995 listing of the '100 Greatest Pop Songs of All Time' by a British panel from *The Times*, the BBC, the music business and the songwriting profession.[10]

In his admirable social history of Aotearoa/New Zealand rock and roll from 1955 to 1988, *Stranded in Paradise*, John Dix describes Split Enz, based outside Aotearoa/New Zealand after 1975, as 'New Zealand's first genuine international rock n roll stars ... [who] proved that a New Zealand band could cut it in the international arena.'[11] Any consequent loss to Aotearoa/New Zealand tended to be compensated by the group's frequent local tours, honours and celebrations. In 1992 Mike Chunn, a former bass player with Split Enz, published a detailed biography of the band, *Stranger then Fiction: The Life and Times of Split Enz*, to mark the twentieth anniversary of the group's first public performance at the Wynyard Tavern in Auckland, an anniversary also marked by a special one-off reforming of the band for a tour of Aotearoa/New Zealand in March 1993, and boxed set CD releases of their complete works. The fact that Neil Finn's receipt of an OBE and the break-up of Split Enz were the subject of an editorial in the *New Zealand Herald* indicate the national importance that both Split Enz and Crowded House assumed in Aotearoa/New Zealand, but both groups had to leave the country to achieve it.

One of the most striking features of Split Enz's music in retrospect is the 'Englishness' of their sound, especially on their early 'art rock' albums. Chunn claims that Split Enz emerged from a musical vacuum in 1972, and had few influences apart from the Beatles and the Kinks: 'we walked in a silent world with nothing but our beating hearts and dreams of a musical evolution; an evolution where all would be unique, individual and pioneering'.[12] None the less there are unmistakable traces of the mellotron-powered 'symphonic rock' of Genesis, Jethro Tull and Roxy Music (whose lead guitarist Phil Manzanera produced their second album, *Second Thoughts*) in their mid-1970s output. One of the group's great regrets was in never managing to crack the British market, an ambition thwarted by the rise of punk rock. (This historical accident also affected their predecessors, Max Merritt and the Meteors, who established themselves in Australia in the late 1960s, before becoming part of the London 'pub rock' scene of the early 1970s, and eventually basing themselves in Los Angeles.) But even prior to punk, when glam-rock groups like Sparks were exploring similar 'arty' gimmicks, Split Enz's eccentric costumes, make-up and hairstyles, concentration on theatrical devices like Noel Crombie's spoons playing, and aspiration to what Red Symons has described as 'the British melodic angst area'[13] seemed very deja-vu in London. They also had to contend with the renowned xenophobia of *Melody Maker*, who warned readers to keep the volume down when playing their 1981 single 'One Step Ahead', 'or you may just find yourself, mere moments later, snoring on the carpet to the naff new sound of dumb New Z-z-z-z-zealand'.[14]

Although they managed to gain a strong following in Canada and Netherlands, Split Enz also failed to make much of a dent in an uncomprehending American market, and their Australasian success was in many ways a rebound consolation. By the end of the 1970s, the band had settled in Melbourne, to be within striking range of Mushroom Records, the only company with whom they could secure a reasonably solid recording deal. The move coincided with a shedding of the more pretentiously 'arty' aspects of their sound and image, and the development of a lighter, more stripped-back, mainstream melodic pop repertoire which won them their wide Australian following and rock legend status in Aotearoa/New Zealand.

In 1985, as Aotearoa/New Zealand rock's next great white hopes the Chills were about to depart for their first tour of England, Neil Finn gave his reasons for staying away from his homeland in the hundredth issue of the monthly Kiwi music magazine *Rip It Up*. He described an Aotearoa/New Zealand music scene stuck in a 'garage mentality', where essential industry support for struggling bands was unforthcoming, there was an urgent need for a 'centralizing figure' and 'musical minorities' were unable to survive. Recording production standards were 'shoddy', management was 'terrible', and the musical environment was 'out of view of the world'.[15] Finn's decision to return to live in Auckland in 1993 and record Crowded House's new album there indicates the degree of progress the local music industry had made in the ensuing decade, although Finn gave his main reasons for returning as family concerns, cultural identity and the strengthening of Maori and Polynesian cultural influences.[16]

Finn chose Kare Kare, the West Coast Auckland beach where Jane Campion's internationally successful film *The Piano* was shot, and a popular artists' retreat, as a recording site for Crowded House's fourth album, *Together Alone*. A recording studio was set up in the house where US actor Harvey Keitel had stayed during the making of *The Piano*, and, according to Finn, the evocative and remote setting had an undeniable impact on the group's music: 'we were definitely influenced by the weather and the atmosphere out there – in the sense that we were looking for sounds that kind of matched the epic nature of what we were looking at every day. When you're gazing out at a view or mist rolling in or rain beating down it does tend to affect your mood which affects what you play.'[17]

The album's opening track is entitled 'Kare Kare', and the recording process was influenced by the 'strange energies' surrounding the area, where a Maori tribe had taken refuge from a warring tribe armed with colonial British guns in a cave in the nineteenth century, only to be burned to death there, the survivors subsequently being marched off a cliff.[18] The album employs the powerful chants and harmonies of Te Whaka Huia Maori Cultural Group Choir, who provide backing vocals on three tracks on *Together Alone*, including the title track, which also features a brass band and a group of Cook Islander log drummers. This conscious reflection of indigenous Maori and Polynesian music provides a distinctive sense of place. As Neil Finn has commented, the title track was a conscious attempt to 'bridge a kind of gap, I suppose, because there's always been the different strands of music or culture here which have been very separate: Polynesian culture, Maori culture and Anglo-Saxon culture all coexisting but not coming together in any significant way. So all we tried to do was write a song that would involve all these strands and make it work.'[19] Finn has continued to promote and support Maori and Polynesian musicians, producing and playing guitar on Maori singer Emma Paki's single 'Greenstone', which Nick Bollinger described as 'a spiritual love song with a haunting chant-like melody, accompanied at first only by hand drums, building to a glorious crescendo of Crowded House guitars and ancient Polynesian rhythms.'[20] Finn used his international experience to act as a catalyst for a distinctive combination of Maori, Pacific Island and *pakeha* musical cultures.

The dependence of Split Enz, Crowded House and many other Aotearoa/New Zealand musicians on overseas markets was partly due to the country's limited domestic market, where touring is an ordeal few groups are able to undertake consistently, and offers few rewards when they do. Trumpeter and vocalist Greg Johnson describes national tours as an unrewarding prospect: 'it only takes two weeks to get from one end of the country to the other and you just can't go back and do it again. It has to go overseas in order to be sustainable as a living.'[21] While this remains an economic reality for Aotearoa/New Zealand musicians, the generation who succeeded Split Enz and Crowded House managed to combine overseas touring with maintaining a fixed base at home, although the Chills became a notable casualty of the pressures of maintaining a profile in the USA.

Dunedin, Noisyland

Aotearoa/New Zealand's relation to the Anglo-American-dominated global economy of rock music is aptly troped in a review by Keith Cameron in the *New Musical Express* of Dunedin group the 3Ds' 1994 album *The Venus Trail*, recorded on Flying Nun:

> Pop's least mannered exponents invariably lurk out on the globe's perimeter edges. The propensity for New Zealand's Flying Nun stable to unearth music so drenched with wide-eyed wonder it might as well emanate from another planet is well-documented, and Dunedin's 3Ds maintain the noble tradition of The Chills, The Clean, Verlaines *et al.*, where the classic guitar blueprint can be made to appear as radical as it ever was. Which is to say that 'The Venus Trail' is unlikely to nudge the world off its axis. Here is a record that could've been made at any time in the last 20 years, yet its creators are blessed with such a lack of premeditation and an abundance of heaven-scented melodies around these mysterious tales that it could just as well be an exotic new species of Antipodean fauna.[22]

The indicators Cameron ascribes to the 3Ds – peripheral, fresh, naive, otherworldy, exotic and outside the largely *NME-* and *Melody Maker*-generated historical continuum of rock music trends – place them in a vacuum of time and place. Given their peripherality and isolation, the safest and most familiar reference points for European and US reviewers referring to the band have become their Dunedin origins and their association with Flying Nun, further proof that local identity is a distinctive marker of Aotearoa/New Zealand music.

By 1994, Dunedin's reputation as the main focal point of both Flying Nun recording artists and the underground label Xpressway, which had been formed in 1988 and quickly became a cult label in the USA, was so strong amongst followers of independent rock music that Bob Nastonovich of popular US 'slacker' band Pavement, which toured Aotearoa/New Zealand in July 1994, indicated the group was 'a little bit anxious about the Dunedin show because that's sort of the centre of where most of the bands we really like in this country are from – the 3Ds and the whole Xpressway scene. It's definitely a real artists' and musicians' community down there and last time we played there we were really nervous.'[23]

In the event, Nastonovich discovered 'there were probably only a few hundred people in Dunedin who have heard of us anyway'. As Colin McLeay has pointed out, the 'Dunedin sound' was generated through a cultural geography of isolation, which produced a 'mythology of a group of musicians working in cold isolation, playing music purely for the pleasure of it'.[24] This mythology of place, assembled by fans, artists, critics, promoters and industry personnel, is, McLeay suggests, comparable, albeit on a much smaller scale, to that of 'the Manchester sound', 'the Seattle scene' of grunge music or the hard-core 'gangsta rap' centre of Compton in Los Angeles.[25] But the fact that it arises from one of the most isolated places within New Zealand, 'with a very low population of Maori people relative to the rest of New Zealand and ... dominated by the descendants of Scottish immigrants'[26] made Dunedin a metonym for Aotearoa/New Zealand music as a whole.

A sense of local and national musical identity in the Dunedin music scene coincided with the formation of Flying Nun in 1981. In 1980 Chris Knox's Dunedin-based post-punk group Toy Love had toured Australia and recorded an album in Sydney before splitting up. The group's stories of their bad experiences in Australia convinced other Dunedin-based musicians that exposure in Australia might not be worth pursuing, while their lack of resources meant that they were forced to construct their own local musical scene. This occurred in an environment where, according to record store owner Roy Colbert, a key figure in the development of the Dunedin music scene, 'there was no rock band of any substance ... before 1980'.[27] Roger Shepherd, also a record store owner, set up Flying Nun with the initial intention of providing recording facilities for Christchurch bands. He ended up signing a significant number of bands from Dunedin, a cold and quiet university town of 100,000 inhabitants situated only twenty degrees north of the Antarctic circle, 1,300 miles south east of Australia, and nearly 1,000 miles away from Auckland, the most important city in terms of the music industry and the mass media. This unspoilt, picturesque but bleakly isolated and uninhabited southern part of the South Island was used by Samuel Butler, who lived there in 1860, as the basis of his Utopian novel *Erewhon* ('nowhere' spelt backwards – a characterization which contributed to a long-standing cultural inferiority complex). Dunedin was described more recently by Canadian writer Paul Theroux as 'cold and frugal, with its shabby streets and mock-gothic university ... It felt like the end of the world, and when I looked at a map this seemed true ... leave the southern tip of New Zealand and the next upright animal you are likely to see is an emperor penguin.'[28] But, as Shepherd has indicated, this isolation contributed to the development of a distinctive South Island sonic identity: 'the North island tended to follow international trends. But on the South Island people were a bit more inclined to write and perform the music they wanted to hear. If others liked what they were doing, that was merely a bonus. It wasn't the only place on the planet where that sort of thing happened, but like different dialects, a unique style definitely emerged.'[29] One of these Dunedin-based bands was the Clean, whose single 'Tally Ho' was the first Flying Nun release in August 1981. Recorded on an eight-track machine at a cost of $50, 'Tally Ho' reached number nineteen in the Aotearoa/New Zealand charts, where it stayed for seven weeks. The Clean's follow-up EP, *Boodle Boodle Boodle*, released two months later, spent six months in the charts, peaking at number five. Reviewing 'Tally Ho' in *Rip It Up* in September 1981, Francis Stark indicated that it was by no means an isolated phenomenon in terms of local musical traditions: 'The Clean bring back the Jansen Transonic sound in what could well be a tribute to the Simple Image, and the days when a local record could be number one for six weeks. "Tallyho" stands with the early Toy Love as an argument for Dunedin as New Zealand's home of the pure pop melody.'[30]

'Pure pop melody' and 'guitar jangle' were to become the most frequently used indicators to describe the Dunedin sound, although in themselves they denote little that is geographically distinctive. In her book *Rock Culture in Liverpool*, Sara Cohen describes the predominance in that city of 'a rather melodic, lyrical style of "pop" music',[31] which suggests that this type of sound may be common to independent, guitar-based bands influenced by the Beatles and 1960s British and American pop throughout the English-speaking world. 'Tally Ho' is no exception. It features a frisky, 1960s-sounding organ riff, played by eighteen-year-old Martin Phillipps, who was later to form the Chills, and who again became an honorary member of the Clean on their 1995 Aotearoa/New Zealand tour. David Kilgour's rather bored-sounding vocals seem to mock the Britishness of the expression 'Tally Ho' and the pukka optimism of much 1960s British music. (The video clip of the song is made in the style of 1960s British pop music films where group members clown around self-consciously and the film is speeded up and bleached out.)

The lead guitarist and chief songwriter of the Verlaines, Graeme Downes, who lectures in music at Otago University in Dunedin and has completed a PhD thesis on Mahler, has written an article analyzing the 'modal conflict and resolution' of the Clean's music. Downes suggests that there are musicological reasons, such as the use of tonal and modal tensions and uncertainties, long-range resolutions and predominantly short songs with a 'failsafe sense of appropriate duration', for the Clean's distinctiveness and popularity. Downes characterizes their music in terms of 'clearly discernible compositional differences that distance them from the mainstream':

> The Clean's music tends to be pigeon-holed in the garage, alternative or underground category, due to a tendency towards abrasive guitars, low-mixed vocals and an overall standard of production that any commercial radio programmer would reject out of hand. That as may be, a Clean song can involve a level of complexity that belies the veneer of simplicity that such unsophisticated production and the sometimes naive style of lyric writing implies.[32]

Downes's analysis of the Clean's ability to ring sophisticated changes on basic rock formulas of what he describes as 'three-chord riffs and inane repetition' gives the group a musical distinctiveness which complements their almost legendary status in Aotearoa/New Zealand music. Initially disbanding in 1982 after releasing only three EPs, owing to a dislike of touring and celebrity, the Clean reunited for a highly successful local and overseas tour in 1989, when they released an album of new songs recorded in three days in London, *Vehicle*. Their individual members continue to pursue careers in the Bats and the Magick Heads (Robert Scott), the New-York-based Mad Scene (Hamish Kilgour) and as a successful solo artist who was featured in a cover story in *Billboard* in 1994 (David Kilgour). They reunited again in 1994 to produce another album with the tongue-in-cheek title *Modern Rock*, and toured Aotearoa/New Zealand in confirmation of their legendary status. (Unlike Split Enz, however, whose anniversary concerts filled sports stadiums and played to audiences of up to ten thousand, the Clean played to audiences of five hundred at the most.) None the less, Aotearoa/New Zealand rock writer Campbell Walker has described them as 'the most important band in Aotearoa/New Zealand history':

> They set off Aotearoa/New Zealand's most productive period of music ever, they managed the feat of selling records at a time when to be an independent band in the charts was quite unthinkable, and they demonstrated perfectly what you do and don't need to be a great band: no background, bugger-all gear, no singing ability, a few songs and a whole lot of passion.[33]

Echoes of US guitar bands of the 1960 and 1970s, which Roy Colbert's record store specialized in – the Velvet Underground, the Byrds and Television, but also the 13th Floor Elevators, Moby Grape, the Electric Prunes and other more obscure bands – are detectable in many of the bands who recorded on Flying Nun in the 1980s. The Chills, whose name evokes the bleak wintry climate and severe landscape around Dunedin which is the source of some of leader Martin Phillipps's songs,[34] as well as the peculiar vowel rotation of the Aotearoa/New Zealand accent, which renders 'i' as closer to 'u', combined this influence with a keyboard-dominated sound. The Chills went through fourteen changes of line-up between 1980 and 1992, recording three albums before splitting up owing to the pressures of striving for international success after signing to a US label and touring Europe and the USA extensively. The Bats, who were formed in Christchurch by Clean bass guitarist Robert Scott and Toy Love bass guitarist Paul Kean, also feature jangling guitars and pleasant melodic lines reminiscent of the Byrds. David Eggleton has characterized the Bats in a way which suggests a link between the group's music and its geographical location:

> Their sweet, sticky pop songs are suffused with the tang of something wild and strange ... capturing a sense of the South Island landscape – the slow turn of the seasons, and of what it's like to live in that landscape ... [Robert Scott's] lyrics are partly southern Gothic, partly quasi-Celtic, folk tales about loss and regeneration, tossed out in fragments which don't quite add up to complete stories. ... They are nothing if not tribal: The Bats are the most representative, the most regional band on that most New Zealand of rock record labels, Flying Nun, and they are also the most long-lived, still possessing the original line-up from their 1982 inception.[35]

The Bats have survived by remaining resolutely based in Christchurch, taking periods of recess while individual members pursue other projects, work or look after family. In 1993 the Bats took part in 'Noisyland', an Australian, US and European tour with fellow Christchurch band the JPS Experience and Dunedin group Straitjacket Fits, which was partly subsidized by the Aotearoa/New Zealand government, with each group promoting its third album to be released on Flying Nun. 'Noisyland' represented a serious, and reasonably successful attempt to promote a national construction of Aotearoa/New Zealand rock music abroad.

Straitjacket Fits evolved out of the Double Happys, featuring an aggressive, 'wall of noise' guitar sound behind Shayne Carter's hard-edged vocals, which Paul McKessar has described as 'highly-charged with emotion and bravely ignor[ing] the trends and fashions of late 'eighties independent rock music'.[36] Carter is virtually the only Dunedin musician of Maori origin, but he has suggested that there are economic and social reasons for the guitar-based rock tradition in Dunedin which are markedly different from the more Polynesian-oriented musical culture of Auckland, where there is a significant hip hop subculture:

> Rap's just not relevant to our lives, the things that shaped it just aren't here. The bottom line is that in our band we are four white boys who grew up in a town where there's no technology available. We had no money, so we've never been able to buy samplers or things like that. So we've basically been stuck with acoustic guitars in our bedrooms. You can't pretend to be what you aren't. I think what we're doing is relevant to what we are and where we come from.[37]

The Noisyland tour was the first international exposure for the Jean-Paul Sartre Experience (JPSE), who combined samplers with a churning guitar-based 'psychedelic pop' sound, slightly reminiscent of British 'indie' groups like Lush and Ride, producing what McKessar has described as a 'multi-hued dream-pop landscape ... with a layer of samples and trickery buried inside that help lift the songs into the spacey, spooky category'.[38] Although both Straitjacket Fits and the JPSE subsequently split up, the Noisyland tour laid an important foundation for the subsequent reception of Aotearoa/New Zealand independent rock bands abroad, giving the country what the US *Rolling Stone* described as 'some real rock & roll credibility'[39] and getting positive reviews in both the USA and the UK.

In a thorough and detailed study of the 'Dunedin sound' from 1978 to 1985, Craig Robertson outlines the small and relatively homogenous music scene in Dunedin, which was given its primary impetus by the late 1970s punk 'do it yourself' ethos and the success in Auckland of Chris Knox's punk group the Enemy (named after the *NME*). Robertson identifies four distinct waves of bands in Dunedin, beginning with the Clean, the Same and Bored Games in 1978, and continuing with the Chills, the Stones, the Verlaines and Sneaky Feelings in 1980, Look Blue Go Purple, Double Happys and others in 1984, and Straitjacket Fits, Stephen and Snapper in 1986. Owing to Dunedin's isolation, the main musical influences on these bands were each other, and Robertson delineates a shared aesthetic which

> valued 'dirty' art over 'clean' art; an approach which saw perfection in the roughness of the music. The aesthetic was based on a belief in the primary importance of the song; the idea that a song is an important entity and a valid statement on its own. The execution of the song, its presentation, did not matter as such. The Enemy and The Clean had inspired the younger musicians with short melodic songs within a strong punk format. Long songs were not something the following waves of bands saw as acceptable. This legacy was imbued with a revulsion towards instrumental solos. Everybody worked within the 'song', there was no hierarchy of instruments.[40]

This aesthetic was complemented by a lack of concern for the bands' image as performers, but a tendency for bands to produce their own album and poster art work, much of it influenced by Chris Knox's work as a newspaper cartoonist. The musical aesthetic involved a total disregard for musical fashions and trends, as well as commercial recognition, 'expressed in the idea of authentic music, which legitimised the ignorance of contemporary musical trends. An adherence to authentic music involved stepping outside the confines of musical fashion and justified an ignorance of any boundaries of what was considered popular.'[41] This authenticity was associated with 'simply writing music for yourself',[42] and was also an expression of the limited musicianship shared by most of the bands, causing them to emphasize melody, while the use of open tuning by Clean guitarist David Kilgour, a prime influence in the Dunedin scene, who was also the first to use the expression 'Dunedin sound' in 1981, resulted from his lack of knowledge of guitar chords.[43] In general little attention was paid to the lyrics of the songs the groups wrote and performed, partly because the poor quality PA systems they had to rely on made the words of songs difficult to hear. Although the Chills' music did express responses to the Aotearoa/New Zealand landscape of the South Island, and Chris Knox's songs often engaged with social and political issues, most of the other groups wrote lyrics that primarily fitted in with the melody and rhythm of the songs they wrote.

Despite few signs of overt engagements with political concerns, Michael Goddard has convincingly suggested that the mutual musical supportiveness and borrowings amongst the South Island bands and Flying Nun performers, and their shared intellectual and cultural environment, provide evidence of a political subculture for which 'the music was only the material trace':

> This eclecticism, coupled with the marginal yet effective system of production and distribution made this music inherently political; instead of producing political songs; i.e. songs about politics, they made music politically ... this was a living network, whose politics lay in the way the music was produced, and whose effects went well beyond music to a wider yet specific community, related to other developments such as feminism and anti-racism.[44]

Goddard's analysis indicates that a sense of local identity may be more evident in the existence of a community infrastructure and shared aesthetic and industrial base than in any identifiable elements within the music itself, its performance or lyrical content.

Flying Nun and the British indie scene

While Flying Nun was the main outlet for the groups involved in the 'Dunedin sound', the label rarely achieved success in Aotearoa/New Zealand commensurate with the predominantly favourable responses overseas. Prior to 1990, only the Clean's *Boodle Boodle Boodle* EP and the Chills' 1990 album *Submarine Bells* had achieved gold record status (7,500 units sold) locally.[45] In 1994 Roger Shepherd confirmed the ongoing necessity for successful Aotearoa/New Zealand artists to leave the country by shifting the label's headquarters to London. In doing so he hoped to capitalize on the continuing success of British 'indie' rock groups like Blur, Oasis and Suede, while also signing a distribution agreement with British band Stereolab and adding US groups Ween, Cul De Sac and Labradford to the label's repertoire.[46] This went counter to the inclinations of many of the label's initial bands, who had found little encouragement in the UK and were more inclined to cultivate the 'indie' cult status they were beginning to achieve in the US. Shayne Carter, for example, had been excited by Straitjacket Fits' reception in America, but saw the days of Aotearoa/New Zealand bands aiming for success in Australia and London as no longer relevant:

> We got a good reception in England and our press was really favourable but there was still this underlying sniff, whether it be the attitude of people giving you amps for hire at the sound company through to that *Time Out* review of the Chills' 'Heavenly Pop Hit' which said 'great song, pity about the New Zealand accents'. Still having to put up with that shit after four years of trying to earn respect – what's the point? Whereas in America you're almost exotic.[47]

In fact, much of the most influential coverage of the Flying Nun bands and the 'Dunedin sound' in *NME* and *Melody Maker* was very positive, even envious in some cases. An *NME* review of the 1986 Flying Nun compilation album *Tuatara* stated:

> Half of today's British indie scene strives for this effect, yet I've heard none to match 'Death and the Maiden' [a song by the Verlaines] . . . [The Chills'] 'Pink Frost', a ghostly carousel of lamenting melody, epitomises how self-effacing need not mean either clumsy or *faux naif*, the besetting vices of Britain's shambling generation whose appearance here is so anticipated (and frequently bettered).[48]

While the post-punk 1980s British 'indie' music of the Smiths, the Cure, the Fall and others championed in *NME* and *Melody Maker* tended to have little direct influence on the 'Dunedin sound', both shared some of the features *Melody Maker* writer Simon Reynolds diagnosed in his 1988 article 'Against Health and Efficiency: Independent Music in the 1980s'. Both could be regarded predominantly as the products of 'a white middle class bohemianism that's cleansed of the fast-living and self-destruction of earlier forms of rebellion', derived from the 'strictly albino roots' of 1960s rock, and aspired to ' "pure" or "perfect" pop'. They also shared inclinations towards a 'head culture' rather than 'bodymusic' (although in live performances groups like the Bats and Headless Chickens place strong emphasis on dancing), and tended to rely on 'low-fi' technology and recording techniques which reproduce a 'bombardment or irradiation of noise'. Their songs often celebrated an 'oppositional return to romance' rather than sexuality or social issues, and often opted for 'a quiet withdrawal, as much from the old youth culture as from straight society'. Where Aotearoa/New Zealand independent music most differed from its British counterpart was in its pragmatic lack of concern with image, as opposed to what Reynolds characterizes as the 'androgynous, childlike and/or anorexic' imagery of British 'indie' bands. Nor was the determination of the Kiwi groups to pursue an uncommercial path and express a sense of alienation the petulant expression of 'a stubborn will to misfit, to cling to one's dissatisfaction' that Reynolds saw in British 'indiepop'. There was also little evidence in Aotearoa/New Zealand music of the ambivalent 'anti-Americanism from within the USA' which Reynolds saw as a fundamentally British resistance to a 'health-and-efficiency culture: a hyper-technical, superabundant society whose underside is the loss of community'.[49] The artists on Flying Nun, by contrast, represented a strong sense of community, as well as a shared aesthetic and industrial infrastructure, as well as coming from a largely similar social experience and music scene.

The predominantly middle-class, university background of most of the Flying Nun groups was one factor in their estrangement from the often sentimental working-class aspirations Reynolds diagnosed in many of the British 'indie' groups. 'Politically correct' social assumptions and concerns tended to be tacit in much of Aotearoa/New Zealand's independent music until the mid-1990s, along with an occasionally self-conscious artistic introspection which led more commercially oriented musicians like Push Push's Mikey Havoc to criticize the polarization of the national music scene: 'what bugs me about New Zealand musicians is everyone's trying so hard to be an intellectual that it makes for some really dull music. ... On the one hand you've got your wimpy chart stuff, which is mostly bad dance music. And on the other there's the Flying Nun "I'm involved in my own trauma" music.'[50]

Push Push, who recorded a heavy-metal-styled cover of the Chills' song 'I Love My Leather Jacket' as well as performing other Chills covers, became a casualty of their attempt to relocate themselves in Australia, where they received an indifferent response. But Havoc's comments serve to indicate that Flying Nun was far from providing a national norm. While Aotearoa/New Zealand independent music tended at first to follow the British post-punk mould of politically oppositional music, partly owing to its almost total lack of support from the local music industry, small labels like Flying Nun managed to preserve a 'non-commercial' approach to a heterogeneous range of recording artists despite the relative commercial success of band like the Chills, the Verlaines and Straitjacket Fits. As such, the label fits Lawrence Grossberg's characterization of independent rock music:

> Independent rock and roll does not present itself as a challenge, either explicitly or implicitly, to the dominant culture although it may function as such. It apparently exists outside of its relation to the dominant culture; it does not want the world. It seeks to escape, to define a space which neither impinges upon nor is impinged upon by the hegemony: 'we want our world'.[51]

But the Aotearoa/New Zealand version of 'self conscious peripheralisation', which Grossberg sees as a determining characteristic of American post-punk music, is a product of geographical and cultural isolation, a turning inwards to a self-enclosed world of rituals of leisure, unemployment and boredom made up of rearranged and often idealized fragments from the Northern Hemisphere. Commenting on the sense of alienation that characterizes many of the lyrics of the work of groups associated with the 'Dunedin sound' (illustrated in the repetitive rhythms of the Chills' song about living on unemployment benefit, 'Dole Drums') Hamish Kilgour of the Clean has stated, 'It's probably the effect of living in a conservative middle-class culture. White culture doesn't encourage free expression or very expressive behaviour.'[52] But the lack of any overtly oppositional stance in the music of many of the Flying Nun bands and the absence of specific political pointers in their lyrics could also suggest a paradoxical 'originality' operating within local 'low-fi' constraints of technology, distribution and creativity. As Goddard commented:

> These bands produced music that abandoned any form of oppositional pose, without being motivated by dreams of commercial success either; a highly unlikely prospect, coming from Dunedin. Their approach was to plunder the musical styles of many different periods and forms, and recombine them, take them in new directions, in order to produce a music that was distinctive and innovative, while still retaining a respect for the classic melodic pop song.[53]

Aotearoa/New Zealand popular music can be regarded as what Mark Slobin has referred to as a Western 'micromusic', in the sense that it is a post-colonial example of 'small musical units within big music-cultures', having developed at a tangent to dominant Anglo-American musical forms which it has 'domesticated'.[54] But the history of rock and pop music in Aotearoa/New Zealand, like that of most other countries outside the British–American nexus, can also be seen as part of a global process of acculturation. As Evelyn McDonnell suggested in a *Village Voice* feature on Flying Nun:

> In many ways, the story of the Flying Nun scene isn't that different from indie/ punk scenes everywhere. When Shayne Carter says of the band he formed when he was 15, Bored Games was a reaction to seeing the Sex Pistols on telly and thinking, My God, we can do this type of thing, he could be the Soviet Union's Boris Grebenshikov, Minnesota's Paul Westerberg, or Australia's Peter Garrett. Wire and Pylon have reformed, why not the Clean?[55]

Recognition overseas had a strong influence on the eventual recognition by the local music industry of groups like the Chills, the Auckland-based Headless Chickens and Straitjacket Fits in the annual New Zealand Music Awards. In 1992 a special award was given to Roger Shepherd for 'outstanding contribution to New Zealand music',[56] and a record number of forty-eight Aotearoa/New Zealand singles reached the local top fifty singles charts – twice the 1991 total. Ten of these were among the top hundred singles of 1992, while seven local albums were in the top hundred albums of the year. Flying Nun also achieved a 300 per cent sales growth in 1992, largely due to export sales and US licensing agreements.[57] In 1995, Shepherd was awarded a Tradenz (Aotearoa/New Zealand Trade Development Board) Export Commendation as Flying Nun was the largest music exporter in Aotearoa/New Zealand, with international record sales for 1994 of over $1 million. This was still a very small amount compared to $7 million earned in exports by Australian independent label Shock, and $6 million by Mushroom Distribution Service, who bought 26 per cent of Flying Nun in 1992.

Flying Nun's path to discreet but substantial international recognition was accompanied by a perceived impression in Aotearoa/New Zealand that the label was undergoing a mid-life crisis. A 1994 article by John Russell in the long-standing Aotearoa/New Zealand music monthly *Rip It Up* pointed to the demise of the Chills, Straitjacket Fits and JPSE, the Verlaines' signing to US label Slash, and the fact that the label had only four musicians under thirty on its books, three of these in one band. Long-standing music critic Colin Hogg suggested that continual 'in-breeding' by Flying Nun bands had weakened the label's output, while Headless Chickens' bass player and manager Grant Fell described a sense of atrophy in Dunedin: 'Dunedin seems to be a very strange place these days, it appears to be a graveyard for old Flying Nun people. I'm not saying that's a bad thing, an absolutely wonderful Flying Nun supergroup may come out one day, but a lot of people seem to return there when things don't work out for them.'[58]

Flying Nun's three-hundredth release in 1994 was *Sassafras*, an album by Dunedin supergroup Chug, comprising members of former Flying Nun bands Look Blue Go Purple, Goblin Mix, Snapper and the 3Ds, and sounding like a pastiche of all these bands. Reviewing the single 'Golden Mile' taken from the album in *Rip It Up*, Russell noted: 'The band are perfectly named, "Golden Mile" swirls/drones on indefinitely, pushed by a drum beat that's well past its sell-by date. ... While this particular Nun sound worked wonders in the '80s, it's incapable of exciting these ears in the '90s.'[59] Ironically, Steve Sutherland, the editor of *NME*, gave Chug's album a hyperbolically enthusiastic review:

> The years keep Flying past, but still the seam of delightful guitar pop unearthed in Dunedin, New Zealand, keeps throwing up gems. After the 3Ds, the Chills *et al.*, meet Chug, a combination of minor players from the incestuous-but-productive smalltown scene, and owners of a sporadically wonderful lo-fi racket. ... If only Chug hailed from Slackville, USA, rather than Hardwork City, Noisyland, the world and its major-backed indie label would surely be queuing up to a) proclaim their 'genius' and b) give them lots of money.[60]

The principal drawback to the Dunedin sound, Sutherland concludes, is its location at the bottom of the world rather than in the USA. But Dunedin's chief importance as a focal point for international recognition of Aotearoa/New Zealand popular music in the 1980s and early 1990s lay in its production of a self-confident, fixed base of production which supplanted the prevailing migratory tendencies, bound up with the need to travel abroad to achieve success, which characterized New Zealand musicians in previous decades.

One Dunedin group which went against the Flying Nun grain in the mid-1990s was the highly acclaimed surf-punk-cabaret group King Loser, who defined themselves as 'more or less a straight rock band. ... We aren't alternative or indie.'[61] King Loser translocated to Auckland to get away from what they saw as the suffocating peer pressure of the small and insular music community of Dunedin, which guitarist Chris Heazlewood estimated to consist of

> 30 or 50 people, or 100 if you take in the peripheral players in the game. You're only going to get by there if you don't get too concerned about seeing the same faces in the crowd each time you play. ... You get judged in Dunedin. Not necessarily badly but you get labelled and people are looking a whole lot more closely at you, often with more intelligent eyes. And you start to feel cornered or cloistered.[62]

While acknowledging the help he received from Dunedin musicians like Shayne Carter, Heazlewood preferred to release the group's first album, *Sonic Super Free Hi Fi*, on an obscure vinyl-only Belgian label, Turbulence, than take the expected Flying Nun option. But the album was eventually re-released on CD by Flying Nun, followed by a second album, and King Loser became the figurehead of a perceived new image for the label, headlining a three-band Flying Nun concert in Sydney in 1995. This concert was reminiscent of the 'Beyond the Jangle' tour of 1993, although it was less well received, and none of the three groups could be associated with the 'Dunedin sound': Garageland, named after a song by the Clash and described by Darren Hawkes in *Rip It Up* as sounding 'like a New Zealand band imitating an American band imitating a New Zealand band'[63] are from Auckland; and Love's Ugly Children, a neo-punk group who blend guitar grunge with gothic pose, are from Christchurch. King Loser's manic cabaret-like style, and wild, slewed rhythms reminiscent of US rock and roll group the Cramps, indicate a definite break with a perceived Flying Nun house style, and a relocation of the capital of Aotearoa/New Zealand popular music from Dunedin to Auckland which has accompanied the emergence of a number of distinctive Maori and Polynesian groups in that city. But the release in 1995 of *Abbasolutely*, a compilation of covers of songs by 1970s Swedish pop group Abba by a number of prominent Flying Nun artists old and new, including Chris Knox, the Able Tasmans, Garageland and Superette, suggested that the label's sense of corporate identity was still under strain. As Shayne Carter, who contributed a version of 'Name of the Game' with former Headless Chickens vocalist Fiona McDonald, commented: 'I think essentially that Abba suck and even the idea of a tribute album is pretty tired as well. When I listen to the Abba compilation the overwhelming feeling I've struck is one of how insipid and annoying all their melodies are.'[64]

A 'Kiwi head' subculture

In relation to Flying Nun, Xpressway, which was established in Dunedin after Shepherd shifted the label's base to Auckland in 1988, had a much smaller but more distinctively marked cult status. Known only to a small group of independent music collectors, mostly in the USA and Europe, this label was set up by Bruce Russell, a former publicist for Flying Nun in Christchurch, and guitarist with Dunedin noise band Dead C, whose album *Eusa Kills* was one of Flying Nun's more adventurous and avant-garde releases. Initially a cassette-only mail order company, Xpressway recorded some groups and artists who had initially been on Flying Nun, but were dropped in the label's shift towards a more mainstream orientation. In the label's 1992 catalogue Russell described Xpressway as 'a Dunedin-based label aiming to present a narrowly focussed section of NZ music – especially South Island music – to the rest of the world. Xpressway is a collective run by artists for artists. Our aim is to make music, not money'.[65]

Xpressway maintained a policy of releasing its output on vinyl, which had become possible only by sending releases to Australia for pressing since Aotearoa/New Zealand's last vinyl-pressing plant had closed in 1987. The label achieved cult status in the USA among a group which Erik Davis defined in the *Village Voice* as 'Kiwi-heads'.[66] Some of its recordings and artists were subsequently released on US independent labels such as Siltbreeze and Ajax. Peter Jefferies became particularly successful in the USA with his 1991 ambient/garage-punk album *The Last Great Challenge in a Dull World*, which covers a musical spectrum from distorted guitars to ambient piano, with sound effects of household appliances added for good measure. Sandra Bell's *Dreams of Falling*, produced by Jefferies, continued in a similar vein, with Bell's vocals reminiscent of Nico, and a range of sounds including Bell playing a didjeridu, recorder and chimes, Snapper's Peter Gutteridge on a distortion unit, Jefferies on digital cello, and 'purrs and meows' from two cats. Two 1991 compilations of Xpressway artists, *Pile-Up* and *Killing Capitalism with Kindness*, the latter released in partnership with Belgian label Turbulence, provided samplings of the range of Xpressway artists, described by US critic Oliver Stead as combining 'the brooding, screaming electronic buzz of Dunedin minimalism with occasional sunbursts of that curious chiming clarity indigenous to the city's music.'[67]

The avant-garde, experimental and often self-indulgently left-field orientation of Xpressway restricted it to a minority audience, and the low-fi, four-track quality of many Xpressway recordings is often almost all that identifies any Aotearoa/New Zealand origin. The Dead C's noise-oriented, distorted drift was compared by Davis to 1970s experimental musicians like Syd Barrett, Nico and Faust, and he portrayed much of the music on the label as exploring inward, obscurantist, non-commercial soundscapes:

> This progressive urge also seeks liberty of a sort, an almost childlike insistence on exploring nooks and crannies the mainstream has no use for. . . . Xpressway releases have ranged from sad-eyed piano ballads to garage fuzz to Eurocentric dirges scored for screechy violins and home appliances . . . if Flying Nun is Aotearoa/New Zealand's fuzzy pop sun, Xpressway is its stark, hermetic moon.[68]

The international profile of Xpressway increased with Russell's decision to operate as an importer of experimental and avant-garde music from the USA and Europe, and its deletion of a number of its local releases. This suggests that the rarity and scarcity value of these groups due to their geographic isolation increased their international commodity value, at least in the USA, where they reached a far bigger market abroad than they did at home. Partly as a result of a number of US, UK and European labels licensing Xpressway's output, Russell decided to close down the label in August 1993, claiming that Xpressway 'has done all it set out to do. It has exposed the underbelly of South Island music with a vengeance'.[69] Its function as a mail order catalogue of obscure underground Aotearoa/New Zealand, US and other independent recording artists was taken over by IMD (Independent Music Distribution), who used a record pressing plant in Canada. In 1994 Russell founded an even more obscure label, Corpus Hermeticum, based in Lyttleton, near Christchurch, dedicating it to 'free noise' and 'live stereo recordings of improvised non-music music',[70] an apt description of the Dead C's output. Another small Dunedin-based independent label, Trinder, was established at the same time by James Cooney, releasing a compilation album of Dunedin musicians, *Does it Float?* which included a number of former Xpressway artists. All three labels ensured the survival of Dunedin as a somewhat mythologized musical production site, at least for underground left-field recording artists.

He waiata na Aotearoa (Maori music in New Zealand)

The appropriation of black American, Jamaican and British musical forms by Maori musicians in the past three decades represents a parallel musical culture to that of *pakeha* musicians, who have tended to build on white Anglo-American musical roots, and, unlike the Maori, lack an indigenous musical tradition to draw on and combine with imported idioms. These parallel cultures, within which the movement towards Maori self-determination and self-celebration is continually strengthening, reflects a binarism of Maori and *pakeha* culture which is becoming more predominant within Aotearoa/New Zealand.

Maori make up an estimated 13 per cent of the 3,360,000 population of Aotearoa/New Zealand, but 40 per cent of Maori are in the lowest income group, and 21 per cent are unemployed, compared with 5.4 per cent *pakeha*. Of the Maori population 75 per cent is under thirty years of age, but 40 per cent of Maori youth are out of work and four out of ten leave school without qualifications.[71] The remainder of the population is made up of 81.2 per cent *pakeha*, and 3 per cent Pacific Islanders, mostly Polynesian migrants from Tonga, Samoa, Fiji, Niue and the Cook and Tokelau Islands.

Since the 1980s, increasing steps have been taken by Maori towards a renewal of their cultural and social traditions, and to regenerate *te reo Maori* (the Maori language). This Maori Renaissance, as it is often referred to, has developed alongside the process of biculturalism in Aotearoa/New Zealand, and has generated an increasing number of Maori land claims which were not appeased by the government's offer in 1994 of a non-negotiable $2 billion 'fiscal envelope' as a bulk land-retribution deal. This became manifestly clear in 1995 with the disruption by Maori militants of the annual Waitangi Day celebration of the treaty signed between Maori and the British government in 1800, and in the rejection of the government's fiscal envelope in a succession of Maori tribal *hui* (meetings). There were also a number of land occupations by militant Maori groups, and racial conflict was exacerbated to unprecedented levels when police began forcibly evicting the occupiers. As James Ritchie, the *pakeha* author of the influential book *Becoming Bicultural*, stated in 1992, 'We face a future in which Maori people will assert their rightful place in this society, with or without non-Maori help. They are fashioning a thoroughly modern, totally viable Maori lifestyle in which the rest of us may participate, if we wish.'[72]

In 1992 a feature article on Maori music by Aotearoa/New Zealand critic Graham Reid in *Billboard* demonstrated how 'Maori artists have readily assimilated the sounds of the wider world and adapted them as their own'.[73] This followed the release of *AEIOU (Akona Te Reo)*, which translates as 'Learn the Language', by the all-women group Moana and the Moahunters, which is addressed primarily to Maori *rangatahi* (young people), many of whom do not speak Maori. (Only 3 per cent of the population of Aotearoa/New Zealand is able to speak Maori fluently.) *AEIOU* is also a plea, mostly in English, to the Maori people of Aotearoa to preserve their native culture (*Maoritanga*), study their history, and take part in the global movement of indigenous peoples for self-preservation.

Receiving an Aotearoa/New Zealand Music Industry award for the song, Moana accused Aotearoa/New Zealand radio of racism, commenting that fewer than twenty people present at the awards ceremony would have heard all three finalists in the Best Maori Recording category, as airplay on national and local radio stations was still a rarity for Maori popular music groups, especially those who sing in Maori.[74] Even the twenty-four *iwi* (tribal) Maori-language radio stations that had been financed by the government-backed NZ on Air since 1990 found it impossible to keep their young Maori listeners by playing Maori music, and most included a high proportion of US and UK music on their playlists.[75]

By 1994, the category of Best Maori recording had been dropped from the NZ Music Industry Awards, owing to the controversy surrounding its perceived tokenism, and acknowledgement by the organizers of the awards that Maori musicians were unhappy with the category. This was accompanied by an offer to assist Maori to set up their own awards. In a letter to *Rip It Up*, Moana Jackson explained how a delegation of Maori musicians sent a recommendation that the Best Maori recording category be retained as an award for music in *te reo Maori*, but this was denied.[76] As a result, the awards for 1994 included seven nominations for four Maori recordings (Emma Paki, 3 the Hard Way, Howard Morrison and the soundtrack to the film *Once Were Warriors*) out of a total of sixty-six, and six nominations for four Pacific Islander artists (Sisters Underground, Purest Form, Stephanie Tauevihi and Sulata Foai). Of these, *Once Were Warriors*, Sisters Underground, Sulata Foai and Purest Form won four out of the twenty-one awards, a significant but still marginal presence.

Moana and the Moahunters achieved Gold record status in 1991 with a version of the Checkmates' song 'Black Pearl', transposed to the context of Maori women, and including a rap segment by Dean Hapeta of the Upper Hutt Posse. Moana began her career singing Madonna covers in South Auckland clubs before joining the Maori reggae group Aotearoa, 'a bilingual, political band, and they kind of inspired me to get into more *kaupapa* music [music with a Maori theme]. . . . The whole point of it was reflecting what Maori people are up to, learning their language and fighting for their land.'[77] Moana and the Moahunters' musical agenda included producing internationally directed, commercially oriented Maori language music: 'We thought Maori music had a lot of international potential because it's something different. We didn't see much point in just being another funk/soul band with Maori artists because Chaka Khan and co[mpany] do it heaps better than we do. But they can't sing in Maori and do the *haka* [a Maori war dance]'.[78]

The group's first album *Tahi* (One) was released in 1993, and contained a wide spectrum of material, including the group's first four singles. It won the Best Maori Recording in the Music Awards for 1993, but was not nominated for best album, nor was Moana nominated for the best female vocalist award, even though she would have been a strong contender. Like the work of a number of their Maori peers in contemporary popular music, Moana and the Moahunters combine pop influences with rap, reggae, funk, soul and aspects of traditional Maori *waiata* (song), with particular emphasis on the latter. Musical styles on the album range from gospel to rock and dance music, along with traditional Maori instruments like the *purerehua* (bull roarer) and the *poi* – a small ball of flax on a string used in traditional dances. Singing styles include *karakia* (prayer chant), *karanga* (call) and *taparapara*, a kind of *haka*, the fierce, rhythmical war dance which is also a welcoming challenge, made internationally famous by its use by the All Blacks rugby team. *Tahi* stands as an album of Maori pop *waiata* as important in the context of indigenous popular music in Aotearoa/New Zealand as Yothu Yindi's *Homeland* and *Freedom* albums in Australia. Moana and the Moahunters' combination of African-American musical influences with Maori *waiata* was recognized by New Orleans soul group the Neville Brothers, who invited them to perform in the New Orleans Jazz and Heritage festival in 1992, and included a Maori welcome chant on the closing track of their 1992 album *Family Groove*.

Historical hybrids

The hybridization of aspects of traditional Maori *waiata* (song) and imported black American crossover musical forms is one which many Maori popular groups and performers have pursued in different ways and to varying degrees throughout the history of Maori popular music. Given the implausibility of entertaining strict notions of authenticity and purity in relation to Maori cultural traditions (or to any contemporary indigenous musical forms), the combination of traditional *waiata* and Anglo-American popular musical forms is part of a cultural project of self-assertion and self-preservation which links itself with a global diaspora of expressions of indigenous ethnic minorities' social struggles through music. But the use by some Maori musicians of a range of white Anglo-American musical influences can also be regarded as part of a bicultural project of interracial harmony, tolerance and respect which has also been expressed through Maori popular music.

Historically, Maori popular music has frequently been associated with novelty entertainment. As Reid has pointed out, the first song to be recorded and pressed in Aotearoa/New Zealand (in 1948) was the strongly Hawaiian-influenced 'Blue Smoke' by the Ruru Karaitiana Quartet, who preserved few traces of traditional Maori influences.[79] This Hawaiian influence continued into the 1950s, and was prominent in 'Haka Boogie', a 1955 composition by Lee Westbrook sung by Morgan Clarke with Benny's Five, which announced a hybridization of traditional

Maori *waiata* and popular dance music, as did Rim D. Paul's 'Poi Poi Twist' in 1962. In 1990 a seven-part television programme, *When the Haka became Boogie*, featured Maori popular entertainment from the 1950s to the 1970s, and proved to be so popular that it expanded into twenty-five episodes, and two albums of its 'greatest Bits' were released by Tangata records in 1992. Featuring cover versions of songs made famous by Frank Sinatra, Bobby Darrin, Elvis Presley, Dean Martin and others, the first album, *Nga matua* (The Stem) focused on the 'golden age' of Maori entertainment in the 1950s and 1960s. It featured groups like the Maori Hi-Five (singing 'That Old Black Magic'), Rim D. Paul (performing 'That's Life'), the Quintikis, Prince Tui Teka, Johnny Cooper and comic impersonators Bill Taitoko with the Maori Volcanics (who jokingly refer to Motown group the Platters as a Maori group, and Johnny Cash and Dean Martin as 'famous Maoris'). As Bruce Morley has pointed out, many of these groups had become almost 'legendary' in Sydney in the early 1960s, in what was essentially a live performance phenomenon; some of them reunited especially to record for the television programme.[80] The second album, *Te Rangatahi* (Modern Youth) featured Maori artists of the 1980s and 1990s, both albums establishing an historical continuity of appropriation of US influences combined with elements of traditional Maori language *waiata*.

Since Victorian times Maori concert parties, featuring the polyphonic harmonies of traditional songs and dances of Maori folklore like the *poi* dance, the *haka*, and the *karanga* (call) have been performed in various colonial contexts, often touring outside Aotearoa/New Zealand or performing for overseas tourists. Within Aotearoa/New Zealand, Maori concert parties began to be regarded by some *pakeha* as unauthentic exponents of *Maoritanga* (Maori culture). In the 1950s, Maori showbands began performing repertoires of largely Anglo-American music on cabaret circuits, sharing the indigenous popular music scene with Hawaiian-styled combos and US-influenced country and Western singers.

In 1955 a Maori country music artist, Johnny Cooper, known as 'the Maori Cowboy', was prevailed upon to record a cover version of Bill Haley's 'Rock around the Clock' in an unsuccessful attempt to launch an indigenous rock and roll scene. The Haley version was prevented from getting a local release so that Cooper's version, released on a 78 rpm record with a song called 'Blackberry Boogie' on the flipside, could gain chart success, a practice common throughout the 1950s and 1960s. John Dix has claimed that Cooper's recording was 'probably the first rock and roll recording made outside the USA.'[81] None the less it failed to have much impact on local charts, and it was not until the film featuring Haley's original version was released that Aotearoa/New Zealand youth of the 1950s discovered rock and roll. Cooper did make a significant contribution to the local rock and roll scene with his own composition,

'Pie Cart Rock and Roll' celebrating 'pea pie and pud' and an Antipodean institution, the pie cart, which exists to this day. He also had a hit with 'Look What You've Done (Lonely Blues)', and tutored the *pakeha* singer Johnny Devlin, who became a rock and roll legend in Australia and Aotearoa/New Zealand in the late 1950s. Cooper set a precedent for Maori musicians playing rock and roll, to the extent that, as Dix has pointed out, 'Any talk of Aotearoa/New Zealand rock 'n' roll cannot by-pass the Maori contribution.'[82]

In the 1960s, Maori recording artist Sir Howard Morrison, comedian Billy T. James and ballad singer John Rowles, who had two hits on the British charts, all achieved local prominence. In the 1970s, the pyrotechnical blues and acid rock of black American guitarists Jimi Hendrix and Carlos Santana were an important influence on Maori guitarists like Billy Tekahika (also known as Billy TK), who combined Hendrix-like inflections with aspects of *waiata* and Polynesian guitar rhythms. Guitarist Tama (Tama Renata), who toured Sydney in May 1993 with shows billed as tributes to Hendrix and Santana, combined Hendrix-like lead guitar with reggae, soul, blues and funk rhythms. His 1989 album *Workshop*, which he recorded and mixed on his own 'three and a half track' equipment, was released on the independent Te Aroha label, with the slogan *He Waiata na Aotearoa* (Maori Music in Aotearoa/New Zealand). Tama was billed in the Sydney weekly music paper *On the Street* in Maori-warrior-like terms, issuing a challenge to all-comers: 'The legendary Maori Acid Rock Guitarist – He blew out Jeff Beck and Frank Zappa, now he'll blow out anyone that's game to turn up with their axe.'[83]

Soul, reggae and *waiata*

The 1980s saw the emergence of soul music as a dominant Maori form. In Auckland the soul scene was spearheaded by Ardijah, who later based themselves in Sydney, where they continue to perform and record a mixture of soul, funk and dance music. But the most distinctive figure in Maori popular music of the 1980s is Dalvanius Prime, who produced 'E Ipo' for the popular ballad singer Prince Tui Teka, a song which won two Record Industry Awards in 1982. This was followed by 'Poi E', written and produced by Dalvanius on his Maui label and performed by the Patea Maori Club, which reached number one in the Aotearoa/New Zealand charts in 1984. 'Poi E' combined traditional Maori vocal chants, *poi* dancing and Polynesian drumming with funk and break-dancing, and was even named 'Single of the Week' by Britain's *NME*. It eventually won the 1988 New Zealand Recording Industry's Best Polynesian Record award, four years after it was first released.[84] The Patea Maori Club, whom Lealand describes as 'the group that comes closest to capturing some of the unique nuances of life here ... due to its unique coupling of two unmatched musical traditions',[85] also won Best Polynesian Record in 1984 for their second single, 'Aku Raukura' (My Feather). They were also the original performers of 'Kua Makona' (Satisfied), which Moana and the Moahunters recorded in 1993. A musical entitled *Poi E* based on the story of the Patea Maori Club, formed when local freezing works (slaughter-house) workers were made redundant, and subsequently performed around the world, was produced at the State Opera House in Wellington in 1995, featuring Dalvanius and Sydney-based Maori transvestite Carmen.[86]

As in Australia, Bob Marley's performances in Aotearoa/New Zealand in 1979 caused reggae music and Rastafarian philosophy to be adopted and adapted by local indigenous musicians. Aotearoa and Dread Beat and Blood (later Dread Beat, who were associated with another Maori reggae group, Sticks and Shanty), were both formed in 1985, combining mellifluous Maori vocal harmonies with Jamaican rhythms. These groups also used reggae rhythms to express Maori militancy in their lyrics, and Aotearoa's 1985 single 'Maranga Ake Ai' (Wake Up People) was a plea to young Maori to become politically aware and 'take up the cause'. It became a top-selling record, despite being banned by local radio stations because of its militant Maori activist content. As Ngahiwi Apanui, former Aotearoa singer-songwriter and founder of Tai E, a Maori music recording label, said of the group: 'We wanted to say, here we are, we are Maori and we don't give a shit about what you think. You disagree with us and you're in for trouble. It was the feeling of the youth at the time. It was a political "hot potato" but it gave us a high profile.'[87]

The Rastafarian collective Twelve Tribes of Israel explored the more religious side of reggae, combining Rastafarian rhetoric with Maori and Pacific Islander elements on their 1990 album *Shine On*, written and produced by Jamaican-born Hensley Dyer. This album featured a song entitled 'The Land of the Long White Cloud' (the literal meaning of Aotearoa), characterizing Maori and Pacific Islanders as children of Jah descended from Abraham and Shem.

Graham Reid has described Ngahiwi Apanui's 1989 solo reggae-inflected mini-album *Te Heno Ki Te Kainga* (The Link with the Homeland) as 'an ambitious and largely successful attempt at blending traditional Maori instruments like the *koauau* (nose flute) and *purerehua* (bull roarer) within the rock context'.[88] Combining songs in Maori and English, the album set an important precedent for the use of traditional Maori instruments in pop and rock. Although not reaching the national proportions of Jawaiian reggae in Hawaii, reggae, ragga and dancehall have been important forces in the hybridization of Maori popular music, which contains a number of examples of what Andrew Weintraub describes as 'the way reggae and its associated images and ideas, when transported to a different social system, take on a different symbolic meaning'.[89] This is evident in the South Pacific reggae of Maori female singer and DJ Jules Issa. Issa has stated that she finds no difficulty in juggling her subordinate status as a woman within orthodox Rastafarianism, her Israelite identity and belief in repatriation to Africa with her Maori tribal status: 'In my tribe, Ngati Porou, women are allowed to speak on the *marae*, there are a lot of *maraes* there that are named after women. Women are very much like warriors, like the men. It's the only tribe in New Zealand that's like that and being of that tribe I'm not afraid to attack an area where there's strictly men involved, like DJing.'[90] The most prominent and longest-surviving Polynesian reggae group is Herbs, who were formed in 1980 and continue to perform. Herbs' first single, 'French Letter', which portrayed the French as 'unwelcome guests making nuclear tests' in the Pacific, went to number eleven in the national charts in 1982, and enjoyed a revival during the anti-nuclear protests against French tests in the Pacific in 1995. Herbs have been described by Duncan Campbell as 'epitomiz[ing] the common purpose of Maori and Islander at a time when the youth of the two communities were more intent on gang warfare', and their 1981 debut EP, *What's Be Happen?* as setting 'a standard for Pacific reggae which has arguably never been surpassed'.[91] Their album *Sensitive to a Smile* won the Recording Industry Album of the Year award in 1987 and two cuts from it also won Best Polynesian record and Video of the Year. Herbs' soft brand of politically oriented Polynesian reggae, which includes the occasional song in Maori, became highly successful throughout the Pacific Island region, where they toured extensively, and in 1986 US blues artist Taj Mahal recorded two of their songs, 'Light of the Pacific' and 'French Letter', on his Pacific-oriented album *Taj*. Herbs also played on Dave Dobbyn's 1987 Australasian number one hit 'Slice of Heaven', which became the theme song of Australian television commercials for the New Zealand Tourist Board throughout the 1990s. Mana, an offshoot of Herbs and the Twelve Tribes of Israel, also combined Maori and Pacific Islander influences in the 'Pacific reggae' of their self-titled 1993 album, which incorporates the sounds of the beach between tracks, and concludes with an exhilarating song sung in Samoan, 'Kolomotu'a', combining the ukulele with Caribbean steel drums.

Perhaps the most internationally successful Maori popular singer of the 1990s is Margaret Urlich, whose first album, *Safety in Numbers*, sold nearly a quarter of a million copies in Australia. But Urlich has indicated that moving to Australia involves both a denial of her Maori and Pacific roots and overcoming antipathy towards soul music.[92] Urlich's increasing tendency to move into a jazz and cabaret idiom is one which many Maori artists before her have shown, but the music of other Maori and Pacific Islander women singers in the 1990s has often tended to incorporate the influences of the black American dance music performed by Paula Abdul and Janet Jackson, or black English groups like Soul II Soul. The disco-soul singer Ngaire (Ngaire Fuata), who is from Ratuma near Fiji, made some impact on the local dance scene with her eponymous album in 1991, featuring a disco cover version of Lulu's 1960s hit 'To Sir with Love', which went to number one on the local charts. Like her backing group D-Faction, who released an album in 1992, Ngaire tends to operate in a dance-disco medium where there is little room for expressing *Maoritanga* through the music, but where she none the less operates as a role model for Maori young people. Maree Sheehan, on the other hand, who records on the Maori Tangata label, combines soul, funk and rap with Maori percussive instruments like the *poi* and sticks, and stresses the importance of using aspects of *waiata* in her music in order to make it distinctively local. The dominance of black American influences over aspects of Maoritanga in the music of a number of Maori female singers brought criticism of cultural imperialism from Mahinarangi Tocker, a respected but commercially unrecognized Maori folk singer-songwriter who is a veteran of the Aotearoa/New Zealand music industry:

> They shouldn't need to pretend to be a Whitney Houston. I feel very sad when I see Maori singers influenced by black singers from America. We're unique, and we have our own style, our own rhythms – we don't need to import a style to copy. Anyway, we're relating to the wrong people: we have far more in common with the indigenous people of America in terms of trying to preserve our culture, than we do with American Blacks.[93]

But the musical paths taken by a number of young Maori and Pacific Islander women are dictated more by musical preferences and the need for a marketable image in the industry than by indigenous ideological choices. Their use of black American idioms is also a response to a global musical culture of sounds and images which relate to a shared black aesthetic, against which local notions of blackness can be defined.

Maori and Pacific Islander hip hop

African-American influences are even stronger in local manifestations of hip hop. Break-dancing was a prominent example of a black American import culture being adopted widely by Maori youth in the 1980s, as a study of break-dance as an identity marker in Aotearoa/New Zealand by Tania Kopytko indicates. According to Kopytko, break-dance first arrived in Aotearoa/New Zealand in 1983 via Western Samoa, and by 1984 local break-dance teams, consisting mostly of young Maori and Pacific Islanders, were appearing on local television programmes, and Television New Zealand even sponsored a national break-dance competition. Kopytko argues that for Maori and Pacific Islander young people with little chance of achieving recognition through conventional channels such as school, sport and social position, 'break-dance provided a very strong and positive identity that did much to raise their self esteem and realise their capabilities'.[94] She also claims that, despite the local mass media's association of break-dancing with street gangs, glue sniffing and petty crime, which gave it pejorative associations and contributed to its decline by 1985, it provided Maori youth in particular with a substitute for their own culture: 'Amongst Maori youth the association with an international Black identity compensates in part for the lack of a thorough knowledge of Maori culture. Also, popular culture movements are more readily accessible without the commitment and effort necessary for a knowledge of Maoritanga.'[95]

In an examination by the Maori cultural magazine, *Mana*, in 1993 of the adoption by Maori youth of African-American music, films, television programmes and clothes such as baseball caps, baggies, T shirts and jackets, Moana Maniapoto-Jackson in part confirms this view by suggesting that this acculturation of the artefacts of another black minority by Maori young people is partly due to the absence of Maori culture from the mass media:

> It comes down to what you see on TV and what you hear on the radio. We don't hear enough of our own culture, so we co-opt the next closest thing. . . . Maori kids identify with the stereotypical Afro-American they see on TV, who's funny, sassy, streetwise, who's funky, who plays sports, who's into music, who's got all the quick one-liners and who's got all the gear on.[96]

In the same article, Maori film maker Merata Mita blamed the absence of strong Maori leadership and the enforcement of *tapu* (taboos) and preservation restrictions on aspects of Maori culture by Maori elders for alienating Maori youth and forcing them to seek black American role models and cultural icons:

> If you put a Maori pattern on your shirt, people accuse you of prostituting the culture or selling out or it's too *tapu*. We've created such a mystique and negative enforcement that it's much easier for young Maori to take Afro-American symbols and wear them. Nobody's going to attack them for it.[97]

But, as Alan Jannson has indicated, the adoption of hip hop by Maori and Pacific Islander youth in Aotearoa/New Zealand is part of a universal youth culture involving the hybridization of US influences with local cultural inflections: '[Maori and Polynesians] can listen to a rap track from the States and straight away they can start rapping too. Rap now is not just an American thing, it's a new universal language.'[98] Rap music and hip hop culture quickly became an inevitable medium for musical expressions of Maori militancy, sometimes expressed in the Maori language. As Kerry Buchanan has argued, hip hop's associations with African American culture quickly became an important reference point and example for musical expressions of a local Maori and Pacific Islander vernacular culture, with which it shared strong roots in church and gospel singing:

> With our links to the land broken, our alienation from the mode of production complete, our culture objectified, we have become marginalised and lost. ... This is not to say beaten. And this is what we have in common with black America. When Maori hip-hop activists Upper Hutt Posse visited America recently, these political, social and racial links were brought into perspective. Upper Hutt Posse were welcomed as people involved in a common struggle, linked symbolically through hip-hop culture.[99]

The Upper Hut Posse's Public Enemy-influenced hard-core rap, featuring Teremoana Rapley (who later joined the Moahunters), first drew attention in both Aotearoa/New Zealand and Australia in the late 1980s. In 1990 the group toured *marae* (traditional Maori community centres) supported Public Enemy on their Aotearoa/New Zealand tour, and played with British-Jamaican reggae artist Macca B and the Bhundu Boys in Australia. Upper Hutt Posse released the first hip hop record in Aotearoa/New Zealand at the end of 1988, the 12-inch single 'E Tu' (Stand Proud), which combined black American revolutionary rhetoric with an explicitly Maori frame of reference. 'E Tu' pays homage to the rebel Maori warrior chiefs of Aotearoa/New Zealand's colonial history, Hone Heke, Te Kooti and Te Rauparaha. It also praises the 28th Maori Battalion, a celebrated volunteer force in the Second World War who suffered high casualty rates which caused the loss of almost an entire generation of Maori men. In a 1989 survey of Upper Hutt Posse, Buchanan commented on their United States–New Zealand hybridity:

> Upper Hutt Posse is modern Maori music with links to the spirit of hardcore black American hip hop, as in the reference in the rap *Hardcore* – 'Like Malcolm X him preach the hard truth / And we'll remember him and what he did contribute'. In the Posse's rap Hone Heke and Malcolm X can exist side by side, because they represent the spirit of resistance against the dominant power structure.[100]

The group's 1989 album *Against the Flow*, delivered in a mixture of Kiwi and American accents, and including a paean to American basketball, combined some rather inchoate political rhetoric with an overriding concern with American hip hop styles. While the singles taken from the album, 'Do It Like This' and 'Stormy Weather', achieved some degree of popularity in Aotearoa/New Zealand and Australia, there was a notable absence of any of the specifically Maori references or use of the Maori language that distinguished the early recordings, as if the group had decided to de-localize their songs in the interests of a broader international appeal, while maintaining a militant rhetorical pose. The video clip of 'Stormy Weather' uses footage of 1977 Maori land rights demonstrations at Bastion Point, protests against the 1981 South African rugby tour of Aotearoa/New Zealand and opposition to French nuclear tests in the Pacific together with scenes of a Kanaka labourers' strike in Queensland and demonstrations in South African townships. This attempt to contextualize the song's claim that 'People's culture's not respected ... madness rules the world' remains an unconvincing domination of hard core rap style and rhetoric over content, as does the fist-pumping but context-free dance track 'Do It Like This'.

Upper Hutt Posse's admiration for Louis Farrakhan and the Black Muslim movement in the USA (they were invited to Detroit by Black Muslims in 1989) extended to an apparent endorsement of Public Enemy's Professor Griff's anti-Semitic rhetorical ploys in an interview in Sydney in 1990. Referring to a query about the song 'Stormy Weather', which begins 'Another dies in Israel / The victim of a bomb / Another burns in a necklace / the victim of apartheid ... Jews are now after Nazis / Blacks and whites still fight', Hapeta claimed that it was 'just about trouble. It's about that sort of strife in the world'. He went on to comment about Public Enemy's anti-Semitic statements: 'Jews control New York ... Jewish people here take me to task over us liking PE, but I hear the other story from black Muslims that Jews have been terrible to black people in New York. It seems that all you hear is the extreme on both sides.'[101] This provoked a sharp rebuke from Naomi Dinnen, the interviewer who had initially queried the sense of the lyrics of 'Stormy Weather'. Pointing out the existence of a number of Jewish American rappers, and that Public Enemy's record producers are also Jewish, Dinnen's criticisms exposed Upper Hutt Posse's endorsement of Public Enemy's rhetoric, and revealed the dangers inherent in the appropriation of African-American nationalist models.[102]

A survey of Aotearoa/New Zealand hip hop in 1995 by Otis Frizzell, of the *pakeha* group MCOJ and Rhythm Slave, featured a dozen groups and individuals and mentioned five more, many of whom have released recordings. Frizzel emphasized the multicultural heterogeneity of the scene, and the importance of Maori and Pacific Islanders in defining its identity.[103] The most successful local hip hop group in 1994 was West Auckland Maori rappers 3 the Hard Way, whose pop-rap single 'Hip Hop Holiday', a hip hop transposition of 10CC's 'Dreadlock Holiday', topped the charts for several weeks and went gold, reaching number twelve on the Australian top twenty. Describing themselves as 'Old School Prankstas' (the title of their debut album), 3 the Hard Way maintain a commercial, accessible sound which suggests that, despite their name, they may have got to the top of the charts the easy way. Their second single was a soft-edged pastiche of UB40's version of Jimmy Cliff's 'Many Rivers to Cross', and much of the album was produced by North Shore musician Anthony Ioassa, who with his two brothers fronts a smooth and silky 'Samoan soul' group called Grace, who have been described as 'a Polynesian

Crowded House'.[104] Few other local hip hop groups have had any comparable chart success, apart from fellow Auckland Deepgrooves label-mates Urban Disturbance, who were voted most promising group at the 1994 New Zealand Music Awards.

Upper Hutt Posse's uncompromising, *kia kaha* (be strong) style of hip hop remains the most distinctive blend of traditional aspects of Maori musical culture, local urban realities and African-American rap music in Aotearoa/New Zealand. Hapeta's 'Whakakotahi' (To Make One) was released in 1993 by E Tu, an offshoot of Upper Hutt Posse, on Tangata Records to mark the United Nations' International Year for Indigenous People. Incorporating quotes from Louis Farrakhan and Khallid Mohammed of the Nation of Islam along with a *haka* (war dance) and *purerehua* (bull roarer), its message of unity to the indigenous people of the world none the less received little media attention. The expletive in the lines 'Fuck New Zealand, ya call me a Kiwi / Aotearoa the name of this country' (sic) necessitated bleeping for radio play.

A definitively hybridized version of 'Whakakotahi' opens the Upper Hutt Posse's powerful 1995 album *Movement in Demand* (a title derived from Louis Farrakhan), wedding together traditional Maori instruments and militant *patere* and *karanga* (raps and shouts), invocations of the spirits of the forest (*tane mohuta*) and the guardian of the sea (*tangaroa*), with Nation of Islam rhetoric. This version also draws on the group's reggae and ragga inclinations (they started off as a reggae group in 1985), funk bass rhythms, blues guitar riffs and hardcore gangsta-style rapping, which switches from English to *te reo Maori*. It ends with a *patere* – for which, like all the other *te reo Maori* lyrics on the album, no English translation is provided – exhorting the *pakeha* to leave the land, the sea, the indigenous people and the world, and to get away from Maori space and children for ever. One of the album's tracks, the *tangi* (lament) 'Tangata Whenua', is entirely in Maori. The cover of the album features fourteen Maori chiefs, warriors, prophets and leaders, from Hone Heke in the early nineteenth century to Princess Te Puea Herangi in the twentieth century, and includes historical notes on all of them, under the banner of a slogan appropriated from Rewi Maniapoto and used in Maori demonstrations: '*Ka whawhai tonu matou, ake, ake, ake*' (We will continue to fight for evermore). Knowledge of past Maori battles, struggles and victories over the *pakeha* informs the whole album, while reference is made in the track 'Hardcore' to Bob Marley, Marcus Garvey and the English dub poet Linton Kwesi Johnson, along with Malcolm X, Steve Biko, Crazy Horse and a number of Maori militants past and present, all of whom D Word claims as part of his *whakapapa* (lineage). The album's musical heterogeneity of influences mirrors its political array of black militant role models, and the track 'Gun in My Hand' disturbingly adapts the violent rhetoric of African-American gangsta rap and ragga boasting into a biblical-styled diatribe against the evils of

Babylon. This is particularly alarming when taken in the light of Hapeta's statement at the end of an Australian Broadcasting Corporation radio programme in November 1995 (which used 'Whakakotahi' as a theme song): 'Guns are going to come into this country sooner or later and they're going to come in a big way, and people should be really thankful they're not here now ... because I just know a lot of brothers who would be shooting people in a big way if they were as available as they are in the States'.[105] Both the song and the statement suggest a rhetorical confluence between the ritualized Maori challenge and the US gangsta rap threat.

Due to their uncompromising political stance of total support by whatever means necessary for *mana* (integrity) and *tino rangatiratanga* (absolute Maori sovereignty), and their musical and political strategy of 'push[ing] it further', the Upper Hutt Posse have never been far from controversy. Hapeta sued the *Auckland Star* (and won) over claims that the group had barred two *pakeha* youths from one of their shows, while in 1990 *The Truth* claimed that the group had behaved in a racist fashion, telling Samoans at a concert to 'go home'.[106] Influenced by his trip to the USA and meeting Farrakhan and hardcore US rappers, Hapeta's comments about the local hip hop scene emphasize its smallness, fragility and deracination, but also rap's compatibility with Maori formations of oral discourse, illustrated by the way concepts such as *patere* (rap), *whakarongo mai* (listen up) and *wainua* (attitude) are easily assimilated into hip hop discourse:

> NZ Hip-Hop is a fallacy! Hip hop is a culture – rap music, break-dancing, graffiti, clothes, language. This country lacks a connection between, and a socialisation of, these components of Hip-Hop. True Hip-Hop will only exist, for the moment at least, in the inner city suburbs of Black America where it was created as an everyday 'living' thing. ... We can emulate certain areas of Hip-Hop, as we do with rap music, and did with break-dancing back in the early 80s, and still do with other components of Hip-Hop today, but, just as experiencing Maori culture today is done best on the Marae, Hip-Hop can only truly be experienced fully at its home. ... Although I love and respect Hip-Hop, being Maori I only take from it what doesn't compromise my own culture. But in spite of this I have found them both very compatible.[107]

Hapeta denies that hip hop is merely a musical style, emphasizing that the music is an expression of a culture and way of life which originated in inner-city black ghettos in the US, making it difficult if not impossible to transpose to an isolated country at the bottom of the world like Aotearoa/ New Zealand. But what Hapeta and other Maori and Pacific Islander rappers and musicians have done is to substitute their own cultural expressions for the black American context of hip hop, while borrowing freely from the hybrid US musical styles of the genre. The result is a further hybridization of an already hybrid form, but one which is capable of having strong musical, political and cultural resonances in Aotearoa/

New Zealand. The importance with which rap music and reggae are regarded by Maori as legitimate forms of expressing official Maori oral *kaupapa* (culture) is illustrated by the inclusion of song lyrics by Hapeta, Herbs and others in *Te Ao Marama* (The Dawning of the Light), a five-volume anthology of Maori literature edited by novelist and former Aotearoa/New Zealand Consul Witi Ihimaera. The Wellington Maori hip hop group Dam Native summed up the appropriation of hip hop in Aotearoa/New Zealand as follows: 'We don't own [hip hop]. All we can do is inject our own culture into it. *Kia kaha.*'[108]

Once Were Warriors and Maori music

The Maori Renaissance in Aotearoa/New Zealand was given an unprecedented boost in 1994 by Lee Tamahori's film version of Alan Duff's controversial novel about a dysfunctional Maori family, *Once Were Warriors*. The film achieved an unprecedented success in its country of origin, being the first film to gross more than $6 million in cinemas (more than *Jurassic Park*), going straight to the top of the national ratings in its first week of release on video, and being seen by almost a third of the population of the country as well as winning nine of the fifteen national film and television awards. It also had some success abroad, winning prizes at the Montreal, Durban and Rotterdam film festivals, being sold to more than twenty countries and running for more than six months in Sydney, and it became an important focal point for current conflicts in Aotearoa/New Zealand over issues of Maori land and cultural rights and social deprivation.

The Maori recording label Tangata Records, which was established in 1991 by Neil Cruikshank in Wellington and George Hubbard in Auckland to record and promote music by Maori musicians, acted as musical advisers to *Once Were Warriors*, and were given a much-needed boost by its platinum-selling soundtrack. This stayed at number two in the Aotearoa/New Zealand album charts for two months, was released in forty-two countries, gaining considerable popularity in Italy, partly due to the popularity of ragga there, and selling 22,000 units in Australia. It received a Recording Industry Association of New Zealand award for best soundtrack album, and was the second-highest selling local album in Aotearoa/New Zealand for 1994.

The Maori musician Hirini Melbourne, who specializes in reconstructing and playing traditional Maori musical instruments from bone, wood, stone, shells and even flax snails, was the film's musical consultant. Melbourne's Maori songs are sung by children in schools throughout Aotearoa/New Zealand, and his demonstrations and recordings with Richard Nunns of the more than seventy traditional Maori musical instruments of thirty-four different kinds Nunns has collected make him the most distinctive indigenous musician in the country. Melbourne and Nunns's work is featured on their 1994 album *Te Ku Te Whe* (The Origin of Sound), the first album of ambient music to feature exclusively pre-European Maori instruments, which Truda Chadwick has described as 'structured by mythology, history and the various moods of nature, evoking the closeness of the Maori to the physical and spiritual elements'.[109] The duo's 1993 album *Toiapiapi* (Mimic of Bird Calls) also features Melbourne's considerable singing, songwriting and guitar playing abilities. The results of Melbourne and Nunns's restoration of *nga taonga puoro* (traditional musical instruments) have also surfaced in recordings by popular Maori musicians like Moana and the Moahunters (*Tahi* opens with Melbourne's composition 'Tihore Mai' (Split Apart)), Hinewehi Mohi (who sang on *Toiapiapi*), Maree Sheehan and Emma Paki, who have all used traditional Maori instruments in soul, dance and rock-oriented contexts, combining *waiata* with pop.

Melbourne's musical presence in *Once Were Warriors* is evident from the opening credits, which introduce the whirring sound of the *purerehua* (bull roarer), an oval or diamond-shaped blade of wood, bone, stone or greenstone, attached to a two-metre rope and swung around the body, and used by different tribes to attract rain, accompany funerals, or lure lizards. The *purerehua* recurs throughout the film at moments of anger and violent confrontation, and serves as a subliminal, elemental commentary on the frequent eruptions of violence in the film. Also used in the main theme and other atmospheric contexts in the film are *koauau*, bone or wooden flutes whose *vibrato* sound is described by their generic name. These join with the *purerehua* and Tama Renata's distorted electric guitar in the main theme to combine the sounds of the earth with an urban rock lament. Melbourne also performs a *patere*, a rhythmic vocal chant (which my Maori dictionary also translates as a 'rap'), on the sound track, while other traditional Maori chants like the *karanga* (call to ancestors), which opens the soundtrack album, and the *haka* (war dance), performed at the funeral at the end of the film, are also included.

The soundtrack's inclusion of a number of important popular Maori recording artists is also indicative of the positive portrayal in *Once Were Warriors* of Maori potential – a theme Duff's book treats from a bleak, victim perspective. As Beth, the victim of domestic violence and other family tragedies in the book, ruminates:

> We're musical people, us Maoris. Comes natural to us; plays a bigger part in our lives ... We got passion, us Maoris. Or maybe it's style. But not like that Negro style you see on the TV of being swank, hip, cool, moving with their black rhythmic groovin, not that kind, but a cross between that and the less showy whites.[110]

The film's soundtrack reflects this 'brown' musical hybridity through the constructed sounds of the streets of South Auckland, using a range of recent (and some not-so-recent) Maori soul, reggae, rap and rock music. Wellington swingbeat group Gifted and Brown perform 'So Much Soul', celebrating Maori and Samoan musicality in a mixture of Maori, Samoan and English, backed by Polynesian drums. Upper Hutt Posse's 'Ragga Girl' demonstrates the ease with which Maori groups incorporate imported Afro-Caribbean rap, soul and ragga styles. Dean Hapeta's ragga-styled rap 'Whakamutungia Tenei Mahi Te Patupatu Tangata' (Stop Killing Our Men), a warning about the dangers of alcohol abuse in Maori communities, is also included as a bonus track on the soundtrack recording, along with Moana and the Moahunters' 'Tahi'.

A reflection of the impact of Maori popular music on Maori communities occurs when the film's protagonists, the Heke family, rent a car to visit their son in remand. They sing Maori group Southside of Bombay's *iwi* station hit 'What's The Time Mister Wolf', evoking a brief moment of family harmony and solidarity. This is so memorable that when Jake Heke later hears the song on the pub jukebox he smashes it into silence. Similarly, Beth and Jake Heke are briefly and harmoniously united in a party scene singing an impromptu duet of 'Here is My Heart', a song written by Herbs, whose song 'HomeGrown' is also featured in the film. Jake and Beth's song is accompanied on acoustic guitar by Tama Renata. In the film the hybrid, Afro-American-influenced music of Maori youth becomes an expression of a vitality in urban Maori culture which has combined with some of the traditional aspects of *Maoritanga* into a vibrantly syncretic mix of old and new. Tamahori indicated that he wanted to show the assertive, hybridized youth street styles of the South Auckland scene in the 1990s:

> I look around the streets. Young Maori look absolutely fantastic. Pride, well-being. A sense of costume. An awareness of how they look. I dare say most of it comes from MTV and other television, but the key is they take all that and change it, make it their own. You'll see bits of black liberation from Africa, a touch of reggae, a touch of East LA, all filtered through their own culture. This picture ... reflect[s] that.[111]

The film takes cues from rap videos and black American hip hop films of urban ghetto life like *Boyz 'n' the Hood*, *New Jack City* and *Menace II Society*, but gives them a distinctively 'urban Polynesian' twist. Generic elements like the Toa (Warrior) gang, who adapt traditional Maori tattoos into a futurist 'Road Warrior' context, and the film's unfussy violent action sequences and music video style, anchored by the predominantly rap, ragga and rock soundtrack, caused it to be immensely popular among young people, particularly those of Maori and Pacific Islander extraction. The film also provided a new source of Maori music in the local popular music scene, as its male star Temuera Morrison, formerly an actor on the long-running Kiwi soap opera *Shortland Street* (notable for its inclusion of Maori characters) released a single in 1995 entitled 'Waiata Poi'. The Upper Hutt Posse's *Movement in Demand* also extends the warrior rhetoric of *Once Were Warriors*; in the track 'Hardcore', D-Word describes himself as 'harder than Jake da Mus' and 'a warrior with knowledge of the past'.

The Proud project and the 'Otara sound'

In 1994 a recording entitled *Proud*, an 'Urban Pacific Streetsoul Compilation' of South Auckland Polynesian rap, reggae, soul, *a cappella*, swing beat and traditional musicians, topped the Aotearoa/New Zealand compilation charts for three weeks. The recording was the result of a community project which involved Samoan, Tongan, Niuean, Fijian and Cook Islander as well as Maori musicians in a twenty-five-date nationwide tour. Produced by Alan Jansson for Second Nature, the Aotearoa/New Zealand branch of Sydney-based Volition records, the album included Sisters Underground, an Otara-based Samoan and African-American *a cappella* duo whose feisty, street-smart rap 'In the Neighbourhood' set the tone for the compilation. With the exception of the Semi MCs, a mixed Maori and Samoan swing-beat group whose 'lover's rap' single 'Trust Me' had been released on Volition in 1993, and DJ Payback, who had been involved in one of Aotearoa/New Zealand's first rap groups, Double J and Twice the T, the groups featured on the album had not previously recorded, and many had been involved in the local Otara Music and Arts Centre in South Auckland. The ironically named Otara Millionaires Club had done a number of live performances, as had the Pacifican Descendants, who were regarded as one of Aotearoa/New Zealand's leading rap performers, along with Radio Backstab and DJ Playback. The Samoan *a cappella* group Di-Na-Ve, the gospel-based Rhythm Harmony and the seven-man team of log drummers Puka Puka completed the line-up.

Proud was regarded by music reviewers as a new landmark in Aotearoa/New Zealand popular music, despite its release on an Australian label and 'cringe' reactions to the final track, an *a cappella* version of the national anthem 'God Defend New Zealand'. This was performed by the Vocal Five, one of a wide range of mainly Polynesian *a cappella* street performers featured along with Di-Na-Ve, Purest Form and others in a TVNZ programme, 'Strictly Acappella' in 1993. Colin Hogg of the *Sunday Star Times* described *Proud* as 'the best compilation of new Kiwi music in a decade'. Hogg also suggested that the album's 'Otara sound' may have ushered in a new era of Kiwi music, displacing and supplanting 'the challenging new sounds of Aotearoa/New Zealand contemporary music ... from the bedsits of Dunedin, the garretts of Grey Lynn [an inner-city Auckland suburb] and the garages of Christchurch'.[112] Russell Baillie in the *NZ Herald* found it 'a truly ground-breaking and purposeful local compilation ... that captures a time and an attitude, and one to point to as a starting point in years to come'.[113]

The extent of young Polynesian musical talent which the project revealed suggested that the hip hop, swing-beat, soul and funk music of the loosely defined 'South Auckland sound' of the 1990s may have replaced the jangling guitars of the 'Dunedin sound'. The 1994 success of the young Auckland-based *pakeha* hard-core funk group Supergroove, who sound a little like a local version of US rappers the Beastie Boys, and sold more albums locally than Crowded House, indicates that a combination of both the areas of American influence to which these two musical directions can be traced has proved to be a successful formula. As Supergoove's singer Karl Steven indicated:

> I think people in and around our age group ... are a bit sick of the black hole in music. There's a separation between the white rock thing and the black dance thing. We were influenced for a long time by the white alternative guitar thing coming from the States and at the same time the Public Enemy thing and the rest of that heavier black American rap thing. A lot of people don't want to subscribe to either completely, instead they want a bit of both and we are a bit of both.[114]

Steven's reference to Supergroove's music solely in terms of American influences runs counter to one of the producers of the Proud project's main concerns. This was to create music that was distinctively local and reflected Polynesian musical traditions and influences such as the ukulele, percussion, acoustic guitars and body slaps. Alan Jansson described how a certain amount of weaning away from American influences and coaching and encouragement in Pacific and Polynesian musical culture was necessary to produce *Proud*:

> A lot of those contributing to the album are Samoans, American Samoans, so they drew off that because they see what's happening in the States with things like Boo Ya Tribe and they think that's what they should be doing. Pacifican Descendants were pressed by a friend of mine, Andy Vann, a white DJ, to come up with something innovative to the region, not just copying the Americans, because that's all we were getting, a lot of cloning. And I've had to turn them around and tell them to get the Polynesian drum thing happening, and we forced Pacifican Descendants to bring the ukulele into it. We were literally about a third of the way into the album when we started to bring the more Pacific elements out of them and then the other bands saw it. Now they've actually started going back and studying their culture, learning about their roots, and I think you'll see more and more of that coming out as it catches on. When the Proud bands started their tour they were wearing Reeboks and Nikes and back-to-front baseball caps, and when they came back they had lava lavas and tapu cloth headgear and I was absolutely blown away. What they discovered when they went on the road is that New Zealand is not

America, and Radio Backstab have written a song called 'This is Not America', so they're really getting into where they're from.[115]

A major contributor to the Proud project and the manager of the Proud tour was the Niuean-Maori musician, songwriter and producer, Philip Fuemana, who fronts the soul group Fuemana with his sister Christina and brother Paul, who also fronts the Otara Millionaires Club. Fuemana's 1994 debut album *New Urban Polynesian* featured covers of Roberta Flack's 'Closer' and Stevie Wonder's 'Rocket Love', and, refusing the 'indigenizing' pressures exerted by Janssen and others, he has pursued a resolutely urban American style of soul and gospel music. Fuemana spoke out about what he regarded as a lack of autonomy in the Proud project due to its *pakeha* producers' pursuit of a strictly Polynesian musical agenda: 'White guys sabotaged the whole thing – hardly any of the bands were happy with the finished product. The Pacifican Descendants hated that version of "Pass It Over". But it was a case of people taking over because they thought they knew better than the band.'[116] Fuemana's view suggests that the pressures exerted by the *pakeha* and *palangi* (European) producers of *Proud* were a form of reverse cultural imperialism which implanted indigenous musical notions for commercial motives. He later cited the fact that by 1995 only one of the groups involved in the Proud project, the Otara Millionaires Club, was still in existence, as an indication of the commercial pressures the musicians involved in were subjected to.[117] His comments illustrate the dangers of pursuing strictly polarized positions for or against the desirability of distinctively local, indigenous forms of popular music in preference to American influences. The American influences in the *Proud* compilation (Arrested Development, Cypress Hill, A Tribe Called Quest, Sly Stone, KRS1, Teddy Riley, etc.) are unmistakable, while the distinctively Polynesian rhythms and harmonies in Fuemana's singing are just as discernible. A desirable solution to the anxieties of influence expressed in the Proud project may be a balance between the indigenous and the imported, as Fuemana stated in an interview in the *NZ Herald* in March 1994, after the Proud tour:

> The performers were all dressed like Americans when we first went out and I don't dis that because we're all affected by American music and culture ... but the trick is to get something of ourselves into the music. It might take a couple of Proud albums to do it, but it'll happen. We are aware that at the moment we are Polynesians using Polynesian culture and it's just a token right now. We can sometimes be accused of using our culture as a fashion and we make no apology for how we sound now because that's where we're at.[118]

Take away the log drums and ukuleles from *Proud* and what is left is a group of English-language songs and raps which reflect the Pacific Island, migrant status of most the performers. Both lyrically and musically it expresses a strong 'urban Polynesian' perspective, but lacks any equivalent to the use of *te reo Maori* (Maori language) by artists such as Moana, Hapeta, Survival and Maree Sheehan, who are all featured performing songs in Maori in styles ranging from soul to hard-core rap on the *Once Were Warriors* soundtrack. Even hybrid Maori–Pacific performers like Fuemana, Gifted and Brown and the Semi MCs tend to be less influenced by Maori culture than by a more generalised 'urban Polynesian' experience.

By 1995 the 'urban Polynesian' label had become a 'buzz word' in the local music industry, and was not always to the liking of the musicians it was used to refer to. The young South Auckland Samoan singer Sulata, for example, who received the award for most promising female vocalist in the 1995 New Zealand Music Awards, indicated her concern at being described in the awards programme as an 'urban Polynesian': 'I went "Uhhh!" I'm trying to get away from the South Auckland scene, away from that music.'[119] Sulata's debut single, 'Never', is an example of 'Samoan soul', with more US than local musical influences, in the style of Fuemana, who co-wrote the B-side, 'Motion'. On the other hand, Wellington-based Samoan recording artist Igelese explores 'Polynesian fusion' on his 1995 debut single, 'Groovalation', which incorporates a native language dialogue between Maori and Samoan rappers with US soul, funk, dance and rhythm and blues influences, as well as including Polynesian log drumming and Maori chants. A church choirmaster, pianist and university music graduate, Igelese claimed he 'had some fresh ideas that nobody else had done and was getting sick of watching Polynesians imitating African Americans'.[120] 'Groovalation' advocates racial unity, reworking the slogan 'One nation under a groove', and its albeit self-consciously national multi-hybridity indicates a possible future musical direction, combining different elements of the multicultural diversity of Polynesian Aotearoa/New Zealand. It certainly represents a benchmark in a historical process in which a complex but distinctively local identity has emerged in Aotearoa/New Zealand music.

Notes

1. G. Lealand (1988) *A Foreign Egg in Our Nest? American Popular Culture in New Zealand*, (Wellington, Victoria University Press), pp. 72, 66.
2. *Ibid.*, p. 75.
3. *Ibid.*, pp. 60–6.
4. R. Watkins (1992) *When Rock Got Rolling (The Wellington Scene 1958-70)*, (Wellington, Hazard Press), and R. Watkins (1995) *Hostage to the Beat (the Auckland Scene 1955-70)*, (Auckland, Tandem Press). The first issue of *Social End Product*, whose title derives from a song by the 1960s Auckland garage band the Bluestars – the first Aotearoa/New Zealand group to be signed to a British label – appeared in October 1995.
5. R. Shuker (1995) *Understanding Popular Music*, (London, Routledge), p. 65.

6. *Ibid.*, p. 68. See also R. Shuker and M. Pickering (1994) 'Kiwi Rock: Popular Music and Cultural Identity in New Zealand', *Popular Music* vol. 13 no. 3, pp. 261–78 for an extended version of this argument.
7. Overseas artists who have done cover versions of songs by Aotearoa/New Zealand groups and performers include the Lemonheads, Superchunk, Barbara Manning, House of Love, the Johnnys, Frente, Paul Young, Belinda Carlisle and Shawn Colvin. In 1995, US independent label Dark Beloved Cloud released a vinyl EP entitled *Cleaned Out!* containing versions of songs by the Clean by Sleepyhead, Uncle Wiggy, Kickstand, Airlines and the Giant Mums.
8. J.Dix (1988) *Stranded in Paradise: New Zealand Rock 'n' Roll 1955-1988*, (Wellington, Paradise Publications), p. 155.
9. M.Chunn (1992) *Stranger than Fiction: The Life and Times of Split Enz*, (Wellington, GP Publications Ltd), p. 117.
10. Unattributed (1995) 'The 100 Greatest Pop Songs of All Time', *The Australian Magazine* (4-5 February), pp. 10–19.
11. Dix (1988), pp. 241, 327.
12. Chunn (1992), p. 2.
13. *Ibid.*, p. 76.
14. *Ibid.*, p. 202.
15. In D. Campbell (1985) 'Neil Finn: The Prodigal Perspective', *Rip It Up*, no. 100, (November), pp. 1, 3.
16. P. Holmes (1994) 'Neil Finn's Homecoming', *Sydney Morning Herald* (5 February), p. 3A.
17. In J. King (1993) 'Distant Son', *Rip It Up*, no. 195 (October), p. 16.
18. In A. Fyfe (1994) 'The House that Roared', *New Musical Express* (11 June), p. 19.
19. In A. Heal (1995) 'The Metro Interview: Neil Finn', *Metro* no. 164 (February), p. 100.
20. A. Bollinger (1994) Review of Emma Paki, 'Greenstone', *Real Groove*, no. 25 (December), p. 25.
21. In J.Taite (1992) 'Cool Thing', *Rip It Up*, no. 183 (October), p. 12.
22. K. Cameron (1994) Review of the 3Ds, *The Venus Trail*, *New Musical Express* (30 April), p. 40.
23. In T. Grimson (1994) 'Elevate me now!' *On the Street* (26 July), p. 33.
24. C. McLeay (1994) 'The "Dunedin Sound" – New Zealand Rock and Cultural Geography', *Perfect Beat*, vol. 2, no. 1 (July), p. 39.
25. *Ibid.*, p. 47.
26. *Ibid.*, p. 41.
27. In S. Coupe (1992) 'Getting Older and Wiser', *Drum Media*, no. 111 (3 November), p. 11.
28. P.Theroux (1992) *The Happy Isles of Oceania: Paddling in the Pacific*, (New York, Putnam), p. 23.
29. In R. Gow (1992) 'Stay Where You Are New Zealand', *On the Street*, no. 619 (November), p. 17.
30. F. Stark (1987) 'The Clean: Tallyho', quoted in *Rip It Up* no.119 (June), p.21.
31. S. Cohen (1991) *Rock Culture in Liverpool: Popular Music in the Making*, (Oxford, Clarendon Press), p. 15.
32. G. Downes (1992) 'The Clean: Modal Conflict and Resolution', *Music in*

New Zealand, no. 16 (Autumn), pp. 21–3.

33. C. Walker (1994) 'Modern Rockers Getting Older', *Real Groove* (October), p. 8.

34. See R. Colbert (1990) 'Singing in My Sleep: Martin Phillipps and the Chills', *Music in New Zealand* (autumn).

35. D. Eggleton (1994) 'The Bats: Hearing Secret Harmonies', *Music in New Zealand*, no. 26 (spring), p. 44.

36. P. McKessar (1991) 'Straitjacket Fits: Another Flying Nun Band Make Their Mark Overseas', *Music in New Zealand* (spring), p. 55.

37. In E. McDonnell (1990) 'Green Grass and High Tides Forever: Rock and Roll is Alive and Well and Living in New Zealand', *Village Voice Rock and Roll Quarterly*, vol. 3 no. 2 (summer), p. 25.

38. P. McKessar (1993) 'The Jean-Paul Sartre Experience', *Music in New Zealand* (winter), p. 44.

39. In *Rolling Stone* (US Edition) (16 September 1993), p. 26.

40. C. Robertson (1991) 'It's OK, It's All Right, Oh Yeah': *The 'Dunedin Sound'? An Aspect of Alternative Music in New Zealand 1978-1985*, BA Honours Thesis, University of Otago, Dunedin, p. 49.

41. *Ibid.*, p. 53.

42. *Ibid.*, p. 54.

43. *Ibid.*, p. 126.

44. M. Goddard (1991) 'It's an Oddity it's True oh Yeah: The Flying Nun Record Label and the Dunedin Sound', *Blunt*, Sydney, Issue 13, pp. 7, 28.

45. Up until 1990, gold record status in New Zealand was 7,500 sales, and platinum 15,000. These figures were then increased to 10,000 and 20,000, but, as Robertson (1991) notes, 'An album receiving gold sales or platinum sales status struggles to pay for itself' (p. 98) in New Zealand.

46. S. England (1995) 'Company Spreads Wings in Britain', *Evening Standard* Palmerston North (15 February), p. 16.

47. In D. Yuzwalk (1990) 'Caught in a Swirl: Straitjacket Fits Resurface', *Rip It Up*, no. 159 (October), p. 16.

48. In *New Musical Express* (11 October 1986), cited in Robertson (1991), p. 134.

49. S. Reynolds (1988) 'Against Health and Efficiency: Independent Music in the 1980s', in A. McRobbie (ed.) *Zoot Suits and Second-Hand Dresses*, (Boston, Unwin Hyman), pp. 246–55.

50. In S. Danielsen (1991) 'Push Have Pull', *Sydney Morning Herald* (15 August), p. 23.

51. L. Grossberg (1984) 'Another Boring Day in Paradise: Rock and Roll and the Empowerment of Everyday Life', in R. Middleton and D. Horn (eds.) *Popular Music 4: Performance and Audiences*, (Cambridge University Press), p. 241.

52. In McDonnell (1990), p. 24.

53. Goddard (1991), p. 7.

54. M. Slobin (1992) 'Micromusics of the West: A Comparative Approach', *Ethnomusicology*, vol. 36 no. 1, (winter), pp. 1, 66.

55. In McDonnell (1990), p. 25.

56. G. Reid (1992b) 'New Zealand Awards Display Diversity', *Billboard*, vol. 104 no. 1 (25 April), p. 36.

57. G. Reid (1993) 'Kiwi Scene Makes Strong '93 Showing', *Billboard*, vol. 105 no. 30 (24 July), p. 93.
58. J.Russell (1994a) 'State of the Indies', *Rip It Up*, no. 205 (September), p. 10.
59. J.Russell (1994b) Review of Chug, 'Golden Mile', *Rip It Up*, no. 206 (October), p. 30.
60. M. Sutherland (1995) Review of Chug, *Sassafras, New Musical Express* (14 January), p. 39.
61. In R. Baillie (1995) 'Flying High in the Face of Fashion', *NZ Herald* (8 September), p. 2:8.
62. In D. Scatena (1995) 'Hi-Fi Way: King Loser', *On the Street* (16 May), p. 19.
63. D. Hawkes (1995) 'Big Day Out', *Rip It Up*, no. 210, (February), p. 18.
64. In R. Pett (1995) 'How Swede it is ...', *Real Groove* (September), p. 9.
65. B. Russell (1992) *Xpressway Newsletter*, p. 1
66. E. Davis (1992) 'Xpressway to Yr Soul', *Village Voice* (11 February), p. 69.
67. O. Stead (1994) 'Xpressway: We Know What's Good for You', *Music in New Zealand*, no. 24 (autumn), p. 40.
68. Davis (1992), p. 69.
69. B. Russell (1992) *Xpressway Newsletter*, (March).
70. A. Yee (1995) 'Dunedin's Musical Low Roads', *Spunkzine*, Sydney, Issue four point five, p. 13.
71. D. Barber (1995) 'Paying for Past Plunder', *The Bulletin*, Sydney (10 January), p. 14, and A. Gifford (1994) 'Warriors Once Again', *Planet*, Auckland no. 14 (spring), p. 41.
72. J. Ritchie (1992) *Becoming Bicultural*, (Wellington, Huia Publishers), pp. 10–11.
73. G. Reid (1992a) 'New Zealand's Maori Music a Genre Melange', *Billboard*, vol. 104, no. 22 (30 May), pp. 1, 34.
74. *Ibid.*, p. 36.
75. See H. Wilson (1994), 'Te Wa Whakapaoho Te Reo Irirangi – Some Directions in Maori Radio' in P. Hayward, T. Mitchell and R. Shuker (eds) *North Meets South: Popular Music in Aotearoa/New Zealand*, (Sydney, Perfect Beat Publications), pp. 99–102.
76. M. Maniapoto-Jackson (1994) 'More on NZ Music Awards', *Rip It Up*, no. 204 (October), p. 8.
77. In W. Dart (1993) 'Moana: A New Song for Aotearoa', *Music in New Zealand*, no. 22 (spring), p. 46.
78. In D. Yuzwalk (1991) 'Black Pearl: Moana and the Moahunters', *Rip It Up*, no. 162, p. 8.
79. G. Reid (1992a), p. 1.
80. B. Morley (1993) 'The Launching of Nga Matua: A Personal View', *Music in New Zealand*, no. 21 (spring), pp. 39–40.
81. Dix (1988) pp. 331, 344.
82. *Ibid.*, p. 330.
83. Advertisement in *On the Street*, (19 April 1993), p. 39.
84. Dix (1988) pp. 331, 344.
85. Lealand (1988), p. 76.
86. P. Walker (1995) 'Under the mountain', *The NZ Listener* (4 February), p. 48.
87. In E. Reedy (1993) 'A Passion for Maori Music', *Mana*, vol. 1 no. 1 (January), p. 67.

88. Reid (1992a), p. 34.
89. A. Weintrab (1993) 'Jawaiian and Local Cultural Identity in Hawaii', *Perfect Beat*, vol. 1, no. 2 (January), p. 78.
90. In J. Campbell (1993) 'Jah Life' and 'Dread Beat', *Planet*, no. 10 (autumn), p. 51.
91. *Ibid.*, p. 51.
92. In Yuzwalk (1992a) 'Margaret Urlich', *Rip It Up*, no. 183 (October), p. 6.
93. In M. Thomson (1991) 'A New Song: Women's Music in Aotearoa', *Music in New Zealand* (winter), p. 23.
94. T. Kopytko (1986) 'Breakdance as an Identity Marker in New Zealand', *Yearbook for Traditional Music*, vol. xviii, pp. 21–2.
95. *Ibid.*, p. 26.
96. J Ihaka (1993) 'Why the kids wanna be black', *Mana* (August/September), p. 12.
97. *Ibid.*, p. 13.
98. In C. Walker, 'Pacific Pride', *Rolling Stone* (Australian Edition), no. 510 (June), p. 28.
99. K. Buchanan (1993) 'Ain't Nothing But a G Thing', *Midwest*, no. 3, p. 27.
100. K. Buchanan (1989) 'The Upper Hutt Posse: Music with a Message', *Music in New Zealand* (summer), p. 35.
101. In *On the Street*, (29 August 1990), p. 24.
102. In *On the Street*, (5 September 1990), p. 36.
103. O. Frizzell (1994) 'Hip hop Hype', *Pavement*, no. 8 (December), pp. 44–50. The rappers featured in this article were Urban Disturbance (European and Niuean), 3 The Hard Way (Maori and Samoan), Upper Hutt Posse (Maori), Dam Native (Maori and Samoan/Maori), Otara Millionaires Club (Niuean/Maori), Ehrman (Samoan), Field Style Orator (Samoan), Rhythm Slave (European), Teremoana Rapley (Maori), Man Chu (Chinese Malaysian), DLT (European/Maori) and Justice (European). Also mentioned were Sisters Underground (Samoan and African-American), Gifted and Brown (Maori and Samoan), Pacifican Descendants (Samoan), Rough Opinion (Maori) and the Semi MCs (Maori and Samoan). Of these, all are from or based in Auckland with the exception of Dam Native, Gifted and Brown and Rough Opinion, who are from Wellington.
104. R. Pett (1995) 'They're by the Grace', *NZ Musician*, vol. 5, no. 4 (March), p. 25.
105. In I. Walker, L. Hakaraia *et al.* (1995) 'Maori Sovereignty', *Background Briefing*, Australian Broadcasting Corporation, Ratio National (November).
106. G. Gracewood (1995) 'What's new Posse cat?' *Real Groove* (August), p. 11.
107. In Frizzell (1994), pp. 48, 50.
108. *Ibid.*, p. 60.
109. T. Chadwick (1994) Review of Hirini Melbourne and Richard Nunns's, *Te Ku Te Whe*, *NZ Musician*, vol. 5, no. 2 (October), p. 9.
110. A. Duff (1990) *Once Were Warriors*, (Auckland, Tandem Press), p. 43.
111. In B. Sheridan (1993) 'Cheering the Good Guys', *Planet*, no. 11 (winter), p. 37.
112. C. Hogg (1994) ' "Otara Sound" Creates Proud New Kiwi Era', *Sunday Star Times* (17 April).
113. R. Baillie (1994) 'Our Streets are Grooving', *NZ Herald* (25 March).

114. In J. Tingwell (1995) 'Groove Mania', *Drum Media* (17 January), p. 25.
115. In M. Smith (1994) 'High on Second Nature', *Drum Media* (21 June), p. 12.
116. In E. Farry (1994) 'The Producers: 5 go Mad in a Studio', *Rip It Up*, no. 204 (August), p. 14.
117. In S. Vui-Talitu (1996) 'AEIOU–Music Video and Polynesian Communication', *Perfect Beat*, vol. 2 no. 4 (January) p. 81.
118. In G. Reid (1994) 'Tour Teaches Pride', *NZ Herald* (25 March).
119. In B. McDonald (1995) 'Now or Never', *Pavement*, issue 11 (June–July), p. 14.
120. In S. Hunter (1995) 'Grooving to Sounds Rooted in the Pacific', *Evening Post* (9 March), p. 24.

Discography

Aotearoa, *He Waiata Mo Te Iwi*, Jayrem, 1986.
Hgahiwi Apanui, *Te Hene Ki Te Kainga*, Jayrem, 1989.
Ardijah, *Take a Chance*, WEA, 1987.
The Bats, *Couchmaster*, Flying Nun, 1995.
—*Silverbeet*, Flying Nun, 1993.
Sandra Bell, *Dreams of Falling*, Xpressway, 1991.
The Chills, *Solid Gold Hits*, Flying Nun, 1995.
—*Soft Bomb*, Slash, 1992.
—*Submarine Bells*, Slash, 1990.
The Clean, *Boodle Boodle Boodle*, Flying Nun, 1981.
—*Modern Rock*, Flying Nun, 1995.
Crowded House, *Together Alone*, Capitol Records, 1993.
Dam Native, *Horified One*, Tangata Records, 1995.
Dread Beat, *All Our Lives*, Jayrem, 1988.
E-Tu, *Whakakotahi*, Tangata Records, 1993.
Fuemana, *New Urban Polynesian*, Deepgrooves, 1994.
—*Closer*, Deepgrooves, 1994.
—*Rocket Love*, Deepgrooves, 1994.
Gifted and Brown, *So Much Soul*, Tangata Records, 1993.
Grace, *Black Sand Shore*, Deepgrooves, 1995.
Headless Chickens, *Body Blow*, Flying Nun, 1991.
Herbs, *Sensitive to a Smile*, Jayrem, 1988.
—*What's Be Happen?*, Warrior, 1981.
Igelese, *Groovalation*, Papa Pacific Records, 1995.
Jean-Paul Sartre Experience, *Bleeding Star*, Flying Nun, 1993.
Peter Jefferies, *Last Great Challenge in a Dull World*, Siltbreeze, 1991.
Greg Johnson, *Vine Street Stories*, Pagan, 1995.
Chris Knox, *Seizure*, Flying Nun, 1990.
—*Song for 1990*, Flying Nun, 1990.
—*Songs of Me and You*, Flying Nun, 1995.
King Loser, *Sonic Super Free Hi Fi*, Flying Nun, 1995.
—*You Cannot Kill What Does Not Live*, Flying Nun, 1995.
The Magick Heads, *Before We Go Under*, Flying Nun, 1995.
Taj Mahal, *Taj*, Ode, 1986.

Mana, *Mana*, Ode, 1993.
Hirini Melbourne and Richard Nunns, *Toiapiapi*, Titi Tangaio, 1993.
—*Te Ku Te Whe*, Rattle Records, 1994.
—*Tahi*, Southside 1993.
—*AEIOU (Akona Te reo)*, Southside, 1992.
Temuera Morrison, *Waiata Poi*, Virgin Records, 1995.
The Muttonbirds, *The Muttonbirds*, Bag Records, 1993.
Ngaire, *Ngaire*, Southside, 1991.
Emma Paki, *Greenstone*, Virgin, 1994.
Patea Maori Club, *Poi E*, Maui Records, 1984.
Purest Form, *Message to My Girl*, Madame X, 1994.
Semi MC'S, *Trust Me*, Volition, 1992.
Maree Sheehan, *Make U My Own*, Tangata, 1992.
—*Dare to be Different*, Tangata 1992.
—*Past to the Present*, Roadshow, 1995.
Sisters Underground, *In the Neighbourhood*, Second Nature, 1994.
Straitjacket Fits, *Blow*, Flying Nun, 1993.
Sulata, *Never*, Deepgrooves, 1995.
Supergroove, *Traction*, BMG, 1994.
3 The Hard Way, *Old Skool Prankstas*, Deepgrooves, 1994.
Tom Thumb, *Ludgate Hill/The Singles*, Jayrem/Legenz, 1992.
Toy Love, *Toy Love*, Deluxe Records, 1980.
3Ds, *The Venus Trail*, Flying Nun, 1994.
Tama, *Workshop*, Te Aroha, 1989.
The Twelve Tribes of Israel Band, featuring Hensley Dyer, *Shine On*, 12 Tribes of
    Israel, 1990.
Upper Hutt Posse, *E Tu*, Jayrem, 1987.
—*Against the Flow*, Southside, 1989.
—*Ragga Girl*, Tangata, 1992.
—*Whakamutungia Tebei mahi Te Patupatu Tangata*, Alcoholic Liquor Advisory
    Council, 1992.
—*Movement in Demand*, Tangata 1995.
Urban Disturbance, *No Flint, No Flame*, Deepgrooves, 1993.
—*37 (degrees) a-ttitude*, Deepgrooves, 1994.
Margaret Urlich, *Safety in Numbers*, CBS, 1989.
Various, *Killing Capitalism with Kindness*, Xpressway/Turbulence, 1992.
—*Nga matua: When the Haka became Boogie's Greatest Bits*, vol. 1, Tangata/
    BMG, 1990.
—*Te Rangatahi: When the Haka became Boogie's Greatest Bits*, vol.2, Tangata/
    BMG, 1992.
—*Once Were Warriors* Soundtrack Album, Tangata Records, 1994.
—*Proud, An Urban-Pacific Streetsoul Compilation*, Second Nature, 1994.
—*The Sound is Out There*, Flying Nun, 1995.
—*Tuatara, A Flying Nun Compilation*, Flying Nun, 1985.
—*Wild Things Volume One: Wild Kiwi Garage 1966-1969*, Flying Nun, 1991.
—*Xpressway Pile = Up*, Xpressway, 1990.
The Verlaines, *Ready to Fly*, Slash, 1991.

Conclusion: Globalization and Local Identity

As Roy Shuker has pointed out in *Understanding Popular Music*, the majority of academic and journalistic studies of popular music still concern themselves with one transnational context, 'the Anglo-American nexus of rock'.[1] This means that the study of local variants on this nexus, in the context of over-arching notions of an Anglo-American rock hegemony, cultural imperialism and globalization, assumes particular importance in defining musical identity. Shuker himself extends the focus of popular music studies to countries such as Canada, Australia and Aotearoa/New Zealand, but remains within a predominantly anglophone sphere of influence where local variants have considerable difficulty asserting their identity within the predominantly Anglo-American forms they appropriate. Even the recent work of Johan Fornas on rock music in Sweden shows the prevalence of this anglophone sphere of influence into non-anglophonic countries.[2] In his book *Producing Pop*, Keith Negus portrays the global apparatus of the popular music industry as follows:

> The global production and consumption of popular music in the 1990s is defined by the North Atlantic Anglo-American cultural movements of sounds and images, and European, USA and Japanese dominance of finance capital and hardware on which to record and reproduce these sounds and images.[3]

It is in this context that notions of globalization of popular music need to be considered, as the maintenance of an Anglo-American dominance over the 'rest of the world', which is divided into the principal market bloc territories of the USA and Canada, Europe, and Japan and South-East Asia. The USA, Japan, Germany, the UK and France account for 70 per cent of world sales of recorded music, which means, as Negus states, that globalization is often little more than a rhetorical 'buzz word' which has 'tended to become a bland wallpaper term used to cover the cracks, conflicts and discontinuities in the world as the planet is reduced to a cosy "global village"'.[4]

Anglo-American dominance has also led to an often idealized, romanticized and nostalgic view of local musics as important oppositional practices which subvert the homogenized mass cultural imperialism represented by the global music market. This view sees local music as representative of an authentic heritage culture and the global as imposing an unauthentic, artificial culture on local markets. The reality, as we have seen, is far more complicated, with local musical forms combining with predominant Anglo-American genres to produce what Negus describes as 'a tension between progress and restoration; between the eclectic, syncretic forms of acculturated expression brought about by the meeting of various musical techniques, technologies and traditions'.[5]

Czech rock, Italian 'rappamuffin', Aboriginal rock and Maori and Pacific Islander soul and hip hop can all be seen as fruitful, positive results of this tension, reinscribing global musical practices in local contexts. But these practices take place on a very small scale in terms of the global picture. Statistics of world sales of records and tapes for 1990 which Negus reproduces indicate that while both Australia and Italy represent only 2 per cent of the global market, the Czech Republic and Aotearoa/New Zealand represent less than 1 per cent, with the USA occupying 31 per cent, Japan 12 per cent, Germany and the United Kingdom 9 per cent, and France, with an unusually high percentage of domestic musical repertoire, 7 per cent.[6] (Although Franco Fabbri has argued that these figures are misleading in the case of Italy, where the revenue received from musical copyright places Italy closer to its designation as the fifth most industrialized nation in the world. The high incidence of pirate recordings in Italy also means that significant sales of local artists are unrecorded.[7] (In this context, the forms of musical expression I have been surveying represent drops in the ocean of the Anglo-US 'global' music industry.

But the impossibility of defining any real sense of 'global identity' in popular music means that local practices and musical idiosyncrasies are increasingly important, not just in terms in providing expression for often problematic notions of national musical identity (as in the case of Australia), but as agents of what Appadurai has called 'repatriation of difference' which adapt homogenized global musical forms into 'heterogeneous dialogues of national sovereignty'.[8] It is arguable that 'global' pop musicians like Madonna and Michael Jackson are often given quite different meanings in different localities, and perhaps even 'misinterpreted' in creative and idiosyncratic ways in some local contexts, which invest their music with new and often more interesting significances. The reception of local musicians in local contexts is even more idiosyncratic, involving an insider field of response and interpretation which is often impenetrable to the outsider. Especially where there are linguistic barriers, as in the case of the Czech Republic, an outsider's understanding of the nuances and local resonances of popular music becomes virtually impossible, and attempts to translate and explain some of them become particularly important.

At the conclusion of their book *Big Sounds from Small Peoples*, Wallis and Malm posit two possible future directions for the ongoing process of transculturation in popular music: that the interaction of global and local musical cultures will increase to the extent that more and more musical features will become common to an increasing range of musical cultures, and a global homogeneity will ensue; or that a variety of different types of music from different living conditions and musical technologies will emerge, adapting traditional musical forms to new environments.[9] Clearly the second option is more desirable than the first, and the emergence of world music as a heterogeneous global marketing category and musical practice can, on the whole, be regarded as evidence of the latter rather than the former. The local forms of musical expressions I have dealt with also exemplify this second option, and are offered as contributions to the study and investigation of music from small countries outside the Anglo-American nexus, which I believe will become increasingly important in the future.

Notes

1. R. Shuker (1994) *Understanding Popular Music* (London, Routledge), p. 284.
2. See J. Fornas (1993) ' "Play It Yourself": Swedish Music in Movement', *Social Science Information*, vol. 32, no. 1, pp. 39–65, and (1994) 'Listen to Your Voice! Authenticity and Reflexivity in Rock, Rap and Techno Music', *New Formations*, no. 24, pp. 155–73.
3. K. Negus (1994) *Producing Pop: Culture and Conflict in the Popular Music Industry* (London, Edward Arnold), p. 14.
4. *Ibid.*, p. 6.
5. *Ibid.*, p. 7.
6. *Ibid.*, pp. 159–60.
7. *Ibid.*, p. 12.
8. A. Appadurai (1990) 'Disjuncture and Difference in the Global Cultural Economy', *Public Culture*, vol. 2, no. 2 (spring), p. 16.
9. R. Wallis and K. Malm (1984) *Big Sounds from Small Peoples* (London, Constable), pp. 323–4.

Index